Liberalizing Foreign Trade

Volume 3

Liberalizing Foreign Trade

Edited by
*Demetris Papageorgiou, Michael Michaely, and
Armeane M. Choksi*

Volume 3

The Experience of Israel and Yugoslavia

ISRAEL   *Nadev Halevi and Joseph Baruh*

YUGOSLAVIA   *Oli Havrylyshyn*

Basil Blackwell

First published 1991

HF
1411
.L497
1989
v. 3

Basil Blackwell, Inc.
3 Cambridge Center
Cambridge, Massachusetts 02142, USA

Basil Blackwell Ltd
108 Cowley Road, Oxford, OX4 1JF, UK

British Library Cataloguing in Publication Data
A CIP Catalogue record for this book is available from the British Library.

Library of Congress Cataloging in Publication Data

Liberalizing foreign trade/edited Demetris Papageorgiou, Michael Michaely, and
Armeane M. Choksi.
p. cm.
Includes index.
Contents: v. 1. Liberalizing Foreign Trade The Experience of Argentina, Chile, and
Uruguay — v. 2. Liberalizing Foreign Trade The Experience of Korea, the Philippines,
and Singapore — v. 3. Liberalizing Foreign Trade The Experience of Israel and
Yugoslavia — v. 4. Liberalizing Foreign Trade The Experience of Brazil, Colombia, and
Perú — v. 5. Liberalizing Foreign Trade The Experience of Indonesia, Pakistan, and Sri
Lanka — v. 6. Liberalizing Foreign Trade The Experience of New Zealand, Spain, and
Turkey — v. 7. Liberalizing Foreign Trade Lessons of Experience in the Developing
World
ISBN 0–631–16666–1 (v. 1).   ISBN 0–631–16668–8 (v.3)   ISBN 0–631–17595–4
(7-vol. set)
1. Commercial policy. 2. Free trade. 3. International trade.
I. Papageorgiou, Demetris, 1938– . II Michaely, Michael, 1928– .III. Choksi, Armeane
M., 1944–.
HF 1411.L497 1989
382′.3—dc19   88–37455
                                                                                        CIP

Typeset in 10 on 12pt Times
by TecSet Ltd
Printed in Great Britain by T. J. Press Ltd., Padstow

Contents

About the Editors

Demetris Papageorgiou is the Chief of the Country Operations Division in the Brazil Department of the World Bank. He has served as a senior economist in the Country Policy Department and as an economist at the Industry Division of the Development Economics Department.

Michael Michaely is the Lead Economist in the Brazil Department of the World Bank. Previously he was the Aron and Michael Chilewich Professor of International Trade and Dean of the Faculty of Social Sciences at the Hebrew University of Jerusalem. He has published numerous books and articles on international economics.

Armeane M. Choksi is Director of the Brazil Department in the Latin American and Caribbean Region of the World Bank. He is co-editor with Demetris Papageorgiou of *Economic Liberalization in Developing Countries*, and has written on industrial and trade policy.

Editors' Preface

The General Objective

"Protection," said the British statesman Benjamin Disraeli in 1845, "is not a principle, but an expedient," and this pronouncement can serve very well as the text for our study of *trade liberalization*. The benefits of open trading have by now been sufficiently demonstrated and described by economic historians and analysts. In this study, we take them for granted and turn our minds from the "whether" to the "how."

The Delectable Mountains of open trading confront the pilgrim with formidable obstacles and there are many paths to the top. The direct route seldom turns out to be the best in practice. It may bring on rapid exhaustion and early collapse, while a more devious approach, skirting areas of excessive transition costs, may offer the best prospects of long-term survival.

Given the sharp diversity of economic background and experience between different countries, and indeed, between different periods in the same country, we should not expect the most favorable route to turn out the same for each country, except perhaps by accident. There are, however, fundamental principles underlying the diversities and it is our thesis that a survey and analysis of a sufficiently broad spectrum of countries over sufficiently long development periods may serve to uncover them.

With this object in view, we set out to study as many liberalization experiences as possible and aimed at including all liberalizations in developing countries in the post-world war period. However, the actual scope of this study had three limitations. First, we restricted the study to market-based economies. Second, experiences with highly inadequate data had to be excluded. Third, to be an appropriate object of study, an experience had to be of some minimum duration. Applying these criteria, we were left with the study of liberalization experiences in the 19 countries listed at the end of this preface. This volume deals with two of these countries (Israel and Yugoslavia). Five other volumes contain the rest of the country studies, and the seventh volume presents the synthesis of the country analyses.

Definitions

"Trade liberalization" implies any change which leads a country's trade system toward neutrality in the sense of bringing its economy closer to the situation which would prevail if there were no governmental interference in the trade system. Put in words, the new trade system confers no discernible incentives to either the importable or the exportable activities of the economy.

By "episode" we mean a period long enough to accommodate a significant run of liberalization acts terminating either in a swing away from liberalization or in a period where policy changes one way or another cease to be apparent.

The "episode of liberalization" thus defined is the unit of observation and analysis employed in each of our country studies.

Identification of Liberalization Episodes

There are three main indicators of a move in the direction of neutrality: (a) a change in the price system; (b) a change in the form of intervention; (c) changes in the foreign exchange rate.

Price System

The prices in question are nominal protection rates determining consumption patterns and, more importantly, effective protection rates affecting production activities. Any change which lowered the average level and distribution of rates of protection would count as a move toward neutrality. Typically, such a change would arise from a general reduction in tariffs, but it might also be indicated by the introduction, rather than the removal, of instruments of government intervention, or even, indeed, by the raising rather than the lowering of the incidence of government intervention. An instance of this might be the introduction of export subsidies in a protective regime previously biased against exports and favoring import substitution. Another instance might be the introduction or increase of tariffs on imported raw materials and capital goods in a regime where tariffs have previously escalated over the whole field, with the zero and lower rates applying on these imports.

Form of Intervention

The form of intervention may be affected by a change in the quantitative restriction (QR) system itself or by replacing QRs with tariffs. Although the actual changes might be assigned price *equivalents*, it is not feasible to assign price equivalents to their comprehensive effects. Moreover, the reactions they induce are so different from responses to price signals that they are better treated as a separate category.

The Exchange Rate

A change in the level of a *uniform* rate of exchange, since it does not discriminate between one tradeable activity and another, is not of itself an instrument of intervention. A move from a *multiple* to a uniform rate would, however, be equivalent to a change in intervention through commercial policy instruments; changes in the rate would modify the effect of commercial policy instruments already in being, for example, where QR systems are operated through the exchange control mechanism itself or where tariffs effective at an existing rate become redundant at a higher rate. Failing detailed studies of the impact of exchange rate changes on QRs or tariffs we take as a general rule that a formal and real *devaluation* constitutes a step towards liberalization.

Policies and Results

We do not take the actual degree of openness of the economy as an indicator in itself of a liberalization episode. Liberalization policies may commonly be expected to lead to an increase in the share of external trade but this is not an inevitable result. For instance, if, starting from a state of disequilibrium, liberalization is associated with a formal devaluation imports may actually fall. Therefore attempts to detect liberalization by reference to trade ratios rather than to policy *intentions* would be misleading. Exceptionally, however, the authors of the country studies have used trade performance as an indication of liberalization, particularly where actual changes in imports can be used to measure the degree of relaxation, or otherwise, of QRs.

Measurement of Degrees of Liberalization

In each country study we have attempted to indicate the degree of liberalization progressively attained by assigning to each year a mark for performance on a scale ranging from 1 to 20. A mark of 20 would indicate virtually free trade, or perfect neutrality, a mark of 1 would indicate the highest possible degree of intervention. These indices are subjective and peculiar to each country studied and in no way comparable between countries. They are a rough and ready measure of the progress, or otherwise, of liberalization as perceived by the authors of the country study in question. They reflect, for instance, assessments of nominal and effective rates of protection, the restrictiveness of QRs, and the gap between the formal exchange rate and its equilibrium level.

Analysis of Successful Liberalization Exercises

To arrive at criteria of what makes for success in applying liberalization policies, the following questions might be asked in our studies.

1   What is the appropriate speed and intensity of liberalization?
2   Is it desirable to have a separate policy stage of replacement of nonprice forms of trade restrictions by price measures?
3   Is it desirable to treat productive activities during the process of trade liberalization uniformly or differentially?
4   If uniform treatment is indicated, how should it be formulated?
5   On what pattern of performance of the economy is the fate of liberalization likely to hinge?
6   Is it desirable to have a stage of export promotion? If so, what should its timing be in relationship to import liberalization?
7   What are the appropriate circumstances for the introduction of a liberalization policy?
8   How important are exogenous developments in deciding the sustainability of liberalization?
9   Finally, what *other* policy measures are important, either in their existence or absence, for a successful policy of trade liberalization?

Lurking behind many of these issues are the (potential) probable costs of adjustment of a liberalization policy and, in particular, its possible impact on the employment of labor.

Scope and Intention of our Study

The general purpose of our analysis is to throw up some practical guidance for policymakers and, in particular, for policymakers in developing countries where the economic (and political) climate tends to present the greatest obstacles to successful reform. It is for this reason that (as already explained) we have based our studies on the experience of a wide spread of countries throughout the developing world. All country studies have followed a common pattern of inquiry, with the particular analytical techniques left to the discretion of the individual authors. This approach should yield inferences on the questions raised above in two different ways; via the conclusions reached in the country studies themselves, and via the synthesis of the comparative experience of trade liberalization in these countries.

The presence of a common pattern of inquiry in no way implies that all country studies cover the same questions in a uniform manner. Not all questions are of equal importance in each country and the same quantity and quality of data were not available in all countries. Naturally, the country studies differ on the issues they cover, in the form of the analysis, and in the structure of their presentation.

The country studies are self-contained. Beyond addressing the questions of the project, each study contains sufficient background material on the country's attributes and history of trade policy to be of interest to the general reader.

The 19 countries studied classified within three major regions are as follows.

Latin America

Argentina	by Domingo Cavallo and Joaquín Cottani
Brazil	by Donald V. Coes
Chile	by Sergio de la Cuadra and Dominique Hachette
Colombia	by Jorge García García
Peru	by Julio J. Nogués
Uruguay	by Edgardo Favaro and Pablo T. Spiller

Asia and the Pacific

Indonesia	by Mark M. Pitt
Korea	by Kwang Suk Kim
New Zealand	by Anthony C. Rayner and Ralph Lattimore
Pakistan	by Stephen Guisinger and Gerald Scully
Philippines	by Florian Alburo and Geoffrey Shepherd
Singapore	by Bee-Yan Aw
Sri Lanka	by Andrew G. Cuthbertson and Premachandra Athukorala

The Mediterranean

Greece	by George C. Kottis
Israel	by Nadav Halevi and Joseph Baruh
Portugal	by Jorge B. de Macedo, Cristina Corado, and Manuel L. Porto

Spain   by Guillermo de la Dehesa, José Juan Ruiz, and
                Angel Torres
Turkey   by Tercan Baysan and Charles Blitzer
Yugoslavia by Oli Havrylyshyn

Coordination of the Project

Demetris Papageorgiou, Michael Michaely, and Armeane M. Choksi of
the World Bank's Latin American and Caribbean Region are the directors
of this research project. Participants in the project met frequently to
exchange views. Before the country studies were launched, the common
framework of the study was discussed extensively at a plenary conference.
Another plenary conference was held to discuss early versions of the
completed country studies, as well as some emerging general inferences. In
between, three regional meetings in each region were held to review
phases of the work under way. An external Review Board consisting of
Robert Baldwin (University of Wisconsin), Mario Blejer (International
Monetary Fund), Jacob Frenkel (University of Chicago and Director of
Research, International Monetary Fund), Arnold Harberger (University
of Chicago and University of California–Los Angeles), Richard Snape
(Monash University), and Martin Wolf (Chief Economic Leader Writer,
Financial Times) contributed in the reviewing process of the country
studies and the synthesis volume.

The Series

Israel and Yugoslavia are presented in this volume. The series' other
publications are the following:
Volume 1: Liberalizing Foreign Trade. The Experience of Argentina,
    Chile, and Uruguay;
Volume 2: Liberalizing Foreign Trade. The Experience of Korea, the
    Philippines, and Singapore;
Volume 4: Liberalizing Foreign Trade. The Experience of Brazil,
    Colombia, and Perú;
Volume 5: Liberalizing Foreign Trade. The Experience of Indonesia,
    Pakistan, and Sri Lanka;
Volume 6: Liberalizing Foreign Trade. The Experience of New Zealand,
    Spain, and Turkey;
Volume 7: Liberalizing Foreign Trade. Lessons of Experience in the
    Developing World.

Demetris Papageorgiou, Michael Michaely, and Armeane Choksi

Part I

Israel

Nadav Halevi   *and*   *Joseph Baruh*
Hebrew University   *Bank of Israel*
Jerusalem   *Jerusalem*

Contents

List of Figures

List of Tables

Acknowledgments

This study could not have been carried out without the assistance of many people and institutions, and it is only to some of them that we can here acknowledge our indebtedness. First, we thank the World Bank, for initiating, supervising, and financing the study, and the secretarial staff of the Bank's Country Policy Division. Research assistance was provided by a number of part-time researchers, students of economics at the Hebrew University. The Falk Institute for Economic Research in Israel undertook to handle all the technical aspects of the study conducted in Israel. Special thanks are due to Margret Eisenstaedt who volunteered to act as word-processing consultant and editor and ended up doing most of the typing as well.

Though much of the statistical analysis is based on published data, several estimates prepared especially for this study were of crucial importance. These could not have been carried out without the active assistance of the Input–Output Research Division of the Central Bureau of Statistics, and especially its director, S. Bar-Eliezer, and the Research Department of the Bank of Israel, in particular Moshe Bar-Nathan.

The process of continuous evaluation and comments devised by the World Bank did much to improve the study. At each conference authors of two other country studies were assigned to comment on each paper: in our case the reviewers were Stephen Guisinger, Oli Havrylyshyn, C. Pertot, and Manuel L. Porto, but additional, often extremely helpful, comments were received from all the other country authors and invited experts, particularly Jacob Frenkel and Martin Wolf, and of course from the project supervisors. Finally, we should like to thank B. Toren of Israel's Ministry of Industry and Trade for his suggestions and comments. Needless to say, the authors are solely responsible for inadequacies that remain despite the unusual outside help that they received.

1

The Israeli Economy: An Overview

Introduction

Israel started a long and fairly continuous process of trade liberalization in 1952. This study of that process was designed to conform to the outline prepared for similar studies on 19 developing economies to facilitate drawing conclusions of a more general nature (see the preface to the volume). For this reason, three subperiods have been singled out as forming separate "episodes" within the continuous process of liberalization. An "episode" is defined as a period with some substantive change. The episodes chosen were 1952–55, 1962–68, and 1969–77.

The study does not cover the liberalization experience after 1977 because it concentrates on *trade* liberalization, whereas in late 1977 the liberalization was mainly in capital transactions. Chapter 2 presents an overview of the liberalization process and the rationale for the choice of episodes.

The study of each episode includes descriptions of the background, the liberalization measures adopted, accompanying policies, an analysis of the effects of these measures, and suggested inferences. Two chapters are devoted to each episode. The first is descriptive: it presents the liberalization and the accompanying policies. The second is more analytic: it considers the economic performance following liberalization, and assesses the liberalization in the light of that performance. The final chapter summarizes the liberalization experience, and offers general inferences suggested by the study.

Trade liberalization is one facet of economic policy, and cannot be understood without reference to the general structure and development of the economy and of economic policy. The remainder of this introductory chapter presents an overview of the Israeli economy.

Modern Israel has its origins in the Zionist movement of the second half of the nineteenth century, in the mounting desire to reestablish a Jewish homeland in Palestine. The practical aspects of this movement consisted of waves of immigration, starting in 1882, that swelled the small long-existing Jewish population of Palestine with immigrants, mainly from Eastern Europe, and of attempts to secure political sanction for a Jewish entity. The latter attempts were not successful while Palestine was under Turkish administration, but with the conquest of Palestine by British troops in World War I, and as a result of the Balfour Declaration of 1917, the stage was set for the creation of a Jewish homeland in Palestine.

The British mandate on Palestine lasted until May 1948. During its 30-year occupation, the British Administration tried to foster the creation of the Jewish homeland while appeasing the aspirations of the native Arab community (which was also growing and developing a national conscious-ness) and attempting to maintain its dominant position in the Middle East. These conflicting aims antagonized both Jews and Arabs, leading to frequent outbreaks of open hostilities. Under international (mainly Ameri-can) pressure, Britain agreed to leave the resolution of the Palestinian question to the United Nations, after creating a separate Jordanian state in the section of mandatory Palestine east of the Jordan river. When the United Nations voted, in November 1947, to partition western Palestine into separate Jewish and Arab states, Britain announced that its adminis-tration would end on May 15, 1948. The local Arab population rejected the partition plan and tried to prevent the creation of a Jewish state by military action; in this attempt they were joined by the neighboring Arab states on May 15. The outcome of Israel's War of Independence was the present State of Israel, with much of what was supposed to have been the Arab state annexed by Jordan.[1] Thus, an independent Jewish state emerged, surrounded by hostile neighbors unreconciled to its existence.

The economy of Palestine, a backwater of the Ottoman Empire, had been quite primitive until the end of the nineteenth century. It began to develop in the early years of the twentieth century, and grew extremely rapidly from 1920, when a civilian British administration took office. The 1920–47 period was one of rapid average growth, marked by sharp cycles. The Jewish and Arab sectors developed separately, and only partially overlapped.

The main stimuli to the development of the Jewish sector were immigra-tion and capital inflows. The Jewish population grew from 57,000 in 1914 to 609,000 in 1947. Jewish capital inflows from 1920 to 1947, mostly private in origin, were some 178 million pounds sterling (Halevi, 1983a). During 1920–47, the economy was transformed. A modern, capital- and water-intensive agriculture was developed, providing local markets with fruit, vegetables, and dairy products, and exporting large quantities of citrus fruit. World War II, which cut off foreign competition and generated war-related demand, saw the transformation of handicrafts into a manufac-

---

[1] This territory has been occupied by Israel since the 1967 war.

turing sector. The housing industry, strongly influenced by the waves of immigration, was the lead sector in the business cycles. These developments were accompanied and facilitated by the emergence of a sophisticated financial sector – commercial and mortgage banks, credit cooperatives, insurance companies, and a stock market – and the transportation and communications infrastructure necessary for a modern economy.

The main institution for fostering development of the Jewish sector was the Jewish Agency for Palestine, which mobilized Jewish immigration and inflows of funds, directed agricultural settlement, and, with other institutions, created a network of health and educational services. A second major institution was the Histadrut, an all-encompassing labor union, which developed economic enterprises and social service activities in addition to its trade union functions. The government of Palestine provided the framework for economic activity, while pursuing a conservative fiscal policy designed to provide the necessary social services not otherwise available. Viewing Palestine as a single economic entity, the tax burden was more on the richer Jewish sector and the poorer Arab sector benefitted more from the expenditures (Metzer, 1982).

The Palestine currency was fully backed by sterling, controlled by a Palestine Currency Board located in London. There was thus no independent monetary policy, but also no foreign exchange problem. Foreign exchange controls were introduced in World War II; as a result, the perennial current account balance-of-payments deficit, financed by capital inflow, became a balance-of-payments surplus covered by blocked sterling balances accumulated in London. Thus, when the independent State of Israel was born, it already had a fairly sound balanced economic foundation. But it had to develop the administrative apparatus for monetary, fiscal, and foreign exchange policy from scratch.

The new state was faced with two major economic problems: waging an all-out war and absorbing mass immigration. The first problem ended in 1949, although several wars have broken out since then and the danger of such conflict has affected the structure of resource use. Israel has remained a small resource-poor "island," surrounded by hostile neighbors, and has had to develop accordingly. Mass immigration came to an end by 1952, but the economic problems of absorption lasted for a full decade and immigration has continued to influence Israel's labor force and economic structure.

These problems reinforced the ideological belief of the dominant political leadership in public responsibility for rapid economic development and substantial government intervention in the economy. Intervention, in addition to the usual fiscal and monetary measures, ranged from outright price controls and rationing (including foreign exchange control) to subsidization and taxation as a means of directing private economic activity, and to high levels of direct government investment, in addition to the usual fiscal and monetary tools.[2] Thus, ideology and history combined to support an unusually large public sector.

A second consequence of these early problems was the mobilization of foreign funds to increase the total resources available to the economy. Whereas during the mandatory period this inflow was mainly private investment and immigrants' capital, supplemented by donations mobilized by the national institutions (whose relative share swelled during and after World War II), the government became the main mobilizer of foreign resources. The obverse side of this inflow is a persistent deficit in the goods and services account of the balance of payments, whose absolute and relative size has been considered *the* major economic problem from time to time and has led to major policy measures.

Another problem of the early years was inflation, which was virtually eliminated by the 1960s but reemerged at unprecedented levels after 1973, reaching an annual rate of some 400 percent in 1984 before being contained. The early inflation had led to a developed system of wage and salary linkages; while these greatly reduced the harm done by inflation to the distribution of income and wealth, they made it harder to cope with inflation itself.

The turbulent early years of mass immigration, price controls, and suppressed inflation came to an end with the new economic policy of 1952, which included severe monetary restrictions as well as gradual devaluation, price increases, and absorption of pent-up inflationary demand.

From 1954 until 1973 the economic development of Israel was a true success story, generally marked by high levels of employment, very high rates of growth of product and income per capita, and the growth of efficient agriculture, modern industry, sophisticated infrastructure, and high levels of social services. During the same period, government intervention, both direct and indirect, decreased steadily. The persisting balance-of-payments problem, however, occasionally elicited more drastic measures: for example, a recession was induced in 1965 which led to interruptions in the trend of growth and prosperity.

Since 1974 the pattern has been different: rates of growth have been much lower, the share of resources devoted to defense has increased, inflation has become an extremely serious problem, and despite continued growth of exports the balance-of-payments deficit has grown tremendously,[3] bringing with it a large foreign debt burden. In recent years, many of the previous liberalization trends have been moderated or even

---

[2] Until 1954 a large private (but publicly controlled) bank handled the issue of currency. The Bank of Israel, founded in 1954, handles all central bank functions.

[3] The developments during the last decade, and contrasts with earlier periods, have recently been examined. These studies are compiled by Ben-Porath (1986).

reversed. Efforts to cope with Israel's serious economic situation have led to greater government intervention and restrictive policies. At the time of writing, inflation has been controlled, but the problems of the balance of payments persist, as does the need for important structural changes in the economy.

Major Economic Attributes and Developments

Population

Immigration and Population Growth

Estimates of the population of Israel for May 1948 give a Jewish population of 650,000 and a non-Jewish population of 156,000.[4] At the end of 1982 the total population was about 4 million, of which 83 percent were Jewish.

The tremendous growth in population is mainly the result of mass immigration between May 1948 and the end of 1951. During those three and a half years about 700,000 Jews arrived – remnants of European (non-Soviet) Jewry and Jews from Arab countries. Jewish immigration dropped sharply after 1951. On occasion, substantial numbers of immigrants arrived, for example some 70,000 in 1957, 60,000 in 1962, 65,000 in 1963, and 55,000 in 1972 and in 1973, but the absolute and certainly the relative volume of immigration has been of a different order of magnitude since 1951. In 1948–50, annual increases in population averaged 26.5 percent, creating economic and social problems that influenced economic policy for many years after the flow of immigrants had declined.

The sources of population growth are set out in table 1.1, which emphasizes the role of immigration. The natural increase in the Jewish population has gradually declined, from about 2.5 percent in the early years to about 1.5 percent in recent years. The rate of natural increase of the Arab population is much higher and, although it has declined somewhat, it has been around 3.4 percent in recent years. After the level of Jewish immigration declined, the different rates of natural increase of Arabs and Jews tended to counterbalance Jewish immigration, keeping the ratio of the two nationalities fairly stable.

Geographic Distribution

Israel is a small country, both geographically and in population. Its total area is only 21,500 km^2, and the Jewish population is concentrated in a narrow coastal strip. The standard distance, defined as the mean square of

---

[4] The Arab population estimates are actually for September, after the departure of many Arabs from the territories included in the State of Israel.

Table 1.1 Population and sources of population growth

Population group	Population at beginning of period (thousands)	Natural increase (thousands)	Migration balance (thousands)	Total increase (thousands)	Population at end of period (thousands)	Average annual rate of increase (%)	Migration balance out of total increase (%)
Jews							
1948–50[a]	649.6	53.8	499.6	553.4	1,203.0	26.5	90.3
1951–60	1,203.0	338.5	369.7	708.2	1,911.2	4.6	52.2
1961–71	1,911.2	412.9	337.9	750.8	2,662.0	2.4	45.0
Non-Jews							
1948–54[a]	156.0	35.8	n.a.	35.8	191.8	3.2	n.a.
1955–60	191.8	47.3	0.1	47.4	239.2	3.7	0.2
1961–5	239.2	57.7	2.5	60.1	299.3	4.6	4.2
1966–71	299.3[b]	91.4	– 0.6	159.4[b]	458.7	4.5	– 0.7
Total population							
1948–82[a,c]	805.6	1,790.3	1,392.1	3,182.4	4,063.6	4.64	3.7

n.a., not available.
[a] 1948 figures are from May 1948.
[b] Including the addition of East Jerusalem.
[c] Excluding the non-Jewish population of East Jerusalem.
Source: CBS, *Statistical Abstract of Israel* 1983, p. 32

the distance between the place of residence of each resident and the center of gravity of the entire population, has generally been about 50–5 km.

The population is predominantly urban: in 1972, 87 percent of the entire population (90 percent of Jews and 55 percent of Arabs) lived in urban localities. These percentages changed little over time for the Jewish population; the Arab population, however, has become more urban. About 28 percent of the Jewish population lived in the three largest cities – Jerusalem, Tel Aviv, and Haifa – at the end of 1981. Since Tel Aviv is surrounded by a number of independent municipalities, the Tel Aviv district alone, that is, the central coastal plain, accounted for some 30 percent of the Jewish population.

For many years, dispersal of the Jewish population throughout the country, particularly in the north where the Arab population is concentrated and in the relatively empty (and barren) expanses of the Negev in the south, has been an important policy objective. For this purpose, new immigrants in the 1950s were sent directly to agricultural and rural settlements, and during the 1950s and 1960s new urban centers were built up throughout the country, and housing and employment incentives were introduced.

In many of these "development towns" employment opportunities were primarily dependent on government-initiated industrial enterprises, mainly in textiles. Though some of these towns have developed, many have not attained viability and, being one- or two-industry towns, are subject to drastic economic fluctuations. The population dispersal objective proved successful in the development of Jerusalem (which received special status for political reasons) and Beersheba, but was much less so in many of the "development towns." On balance, there has been internal migration from these new towns to the established urban centers. The small size of the country makes such internal migration – and commuting – relatively simple; the main impediments to mobility have been in housing.

The Labor Force

Labor Force Participation and Employment

The labor force reflects changes in population. The important role of immigration in population growth affected the labor force in several ways: the age and sex structure and the ethnic origin of the population influenced labor force participation, and education levels and occupational background of immigrants affected quality.

The mass immigration of the early 1950s, consisting largely of Jews from North Africa and the Middle East, raised the share of children in the population and thus reduced the share of the working-age bracket. Table 1.2 shows labor force participation rates in selected years for the popula-

Table 1.2 Labor force participation rates by sex and age,
1955–1982 (percent)

Sex and age group	1955	1960	1965	1970	1975	1980	1982
Men							
All	80.1	78.1	76.1	69.2	64.9	63.7	63.4
14–17	42.2	32.1	38.1	27.3	18.5	14.2	16.2
18–24	80.9	79.5	76.2	46.0	40.3	41.3	40.3
25–34				91.1	86.7	84.7	84.2
35–54	96.4	96.3	96.4	94.9	93.3	90.8	90.4
55–64	82.3	84.3	91.0	88.5	84.3	82.4	79.4
65+	38.3	35.5	39.7	33.8	29.2	27.9	25.0
Women							
All	26.5	27.3	29.4	29.3	31.6	35.7	36.1
14–17	31.7	21.1	27.1	18.1	11.3	10.9	9.7
18–24	32.2	33.2	37.5	44.9	40.4	39.9	38.4
25–34				32.6	44.2	52.6	53.7
35–54	26.2	30.1	30.9	32.8	38.8	46.0	48.7
55–64	17.0	18.5	22.9	22.1	22.4	26.0	25.1
65+	(5.1)	(7.3)	(6.0)	5.0	6.0	6.6	6.4

Source: Ben-Porath, 1985

tion aged 14 and over. The participation of men has declined steadily, while that of women has correspondingly increased, reflecting changing work habits of women from Arab countries, despite a decline in the 14–17 year bracket. The average participation rate in 1965 was 76.1 percent for men and 29.4 percent for women, both low by comparison with international levels.

Most labor is organized. The dominant union, the Histadrut, is a confederation of trade unions, and the vast majority of workers pay dues, if only to benefit from the union's health services. In 1965, for example, there were some 650,000 people paying dues to Histadrut (excluding family members enjoying Histadrut social services), three quarters of the total labor force. The Histadrut is consequently a powerful institution, whose primary concerns are employment and wages, the latter being particularly problematic because of conflicting interests among the Histadrut unions.

Unemployment has always been a politically sensitive issue, in particular because the first and hardest hit are relatively new immigrants in development towns, where one or two industries – usually in textiles – account for a major share of employment. Since the mid-1950s, when mass immigration had been absorbed and unemployment had been brought down to 3.3 percent, economic policy that involved unemployment has been adopted reluctantly, as a last resort. The recessionary policy adopted in late 1965 for balance-of-payments purposes swelled unemployment temporarily to over 10 percent in 1967. In the 1970s, unemployment insurance was added to the National Social Insurance. Since 1975, unemployment has fluctuated, rising to 5–6 percent in mini-recessions and reaching 7 percent in 1985.

Level of Schooling
In the pre-State period the Jewish population of Palestine had one of the highest education levels in the world. Mass immigration drastically lowered the average education level: whereas men aged 14 years and over who had arrived before 1947 had an average of 9.9 years of schooling, those who arrived in 1948–51 had an average level of only 7.7 years. From 1954, the Israeli education system has gradually raised the average level of schooling, and by 1982 only 3.2 percent of men and 21 percent of women (both over 14 years of age) had less than 12 years of schooling.

There has been a great divergence in levels of education among different ethnic groups. In 1961, only 1.5 percent of immigrants from Asia and Africa had 13 or more years of schooling, slightly less than the non-Jewish population and very much less than that of immigrants from Europe and America and of native-born Israelis. More than 43 percent of these immigrants (and almost half of the non-Jews) had no schooling at all. By 1982, there had been a dramatic change: although the high levels of schooling are still more pronounced for native-born Israelis of European and American origin, the disparities between the ethnic groups had narrowed considerably, and the percentage of the population with no schooling dropped markedly as a result of compulsory primary education, introduced in 1954 (see Halevi and Baruh, 1988, appendix table A.14).

Data for 1965 on the population and labor force by years of study are presented by Halevi and Baruh (1988, appendix table A.15). They point to the great disparity that existed between the levels of education of men and of women, the extremely low participation rates of women with low levels of education, and the strong correlation among women between participation rates and levels of education. These data help to make clear the trends both of higher levels of education for women and of their participation in the labor force.

Table 1.3 presents data on the branch distribution of employment. The relative growth of employment in the public sector, particularly in the 1970s, is in part associated with the growing share of women in the labor force. Financial services, too, have been a growing sector. The high concentration of labor in services in general – defined to include everything other than agriculture, manufacturing, and construction – has been a distinguishing feature of the Israeli economy since the mandatory period,

Table 1.3 Industrial composition of civilian employment (percent)

Sector	1951	1955	1961	1968	1972	1977	1981
Total	100.0	100.0	100.0	100.0	100.0	100.0	100.0
Public sector	18.2	21.0	22.8	22.5	22.9	24.6	28.2
Business sector	81.8	79.0	77.2	77.5	77.1	75.9	71.8
Total business sector	100.0	100.0	100.0	100.0	100.0	100.0	100.0
Agriculture	16.9	22.1	22.2	13.4	11.3	9.2	8.9
Manufacturing	28.8	27.0	30.8	30.9	30.3	32.6	32.0
Financial services	n.a.	2.2	2.7	3.6	3.6	4.8	6.3
Business services[a]	n.a.	n.a.	n.a.	2.4	3.5	3.7	4.5
Transportation	8.5	8.5	8.2	9.7	9.0	8.9	8.7
Other	45.8	40.2	36.1	40.0	42.3	40.8	39.6

n.a., not available.
[a]Included in public sector prior to 1968.
Source: Klinov, 1984

and has aroused much interest. Ofer (1967, 1976) has analyzed the influence of supply conditions on this phenomenon, whereas Klinov (1984) has emphasized demand conditions.

Concern about overconcentration in services arises mainly from the association of services with nontradeables, and consequently with the balance-of-payments position. Klinov (1984) classified employment into public services, other nontradeables, tradeables, and semitradeables, and found that the first two together accounted for 34 percent of employment in 1947, 50 percent in 1955, 53 percent in 1972, and 66 percent in 1981. The share of employment in agriculture rose in the early years, but since 1961 it has declined to less than 7 percent of total civilian employment. Manufacturing increased its share in the 1950s, but not since then.

Occupational Structure

Many of the immigrants to Palestine in the pre-State period changed their occupation, shifting from the liberal professions and trade to manual labor either for ideological reasons or because of inadequate employment opportunities. The immigrants in the years of mass immigration generally had lower skill levels than the earlier immigrants: close to half had previously been employed in industry, crafts, and construction, and only about a fifth had been engaged in the liberal professions or as clerks and administrators (Sicron, 1957). By 1954, fully 60 percent had changed their occupations, mainly moving into the class of unskilled workers and into agriculture.

Over time there was upward mobility; the unskilled categories changed to some extent, with Israeli Arabs replacing immigrants and in turn being replaced by Arab workers from the administered territories.

Capital

The Growth of Capital[5]

The tremendous population increase in the early years required very heavy investments in housing. It is not surprising, therefore, that real fixed capital in dwellings doubled between 1950 and 1955, and more than doubled again by 1963, and that dwellings have always accounted for a very high share of total fixed capital.

However, the absorption of the large increases in the labor force in productive employment, let alone their absorption without sharp declines in output per capita, could not have been possible without large-scale capital formation other than dwellings. Israel was able to mobilize resources for such capital formation. Between 1950 and 1960, the gross fixed reproducible capital (excluding dwellings) increased fourfold. From 1950 to 1960, capital grew so much faster than employment that capital per employed person increased at a rate of 10.2 percent in 1950–5 and 6.9 percent in 1955–60. In the 1960s and 1970s the rates of growth of capital stock were much lower than in the 1950s (9 percent in 1961–72 and 6 percent in 1973–81), but since the labor force also grew more slowly, capital per employed person continued to grow at rates of 4.5–5.0 percent.

In 1965, some 37 percent of the capital stock was in dwellings. Of the remainder, 25 percent was in manufacturing, and slightly more than 25 percent in agriculture. This unusually high proportion in agriculture reflects both the desire to expand agriculture and the relatively high proportion of capital stock in irrigation: one third of the total in agriculture. About a quarter of Israel's land area is arable, most of it only under irrigation, and water resources suffice for only half this area. Since the water sources are located in the north and much of the arable land is in the south, heavy investments were made, until the early 1960s, in national irrigation projects. Since then the share of the capital stock in agriculture has steadily declined.

Savings and Investment

The rapid increase in capital stock is, of course, the result of high rates of investment. Net domestic capital formation as a percentage of gross

---

[5] These and the following figures on capital formation until 1966 are based on Gaathon (1971). Detailed figures are shown in Halevi and Baruh (1988, appendix table A.3).

national product (GNP) averaged 25.5 percent in 1950–4, and 21.9 percent in 1955–9 and again in 1960–4 (Halevi and Klinov–Malul, 1968, p. 58). Thereafter, the net investment rate declined: it was about 15 percent in 1965–9 and about 14 percent in the 1970s, with large annual fluctuations.[6]

How was Israel able to achieve such high rates of capital accumulation? Not by domestic saving: most years, savings, defined as the difference between net national product (NNP) and total consumption, were negative or close to zero. The answer lies in the import surplus: the addition to total resources made available by an excess of imports over exports was roughly equal to investment. To be sure, in the early years of the highest investment rates, it was only as a result of policy that these resources were mobilized and directed to investment rather than to consumption. In later years both consumption and investment increased, but investment was frequently more susceptible to squeezes. In the 1970s, there was a squeeze on resources, a combination of worsening terms of trade, slower product growth, and growing allocations to defense. These reduced the share of total resources allocated to capital formation (see Mayshar, 1984). Table 1.4 shows the allocation of resources in selected years.

Private savings, as opposed to total savings, have always been quite high: average gross domestic savings out of disposable income rose from less than 20 percent in the 1950s to over 35 percent in the early 1970s (Mayshar, 1984, p. 96). Part of this is a result of institutional factors such as provident

Table 1.4 Total resources and their uses (percent)

Use category	1950	1955	1960	1965	1970	1975	1980
Private consumption	57.7	53.1	52.6	49.6	39.8	35.6	36.4
Public consumption	15.6	14.4	14.1	15.2	23.6	26.1	21.3
Gross capital formation	24.2	23.8	20.7	19.8	18.8	18.9	13.7
Domestic use of resources	97.5	91.3	87.4	84.6	82.2	80.6	71.4
Exports	2.5	8.7	12.6	15.4	17.8	19.4	28.6
Total use of resources	100.0	100.0	100.0	100.0	100.0	100.0	100.0
GNP	77.5	71.8	74.1	70.7	65.0	58.9	58.8
Imports	22.5	28.2	25.9	29.3	35.0	41.1	41.2

Computed from current price data.
Source: 1950–65 Halevi and Klinov-Malul, 1968, p. 95; 1970–80, CBS, Statistical Abstract of Israel, 1983, table VI/2

[6] These figures are only rough approximations computed from different series: investment from CBS, Gross Domestic Capital Formation in Israel, 1950–1978, Special Series 635; GNP from CBS, Statistical Abstract of Israel, 1983; the depreciation figures for recent years are somewhat problematical.

and pension schemes and of widespread home ownership, but the main reason for the rise in private savings is probably rising per capita income levels.

The public sector is a net dissaver. The government deficit was not large before the Six Day War of 1967, but since then defense spending has increased tremendously – to a new plateau as a result of the 1967 war, and to a higher one as a result of the 1973 war (Berglas, 1983). This has been the principal cause of government deficits of 25–30 percent of GNP. Mayshar (1984) has pointed out that "whereas in the 1950s savings generated by the public sector (including its foreign transfers and loans) contributed about half of gross domestic capital formation, in the period since 1966 the government had to draw on private savings as well."

Financing Investment

The size and allocation of investment was strongly influenced by government policy. The large (perhaps excessive) investment in private dwellings was largely due to direct construction by public or semipublic mass housing companies, and even more to subsidies for the purchase of such homes. Investment in communications, transportation, and power and water has been almost exclusively public, and even most of agricultural and much of manufacturing investment was the result of government-directed finance. Much of the capital inflow from abroad – donations to public institutions, sale of government bonds, international loans and foreign aid, and German reparations – went to government or public institutions, and several categories were earmarked to finance investment projects. The government also dominated the capital market as a financial intermediary. Whether the Government Development Budget allocates these funds to private or public firms, as grants or as subsidized loans, directly or via investment institutions, affects the technical classification of investment funds by source but not the real nature of the government's crucial role.

Table 1.5 presents some indicators of public finance of the business sector's investment. Contrary to expectations, the role of government has not declined with the growth and sophistication of the economy. Even in manufacturing, which surprisingly has maintained a fairly stable share of the gross capital stock and an investment share of only about 4.2 percent of GNP, the role of government finance has risen rather than fallen since 1975.

The government tried to attract private investment from abroad not only to provide more funds but primarily to import industrial and marketing expertise. Laws to encourage investment were passed, granting special status with regard to subsidization, taxation, and profit repatriation for investments in government-approved projects. Though foreign private investment has been of some quantitative importance, particularly in the early 1960s, it has not become a major factor either in investment in

Table 1.5 Indicators of public finance and business investments (percent)

Years	Share of gross investment financed by public loans		Share of explicit grant to gross investment in manufacturing	Real interest rate on average industrial development loans[a]
	Agriculture	Manufacturing		
1956–60	73	39	n.a.	4.6
1961–5	85	20	n.a.	3.5
1966–9	93	40	4	3.8
1970–2	n.a.	35	7	− 2.5
1973–5	71	39	5	− 16.6
1976–8	72	49	10	− 16.6
1979–82	130	71	13	n.a.

n.a., not available.
[a] $(1\ r) / (1 + P) -$, where r is the nominal interest rate on development loans in zone B and P is the rate of increase in GNP
Source: Mayshar, 1984

general or in investment in manufacturing. There are no reliable estimates of the proportion of foreign ownership of Israeli firms, but it is not very large. According to balance-of-payments estimates, annual earnings (whether transferred abroad or reinvested) accruing to foreign direct investment in Israel in the 1970s did not exceed US$70 million annually.

Growth and Structure of National Product

Growth of Income

During the mandatory period, Jewish Palestine attained a very high rate of growth of national income and per capita income, both in absolute terms and relative to other countries, decreasing the gap with Western European countries and widening it relative to other developing countries.

The mass immigration of 1948–51 posed the problem of how to absorb the new immigrants in productive employment without decreasing output per capita and consequently lowering standards of living. The rapidly expanding labor force could not be quickly absorbed, and some 14 percent was unemployed in 1949. This unemployment was gradually reduced to 8.1 percent in 1951 and 1952, but jumped to 11.5 percent in 1953 as a result of drastic changes in economic policy. Thereafter, as previously stated, there was a gradual reduction in unemployment, which virtually disappeared by the early 1960s (though it reappeared in the recession of 1966–7) (see Halevi and Klinov-Malul, 1968).

The absorption of such an increase in the labor force without a drastic drop in income per capita would, in itself, have been no mean feat. In fact, income increased very rapidly, and sufficiently to raise per capita income significantly. The average rate of growth in GNP was 9.7 percent in 1950–70, and although this period was one of worldwide growth, very few other countries – Japan and Taiwan – even approached such high rates of growth (Syrquin, 1984). Per capita income grew at a rate of 5.2 percent during the same period, slightly ahead of Korea, Yugoslavia, and Italy; income per capita was much closer to that of Western Europe than to that of the developing countries. In the 1970s, growth of product in Israel was only about 5 percent – some 2 percent in per capita terms. This slowdown was more pronounced than in other newly industrialized economies and some developed European countries. In 1980, per capita income in Israel was about half that of the United States and three quarters that of Western Europe.

Structure of Product

The branch composition of net domestic product in selected years is presented in table 1.6. Despite the original aspirations that agriculture would be a major sector, its weight in total product declined to only 6 percent. Manufacturing, the branch receiving most encouragement in the past two decades, did not show any relative growth in that period, and appears to have declined. Proper allocation of subsidies may show a smaller decline. Gross domestic product (GDP) in manufacturing grew faster than the average for the total business sector in 1961–72 but more slowly in 1972–81 (Metzer, 1983, p. 52).

Table 1.6 Branch origin of net domestic product (percent)

	1952	1955	1960	1965	1970	1975[a]	1980[a]
Agriculture	11.4	11.3	11.7	8.5	6.4	6.0	5.9
Manufacturing	21.7	22.5	23.8	24.2	24.1	20.4	18.7
Construction and public utilities	10.9	10.1	9.5	9.2	12.0	12.2	11.6
Transportation and communications	7.4	7.4	8.0	8.8	8.8	7.5	6.2
Trade, finance, and other services	25.2	23.3	22.4	23.1	22.7	25.5	29.0
Ownership of dwellings	5.2	5.4	5.9	7.5	6.9	9.0	6.6
General government and non profit institutions	18.2	20.0	18.7	18.7	19.1	19.4	22.0
Net domestic product	100.0	100.0	100.0	100.0	100.0	100.0	100.0

[a] Estimates are very rough because subsidies and imputed bank charges were not allocated by branch.
Source: 1952–65, Halevi and Klinov-Malul, 1968, p. 104; CBS, *Statistical Abstract of Israel*, 1973, p. 167; 1975, 1980, CBS, *Statistical Abstract of Israel*, 1983, p. 177

Whereas in the 1950s and 1960s industrial development was mainly concentrated in light industries – food, clothing, and textiles, together with exploitation of Israel's main mineral resource, Dead Sea potash – in the 1970s there was greater diversification of manufacturing and relative growth of more sophisticated education-intensive branches such as electronics and machinery.

Table 1.6 illustrates the relative growth of public services and trade and other private services. The banking and insurance sector is among those that show the most relative growth. Thus, despite all official efforts, the nontradeable or semitradeable sectors did relatively well.

Factor Inputs and Productivity

Output grows as a result of increased inputs of labor and capital and of more efficient use of inputs. The residual increase in output not "explained" by increased inputs is defined as growth in total factor productivity. Table 1.7 summarizes the growth of output, inputs, and total factor productivity.

In the 1950s, labor inputs grew substantially, but capital inputs grew even faster, thus raising capital-to-labor ratios. Productivity grew at an unusually high rate – 4.7 percent – and accounted for 43 percent of total output growth. In the 1960s, all rates of growth were somewhat lower, particularly that of capital formation, and yet productivity growth remained high and accounted for about the same share of total output growth. International comparisons show that, during the same period, developed economies tended to have low input and high productivity growth rates while most middle-income countries tended to have high input and low productivity growth rates, and several – Japan, Hong Kong, Korea, Spain, Taiwan, and Israel – had high rates of both inputs and productivity (see Syrquin, 1984, for a classification of countries based on Chenery, 1983).

Table 1.7 Growth of output, input, and total factor productivity (percent)

Parameter	1950–60	1961–72	1973–81
Output	11.2	9.7	3.4
Labor	4.3	3.9	1.0
Capital	13.5	8.9	6.0
Total input	6.5	5.5	2.8
Total factor productivity	4.7	4.2	0.6
Total factor productivity relative to output	0.42	0.43	0.18

Source: Syrquin, 1984

Israel's performance is usually explained by increases in human capital – much of which is the result of on-the-job training rather than formal education, which is what is generally included in estimates of human capital – and in the exploitation of opportunities for massive development starting from a relatively low level. The exhaustion of the latter opportunities is suggested as a major reason why productivity and total output grew much less in the 1970s, despite continued growth in capital per worker.

Table 1.8 presents estimates of the components of growth by branch in 1961–72 and 1972–81. In both periods, capital and productivity rather than labor inputs accounted for growth in agriculture. In manufacturing, all three factors contributed to growth in 1961–72, but capital per worker was the main factor accounting for growth in 1972–81, and productivity actually decreased. There was also a marked decline in capital utilization.

Table 1.8 Components of growth by industry, 1961–1981 (average annual rate of change, percent)

Components	Years	A/F	MFG	CON	T/C	CPS	TBS
GDP	1961–72	6.6	11.8	10.4	10.8	7.5	9.7
	1973–81	6.1	3.9	− 1.6	4.0	3.8	3.4
Hours of work	1961–72	− 1.7	4.4	7.1	5.4	5.0	3.9
	1973–81	− 0.6	1.5	− 1.0	0.1	2.1	1.0
Capital	1961–72	4.5	8.3	7.7	13.4	12.0	8.9
	1973–81	4.5	7.4	4.7	5.5	6.7	6.0
TFP	1961–72	5.6	6.0	2.7	2.6	− 0.1	4.2
	1973–81	4.3	− 0.2	− 2.2	1.1	0	0.6
Capital per manhour	1961–72	6.2	3.9	0.6	8.0	7.0	5.0
	1973–81	5.1	5.9	5.7	5.4	4.6	5.0
GDP per manhour	1961–72	8.3	7.4	3.3	5.4	2.5	5.8
	1973–81	6.7	2.4	0.6	3.9	1.7	2.4
GDP per unit of capital	1961–72	2.1	3.5	2.7	− 2.6	− 4.5	0.8
	1973–81	1.6	− 3.5	− 6.3	1.5	− 2.5	− 2.6
Share in the business sector's GDP current prices	1961–72	11.4	31.6	11.7	13.2	32.0	100.0
	1973–82	8.3	32.8	12.6	13.7	32.5	100.0

A/F, agriculture, forestry, and fishing; MFG, manufacturing and mining; CON, construction; T/C, transport, storage, and communication; CPS, commerce and private services (including electricity and water); TBS, total business sector.
Source: Metzer, 1983, p. 52

Sources of Output Growth

The structure of output is a product of both supply and demand conditions. Syrquin (1984) has attempted to allocate output growth among four sources: domestic demand expansion, export expansion, import substitution, and changes in input–output coefficients. His estimates for 1958–1965 and 1965–72 by a three-branch classification – primary, manufacturing, and services – are presented in table 1.9 as are previous estimates by Pack (1971) for 1951–8 (where agriculture rather than primary production is shown, that is, mining is excluded).

In services, the dominant factor in all periods was expansion of domestic demand. The same is true for agriculture and all primary output until 1965.

Table 1.9 Sources of output growth, 1951–1972

Sector	Average annual rate of growth (%)	Percentage of total share				Share in output growth
		Domestic demand expansion	Export expansion	Import substitution	Change in input–output coefficients	
1951–8						
Agriculture	15.8	72	23	− 9	14	18
Industry	14.6	48	14	24	14	43
Services	7.5	60	20	− 31	51	39
1958–65						
Primary	7.3	63	38	− 11	− 12	7
Manufacturing	13.6	57	26	12	5	39
Services	9.9	93	23	− 4	− 12	54
1965–72						
Primary	5.6	32	90	− 18	− 4	5
Manufacturing	11.3	76	50	− 37	11	46
Services	7.9	66	30	− 2	6	49

Source: Syrquin, 1984

Thereafter, export expansion became the overwhelming factor. In manufacturing, domestic demand expanded from 48 percent in 1951–4 to 76 percent in 1965–72. More interesting is the fact that import substitution accounted for almost a quarter of manufacturing output growth in 1951–8, compared with only 14 percent for export expansion, but these shares were virtually reversed in 1958–65. (This was one of the major conclusions of Pack's, 1971, study.) In 1965–72, export expansion accounted for 50 percent, with import substitution becoming a negative factor.

Industrial Concentration and Ownership
In the pre-State period the Histadrut, through its corporate entity Hevrat Ovdim, undertook economic activity in many areas. It was particularly

important in agriculture (noncitrus) because most agricultural villages, collective and cooperative settlements, were Histadrut affiliated. It operated a major construction company and developed a large manufacturing conglomerate. Its health services (Kupat Holim) dominated that social service. With independence and the establishment of a government that until 1977 was controlled by a political party adhering to socialist principles, the State undertook many economic enterprises. The question of what should be government's and what the Histadrut's role has never been resolved. In practice, the government and public institutions tend to fill gaps on a pragmatic basis rather than adhering to some ideological pattern.

By the end of the 1950s about a fifth of net domestic product originated in enterprises controlled by the public sector, which accounted for a large share in transport and communications (40 percent) and almost the entire public utilities and government service branches. The Histadrut accounted for another fifth, but not dominating any one branch (Barkai, 1964).

In manufacturing, the share of product originating in Histadrut enterprises was 22 percent, and that of public enterprises only 4.3 percent. Comparisons of the shares of the public sector in manufacturing establishments and in employment in the mid-1960s show that the government ran a small number of relatively large enterprises. The Histadrut tended to control larger enterprises. Though over 90 percent of the establishments were privately owned, they included very many small firms.

Data on the geographic distribution of manufacturing establishments and employment in the mid-1960s clearly bring out the dominant economic importance of Tel Aviv and the central district. The Haifa Bay district, where the petrochemical industry is located, had almost one fifth of the establishments and a higher than average ratio of workers to establishment. On an almost straight line, some two hours' drive away, lay four fifths of Israel's manufacturing establishments, accounting for an almost equal share of employment.

Is Israel's manufacturing highly monopolistic, with many branches dominated by one to three firms, as is widely believed? The subject is now being studied in the Bank of Israel, and preliminary data indicate that in 1965 high concentration was the exception. For most subbranches, only a very low percentage of sales in the domestic market originated in the three largest firms; much of the competition was from imports, but even without imports the same general conclusion holds.

Trade and the Balance of Payments[7]

In the area of international economic relations, the Israeli economy has two distinguishing features. First, it is very open, in the sense that foreign

[7] This section is based on Halevi (1983b).

trade is large relative to GNP. This is to be expected in a small economy, with scarce raw materials. Second, imports of goods and services have consistently exceeded exports; this import surplus has added greatly to the resources available to the economy.

The Balance of Payments and Economic Dependence

Israel's balance of payments situation in 1952–77 is summarized by Halevi and Baruh (1988, appendix table A.23). Imports of goods and services exceeded exports by US$250–350 million in the 1950s, by US$450–600 million during most of the 1960s, and then by new levels of about US$1 billion (one thousand million) in 1970–2 and US$2–4 billion since 1973.

The import surplus provided additional resources, but its economic implications have been a source of concern. Much of the deficit was financed by unilateral transfers – from World Jewry, the US government and the Federal Republic of Germany. The difference was made up by loans and foreign exchange reserves. In 1949–51, depletion of reserves was a main source of finance. Later, long-term borrowing was developed; among the major sources were sales abroad of State of Israel Bonds and borrowing from the US government. In the past decade US aid, both grants and loans, has become the major source of finance, covering more than half the total deficit.

Table 1.10 presents some indicators of Israel's economic dependence. Row 1 shows that the total addition to resources, computed in current price values, is about 20 percent, and no trend is apparent. This illustrates the importance of a sudden drastic cutback in the size of the import surplus. Such a cutback could actually decrease output, in view of Israel's reliance on imports. Row 2 illustrates this aspect of dependence: the share of imports financed by exports has risen from 20 to 70 percent; thus total imports are less dependent on other sources of finance.

Table 1.10 Ratios indicating economic dependence, selected years

Indicator	1952	1958	1964	1970	1975	1980	1982
1 Import surplus to resources	0.21	0.17	0.19	0.21	0.27	0.17	0.20
2 Exports to imports	0.22	0.34	0.52	0.53	0.49	0.72	0.68
3 Debt-financed import surplus to resources	0.07	0.04	0.08	0.11	0.15	0.06	0.09
4 Interest to exports	0.14	0.13	0.09	0.10	0.11	0.09	0.11
5 Interest and debt repayments to exports	0.49	0.67	0.37	0.31	0.26	0.22	0.23
6 Gross investment to import surplus	1.30	1.41	1.96	1.09	0.87	1.08	0.96

Source: Halevi, 1983b, table 6

A second aspect of concern about economic dependence is illustrated in rows 3, 4, and 5: the "future burden" aspect. Much of the import surplus is financed by unilateral transfers. The growing reliance on debt financing in the past decade has increased the interest and repayment burden, but export growth has been fast enough to prevent any increase in the repayment-to-exports ratio.

Row 6 shows that the allocation of the import surplus has changed; whereas gross investment was much larger than the import surplus until the mid-1960s, it has more or less matched it since then. Thus net investment is considerably less, that is, part of the import surplus (equal to negative savings) finances consumption.

The growth in Israel's foreign exchange obligations is summarized by Halevi and Baruh (1988, appendix table A.25). The figures point to the rapid increase in long-term obligations in the last decade. In the same period there was rapid growth in short-term assets and liabilities, reflecting the activities of Israeli banks in the world money markets. Although table 1.10 does not show the repayment burden as significant, the structure of foreign debts indicates Israel's susceptibility to withdrawal of short-term funds or failure to renew debt.

Imports

Imports of goods and services have always been large relative to GNP. In the 1950s this ratio was 30–40 percent, in the 1960s it was usually 40–50 percent, and it has risen since 1973 to about 70 percent. The share of consumer goods in total imports of goods and services dropped rapidly during the 1950s, and has been less than 5 percent since 1960. Final investment goods show a similar but less dramatic trend, falling in recent years to about 7 percent. Defense imports have fluctuated considerably from year to year but have been a substantial factor since 1967. Raw materials and semiprocessed goods have been the main imports throughout, growing in relative importance as Israel deepened its production processes. Since 1973, the share of fuel in this category has risen. Services make up a quarter to a third of all imports, with the most dramatic growth trend evident in "investment income," mainly interest charges.

Input–output studies estimate the import component in final uses. For 1964 (Bank of Israel, 1964, p. 17), this was estimated to be 29.3 percent on average, and the percentages for the various components were as follows: 22.0 in private consumption, 29.8 in public consumption, 33.6 in gross investment, and 44.9 in exports.

Exports

Exports have grown relative to imports, and have risen to about 40–50 percent on GNP. Over the years, exports have not only grown rapidly but have become greatly diversified.

Agricultural exports, mainly citrus fruit, were the major single category until the 1960s. They were then replaced in relative importance first by cut and polished diamonds and then by manufactured goods. Some two fifths of total exports have been made up by services. The growing share of "investment income" is the obverse side of part of the increased interest charges: both reflect the matching growth in short-term assets and obligations. More important is "foreign travel," Israel's receipts from tourism. Though this reached 8–10 percent of total exports (about $900 million) in 1980, it falls far short of what most observers consider Israel's potential to be.

The exports differ greatly in their net foreign exchange contribution, that is, value added. The value added percentage ranges from about 20 in diamonds to about 80 in citrus exports. For industrial exports, value added is around 50–58 percent.

The development of industrial exports was marked by growing export diversity and a relative increase in the share of sophisticated industries. The latter development was most striking in the 1970s. Whereas the less-sophisticated branches – mining, food, textiles, clothing, wood, and rubber – accounted for over 60 percent of total manufactured exports (excluding diamonds) in 1970, their share fell to less than 36 percent in 1980 (see Halevi and Baruh, 1988, appendix table A.36).

Early studies of the factor content of Israel's trade (Bruno, 1962) found a "Leontieff paradox": exports were relatively capital intensive. Later studies of the factor content of Israel's exports of manufactured goods have stressed the growing importance of human capital. Fishelson et al. (1979) found that in the early 1970s Israel exported skill-intensive goods to countries less developed than itself, and imported skill-intensive goods from more developed countries.

Estimates of relative tangible and human capital intensities in Israel's imports (table 8.5 later) show that tangible capital per worker was indeed greater in exports in 1965, but this paradox disappeared by the 1970s. Human capital per worker was somewhat higher in imports than in exports in the 1960s but there was virtually no difference by the late 1970s.

The Geographical Structure of Trade
The geographical pattern of Israeli trade could not but be very different from that of pre-State Palestine. World War II and its aftermath reduced the economic importance of the United Kingdom, with which Palestine was very closely linked economically, and the War of Independence severed Israel from the neighboring Arab states.

The geographical structure of trade in goods is shown by Halevi and Baruh (1988, appendix table A.39). The changing patterns reflect not only comparative advantage in production, but also methods of finance. Thus US grants and loans in the early 1950s tended to finance imports from the United States, and the sudden growth of West Germany as a supplier in the mid-1950s reflects the Reparations Agreement, since reparations were received in the form of goods. Similarly, the relatively large share of imports from "other countries" in the early years is a result of reliance on trade and payments agreements with other soft-currency countries.

From the 1960s, the changing patterns of imports reflects more basic economic considerations; tied aid and trade agreements declined in importance. The United States has been Israel's main supplier throughout, though its share has steadily declined. The shares referred to above do not include figures for direct imports for defense, whose presence would raise the share of the United States since 1973. The United Kingdom's share rose gradually to about a fifth, where it remained during most of the 1960s, without benefit of special agreements. During the 1970s, the United Kingdom's share declined and West Germany's fluctuated, while the total European Economic Community (EEC) share grew. In 1975–80 there was a resurgence in the share of "other countries," primarily because of changes in the price and source of oil. At the end of the 1970s West Germany and the United Kingdom each supplied a little over one tenth of Israel's imports, the rest of the EEC about a fifth, and the United States close to a quarter. Thus a small number of developed countries provided 70 percent of Israel's imports.

The pattern of exports shows that the share of the United Kingdom declined steadily, from close to 30 percent in the early 1950s to less than 10 percent in the 1970s. West Germany and the other EEC countries grew in relative importance until the mid-1960s at the expense of other European countries and the United States, but their share has not increased since then, despite preferential tariff agreements with the EEC. The United States has remained a major buyer, particularly of diamonds. Especially striking is the increased share of "other countries" in the 1970s. Part of this growth results from the inclusion in this category of goods not classified by country, a main component of which is military equipment, but the same trend is evident even when the unclassified group is excluded.

Since 1967 Israel's trade relations with the territories occupied in the Six Day War have grown. By 1980 exports of goods and services to these areas had grown to some $700 million, but this was only about 7 percent of total exports. Imports were only about $500 million, less than 4 percent of total imports, and some 36 percent of this was payment of wages to workers from the territories employed in Israel.[8] Thus these territories have only a marginal impact on Israel's balance of payments, though here Israel has an export surplus. However, Israel is the main trading partner of the occupied territories, but its importance is greater in the territories' imports than in their exports.

The developments in the balance of payments were both a result and a determinant of trade policy. We turn now to an overview of related policy.

---

[8] Unpublished figures estimated by the CBS balance-of-payments division.

2

Trade Policy: An Overview

Israel has had continuous deficits in the goods and services account of its balance of payments, as we have seen in chapter 1. A combination of five types of major policy measures was used to deal with the balance-of-payments problem. The first was to mobilize foreign funds – unilateral transfers and long-term capital inflow – to finance the import surplus. The fact that the import surplus persisted for so long is clear evidence that this financing succeeded. The other four groups of measures were all intended to reduce the import surplus by affecting exports or imports: investment incentives (primarily through funds from the development budget) to encourage export and import substitution industries; occasional drastic demand-curtailing macroeconomic policy designed to decrease imports and push products into export markets; exchange controls and quantitative restrictions (QRs) to curb imports; the use of exchange rates, import taxes, and export subsidies to affect trade via the price mechanism.

This study concentrates on the interrelationship between QRs, exchange rates, customs duties, and export subsidies. Customs duties and subsidies are often intended as price incentives for individual commodities or commodity groups. However, in Israel these have been used as "nonformal components" of the exchange rate.

Israel was officially on a fixed exchange rate standard – the adjustable peg – until late 1977, when it adopted a fluctuating rate system. Until 1975, when the crawling peg was adopted, changes in the formal rate of exchange were infrequent. Formal devaluation was considered a sign of weakness, and was usually deferred long past when it was due; taxes on imports and subsidies to exports were used as partial substitutes for devaluation. These "nonformal" components of the exchange rate created multiple effective rates of exchange that differed not only between goods, services, and transfers, but also between exports and imports, with great divergences between commodities. This multiple rate system has been studied by Michaely (1971); its role in the liberalization process is considered in greater detail below.

The Trade Policy Regime before 1952

The economic conditions facing Israel at the end of its War of Independence (1949) made government controls over foreign trade (especially
imports) inevitable. In early 1948 Palestine was expelled from the sterling
area and its sterling assets in London were temporarily frozen. Israel's
exports (mainly citrus) dropped drastically in the course of the 1948
fighting. The disruption due to the war, the war effort itself, and the
post-war wave of immigrants led to a considerable increase in the demand
for imports.

The ensuing gap in the current account and the dwindling foreign
exchange reserves in the post-independence period (1949–51) were met by
a system of very stringent trade and payments restrictions, but not by
adjusting the price of foreign currency.[1] The framework of these controls
was inherited from the mandatory regime. As we shall see, 1949–51
qualifies as the period of least "trade liberalization."

The restrictive system consisted of a licensing system for all imports,
with the government allocating foreign currency for most imports.[2] Export
receipts had to be turned over to the authorities at rates somewhat higher
than the official rate. Private capital outflows were not permitted, while
capital inflows (loans) were strictly controlled so that they would not
interfere with the conduct of monetary policy.

On the import side, the restrictions worked as a system which allocated
among various uses a resource in short supply – foreign currency – whose
price was kept lower than the level at which an equilibrium could be struck
between supply and demand. This QR scheme was accompanied by
rationing and price controls in the local market. The protection of local
industries (mainly final consumer goods industries) from competing imports was almost absolute: in general, the import of any good produced in
Israel was simply barred. Furthermore, declaration by a domestic firm of
its intent to produce a given good led, in most cases, to the prohibition of
that good's import. Importers could appeal to a Customs Committee,
whose duty was to withhold protection from goods with excessive local–
foreign price differentials. The bias in favor of local production is evident
from the fact that the Committee very rarely decided in favor of importers.

---

[1] The formal rate remained at the IL 0.357 per US dollar level from September 1949 to the
end of 1951 (the rate was slightly lower in the first nine months of 1949). Furthermore, the
import effective rate (formal rate plus import tax rate) rose by only 2 percent during those
three years.

[2] Some commodity imports (about 17 percent) were financed by gifts, immigrants' capital,
and foreign capital transfers, and were termed imports without payment. The decision as to
which goods could be imported under this scheme rested with the government through the
licensing process.

QRs on imports of raw materials and investment goods that could not, in general, be produced in Israel operated mainly as a foreign currency rationing device.

Lack of relevant data (mainly price comparisons) makes it impossible to calculate effective or even nominal protection rates for import substitutes for this period. For exports, the nominal protection rates (NPRs) were around 10–15 percent (the export subsidy rate).

In 1949–51 the export effective exchange rate (EER) (formal rate plus subsidy rate) was not very different from the import EER (formal rate plus import taxation rate). Since the latter rate drastically understates the effective protection rates of import substitutes, it is clear that export production was grossly discriminated against compared with production for the local market. As we shall see, this discrimination was maintained until the 1970s, with a tendency for the protection gap to narrow over the years.

Trade Policy in 1952–1961

In 1949–51 the policy of keeping the price of foreign currency nearly constant and the pressure on domestic prices due to expansionary fiscal and monetary policies affected rationing and price controls adversely and led to the development of black markets. The cure took the form of a drastic devaluation process which began in early 1952 and ended in 1955 when the exchange rate reached IL 1.80 per US dollar[3] (five times the pre-devaluation level of IL 0.357 per US dollar). At the same time controlled prices in the local market were allowed to rise, doubling consumer prices from the end of 1951 to the end of 1954. This "real" devaluation[4] (carried out in the context of a restrictive demand policy) put an end to the state of disequilibrium. The tripling of the relative price of imports permitted the relaxation of QRs on raw material imports and gave a greater role to the price mechanism in controlling import quantities.

The relaxation of QRs on raw material imports took the form of a move from specific to general import licenses. Furthermore, the ratio of allowed imports to total applications was increased. Special levies were imposed on these imports to help control their volume. A study carried out on Israel's tariff structure in 1955–6 reveals that about 25 percent of imports (mainly noncompetitive) were limited in that year by taxes rather than by quotas (Gafni et al., 1963).

---

[3] Customs and other import tax rates were also raised, but most of the changes in the EER for imports were due to changes in the formal rate.
[4] The indices for the EER of the Israeli pound and for the consumer price level were 537 and 217 respectively in the last quarter of 1954 (end of 1951 = 100) (Michaely, 1975, table 5.5).

The removal of QRs on imports of raw materials and to a lesser extent on imported investment goods, and their replacement by the price mechanism, was carried on from 1955 until the early 1960s.

Two categories of goods remained outside this general drift away from QRs. The first included certain raw material imports, for instance, for textiles, which were restricted in order to allow quota profits to exporters. This import entitlement subsidization scheme, confined to the manufacturing sector (excluding diamonds), was instituted in 1953 and ended by 1959. The decline and demise of this scheme was due to the disappearance of quota profits as QRs on imports were lifted and to their replacement by a general direct export subsidization scheme.

The second category of goods whose imports continued to be restricted were raw materials for food industries and fuel. The government imported nearly 80 percent of the former and all the latter, for reasons of security and monopsonic power. Bulk purchase of these commodities by the government is still prevalent in Israel.

Final consumer goods produced in Israel continued to be protected through import prohibition. A few intermediate and investment goods which could be produced locally were also granted this type of protection, but the fact that these goods constituted inputs to the production of final consumer goods militated against their inclusion in the protected goods list.

In 1955–61 the formal rate of exchange of the Israeli pound remained unchanged at IL 1.80 per US dollar but creeping devaluation was introduced by gradually increasing various taxes on imports and subsidies on exports. The end result (in 1961) was a multiple exchange rate system with a high degree of dispersion in import tax rates and with a far more moderate dispersion in export rates.

In 1955, the nonformal component (subsidy) of the export EER amounted to only about 1.5 percent of the overall rate (including both the formal and the nonformal components). By 1961, the share of the nonformal component had grown to 32 percent. This rise in the export subsidization rate was effected by introducing value-added premiums payable to industrial exports (excluding diamonds) that subsidized the local value-added component of the exported output rather than the value of the total output.

The export subsidy schemes narrowed the gap between import and export EERs from 20 percent in 1955 to zero by 1958. Still, this equalization of effective exchange rates does not imply an equalization of protection rates. On this score, exports were discriminated against since the QRs in the import substitution sector brought about very high (unmeasured) protection levels.

During the early 1950s allocations for some services imports (for instance tourism) were severely restricted, and some necessary expenditures (for instance transportation) were allowed, but foreign companies had to work through blocked accounts. These restrictions on services were gradually relaxed, and allocations for tourism were increased.

From 1952 through 1961 the liberalization process, when various aspects are considered, was continuous: the price mechanism was used more frequently for affecting noncompetitive imports; the bias against exports relative to import substitution was partly eliminated; measures were taken to decrease intra-export discrimination in subsidies; and there was greater liberalization of services. The process can be seen as two distinct stages: 1952–5 witnessed the rejection of the previous trade regime and a switch to effective exchange rates as the major tool for curbing noncompetitive imports; the 1956–61 subperiod was one of more gradual nondrastic continued liberalization.

The Trade Regime in 1962–1977

In the early 1960s the misallocation of resources arising from the near prohibition of imports of goods produced in Israel began to be recognized and discussed.

In February 1962 a "new economic policy" was instituted. It consisted of a devaluation of the Israeli pound and a declaration of intent to allow imports to compete with local production. This announcement initiated a liberalization policy which continued through 1977. The policy consisted of two stages: in the first, completed by the end of 1968, QRs on commodities produced in Israel were replaced by tariffs granting similar protection levels. During the second stage, from 1969–1977, tariffs were scaled down to allow import competition. Because of the basic differences in these stages, we consider them as separate liberalization episodes.

The 1962 devaluation increased the formal price of the US dollar from IL 1.80 to IL 3.00 (67 percent). This step was taken in order to move from the multiple exchange rate system toward a unitary system and to forestall balance-of-payments difficulties. The former objective was looked upon as a necessary first step in a program of import liberalization.

The devaluation was indeed accompanied by a reduction in tariff rates, which not only lowered the effective devaluation from 67 to 37 percent but also considerably reduced the dispersion within the import tax rates system.[5] On the export side, nearly all export subsidies were abolished, which meant that exports were given no nominal protection whatsoever.

The 1962 devaluation left the protection levels for import substitutes unchanged, since these were effected through quantitative controls (import

[5] The coefficient of variation of the EERs of imports went down from 0.435 in 1961 to 0.268 in 1962.

prohibition) rather than tariffs and other import taxes. Again, no estimates of nominal and effective protection rates on import substitutes for this point in time are available, since no price comparisons were made at the time between prices received by local producers and the cost, insurance, and freight (c.i.f.) prices of corresponding goods had they been imported.

The first step in the post-1962 liberalization policy was to set up a public commission empowered to replace QRs on imports with equivalent tariffs. The latter were set, at the outset, at levels as restrictive as the QRs. This first step cannot therefore be credited with having actually liberalized the import trade, though it was a necessary one if import liberalization was to proceed to a second stage, namely, tariff rate reductions.

The public commission completed work by the end of 1968; from then on a significant import liberalization process began to gain impetus. Since the process consisted of reductions in the tariff rates, more and more import substitutes became subject to various degrees of competition from imports.

The trade liberalization policy adopted in 1962 was explained to the public as being related to Israel's need to become competitive with Europe. As early as 1958, governmental committees had been set up to examine the implications of the formation of the EEC for the Israeli economy. The initial motivation for some kind of association with the EEC – ultimately complete integration – was political. The main economic selling point to local economic policymakers was the potential for Israeli exports arising from an integrated European market. Opinions on the consequences of unhindered imports of Israel's industrial development were divided: "free-traders" welcomed this new external reason for liberalization, whereas "protectionists" feared the effects of import competition. The 1962 policy of trade liberalization preceded the negotiations with the EEC; consequently, negotiators could adopt the view that concessions granted in the form of reduced protection were not really concessions but rather were part of an announced process already accepted, with only the timing influenced by the negotiations.

The first agreements with the EEC – a trade agreement signed in 1964 and a five-year preferential agreement signed in 1970 – did not involve any significant Israeli concessions. In 1973 and 1974 new negotiations culminated in an agreement on a free-trade area in industrial goods, entered into in 1975. The EEC eliminated duties on almost all industrial imports from Israel by July 1977 and agreed to reduce tariffs on some agricultural goods. For its part, Israel was gradually to reduce all duties on 60 percent of industrial imports from the EEC by January 1980, and, starting in July 1977, gradually to reduce tariffs on most of the remaining 40 percent, which were deemed "sensitive" because they competed with domestic product. These reductions were originally to be completed by 1985, but the time period could be extended to 1989.

Thus the agreement with the EEC was not the initiator of liberalization on sensitive imports, but served more as a block against reversal of liberalization policy. It was indeed a major factor in the liberalization of noncompetitive imports.

The liberalization process in 1965–77 can be analyzed using two sets of data: estimates of nominal and effective protection rates (NPRs and EPRs) and import penetration ratios (MPRs), defined as CM/(TO − X +CM) were TO is the total output of an industry, CM are the imports competing with that industry's output, and X are the exports of that industry (for details of methods of estimation and earlier studies, see Baruh, 1976, 1979, 1980).

The year 1965 is chosen as a benchmark since it was the first year for which NPRs and EPRs were systematically estimated for Israel's tradeable commodities. The NPR and EPR estimates are based on import tax rates (when competitive imports constituted a significant ratio of the total availability of a given good in the local market) and on price comparisons (when import tax rates or remaining QRs did not allow significant import penetration).

The first point to be made about the benchmark year of 1965 is that, for about 62 percent of the industrial output destined for the local market in that year, the MPR was less than 10 percent.[6] The high proportion of import-substituting output that was shielded from competing imports shows that effective liberalization had not yet begun in 1965. By 1977 the proportion of industrial output with an MPR of less than 10 percent fell to about 14 percent, indicating that liberalization was under way in the period surveyed (1965–77).[7]

Estimates of effective protection indices for 1965 show high bias in favor of import substitution, whose average effective protection index was about 50 percent greater than the export index. This effective bias was due to the higher nominal protection levels afforded to import substitutes and the escalation effect in the import substitutes sector, which arose from the large differential between the NPR on outputs compared with the rate for inputs. No such escalation effect could arise in the export sector, where the output–input differential in NPRs was rather low.

It should also be pointed out that these estimates are based on the assumption that the exchange rate of the Israeli pound remains unchanged on moving from a protected system to one in which the ruling prices are

[6] Local outputs exclude nontradeables like clay, sandstone, cement, baked goods, soft drinks, repairs, etc. Nontradeability is due to high transport costs.

[7] Estimations of MPRs require detailed (by commodity) data on industrial output and corresponding import data. In Israel, such data are collected only in years for which input–output tables are constructed. The most detailed estimates can be found in Halevi and Baruh (1988, appendix table A.32).

world-market prices. Estimates of net protection rates, which take into account the devaluation required to keep the current account constant on moving to a free-trade regime, show that on average exports in 1965 did not enjoy any effective protection. This implies that export industries with lower than average effective protection levels must have faced negative rates of protection.

The introduction of a new export subsidy scheme in 1966 (the "indirect tax refund" scheme), which granted subsidies at nearly equal rates to all the exports that did not enjoy any nominal protection in 1965, raised net NPRs in the export sector to about 7 percent in 1968. This subsidization scheme narrowed the dispersion among the export protection rates.

To summarize, 1965 was still a year in which most Israeli industrial import substitutes did not face external competition. In terms of protection levels (both nominal and effective), exports were grossly discriminated against compared with import substitutes. Furthermore, the dispersion of protection rates in both sectors was quite pronounced. On these counts, 1965 is still a year with low marks on trade liberalization. By 1968, there was no reduction in the bias against exports in terms of nominal and effective protection levels. In the import substitutes sector no narrowing occurred in the dispersion of protection rates; for exports, however, the dispersion of the protection rates did diminish.

Thus the changes between 1962 and 1968 were essentially in the form, rather than the level, of protection. In 1968 a new policy of reducing protection levels was introduced, which operated over the 1969–77 period. During this period there was more rapid reduction of protection rates on import substitution in the earlier years (1969–72) than between 1972 and 1977, but there was a greater reduction of anti-export bias in terms of rate differentials in the second subperiod. By 1977 a considerable degree of import liberalization had already been achieved.

The next major change in Israeli trade policy occurred in October 1977. Israel moved from a fixed to a floating exchange rate system and controls on capital movements were considerably liberalized. These steps were accompanied by a 26 percent devaluation of the Israeli pound (from IL 11.90 per US dollar to IL 15 per dollar), by an abolition of all export subsidies and by some import tax reductions that decreased NPRs for manufactured import substitutes by an average of 4 percent. Much of the remaining licensing apparatus, which was burdensome although it had little economic impact, was abolished. Thus the reforms of late 1977 were a new liberalization episode. However, because their impact was greater on capital movements than on trade, this episode is not included in this study.

In the following years tariffs were gradually eliminated or reduced in accordance with the EEC agreement. However, the deteriorating balance-of-payments situation in the early 1980s led to regression in liberalization policy, including the imposition of nontariff barriers. The continuous process of liberalization, lasting some 30 years, came to a (temporary) halt.

Liberalization Episodes

From even a brief survey of trade policy it is clear that in 1952 Israel embarked on a long process of trade liberalization, and, though the situation in 1977 was still far short of complete liberalization, the progress made from the very highly controlled pre-1952 trade regime was immense.

The term "trade liberalization" encompasses several components: greater reliance on exchange rates and the price mechanism as determinants of foreign trade in general; changes in the form of protection of import substitutes; lowering of actual levels of protection; reductions of bias in protection between import substitutes and exports, and between commodities in each group. Even the announcement of intentions regarding these components has an element of liberalization. Israel's liberalization measures did affect all the components, but progress was not uniform in all; in fact, frequently major advances for one component were accompanied by regression in others. The nonuniformity of the period of liberalization is illustrated in the following chronology.

1949–51   Most highly controlled trade regime. QRs on all imports. Considerable bias against exports.

1952–5   Devaluation and relaxation of QRs on noncompetitive imports (mainly raw materials) and their replacement by import levies (use of price mechanism). Import prohibition of goods produced locally. Still considerable bias against exports.

1956–62   Gradual removal of QRs on noncompetitive imports and their replacement by tariffs amid widespread liberalization of services imports. Continued near prohibition (through QRs) of imports of locally produced goods. Continued bias against exports despite various export subsidization schemes, with some reductions in intra-export bias.

1962–8   Devaluation and abolition of export subsidies. Gradual replacement of QRs on imports of locally produced goods by equally restrictive tariffs (by 1966). The beginning of a slow scaling of tariffs on competitive imports (by 1968). Continued bias against exports, though bias reduced in the 1965–8 period through export subsidization. High dispersion in protection levels afforded to import substitutes.

1969–73   Program of across-the-board reductions in protective tariffs but persistent and high dispersion in the protection levels in the import substitute sector. Reduced dispersion in protection levels for exports.

1974–7   Continued across-the-board reductions in protection levels from 1975 in accordance with the EEC agreement; reduction in anti-export bias.

Post–1977   A policy change at the end of October 1977 led to an increase in the nominal protection gap between import substitutes and exports, a reduction in dispersion in export rates, and reduced differentials between the effective rates of commodities, services, and capital transactions. Mounting balance-of-payments problems from 1980 led to regression in liberalization policy.

The comparison of experience in trade liberalization with other studies in the project required analysis of liberalization "episodes" (see the preface to the volume). The Israeli experience does not show dramatic brief episodes, but rather a prolonged process. Our concern is therefore to choose subperiods in which more basic changes took place, and to consider them as episodes. To help choose these episodes, an arbitrary index of trade liberalization was constructed, based on the authors' subjective weighting of the various components of liberalization. For international uniformity, a scale of 0 to 20 was adopted, and only discrete integers were allowed. This has the advantage of highlighting changes but, given the narrow range of the index, sometimes leads to an arbitrary choice of attributing to a particular year of change which was actually more gradual. Thus, what figure 2.1 purports to point out is not the year-to-year changes, nor the

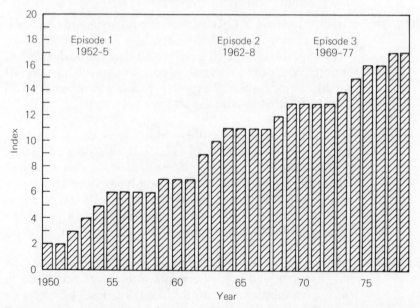

Figure 2.1 Index of trade liberalization, 1950–1978

absolute values of liberalization, but rather turning points and trends. Three subperiods were chosen as episodes:

1952–5   marked by a general switch to greater reliance on the price mechanism;

1962–8   marked by changes in the form of protection;

1969–77   marked by reduced levels of protection.

3

Liberalization and Accompanying Policies, 1952–1955

The Introduction of Liberalization

Economic Circumstances

During the three and a half years between the creation of the State in May 1948 and the end of 1951, the magnitude of Israel's economic problems reinforced by the government's ideological predilection engendered major intervention in the economy. In foreign trade, this intervention took the form of strict exchange control and foreign exchange rationing. The exchange rate was maintained at an unrealistically overvalued level; import licenses were issued to recognized traditional importers.

The tariff level in 1951 was low, averaging only IL 0.038 per US dollar or 10.6 percent of the official exchange rate (Michaely, 1971, pp. 12–13). To avoid complete deterrence of private capital inflows some imports could be financed without allocation of foreign exchange, under the misnomer "imports without payment" (IWP), with higher domestic prices providing a more reasonable rate of exchange to suppliers of such funds. These imports included some "luxury" items (for instance, tires) and some more essential imports, mainly building materials. The effective premium on these goods, which at their peak amounted to 20 percent of total imports, has been estimated at 12.9 percent of the total value of imports in 1951 (calculated from Gaathon, 1959, pp. 66–8). If these premiums were added to the EERs, made up of the formal rate *plus* import duties, the average EER for imports (EERM) would be higher than suggested by the low tariff levels, and rate dispersion would be much larger. Exports received an average premium of 14 percent in 1951 (Michaely, 1971, p. 85), but total exports were quantitatively small.

The trade restrictions were part of a general system of price control and rationing. Thus the QR system gave widespread protection to domestic production and, except for the IWP scheme, quota profits were passed on to the consumers in the form of lower controlled prices.

Unable to prevent the build-up of excess demand resulting from wartime finance and mass immigration, the government "repressed" inflation. Price controls and rationing, based on mandatory experience, became extensive after the announcement of an austerity program in April 1949 (see Weiss, 1964, for a comprehensive study of the price-control system). Their purpose was to ration scarce resources, including foreign exchange, to guarantee an equitable distribution of essential commodities among the rapidly growing population. Additional objectives were the expansion of domestic output and the fostering of investment.

This program did achieve some success: firstly, mass immigration was fed and clothed (though inadequately housed), and for several years the control and rationing system did maintain a fairly equitable – though hardly economic – distribution of the most essential commodities. Secondly, resources were directed to capital formation. The ratio of net capital formation to total resources available to the economy was 21.7 percent in 1950 and 24.1 percent in 1951; a ratio as high as 20 percent was never achieved after 1952.

The repressed inflation was accompanied by continuous monetary expansion; thus the "anti-inflation policy" was merely curbing inflationary symptoms while creating a financial time bomb (see Patinkin, 1956). By late 1950, the excess demand led to rapidly expanding black markets, and increasing segments of the public lost faith in the government's ability to control prices and guarantee an equitable distribution of commodities. A year of political instability, from October 1950 to October 1951, did nothing to improve the control apparatus or its image.[1] Paradoxically, a vigorous return to the political scene of the minister who originally administered the controls (in October 1951) coincided with the realization on the part of other policymakers that the system could not be maintained and that the inflationary demand must be absorbed rather than repressed.

While disillusionment with the distribution system grew, the balance of payments deteriorated drastically. The deficit in the goods and services account, estimated at US$220 million in 1949, rose to some US$280 million in 1950 and swelled to almost US$370 million in 1951.[2] Part of the increase reflected the rise in import prices induced by the Korean War, estimated at 21.5 percent between the second quarter of 1950 and mid-1951 (Gaathon, 1959, p. 5). Despite net unilateral transfers (some US$137 million) and long-term official loans (US$78 million), the short-term position

---

[1] Patinkin (1956, p. 49) presents estimates of black-market prices for foodstuffs. In September 1951, the ratio of black-market prices to controlled prices on selected food items ranged from 2.7 to 9.3. Similar ratios are reported by Weiss (1964) for the main controlled sector: building materials.

[2] The 1949 figure is from Michaely (1963, p. 58). The 1950 and 1951 data are from Halevi (1956, p. 133).

deteriorated sharply, with liabilities increasing and reserves falling to only US$34 million.[3]

Whereas the official rate of exchange was maintained at US$2.80 to the Israeli pound, the black-market rate fell to US$1.20 at the end of 1950, and to an average of US$0.63 in 1951 (Gaathon, 1959, p. 7).

From 1949 to 1951, immigrants arrived faster than they could be absorbed in terms of housing and employment. Abandoned Arab property was used for housing at first, but soon many immigrants were held in transit camps and in temporary housing. In terms of unemployment, the situation in 1951 was better than in 1950: average unemployment, including potential workers in immigrants' camps who were prevented from actively seeking work, fell from 11.2 to 8.1 percent (computed from Hovne, 1961, pp. 12 and 82). However, the absolute magnitude of "unabsorbed" immigrants was so large that immigration policy was changed the following year from openly soliciting mass immigration to being much more restrictive.

Thus the principal economic problems were internal: mass immigration, unmatched by increased output and housing facilities; suppressed inflation, fueled by monetary expansion, that created black markets; a serious balance-of-payments problem; and an unrealistic exchange rate. Clearly, major changes in economic policy were called for.

Some important changes were already introduced in late 1951, notably a curtailment of monetary expansion. From September, the monthly rate of monetary expansion fell from 2.5 to 1.5 percent, and some effective devaluation was achieved by raising the valuation of imports for customs purposes and by imposing additional import levies (Patinkin, 1956, p. 29). However, the official announcement of a new policy was delayed until February 1952.

Nature and Targets of the Policy

On February 13, 1952, a new economic policy (NEP) was announced, introduced by the Prime Minister himself – who was usually unconcerned with economic matters. Ben Gurion stated the aims of the NEP as being to encourage the inflow of foreign capital, to stabilize the currency, to increase exports of agricultural and industrial products, and to prevent the rise in prices of essential goods. The major innovation was the replacement of the single official exchange rate of IL 0.357 to the US dollar by three *formal* rates: the previous rate, plus two additional "formal" rates (IL 0.714 per dollar and IL 1.00 per dollar). Different types of transactions were conducted at one of these rates. Since most imports, except for some

---

[3] Long-term inflow figures are from Halevi (1956, pp. 108 and 119); reserves data are from Michaely (1975, p. 35).

essentials, were now charged a higher rate of exchange, the effect of the NEP was to raise the price level. This was clearly its intention: to reduce the real value of accumulated cash balances held by the public.

Was the NEP really a liberalization policy? At its introduction, it made no claims either to reduce domestic protection or to dismantle the existing licensing system, replacing QRs by tariffs. It was essentially an anti-inflation policy, replacing repressed inflation by a higher price level and lowering real purchasing power. Formal devaluation was designed to improve the balance of payments through both income and relative price effects. Mere devaluation cannot be considered as "liberalization," but if it also leads to considerable narrowing of rate dispersion it does contain a strong element of liberalization. Initially, the NEP of 1952 did not do this: the gradualism in the transfer of imports from lower to higher formal exchange rates led to marked rate dispersion. Nonetheless, the NEP was an announcement of a new more liberal approach. Though the import-licensing system was not replaced by fiscal restrictions on imports, the drastic increases in EERs reduced much of the excess demand for imports, and in some cases made the QRs redundant. For this reason, and because it signaled greater future reliance on the price mechanism, we view the NEP of 1952 as a bona fide liberalization episode.

Political Circumstances

Drastic changes in economic policy were delayed by political instability until October 1951, when a new government was set up, again dominated by the MAPAI labor party. Though there was no change in economic ideology as a result of the change in the composition of the government, the ideology of the ruling party had itself changed. The minister in charge of rationing and price control was determined to reaffirm and improve the control mechanism, and indeed improved methods were employed (Weiss, 1964). However, the other MAPAI ministers, most importantly the Minister of Finance, realized that the entire system of repressed inflation had reached an impasse. The change in policy starting in October 1951 and culminating in the NEP of 1952 was entirely at the initiative of the same MAPAI party, but reflected the public disaffection evidenced in the 1951 municipal elections. In December 1952 there was a government crisis, completely unrelated to economic matters, which resulted in a new coalition government in which one of the religious parties was replaced by the General Zionists. The General Zionists, for whom economic liberalism was a major tenet of faith, received the Ministry of Commerce and Industry, second only in importance among economic ministries to the Ministry of Finance. Consequently, the main ministry issuing import licenses was now controlled by people who viewed controls as a necessary, but temporary, evil. The allocation of foreign exchange remained in the hands of the MAPAI-held Ministry of Finance.

Public reception of the NEP was mixed. For several weeks, the details wer not clear even to informed segments of the population (see, for instance, *The Jerusalem Post*, February 18, April 8, and April 18, 1952). The press reacted partly along ideological lines, reflecting the debate in the Knesset – the more left-wing papers saw the policy as a sell-out to foreign (American) investors, and the more right-wing saw no real changes. The MAPAI-connected paper *Davar* (February 14, 1952) clearly saw the NEP as leading to a more liberal economic regime, granting more freedom to consumers, workers, and producers.

Israel applied for membership in the International Monetary Fund (IMF) in late 1953, while the NEP was under way. Though it was felt at the time that IMF membership would entail certain restrictions on foreign exchange policy (*Israel Economist*, October 1953, p. 213), this liberalization episode was neither initiated by nor "sold" to the public as being compelled by foreign pressure. Undoubtedly, however, this move to a more liberal economic regime was partly a response to the desires of the American Jewish community and the US government, the main providers of foreign assistance.

Implementation of the Liberalization Policy

The keystone of the liberalization policy was the introduction of a multiple formal exchange rate system and the gradual substitution of the higher rates (that is, more Israeli pounds per US dollar) for lower ones. Initially, essential imports such as basic foodstuffs and uncut diamonds (for reexport as polished diamonds) continued to be charged at the old low rates. Less essential imports were charged the higher rates. Gradually, the higher rates were applied to more and more items. Exports, too, were subject to the three rates: only diamonds received the lowest rate; other exports received the higher two, although some subsidies were reduced. The process of shifting transactions to the highest rate continued through 1952 and 1953.

The implicit assumption, by both policymakers and the public, when the first three-formal-rate system was adopted, was that the highest rate would become the only rate. In fact, before this target was achieved, increases in the domestic price level forced the adoption, from February 1953, of an additional higher rate; thus, when the lowest rate was dropped, a new three-rate system came into existence. In late 1954, the highest formal rate applied to all commodities and to most services. Only in 1955 was a unitary formal rate system reinstated, with the highest formal rate, IL 1.80 to the US dollar, becoming the official rate.

Exchange Controls

Fundamentally, exchange control was unchanged. In fact, the worsening foreign exchange situation in late 1951 led to tightening of the foreign exchange control regulations. Many believed, however, that the first steps were necessary preconditions for actual liberalization of controls, which would follow.

The entry of the General Zionists into the coalition strengthened these expectations. A public committee set up to examine the whole idea of exchange control presented its report in July 1953. All the members agreed that the time was not yet ripe for complete abolition of exchange controls, particularly for capital movements. A majority felt that current account transactions had to be licensed, with a gradual changeover to open general licenses. The minority advocated freeing most current account transactions, for which the foreign exchange should be bought at auction. It also advocated using tariffs and subsidies rather than licenses to distinguish between essential goods and others. The majority called for ending the multiple formal rate system and establishing a single rate.

The 1952–5 liberalization took the form neither of an official reduction in protection from competing imports nor of an official transformation from QRs to fiscal protection. However, rising domestic prices of imports via higher EERs reduced demand and made many of the surviving QRs ineffective. Thus, whereas fiscal control of imports is usually defined as the import-reducing effect of customs duties, in the case of the NEP the same effect was achieved by increasing the formal exchange rate.

Most imports of services were limited by QRs. The severity of restrictions depended on the type of service. Foreign loans were subject to control, but interest charges on permitted loans were paid at the official rate of exchange. Profits on foreign investments could be repatriated within limits (only in 1968 was this allowed for non-"approved" investments). Foreign shipping, airline, and insurance companies could operate, but only through blocked accounts, with severe restrictions on transfers of profits. These transfers were eased only in the mid-1950s. The restrictions clearly helped promote domestic companies. Other service expenditures were subject to very strict controls and meager allocations of foreign exchange.

Passenger transport and tourist expenditures were the only service expenditures not charged the official exchange rate. Passengers were charged a travel tax, with different *ad valorem* rates depending on means of transport and class. This limited expenditure but did not discriminate between foreign and domestic carriers. Thus the NEP did not include liberalization of service imports. Only from the late 1950s, with an improved foreign exchange position, were QRs for services significantly reduced. Gradually foreign shipping, airlines, insurance companies, and other foreign services (for instance, film rental) were given greater freedom in using foreign exchange accounts and in transferring profits. The same was true for approved investments. Allocations for various purposes became more generous, and the banks were used as official foreign exchange dealers to control allocations under general directives, replacing individual applications to officials. However, since receipts from service exports had not received subsidies, the effective devaluation did improve their relative position.

Formal and Effective Exchange Rates

The multiple formal rate system continued until July 1955, when the rate of IL 1.80 to the US dollar was made official.[4] The formal rates are compared with black-market rates in table 3.1 and column 4 provides a measure of

Table 3.1 Formal and effective exchange rates for imports, and black-market rates, 1951–1956 (average rates, Israeli pounds per US dollar)

Year	1 Formal rate[a]	2 Effective rate	3 Black-market rate	4 Rate disparity	5	6 Coefficient of variance of importers' rates
1951	0.36	0.40	1.96	0.82	0.80	0.14
1952	0.69	0.81	2.53	0.73	0.68	0.32
1953	0.83	1.17	2.13	0.66	0.52	0.47
1954	1.51	1.80	2.58	0.44	0.30	0.29
1955	1.80	2.21	2.32	0.22	0.04	0.31
1956	1.80	2.26	2.47	0.27	0.09	0.45

Column 4 is column 3 minus column 1 divided by column 3; column 5 is column 3 minus column 2 divided by column 3.
[a] Excludes IWP differential.
Source: Formal and effective rates Michaely, 1975, pp. 107 and 93; Black-market rates, computed from Patinkin, 1967, p. 143; column 6. Michaely, 1971, p. 105.

rate disparity: the difference between the black-market and formal rates as a ratio of the black-market rate. The black-market rate cannot be taken as a measure of the "real" rate of exchange and therefore this ratio is not a

---

[4] A lower rate (IL 1.50 to the US dollar) for institutional transfers remained in force until 1958.

correct measure of departure from the "real" rate, but it is one measure of "intensity of control."[5]

As well as gradually transferring imports from lower to higher rates, the government levied additional charges on imports. Thus the average *effective* rate for imports (EERM) rose more than the average formal rate. Table 3.1, column 2, presents data on average effective rates for 1951–6. The black-market rate exceeded the average EERM throughout this period, but the black-market rate fluctuated whereas the average EERM rose steadily, and, as columns 4 and 5 show, the relative disparity between the black-market rates and the formal and effective rates decreased dramatically.

The average effective rates conceal disparities between commodities; in fact, the whole idea of the multiple rate system was to permit discriminating rates. Table 3.1, column 6, shows Michaely's estimates of the coefficient of variance among EERMs. In 1951 this coefficient was very low, but the NEP raised it to a high of 0.47 in 1953. Substantial fluctuations followed, but even the lower coefficients indicate considerable scatter among rates. However, it must be recalled that these estimates do not include the IWP differentials, nor estimates of quota profits, whose inclusion would probably increase the variance.

Exchange Rates, Tariffs, and Quotas[6]

The nature of Israel's tariff structure has been examined for the fiscal year 1955–6, that is, the end of this liberalization episode. Because QRs were extensively used in conjunction with tariffs, only one of these forms of limiting imports could be effective. Consequently, when a tariff was levied on a good whose imports were limited by an effective QR, the tariff merely brought in revenue, without affecting the pattern of trade or domestic output. If we call such tariffs "revenue tariffs," those duties that limited imports but did not protect domestic output "import-reducing tariffs," and those that *did* protect domestic output by reducing imports' "protective tariffs," Israel's tariffs can be classified by their effects.[7]

Of total imports subject to customs duties in 1955–6, and for which information existed to classify the tariffs by effects,[8] 43 percent were subject to revenue duties, that is, their importation was effectively limited

---

[5] This measure is used by Weiss (1964, p. 133A). The figures here differ somewhat from his because slightly different average formal rates are used.

[6] This section is based on Gafni et al. (1963).

[7] Obviously, this classification does not imply that no revenue is collected by tariffs not classified as "revenue tariffs," nor that imports are not reduced by tariffs classified as "protective" rather than as "import reducing."

[8] Tariffs classified by function applied to only 44 percent of imports; another 30 percent had differing rates depending on sources of finance, and 26 percent were not classified.

by QRs. Since 24 of the 43 percent were domestically produced goods, removal of QRs would have made the tariffs protective. Only 7 percent of imports were competitive imports, protected to some extent by tariffs and not by QRs. Thus at the end of this liberalization episode protection of domestic production was still widespread, but essentially by QRs, not tariffs.

Table 3.2 shows the composition of imports subject to tariffs classified by function. Protective duties were imposed on foodstuffs and on processed goods. The imports subject to import-reducing (but not protective) duties were in all categories, but more than half were processed goods. Imports subject to revenue duties were predominantly processed goods. Whereas raw materials and semiprocessed goods made up about two thirds of total imports, very few were subject to revenue duties. In other words, by 1955–6, many of these goods were not subject to QRs and their import was controlled by the price mechanism.

Table 3.2 Imports in 1955–1956 according to classification of tariffs (percent)

Imports	Revenue tariffs	Import-reducing tariffs	Protective tariffs
Food, drink, and tobacco	6.7	14.1	64.1
Raw materials and semiprocessed goods	1.4	31.5	—
Processed goods	91.7	54.4	35.9
Total	99.8[a]	100.0	100.0

—, not applicable.
[a] 0.2 percent do not fit any of these categories.
Source: Gafni et al., 1963

Though the divergence between the official rate of exchange and the average effective rate was mainly the result of multiple formal rates until 1955, import duties added to this divergence. Weinblatt (1972) aggregated Michaely's (1971) EERs into classes of commodities; his figures are reproduced in table 3.3. In 1951, the average rates for consumer goods, investment goods, and inputs were fairly close; by 1952 investment goods had a relatively lower rate. By 1954, the average divergence had been reduced, but not in all subcategories; for example, durable consumer goods were charged a much higher rate, as was fuel. It should again be stressed that the effective rates are for goods actually imported; they do not take into account the effective rate on goods produced domestically

Table 3.3 Effective exchange rates by type of import, 1951–1955 (Israeli pounds per US dollar)

T-y-p-e- of import	1951	1952	1953	1954	1955	Ratio of 1952 to 1951 values	1955 to 1952 values
A Total imports	0.40	0.83	1.16	1.79	2.03	2.08	2.45
B Total consumer goods	0.43	0.85	1.22	1.73	2.05	1.98	2.41
Current consumption	0.42	0.85	1.20	1.63	2.01	2.02	2.36
Food	0.41	0.79	1.20	1.56	2.03	1.93	2.57
Durables	0.47	0.85	1.35	2.41	2.26	1.81	2.66
C Investment goods	0.39	0.75	1.00	1.88	1.93	1.92	2.56
Agriculture	0.40	0.74	0.99	1.82	1.85	1.85	2.50
Industry	0.37	0.69	0.89	1.77	1.84	1.86	2.67
Transport	0.40	0.83	1.16	2.04	2.03	2.08	2.45
Trade and services	0.42	0.92	1.10	1.93	1.84	2.19	2.00
D Inputs	0.39	0.86	1.19	1.79	2.06	2.21	2.40
Agriculture	0.37	0.87	1.06	1.31	1.69	2.35	1.94
Industry	0.39	0.81	0.99	1.63	1.87	2.08	2.31
Construction	0.39	0.77	1.39	2.17	2.61	1.97	3.90
Fuel	0.43	1.06	1.92	2.56	2.91	2.46	2.75

Source: Weinblatt, 1972, table C-1

that received complete protection by means of QRs. A basically new approach to protection was not adopted until the second liberalization episode, starting in 1962.

During 1952, the entire foreign exchange licensing system was reformulated and related to a foreign exchange budget. A department of the Ministry of Finance estimated foreign exchange receipts for the coming fiscal year, to establish a framework for foreign exchange budgetary allocations. Each ministry dealing with imports or other expenditure licensing would file its request; the Ministry of Finance then constructed the budget, which was formally approved by the Council of Economic Ministers.[9] Three types of receipts were included: income from exports of goods and services, unilateral transfers (excluding private gifts), and major long-term loans and private investment. Planned expenditures were classified by the final use of the imports: for instance, for investment, consumption, and exports. The licenses would then be issued by the ministries, and when validated by the Ministry of Finance – that is, when

[9] Unlike the State Budget which is approved by the Knesset.

an authorized allocation of foreign exchange was specified – the budget was debited.

Table 3.4 shows the ratio of the realized foreign exchange budgets to the planned budgets. The basic idea was to have a more rational expenditure policy but also to allow a margin of safety. In the first two years, 1952–3 and 1953–4, receipts fell short of expectations, but expenditures were kept within bounds. Thereafter, actual receipts always exceeded expectations, but expenditures exceeded receipts (until 1958–9).

Table 3.4 Ratio of foreign exchange budgetary performance to approved budget, 1952–1953 to 1956–1957[a]

Item	1952–3[b]	1953–4[b]	1954–5	1955–6	1956–7
Total receipts	84	82	112	103	108
Exports of goods and services	94	146	133	103	117
Other receipts	82	106	106	103	104
Total expenditure	100	82	115	115	110
Consumer goods[c]	99	86	117	110	140
Capital goods	118	108	104	118	90
Imports for exports	95	152	133	137	103

[a] Budget years, usually April 1 to March 31.
[b] Budget year nine months.
[c] Includes services.
Source: Halevi, 1971, p. 47

Accompanying Policies

Export Promotion Policy

Promotion of exports in Israel has always consisted of two separate sets of policy measures. The first is related to investment policy: the growth during the 1950s of external funds mobilized by the government and public institutions and channeled to investment, played a crucial part in economic development. There is no evidence, however, that export potential was an important criterion for the allocation of funds from the development budget before the late 1950s.

The second set of policy measures relates to EERs. Premiums were paid on exports before the 1952 devaluation – on gross export proceeds until May 1950, and on added value added thereafter (Rubner, 1961, p. 138). These "premiums" were not really subsidies, but rather partial compensation for an overvalued exchange rate. The new system introduced in February 1952 moved most export items to higher rates, which replaced the previously existing premiums (diamonds retained the lowest rate). By the end of 1952 all exports received the highest rate, and in 1953, the IL 1.80 per US dollar rate began to be applied.

In 1951, some exporters were permitted to retain part of their export earnings for purchasing raw materials. From May 1953, this export retention scheme, called PAMAZ, was widely extended. Exporters were permitted to use their export earnings to import raw materials in their "line of production and exports" (this was intended to prevent trade in these accounts). The value added from exports financed imports for production for the local market. Producers were thus given access to a protected market; they received quota profits, and in effect the domestic consumer subsidized the exports.[10] In 1954–5 the PAMAZ system was the main subsidization scheme for exports, once the IL 1.80 per US dollar rate became generalized. Some exports that could not benefit from the PAMAZ system (such as citrus and diamonds) received direct premiums. From 1956, direct premiums on computed value added grew to become the main subsidization program for exports.

Comparison of the EERs for imports and exports (EERM and EERX) gives the impression that exports received a more favorable rate than imports until 1955. However, the EERMs measure the average rates actually paid by importers, and thus serve to evaluate imports,[11] but they do not include quota profits and therefore do not reflect the true protection given by the almost complete exclusion of competitive imports. Thus, in marked contrast with what the above comparison implies, the producer comparing the relative profitability of production for the local market or for exports would find very marked discrimination in favor of the domestic market.

No reliable estimates on the dispersion of EERX for the early 1950s are available. Citrus exports received a lower rate than diamonds – the other "traditional" export – in 1952, and again in 1955–6, with a slightly higher rate in 1953–4. Other merchandise exports received slightly more favorable rates after 1952, according to estimates that do not fully take into account the subsidies received by exporters from the domestic market via the PAMAZ arrangement (Michaely, 1971, p. 102). Estimates of the subsidy arising from this foreign exchange retention scheme in the fiscal year 1954–5 suggest that industrial exports (other than diamonds) received considerably higher rates than citrus and diamonds (Gottlieb, 1957, p. 27). The PAMAZ subsidies ranged from IL 0.75 per US dollar (chemicals) to IL 2.00 per dollar (food), and averaged IL 1.24 per dollar value added. These dispersions probably increased during 1955, but with the gradual

---

[10] The most extensive treatment of export subsidization in Israel is given by Pines (1963).
[11] For a discussion of the use of EERM in national income accounting see Halevi (1971).

curtailment of the PAMAZ in 1956–8, concomitant with greater import liberalization, the dispersion in export subsidization decreased.

Monetary Policy[12]

After the creation of the State the government signed an agreement with the Anglo-Palestine Bank (later renamed Bank Leumi Le-Israel) whereby the bank set up a separate department that issued currency backed by foreign exchange balances frozen in London and exchanged for the Palestine pounds held by the public. Additional currency was created by permitting 50 percent of the backing to be in the form of Treasury Bills. In 1949 an agreement was reached with the British government on "thawing" the balances in London, and it became necessary to find alternative backing for the currency so that the foreign exchange balances could be spent. Consequently, Land Bonds were introduced as formal backing, and by mid-1951 the foreign exchange backing was almost depleted. The inflationary pressures of growing liquidity were repressed by price controls.

In April 1951 the government stopped the discounting of Treasury Bills and, at the end of August, halted financing by issue of Land Bonds. Liquidity ratios – without binding legal power – were used in an attempt to keep down private credit. From September 1951 the rate of monetary increase was sharply reduced. In June a 10 percent compulsory loan was levied on all means of payment, but this was primarily a fiscal measure, and the funds collected were quickly spent.

Monetary restrictions by means of liquidity ratios became effective only from April 1953, that is, more than a year after the 1952 devaluation. Reserve requirements were raised to 90 percent on deposits created after December 1952 or March 1953 (at the bank's discretion). In early 1954, the government set credit ceilings at the level of November 1953; this level was slightly raised during the year.

In December 1954, a central bank, the Bank of Israel, was established. It relied on two main instruments to control the money supply. Liquidity ratios were now legally binding, and set at once at 50 percent for deposits existing before April 1951, 75 percent on deposits added before the end of 1952, and 90 percent on deposits created after that date. The government credit ceilings were retained until 1958. From 1956, the liquidity ratios were the major restrictive instrument. From the end of that year, and especially from 1958 when the complex liquidity ratios were revamped, exemptions from liquidity requirements were used as an instrument for directing credit toward desired objectives.

---

[12] This section relies heavily on Patinkin (1956, 1967), Genihowski (1965), and Halevi and Klinov-Malul (1968).

Open-market operations were not used at all before the establishment of the Bank of Israel, and the bank used them for directing credit rather than as an instrument for control of the money supply.

Tables 3.5 and 3.6 present data on the supply of money and the sources of its growth. The very rapid growth in the money supply in 1949–51 was due to bank lending to the government and to the public; the decrease in foreign exchange reserves was an offsetting factor. In 1952, the rate of

Table 3.5 Money supply, 1949–1956 (end-of-year data) (million Israeli pounds)

Year	1 Currency held by the public	2 Liquid assets held by banks	3 Total monetary base (1 + 2)	4 Money supply M1	5 Percentage change in money supply
1949	43.3	51.3	94.6	128.9	39.1
1950	64.8	65.1	129.9	169.7	35.4
1951	91.0	75.6	166.6	224.0	27.2
1952	106.0	62.9	168.9	247.3	6.5
1953	128.0	62.3	190.3	290.1	24.5
1953[a]	—	—	—	262.7[a]	—
1954	146.6	113.8	260.4	330.5	20.1
1955	172.6	181.2	353.8	398.1	20.4
1956	228.4	205.5	433.9	469.4	23.3

—, not applicable.
[a] From 1953, the new series excludes demand deposits in foreign currency.
Source: columns 1 and 2, Zanbar and Bronfeld, 1973, p. 7; columns 4 and 5, Halevi and Klinov-Malul, 1968, p. 251

Table 3.6 Sources of changes in the money supply, 1949–1956

Year	Percentage change in money supply due to changes in			
	Net foreign balances	Bank credit		Other factors (residual)
		To government	To public	
1949	− 13.7	78.4	47.2	− 11.9
1950	− 33.5	104.0	57.9	− 28.4
1951	− 17.0	86.8	54.0	− 23.8
1952	− 17.2	26.1	186.0	− 94.9
1953	24.4	7.6	87.6	− 19.6
1954	106.8	− 31.8	46.6	− 21.6
1955	27.8	66.1	35.7	− 29.6
1956	15.8	64.8	49.8	− 29.9

Source: Patinkin, 1967, p. 112

growth of the money supply decreased sharply, clearly as a result of decreased government borrowing; private borrowing was not curtailed. In fact, much of the "private" borrowing was authorized by government letters of obligation to the bank. By 1953, rapid monetary expansion had resumed; only from 1955 did government borrowing regain its dominant role.

Real monetary balances are derived by deflating the money supply by a price index. In table 3.7 three alternative indices are used for this purpose. With the official consumer price index (CPI) used by Patinkin (1967, p. 110), real cash balances increased in 1951 and decreased in 1952 and 1953, most severely (over 30 percent) in 1952. However, the official index used to determine cost-of-living wage allowances was very limited in coverage, and dominated by controlled food prices. Weiss (1964) made

Table 3.7 Changes in real cash balances, 1949–1955

Year	1 Nominal money supply	2 Official CPI	3 Adjusted CPI	4 Implicit GNP deflator	5 Real cash balance[a] A	6 B	7 C
1949	39.1	3.4	1.0	—	34.0	37.7	—
1950	35.4	− 5.0	20.4	—	38.6	12.4	—
1951	27.2	10.5	44.9	16.3	19.4	− 12.2	9.3
1952	6.5	58.7	21.6	39.3	− 30.5	− 12.4	− 23.6
1953	24.5	28.0	2.9	24.3	− 8.4	21.0	0.2
1954	20.1	12.5	12.2	7.7	11.8	7.0	11.5
1955	20.4	5.6	5.9	10.3	14.2	13.7	9.2

—, not applicable.
[a] A is deflated by the official CPI; B is deflated by the adjusted CPI; C is deflated by the GNP price index.
Sources: column 1, Halevi and Klinov-Malul, 1968; columns 2 and 4 CBS, Statistical Abstracts of Israel; column 3, Weiss, 1964, columns 5, 6, and 7, computed from indices

several estimates of an adjusted index, reflecting higher food prices in uncontrolled markets. His most conservative estimate of uncontrolled prices, shown in table 3.7, column 3, implies that food prices rose dramatically in 1951, and that the official CPI in 1952 reflected much of the illegal price increases in 1951. This index (column 6) shows real balances already decreasing in 1951, a similar decrease in 1952, and an increase in 1953.

A more useful index for this purpose, because of its much broader coverage, is the implicit GNP deflator shown in column 4. Use of this index shows that real balances decreased only in 1952; thus, the shift of imports to higher exchange rates and the increase in controlled prices did have a strong deflationary effect. In this respect 1953 was neutral, while in 1954 real monetary expansion resumed.

Throughout this period interest rates were still subject to an old Ottoman law and were restricted to 9 percent (from 1957 to 1970 the legal limit was 11 percent). Until 1953 the official ceiling was not effective, and thereafter it was clearly too low: those receiving loans at that rate or less were being subsidized, there was excess demand for credit, and black markets for credit developed. When the Bank of Israel was set up, its governor was empowered to penalize financial institutions that exceeded the legal interest rate limit; however, he did not do so, as he himself opposed the idea of an interest ceiling (according to Genihowski, 1965).

From 1950 to 1956 average nominal interest rates crept up towards 7 percent; they were well below the interest ceiling because of the low rates charged on government-directed controlled credit. Because of the high rate of inflation, the real rate of interest was negative. Table 3.8 presents two estimates of real average interest rates on legal commercial credit: deflation by the CPI and deflation by the implicit GNP deflator. The latter, because of its broader coverage, seems appropriate; it shows high negative rates in 1951–3, and low negative rates in 1954–6.[13]

Table 3.8 Average interest rates on commercial credit, 1950–1956

	1	2	3	4
Year	Total credit (million IL)	Average interest rates (%)		
		Nominal	Real A	Real B
1950	85	4.62	11.2	n.a.
1951	100	5.24	− 7.8	− 9.5
1952	124	5.79	− 33.0	− 24.1
1953	232	6.05	− 17.3	− 14.7
1954	308	6.04	− 5.2	− 1.5
1955	337	6.56	0.6	− 3.3
1956	387	6.74	0.3	− 3.1

n.a., not available.
Real A, deflated by the CPI index; real B, deflated by the implicit GNP price index.
Sources: columns 1–3, Ben-Shahar et al., 1971, pp. 292 and p. 319; column 4, column 2 deflated by the GNP price index in Halevi and Klinov-Malul, 1968, p. 282

[13] The CPI-deflated rates show a very high positive real rate in 1950 – when the CPI was artificially reduced – and an exaggeratedly high negative rate in 1952.

No such detailed estimates are available for long-term credit, which mainly took the form of government development budget loans. Table 3.9 presents Ben-Shahar's estimates for the period 1949–50 to 1953–4 and for the next two-year period, by main branch. Here, deflation is by the CPI only. In the first period, average nominal rates did not vary much between sectors – though agriculture generally received preferential treatment – but differences in the timing of loans to various sectors relative to price increases led to significant variation in real interest rates, with manufacturing enjoying the largest negative rate.

Table 3.9 Average interest rates on development budget loans (percent)

Sector	1	2	3	4	5
	1949–50 to 1953–4		1954–5 to 1955–6		
	Nominal rate	Real rate	Nominal rate	Effective rate[a]	Real rate[b]
Agriculture	4.7	− 7.2	4.5	5.6	0.1
Manufacturing	5.5	− 10.5	7.3	8.1	1.3
Mining	5.5	− 6.3	5.5	7.0	1.1
Electricity	4.5	n.a.	4.5	5.6	n.a.
Housing	5.7	n.a.	6.0	8.0	n.a.
Others	4.8	n.a.	5.8	8.0	n.a.
Total	5.0	− 6.7	5.2	6.0	0.5

n.a., not available.
[a] Including linkage provisions.
[b] Effective rates deflated by the CPI.
Source: Ben-Shahar, 1965, pp. 39, 44, and 83

To counteract the effect of inflation on loans, linkage was introduced in 1954: loans were linked either to the CPI or to the foreign exchange rate. Table 3.9, column 4, adds the linkage component to the nominal interest rate to arrive at the "effective rate." The deflated effective rate shows that by this period real interest rates were no longer negative. The 1952–4 effective devaluations, which were accompanied by rising domestic prices, were not matched by increased nominal interest rates; only when the rate of price increases declined were negative interest rates eliminated.

Fiscal Policy

The public sector in Israel includes not only central government and local authorities but also national institutions run by the Zionist Organization. Total public sector consumption as a percentage of available resources reveals no trend during this period: it was consistently high, generally 15–16 percent in 1950–1, and slightly lower in 1952–4. The decline was due primarily to decreased central government expenditures; clearly, the latter is related to the NEP.

The structure of government receipts and expenditures is shown in table 3.10. Total government expenditure increased throughout the period. The smallest relative increase occurred in 1951–2 and 1953–4; taking price increases into account, real expenditure probably did not increase in those years. External resources fluctuated between 21 and 35 percent of total receipts (from 1949 to 1950); they were relatively most important in the three years of the NEP. By 1952–3, taxes were providing four fifths of total internal resources. Expenditure taxes (mainly customs duties) were the main source of revenue until 1955–6; by then, income taxes had attained equal importance. This general trend is not a result of a new philosophy of taxation, connected with the NEP. The effects of the NEP are, however, reflected in the compulsory loan imposed in 1952–3, which resulted in a one-time jump in the relative share of property taxes, and in the decline of customs duties, which resulted from the decrease in imports.

The growth of foreign capital inflows to the government, in particular from State of Israel Bonds, German reparations, and US aid – all foreign exchange receipts that granted counterpart funds in the development budget – could not but lead to a large governmental presence in financing investment. The Jewish Agency's continued investment in housing and agricultural settlement also increased the role of the public sector.

The role of the public sector in investment finance is shown in table 3.11. The level of total investment fell drastically in 1952 and further still in 1953, recovering substantially only in 1955. The figures underestimate the extent of indirect government investment financing in 1950–1; thus the increase in total public financing of investment in 1952 is exaggerated, but not the relative increase in 1953 and 1954. Yet in 1952 there was a drastic decline in the absolute level of direct government investment, and only slight increases in 1953–4. In 1955–6 total investment increased, but not as a result of public financing. Clearly, after the NEP readjustments, private investment rose, both absolutely and relatively.

While in the very early years there were ideological preferences for direct government investment, or Histadrut control, necessity led to a more pragmatic approach: direct government investment would go to areas where private ventures were not forthcoming. Whereas foreign exchange controls, particularly on capital outflows and profit repatriation, were still fairly strict, special privileges were granted to encourage investment in general, and foreign investment in particular. To benefit from privileges granted under the law for the encouragement of investment, investment ventures had to be approved by the Investment Center. By the end of 1954, 360 approved enterprises were in operation; of these, 285 were new

Table 3.10 Structure of government budgetary receipts and expenditures, fiscal years, 1948–1949 to 1956–1957

Item	1948–9	1949–50	1950–1	1951–2	1952–3	1953–4	1954–5	1955–6	1956–7
A Total budgetary and extra-budgetary expenditure (million IL)	74.4	175.2	252.7	296.1	400.4	483.2	867.7	845.9	1,222.8
B Sources of receipts (%)									
Internal	98.1	69.8	78.5	76.7	70.6	67.9	64.6	70.0	76.2
External	1.9	30.2	21.5	23.3	29.4	32.1	35.4	30.0	23.8
Total	100.0	100.0	100.0	100.0	100.0	100.0	100.0	100.0	100.0
C Type of interest receipts (%)									
Taxes	n.a.	60.1	53.1	68.4	83.4	84.9	73.0	80.9	79.8
Other	n.a.	39.9	46.9	31.6	16.6	15.1	27.0	19.1	20.2
Total	100.0	100.0	100.0	100.0	100.0	100.0	100.0	100.0	100.0
D Type of tax (%)									
Income	25.5	26.0	33.3	34.5	35.4	35.7	45.7	45.5	47.3
Property	4.3	3.9	3.0	3.4	16.2	7.2	5.8	4.0	2.8
Expenditure	62.5	61.7	55.9	55.7	43.4	52.3	43.6	46.2	45.3
Transactions	7.7	8.4	7.8	6.4	5.0	4.8	4.9	4.3	4.6
Total	100.0	100.0	100.0	100.0	100.0	100.0	100.0	100.0	100.0

n.a. not available.
Source: Halevi and Klinov-Malul, 1968, pp. 182, 184, and 188

Table 3.11 Indicators of public investment financing, 1950–1956

Year	Index of real fixed investment (1950 = 100)	Percentage of total fixed investment			Percentage of resources		
	Total	Financed by public sector[a]	Financed by public sector	Direct government investment	Total fixed investment	Financed by public sector[a]	Government investment
1950	100	100	42[b]	42	24.1	10.5	n.a.
1951	119	110	39[b]	39	26.8	10.7	n.a.
1952	96	119	49	24.6	24.3	13.0	6.0
1953	82	140	69	29.5	22.4	16.5	6.6
1954	90	183	81	31.8	22.2	19.3	7.1
1955	107	148	59	n.a.	23.5	13.8	n.a.
1956	107	130	52	n.a.	21.3	11.1	n.a.

n.a., not available.
[a] For 1950–4, based on total, not fixed, capital formation.
[b] Direct government investment only.
Source: Halevi and Klinov-Malul, 1968, p. 205

enterprises approved since 1951–2.[14] In general, the Center reserved its approval for new firms, believing that the expansion of existing firms was adequately provided for by subsidized government aid. Major criteria for approval of new firms were the "necessity" of the product, export potential, and location in development towns.

Domestic Price Controls

As already mentioned, a basic reason for the liberalization policy was the failure of price controls and the growth of black markets. Weiss (1964) constructed indices to measure the extent of price controls and the importance of rationing. By all measures, maximum controls were applied in 1951. Thereafter there was a gradual reduction. While in 1954 some 70 percent of all goods consumption was still subject to rationing, half the consumption of these items was purchased at uncontrolled prices, and there was already a sharp drop in the difference between controlled and uncontrolled prices. Controls were still very extensive on many food items.

The effect on controls of nonfood items was much more significant. During 1952–4, price controls were eliminated for almost all industrial and intermediate goods. Raw materials were still rationed, but the rationing was less comprehensive than before and now depended on plant efficiency rather than past history (Weiss, 1964, p. 98).

---

[14] These figures and the following conclusions are based on Citron and Kessler (1958).

During the second half of the 1950s, direct controls declined, though they were not eliminated. For some major items, for example, wheat, grains, meat, and oil beans, the government was the importer and set the prices. Final basic products such as bread, oil, and dairy products were subject to controls, and these products were highly subsidized in order to keep the CPI low. Indirect controls, such as "persuading" certain industries to keep prices low, were more extensively used: this was easier to do when the producer relied heavily on government ministries for licenses, subsidized credit, and other benefits.

4

Economic Performance and Assessment of Policy, 1952–1955

The 1952–5 liberalization was not a passing episode, and it was a sufficiently drastic departure from previous policy to have tremendous influence on economic developments in the 1950s. In this chapter the economic performance of the major macroeconomic variables during and following this period is discussed first, and then the role of liberalization in these developments is assessed and inferences are drawn.

Economic Performance Following Liberalization

Relative Prices

The anti-inflationary policy of sudden drastic price increases to absorb inflationary pressures was obviously reflected in sharp increases in the price indices. Of particular interest is the change in relative prices accompanying the rise in the general price level. Table 4.1 presents data relevant to assessing changes in real wages, both from the point of view of wage earners and as relative costs. The CPI rose 58 percent in 1952 and another 28 percent in 1953. As already described, however, this index does not reflect earlier increases in black-market prices. The implicit price index for the GNP is much broader in coverage than the CPI and also reflects more accurately the noncontrolled prices. It shows a smaller – though absolutely large (39 percent) – jump in 1952, and lower rates of increase in 1953 and 1954. In 1955 and 1956, this index shows price increases of 10 percent, compared with 6 percent in the CPI.

Wages in Israel are determined by collective bargaining. Since the inflation of World War II, automatic cost-of-living adjustments, based on the CPI, have been a major component of wages and of collective bargaining agreements. Yet the wage bargaining process cannot lead to more than temporary departures from what basic market forces determine.

Table 4.1 Annual changes in prices and wages, 1951–1956

Year	1 CPI	2 Prices	3 Nominal average wage in industry	4 Nominal wage index relative to CPI	5 GNP pricesª	6 GNP pricesᵇ	7 Price of industrial equipment
1951	14.6	16.3	19.5	4.3	2.8	− 2.0	9.4
1952	58.0	39.3	59.0	0.8	14.1	5.4	− 41.3
1953	28.1	24.3	32.8	3.7	6.8	6.2	− 11.3
1954	12.4	7.7	15.5	2.8	7.2	12.1	− 12.9
1955	5.9	10.3	11.8	5.6	1.4	4.3	2.6
1956	6.4	10.2	14.0	7.1	3.4	3.4	6.5

ª The implicit GNP deflator.
ᵇ Index of GNP prices excluding the effect of import prices (from table 5.1).
Sources: column 1, computed from CBS, *Statistical Abstract of Israel*, 1960;
column 2, computed from Halevi and Klinov-Malul, 1968, column 4,
computed from Bahral, 1965, p. 75

Mass immigration in the early years, which added a relatively large proportion of low-skill workers to the labor force, could not but have repercussions on wages in the later 1950s.[1]

Nominal wages in industry, shown in table 4.1, column 3, rose steeply in the early 1950s, almost 60 percent in 1952 alone. Real wages, from the point of view of the worker, are nominal wages deflated by a price index. Column 4 deflates nominal wages by the CPI. This gives a misleading measure of real changes, and deflation by the broader GNP price index (column 5) is preferable. The rise in real wages was greatest in 1952 (14 percent), and substantial in 1953 and 1954. Clearly, the link of wages to the CPI led to larger increases in nominal wages and therefore in real wages when the CPI increases overestimated real inflation. However, the general trend, no matter how estimated, was substantial increases in real wages, even in years when unemployment rose.

From the point of view of producers, nominal wage increases must be compared with other prices. Bahral (1965, pp. 4 and 75) found that nominal wages rose less than import and export prices; thus he concludes that the price of labor relative to product prices in exports and import substitutes declined after 1952, a result to be expected in a period when the real exchange rate doubled.

An alternative measure of such a relative change in wages is shown in table 4.1, column 6. Here Michaely's index of domestic product prices, which excludes the influence of import prices on imports for domestic use,

[1] This is the subject of Bahral's study (1965); this section draws on his conclusions.

is used. Nominal wages deflated by domestic prices (excluding the effect of import prices) reflect no relative decrease in labor costs after 1951. Finally, in column 7, changes in nominal wages are compared with changes in the prices of industrial equipment to show a measure of changes in relative labor costs. Here there is a drop in relative labor costs in the three-year period 1952–5. Use of the problematic index of equipment prices is far from ideal for this comparison; nevertheless, the data are adequate to show clearly that the more realistic exchange rate did much to correct the imbalance in the relative price of labor and equipment.

Table 4.2 presents indices of EERM and EERX, GNP prices, and exchange rates relative to domestic prices and to purchasing power parity (PPP) rates.[2] The rapid rise in the EERM in 1952–4 and accompanying increases in controlled prices led to rapid but smaller increases in GNP prices. Thus, as shown in column 7, deflated EERM increased significantly – 36 percent in 1952, 16 percent in 1953, and 50 percent in 1954. "Real devaluation" refers to a devaluation greater than the PPP rate; this is shown in column 8. There was a significant real devaluation in 1952–5. Thereafter, there was no significant real devaluation (until 1962).

The EERX deflated by GNP prices shows very substantial increases in 1952, 1953, and 1954, and practically no change in 1955. Thus the NEP went a long way towards correcting the previous penalizing of exports.

Table 4.2 Indices of the effective exchange rate, the domestic price level, and purchasing power parity, 1950–1956

	1	2	3	4	5	6	7	8
Year	EER		GNP prices[a]	PPP	Exporters' rate relative to		Importers' rate relative to	
	Exporters'	Importers'			Domestic price	PPP	Domestic price	PPP
1950	100	100	100	100	100	100	100	100
1951	106	98	122	103	87	103	80	95
1952	210	200	184	154	114	136	109	130
1953	331	290	230	208	144	159	126	139
1954	448	447	237	222	189	202	189	201
1955	474	550	254	223	187	212	216	247
1956	532	563	280	234	190	227	201	240

Column 5 is the ratio of columns 1 and 3; column 6 is the ratio of columns 1 and 4; column 7 is the ratio of columns 2 and 3; column 8 is the ratio of columns 2 and 4.
[a] This is an index of domestic product computed by taking prices of domestic uses of resources and subtracting the influence of import prices on imports for domestic use. Thus it is not the same as the implicit GNP deflator used in table 6.2
Source: Michaely, 1971, p. 94

[2] The PPP rates take foreign prices into account. Thus, PPP is maintained when the ratio of the new to the old exchange rate is the same as the ratio of domestic to foreign price indices.

Column 6 shows a truer measure of real devaluation, that is, relative to the PPP rate.

External Transactions

Imports

Imports of goods (c.i.f.), measured in current US dollars, declined by 17 percent in 1952, and by another 13 percent in 1953 (but only 2.3 percent in constant dollar prices). In 1954 the trend reversed, and 1955–7 were years of significant growth in imports. Goods and services data – less reliable, especially before 1952 – show similar directions of movement. When current price data are used to compare imports of goods and services (converted at EERs) to GNP, there is no declining trend during the NEP years but rather the reverse: the relative increase in exchange rates gives a greater weight to the smaller dollar volume of imports (table 4.3, column 7).

Table 4.3 Imports of goods and services, 1950–1956

	1	2	3	4	5	6	7
Year	Imports[a] (million US$)			Annual rate of increase			Ratio of imports to GNP[b]
	Goods	Services	Total	Goods	Services	Total	
1950[b]	300	30	330	—	—	—	0.28
1951[b]	389	36	425	29.7	20.0	28.8	0.23
1952	323	69	392	– 17.0	91.7[c]	– 7.8	0.33
1953	281	84	365	– 13.0	21.7	– 6.9	0.35
1954	291	82	373	3.6	– 2.4	2.2	0.35
1955	337	95	432	15.8	15.9	15.8	0.39
1956	367	169	536	8.9	77.9[c]	24.0[c]	0.41

—, not applicable.
Computed from current local currency price data.
[a] Based on c.i.f. recording of imports.
[b] Estimates of services incomplete in 1950 and 1951; therefore increase in 1952 overestimated.
[c] Mainly due to increase in defense expenditure.
Source: Halevi, 1983b, p. 79 and data from figure 1

The composition of commodity imports, measured in current dollar values, is shown in Halevi and Baruh (1988, appendix table A.30). Final consumer goods, which were a quarter of total imports in 1950–1, fell to 15 percent by 1955. The share of final investment goods declined during this period, and that of raw materials and semiprocessed goods grew from 43.7 percent in 1951 to 56.6 percent in 1954.

An empirical analysis of the factors affecting imports of commodities for the 1950–67 period (Weinblatt, 1972) found that total imports were positively correlated with national product and negatively correlated with the EER. The elasticity of the latter was − 0.35. Weinblatt explained this low elasticity as resulting from the fact that some classes of imports were not responsive to relative prices. In his examination of subcategories of imports Weinblatt found that relative prices were a very strong factor for final consumer goods: the elasticity was − 2.56. Surprisingly, nondurable consumer goods were even more responsible than durable consumer goods to change in relative prices. Raw materials were not responsive to changes in relative prices, while final investment goods were responsive, but with a low elasticity.

In view of the NEP these findings suggest that the decline in imports, particularly of consumer goods, in 1952 and 1953 had two causes: a real devaluation and a slowdown in economic activity. In 1954 and 1955 real devaluation continued, and would have cut total imports further had not renewed economic growth more than counteracted this effect. Import substitution continued, however, even as total imports increased.

Exports

In the early years, total exports were very small, both absolutely and relative to GNP and to imports (table 4.4); commodity exports did not increase in 1952, but grew very rapidly – of course, from a very low base – in 1953 and 1954, reaching US$88 million in 1954. Real commodity exports grew at rates of 33 percent in 1953 and 50 percent in 1954. The following year real exports declined, but they resumed rapid growth in 1956.

Table 4.4 Exports of goods and services, 1950–1956

Year	Exports (million US$)			Annual rate of increase			Real commodity exports	Ratio of exports to GNP[b]
	Goods	Services[a]	Total	Goods	Services	Total		
1950[c]	35	10	45[c]	—	—	—	—	0.04
1951[c]	47	9	56[c]	34.3	c	c	27.3	0.03
1952	44	42	86	− 6.4	c	c	− 4.5	0.07
1953	56	46	102	27.2	9.5	18.6	32.9	0.10
1954	88	53	141	57.1	15.2	38.2	50.0	0.13
1955	86	59	145	− 2.3	11.3	2.8	− 7.0	0.12
1956	110	68	178	27.9	15.3	22.8	27.5	0.13

—, not applicable.
[a] Estimated to correct for c.i.f. recording of imports.
[b] Under-estimates of services in 1950 and 1951; therefore rates of growth inaccurate.
[c] Computed from current prices, local currency data.
Source: Halevi, 1983b, p. 78 and data from figure 1

Exports of services were probably underestimated before 1952; thus their growth in 1952 is exaggerated. Between 1952 and 1955 service exports grew modestly, reaching US$59 million in 1955.

During this period agricultural exports provided a fairly steady two fifths of total receipts from commodity exports, and higher proportions of net foreign exchange value added: 54–60 percent. Diamonds were generally (except in 1954) 22–5 percent of exports, but because of their very high import component they never provided as much as 10 percent of total net receipts. Industrial exports declined relatively both in total receipts and in value added until 1956; their signficant relative growth did not occur until later.

In a study of the factors explaining the growth of exports Halevi (1972) found that in the 1950s total exports value added was responsive to changes in relative prices; this elasticity was not constant but increased during the period. Economic growth, as measured by capital formation, was not export biased, as it was in the 1960s. The NEP on prices can therefore be assumed to have stimulated exports (and all traded goods), as it covered the period of greatest relative devaluation; however, the effects on exports were not dramatic during this period. The influence of devaluation must have had a considerable lag in those years, both in its direct effect and through the increased relative profitability of exports (and import substitutes) as a stimulus to investment in such industries.

Balance of Payments and Foreign Indebtedness

The changes in imports and exports are reflected in the excess of total imports over total exports (table 4.5, column 2), that is, the import surplus, which has been a permanent feature of the economy. This fell from some US$370 million in 1951 to some US$230 million in 1954, and then started

Table 4.5 Measures of openness of the economy, 1951–1956

Year	1 Exports plus imports (million US$)	2 Imports minus exports (million US$)	3 Ratio of total trade to GNP (current prices)	4 Ratio of import surplus to GNP Current prices	5 1955 prices
1951	481	369	0.26	0.20	0.52
1951	478	306	0.40	0.26	0.39
1953	467	263	0.45	0.25	0.35
1954	514	232	0.48	0.22	0.27
1955	577	287	0.51	0.27	0.27
1956	714	358	0.54	0.28	0.30

Source: computed from data in Halevi and Klinov-Malul, 1968

to rise again in 1955 and 1956, to almost the peak of 1951. Thus the NEP did reduce the deficit sharply, via the curtailment of imports and the expansion of exports, but the improvement in dollar values was short lived. Whereas the ratio of this deficit to GNP fluctuated in 1952–6 when measured in current prices, it dropped dramatically from over a half in 1951 to about a quarter in 1954 and 1955 when measured in constant prices. Exports rose to 36 percent of imports in 1954, declined to 33 percent in 1956, and then rose steadily (to about 50 percent in 1960). The rise in exports was sufficient to increase the total trade-to-GNP ratio from 1951 to 1956.

The large deficits before 1952 were financed by grants, loans, and depletion of foreign exchange reserves. By the end of 1951, foreign exchange reserves had been depleted and Israel had incurred substantial short-term obligations. The improvement in the balance of payments in 1952 and 1953 was not sufficient to improve the foreign exchange position: foreign exchange reserves at the end of 1953 were US$40 million less than short-term obligations (Halevi and Baruh, 1988, appendix table A.25). Though interest payments were not yet large, annual repayments of debts plus interest charges were already substantial relative to exports. To alleviate short-term indebtedness, philanthropic institutions who were raising funds abroad for transfer to Israel were asked to take a "consolidation loan," that is, to borrow from foreign banks against future collections and to transfer this loan to Israel as an additional unilateral transfer in 1954. Consequently, the net short-term position was improved. Though this improvement resulted from a special action unrelated to the NEP, the financial position in the mid-1950s would have been much worse without the decreases in the deficits in 1952–5.

Input, Output, and Productivity

In the years following the NEP there were dramatic changes in employment, output, and productivity. These are shown by the data in table 4.6. The recessionary policies of the NEP are reflected in increased unemployment – from some 8 percent in 1951 and 1952 (after having fallen from some 14 percent in 1949) to 11.5 percent in 1953. They are also reflected in the slower increase in real GDP, from almost 30 percent in 1951 to 8.4 percent in 1952, and in a *decrease* of 6.4 percent in 1953.[3] While output and labor input declined in 1953, capital inputs kept growing, but at a slower rate than earlier: 15.7 percent in 1953, compared with 24–5 percent in 1952 and 1955. The change in factor productivity was slightly negative in 1952

[3] These are based on Gaathon's adjusted GDP estimates (Gaathon, 1961). The real GNP estimates (Halevi and Klinov-Malul, 1968) show no decrease in 1953 with a 1.3 percent fall in GNP per capita.

Table 4.6 Inputs, product and productivity, total economy, 1951–1956

Year	1 Annual growth rates (%) Unemployed as percentage of labor force	2 Real GDP	3 Labor input	4 Capital input	5 Factor productivity
1951	8.1	29.5	22.1	25.4	5.5
1952	8.1	8.4	5.8	24.3	− 1.5
1953	11.5	− 6.4	− 2.0	15.7	− 8.7
1954	9.2	17.8	4.3	11.1	10.8
1955	7.4	15.9	3.7	10.9	9.5
1956	7.8	9.0	4.7	11.9	1.9

Source: Column 1, Halevi and Klinov-Malul, 1968, p. 66; columns 2–5, computed from Gaathon, 1971, appendix tables

and − 8.7 percent in 1953. Thus the necessary readjustments of the economy involved real costs.

These costs began to pay off in 1954. Real GDP grew by almost 18 percent in 1954, and by another 16 percent in 1955. Labor inputs grew at rates of about 4 percent, and capital inputs at about 11 percent. Consequently, factor productivity grew at around 10 percent. From 1956, rates of growth of product and factor productivity were much more moderate.

The development of agriculture and of manufacturing does not show a similar pattern. Agricultural product rose slightly in 1951, and tremendously (40 percent) in 1952. Even allowing for problems of estimation in the period of controlled prices, there was certainly a large real growth of product, no doubt reflecting more realistic pricing. Several years of marked fluctuations followed: almost no growth in 1953, major growth in 1954, no growth in 1955, and major growth again in 1956. These fluctuations cannot be associated with the liberalization policies.

Industrial product was high in 1951 but declined by 15 percent in 1952, rose by 5 percent in 1953 – while total product fell – and rose at fairly steady high, but not exceptional, rates thereafter. Labor inputs into industry grew more than in agriculture from 1953 (except in 1955), and capital inputs grew more from 1954. Is this a result of the liberalization policy? Liberalization certainly provided a better general climate for investment in industry, and the more realistic exchange rates made possible more rational planning; but these developments no doubt are more the result of other policies, particularly the realization that greater emphasis, and more public investment activity, should be directed to industry. Substantial changes came much later. Public investment continued to favor agriculture owing to heavy investment in irrigation projects, and the share of industry in total fixed capital formation overtook agriculture only in the late 1950s.

Income Distribution

Income distribution in the Jewish sector of Palestine is believed to have been extremely egalitarian by international standards. Several factors accounted for this: there was no traditional landed aristocracy or large property holdings, egalitarian principles were prevalent, and social and economic mobility of labor was high. This income equality is still present in the first estimates for Israel for 1950–1, although the estimates exaggerate the equality because they exclude the thousands of new immigrants in transit camps or otherwise unemployed. However, the austerity system and its rationing program guaranteed a much more egalitarian distribution of consumption than the distribution of money income would have provided.

In the following years the new less-skilled immigrants were absorbed into the working population, affecting the distribution of wages, and market forces became more potent in the distribution of welfare. Hanoch (1961) found that between 1950 and 1956 the general rise in income was accompanied by wider differentials: the real income of the lowest fifth did not increase. However, since many of those in the population in 1956 were not in the working population in 1950, it is possible that the lower fifth of 1956 were much better off than those same individuals had been in 1950.

Did the NEP affect the distribution of welfare? Between 1954 and 1957–8 the real income of the lower two fifths did not increase (Hanoch, 1961). Certainly, the gradual elimination of rationing reduced equality of consumption; thus the widening of income inequality is not mitigated by the qualification suggested above. The rise in the level of prices – the essential element in the NEP – probably strongly affected welfare distribution in 1952–4, but after 1954 there were no significant differential price movements in the consumption of various income groups (Landsberger, 1963).

Inferences from the Liberalization of 1952–1955

The liberalization episode of the early 1950s was part of a macroeconomic policy package. In fact, the results of the macro policy have led to some doubt whether a liberalization episode, in the more conventional sense of the term, occurred at all. Before assessing the specific liberalization aspects of this policy package and drawing inferences for sequencing liberalization policies, it is advisable to assess the achievements of the macroeconomic policy package as a whole.

Assessment of the Macroeconomic Policy

The policy package adopted in late 1951 and early 1952, and carried on for three years, was designed to deal with two main problems; high inflation pressure and a severe deficit in the goods and services account of the balance of payments. As described in some detail above, the main tools used were a restrictive monetary policy and sharp increases in controlled prices, particularly those related to the effective rates of exchange which were increased by the adoption of a multiple formal exchange rate system. The decline in real cash balances was designed to absorb inflationary pressure, only partly contained by price controls, which had been losing their effectiveness. These income effects, and the relative price effects achieved by real effective devaluation, were to decrease the deficit in the goods and services account.

Data on annual rates of change of some relevant macro variables presented and discussed above are summarized in table 4.7. The price level, here measured by the implicit GNP deflator, rose by 16 percent in 1951; the intentional raising of prices resulted in a tremendous increase (close to 40 percent) in GNP prices in 1952 and a 24 percent increase in 1953. In 1954, the inflation rate dropped to less than 8 percent, but was back to the 1951 rate in 1955. Prices rose much faster than the money

Table 4.7 Annual rates of change of some macro variables, 1951–1956

Variables	1951	1952	1953	1954	1955	1956
Real money supply[a]	10.5	− 32.9	− 11.2	5.2	8.0	5.9
GNP prices	16.3	39.3	24.3	7.7	16.3	10.2
EERM relative to PPP	− 5.0	36.8	6.9	44.6	22.9	2.5
Import surplus	30.4	− 17.1	− 14.1	− 11.8	23.7	24.7
Real product[b]	29.5	4.1	− 4.7	21.0	13.0	10.0
Labor input[b]	22.8	5.0	− 5.2	1.8	0.4	4.6
Capital inputs[b]	21.9	30.0	15.7	11.6	9.8	10.7
Productivity[b]	5.5	− 3.4	− 3.6	15.8	10.0	3.6

[a] Average year M1 deflated by implicit GNP deflator.
[b] Non-dwelling private economy.

supply in 1952; money balances decreased by one third. They fell another 11 percent in 1953, but thereafter monetary expansion outpaced price increases, and in fact contributed to renewed inflation. Thus the anti-inflationary policies were successful in eliminating repressed inflation and replacing it by a protracted rate of inflation which was "moderate" by Israeli standards.

The nominal devaluations contributed to the increase in GNP prices, but outpaced them; thus real devaluation was achieved, as shown by the changes in the average EERM relative to the PPP rate. After real appreciation in 1951 there was a tremendous real devaluation in 1952 (almost 37 percent), a modest devaluation in 1953 (44.6 percent), a tremendous devaluation again in 1954, and substantial devaluation in 1955. In all, there was a four-year period of sustained real devaluation.

The combined effects on income and relative prices did substantially decrease the goods and services deficit, which declined in each of the three years 1952, 1953 and 1954. The total deficit, in current US dollars, was US$137 million less in 1954 than in 1951, a drop of 37 percent. Imports fell by US$52 million, and exports rose by US$85 million. Thus, increased exports accounted for 62 percent of the improvement.[4]

The cost of this improvement in the balance of payments was severe. Product, which had grown very rapidly in 1951, grew only 4 percent in 1952, and actually declined in 1953. Per capita product declined in both years. Unemployment increased in 1953, and productivity declined in both years. In 1954 product grew by more than 20 percent, and the economy entered a period of sustained growth. Inputs of labor did not increase significantly until 1956, although productivity rose substantially in 1954 and 1955. With economic recovery, however, imports again increased, and since they were so much larger than exports, their growth, though slower than export growth, was sufficient to increase the absolute value of the import surplus.

Macro policy lowered inflation and improved the balance of payments through 1954 but, partly because of the Sinai campaign, these objectives were not attained in the two following years, despite continued real devaluation.

Assessment of Liberalization

One important attribute of a liberalization policy is that it indicates an "outward look," manifested by increased trade, both export and import. In 1952–5 Israel's exports did increase, but imports fell during the first three years. By this indicator, the NEP could be considered "antiliberalization." Our view, however, is that the criterion of increased imports is not relevant for this period. When liberalization consists of decreasing import barriers – whether QRs or tariffs – imports will indeed increase. Throughout the 1950s, however, domestic production was almost completely protected from competitive imports; there was little liberalization, in the sense either of changing the form of protection or of reducing protection. Most imports

---

[4] Part of the increase in exports in 1952 reflects better coverage of service exports; this is not a factor in 1953–4.

were therefore of goods not produced domestically; their imports had been controlled by QRs. Whereas the licensing system remained in force during and after the NEP, the changes in EERs in 1952–5, via devaluation and use of duties, were in fact a switch in the form of controlling imports, from QRs to price measures. This is liberalization, despite the import-decreasing effect of real devaluation.

A second important aspect of liberalization concerns divergence in EERs. Indicators on some relevant divergences in the rates are summarized in table 4.8. All the measures are biased, to a greater or lesser extent, by the fact that the average EERs for commodity imports relate to actual imports. They are not EPRs for domestic import substitutes protected by QRs.

Table 4.8 Some measures of exchange rate divergence, 1951–1955

Measure of divergence	1951	1952	1953	1954	1955
1 Disparity between black-market exchange rate and EERM	0.80	0.68	0.52	0.30	0.04
2 Ratio of EERX to EERM	1.02	1.00	1.09	0.96	0.82
3 Coefficient of variance of importers' rates	0.14	0.32	0.47	0.29	0.31

Source: Rows 1 and 3, computed from table 3.1; row 2, computed from Halevi and Baruh, 1988, appendix table A.22

Though the black-market exchange rate is not an accurate measure of the "real" rate of exchange, the disparity between the black-market rate and the average EERM does indicate the extent to which the EERMs are out of line. There was a continuous decrease in this disparity from 1951 to 1955; at the end of that period, the difference between the two rates was very slight. If the average EERM had been a single uniform rate, there would be no doubt that a major step had been taken towards liberalization, in the sense that the exchange rate would serve as a measure for deciding on present and future activities. Such a conclusion must be tempered by consideration of rate divergences.

The ratios of the EERM to the EERX show that exports had a higher average rate in 1952, but this fell relative to the EERM in 1953, and again in 1954. However, this was still a period of strict controls and allocations of foreign exchange. Since the unmeasured EPR must surely have been much higher than the average EERM, the higher EERX in 1952 only partially corrected the relative preference given to import substitutes. The fall in the ratio in the next two years clearly indicates additional bias in favor of import substitutes and against exports. The coefficient of variance of the EERM rose through 1953, but fell to a lower level in 1954 and 1955. As previously mentioned, one objective of using a multiple rate system was to permit discriminatory rates; but even though the data show that such discrimination was indeed applied, it may be argued that an intentional discriminatory system via the price mechanism is preferable to the unintentional discrimination provided by a QR system. In 1955, with the adoption of a single formal rate of exchange, discrimination, at a lower level, was achieved by use of the nonformal components of the EER.

Some Conclusions

The distinctive character of the liberalization episode of the 1950s limits the inferences relevant to other episodes. The main gain from the liberalization can be suggested in a qualitative sense but cannot be quantified: it lies in the greater reliance on the price mechanism, whose benefits would be influential over a long time. This liberalization was not in the trade sector alone, but was part of a general easing of intervention in pricing, the result of disillusionment with controls. No immediate losses resulted from the liberalization as such. Unemployment increased, but as a result of deflationary policy, not of increased imports. In fact, the increase in imports towards the end of the period was part of a general upswing in activity rather than a substitute for domestic production.

The main effects of liberalization were the outcome of a process of formal devaluation, undertaken mainly for macroeconomic reasons. When formal devaluation ended with the adoption of a single rate, this itself diminished disparities in effective rates among imports of commodities, between imports and exports, and between transactions in goods and in services.

Devaluation was accepted as a necessary evil; it was believed that once the process ended it would not be necessary again. In fact, rising domestic prices made compensatory changes necessary in EERs, but eschewing formal devaluation predicated use of nonformal components, which by their very nature tend to be applied in a nonuniform manner and thus to increase rate disparity. In this respect, this liberalization period was followed by one of antiliberalization, mitigated by attempts to make export subsidies more uniform in foreign exchange value added. Though no stages were formally announced, the general impression during the liberalization period was that a new approach, with a trend of gradual liberalization, had been embarked upon, marked by less overt governmental interference in the economy and wider reliance on the price mechanism. The impression proved to be correct: in this sense, the 1952–5 period was not a transient episode.

Could wider liberalization have been expected? Significant segments of the population supported political parties ideologically committed to the idea of a free-market economy, and when the General Zionists joined the coalition government in December 1952 there were grounds for believing that the first year of the NEP would be followed by more drastic liberalization. In fact, there was a trend of easing price controls and less reliance on rationing, but in the area of foreign exchange control a major change was not forthcoming.

We believe that two separate reasons combine to explain why further rapid liberalization did not take place. One was the assessment of Israel's economic situation. The 1953 committee that examined whether exchange control could be abolished included several members who, in their minority report, strongly advocated much more liberal measures for trade (but not for free capital movements). The majority of the committee, including professional economists who favored the market mechanism, were convinced, both by their own understanding of the existing economic situation and by the analysis of a host of witnesses who presented various views, that drastic rather than gradual liberalization could seriously disrupt the economy and cause a balance-of-payment crisis. They all favored use of a single rate of exchange and minimum divergence in effective rates.

The second reason was that many of the leaders of the MAPAI labor party, the dominant party in the coalition, were reluctant to relinquish the idea of government domination and direction of the economy. Of necessity, they realized that the pre-1952 system had to be drastically revised – hence the NEP. But the acceptance of greater reliance on the price mechanism as an allocative instrument was seen as a tool of central planning: the economic ministers felt entirely justified in using discriminatory prices to foster developments they deemed desirable. Their objectives were still biased in favor of agricultural development, fostering economic growth, and balance-of-payments improvement based on import substitution. Many years elapsed before the latter predilection was, reluctantly, abandoned; until then, the idea of allowing wide-scale competitive imports found very litle support in governing circles.

5

Liberalization and Accompanying Policies, 1962–1968

Introduction of the Liberalization Policy

Economic Circumstances

The 1955–61 period has been a fairly stable one for the Israeli economy. Immigration ranged between 24,000 and 71,000 annually (the latter in 1956), and was much less of an economic burden than in the early years. National income per capita grew at an annual rate of 7.2 percent. Agriculture and industry were growing rapidly, productivity growth was high, and there was virtual full employment. Inflation rates were much lower than in the past: after 1955, they dropped to one-digit rates, usually in the 3–6 percent range.

Even the balance of payments – the perennial problem – seemed less formidable. Imports grew at an average rate of 10 percent in 1955–61, whereas exports grew at over 15 percent. Moreover, there was a continuous increase in export diversity, particularly of industrial exports. The foreign exchange budget presented a framework for expenditures limited by expected export earnings and foreign unilateral and capital transfers. Toward the end of the period total receipts exceeded expenditures. For the period as a whole, unilateral transfers covered some three quarters of the deficit in the goods and services account, and long-term capital, including substantial direct private investment, more than made up the difference, building up foreign exchange reserves. In 1961, the import surplus rose to its highest level – US$443 million – but foreign exchange reserves were at their highest level, so there was no real concern for the immediate future. In fact, the economy seemed to have entered a prolonged period of prosperity.

Thus, although, as usual, immediate balance-of-payments problems helped precipitate action, the 1962 change in policy appears to have been motivated by two other major concerns. The first was related to the long-term balance-of-payments prospects. With the Reparations Agreement with West Germany coming to an end, and with no alternative sources of unilateral transfers, it was felt that measures to hasten economic independence should be adopted while the economy was strong.

The second concern stemmed from the exchange rate and protection regimes. The use of nonformal components of the EER made it possible to delay formal devaluation without impeding the growth of exports or import substitutes. From 1956 on, direct subsidies were increasingly used on computed value added in foreign exchange and fewer exports were subsidized by the PAMAZ system; this decreased the dispersion among effective rates for exports. However, the nonformal component exceeded 30 percent of the effective rate for both imports and exports in 1961. Although some services, unilateral transfers, and capital transfers received subsidies in one form or another, these were smaller than those for goods, and many transactions were conducted at the official, overvalued, rate. This policy decreased desirable transfers, and encouraged black-market transactions.

Though the computed average effective rates for imports and exports were quite close, the dispersion among imports was very wide: raw materials and investment goods enjoyed much more favorable rates than consumer goods. Moreover, since much of domestic production was protected by QRs, the EPRs for import substitutes were much higher than the EERM. Though we do not have estimates of the EPR for import substitutes in 1961, we know that little actual liberalization took place before 1965; in that year, the ratio of the protection index for imports to that of exports was 1.5. The effects of this multiple rate system on the efficiency of economic activity, and in particular on projected development, were being appreciated by a widening circle of people.

There was also considerable pressure from the IMF to change the multiple rate system. In addition to the actual rate disparities of the system, the IMF objected to a basic feature which in fact was beneficial: the subsidization of value added in exports. This method of subsidization eliminated horizontal and vertical distortions among exports to the extent that exports received the same subsidy per US dollar value added in foreign exchange. However, the uniform subsidy per dollar value added implied a multitude of rates per dollar of gross exports. It was to this feature of the system that the IMF objected. Clearly, a uniform rate of exchange applicable to all transactions would have been a nondistortionary alternative.

Nature and Targets of the Liberalization Policy

The second new economic policy (hereafter NEP II) announced by Finance Minister Eshkol on February 9, 1962, was heralded as a policy designed to strengthen the competitiveness of the Israeli economy. Its proponents justified the new policy in terms of developments in the EEC and Israel's need to adjust its economy so that the "blessing for Europe would not be a curse for Israel." Israel would make approaches to the EEC, but could not do so without becoming competitive with Europe. The Governor of the Bank of Israel specified three purposes: to eliminate price distortions, to increase competitiveness, and to attain economic independence.

The 18 points of the announced policy contained three major components: (a) a substantial formal devaluation and concomitant reductions in import duties and export subsidies, thus changing both the level and the dispersion of EERs; (b) a gradual reduction in the protection of domestic industry from import competition; (c) an anti-inflationary policy, to prevent price increases from following close upon the devaluation and thereby nullifying it.

The first two components are clearly "liberalization policy." The devaluation, partial reduction of import duties, and complete elimination of the existing subsidies to export value added were immediate. The reduction of protection was to be gradual. The Minister of Finance was empowered to set up a committee on protection to advise on whether to allow competitive imports and, if so, at what level of import duties. Since neither a timetable nor clearly specified final objectives were announced, the future course of the liberalization policy was left vague. Two stages were implied: a shift from QRs to fiscal protection, and the reduction of protection rates. Since, contrary to expectations, many years elapsed before the second stage was activated, we have chosen to consider the two stages as separate liberalization episodes.

Though not originally intended, it quickly developed that items to be "liberalized" were to be examined individually; thus the system was interpreted as a nonuniform liberalization. However, no pre-announced discrimination was proclaimed, with one major exception: agriculture was not included; the liberalization applied only to industry.

Political Circumstances

At the time that the new policy was announced the political structure was regarded as extremely stable: the MAPAI party, dominant in the coalition, were confident that the government would be able to withstand any objections to NEP II. The opposition parties were too weak to be a threat. A more "leftist" coalition partner expressed reservations concerning certain aspects of NEP II, but the terms of its entrance into the coalition did not grant its members freedom to vote against government decisions except in certain specific noneconomic matters.

Of greater concern was how the public, and predominantly MAPAI supporters, would accept the decisions. The chief source of possible opposition was the MAPAI-dominated labor organization, the Histadrut, which frequently objected to measures suggested by their fellow party members in government. However, official Histadrut objections were not forthcoming; on February 11, 1962, the Executive Committee of the Histadrut voted to support NEP II.

What was the perception of the general public? Even though the official spokesmen for NEP I – the Finance Minister, the Governor of the Bank of Israel, and the Chief of the Planning Authority – all stressed that the specific liberalization aspects of the new policy were equal in importance to the devaluation, the general public focused almost exclusively on the latter effects on the price level and implications for dollar-linked loans (particularly mortgages). These were the subjects of debates, petitions, and consequent government efforts to alleviate hardships. The more economically sophisticated circles also debated the monetary implications of the devaluation – the possibility that higher valuation of dollar-linked assets would lead to demand inflation, quickly making the devaluation nominal but not real.

As for the liberalization aspect of NEP II, it soon became evident that there were differences of opinion within the government as to what was meant, and how to implement it. The Ministry of Finance clearly wanted rapid lowering of effective protection, though it did not set a timetable. It is probably fair to say that policymakers in that ministry thought the opportunity was ripe to implement a policy that reflected this new ideological concept. However, the Ministry of Commerce and Industry was in charge of import licensing of most goods, and responsible for the development of industry, and had a very different ideological approach to protection. The NEP II was accepted as a necessary correction of excessive distortions, but this ministry's efforts would be directed toward creating a very gradual process, with case-by-case decisions in which prevention of damage to local industry would be accepted as the main criterion.

Industrialists, who had most to lose by real liberalization, were worried by the general approach declared by the Ministry of Finance, but were quickly reassured by the Ministry of Commerce and Industry, which, after discussions with the Manufacturers' Association, adopted and announced the commodity-by-commodity approach. Various branches, for instance, textile and metal products, protested occasionally that they were being subjected to more competition than others, but it was understood that there was no intention of destroying industries.

Implementation of the Liberalization Policy

The process of liberalizing competitive imports was started by setting up a public committee (the Committee for the Protection of Local Industry), which began its work in May 1962. This committee included representatives of the government (the Ministry of Finance, the Ministry of Trade and Industry, and others), the Histadrut (trade unions), and the Manufacturers' Association. Subcommittees coordinated by the Ministry of Trade and Industry prepared reports on a commodity-by-commodity basis which were brought to the Public Committee for a decision.

This procedure meant that the Ministry of Trade and Industry decided which commodities were to be considered by the Public Committee. For each commodity, the Committee had to decide whether to rescind the QRs on its imports, and what tariff rate to set if the restriction was lifted.

No timetable was set for the Committee's deliberations, and discussions on each item proceeded slowly. The Committee completed most of its work by the end of 1967.

The liberalization was confined to the industrial sector: the agricultural sector was excluded from the outset. Part of the agricultural output was nontraded because of transport costs (vegetables, fruit). Some agricultural commodities were produced locally but not in quantities that could meet local needs (wheat, fodder, sugar); these goods were imported by the government and their implicit protection rates (low for wheat and fodder and very high for sugar) were a function of the prices set by the government. Other goods like meat and dehydrated milk continued to be protected by QRs.

Within the industrial sector, the output of various branches was liberalized to varying degrees. Food processing remained practically unliberalized: the continued controls were justified on religious dietary grounds. Motor vehicles and motor parts industries were exempt from the liberalization process.

In this period (1962–7) there was no intention of allowing imports to compete seriously with local production. The object of the exercise was to replace the implicit protection afforded by QRs by explicit protection levels – through tariffs and other import taxation measures as prohibitive as the QRs they had replaced.

This type of "nominal" liberalization does not affect the immediate performance of the various sectors of the economy, nor need it be affected by developments in the economy. Yet the rate at which the program was implemented varied over the period. The three years in which considerable liberalization took place were 1963, 1964, and 1965. By the end of 1965, 40–50 percent of the relevant local output (industrial output excluding diamonds and nontradeables) was protected by tariffs rather than QRs.

The years 1966–7 saw a slowing down of the liberalization process – presumably because of recession in those years and the fear of adding to uncertainty among industrialists which would lead to unemployment. By 1969, imports of about 90 percent of the "relevant" industrial output were liberalized so that QRs in that sector were more or less eliminated.

It is difficult to be precise about the relationship of the actual to the planned length of this first stage of liberalization (1962–8) though some contemporary documents speak of three years as the planned period. It was hoped that the industrial output defined as "relevant" would be liberalized by the end of 1965. It is even more difficult to say anything about the planned magnitudes of the nominal and effective protection rates in this first stage of liberalization. There was no general policy, no overall ceilings for protection rates. As stated, these rates were set on a commodity-by-commodity basis, with protection levels[1] for each commodity that ensured continued local production unthreatened by competing imports.

The actual nominal and effective protection indices for import substitutes in 1965 and 1968 are shown in table 5.1. Comparison of the rates in 1968 with those in 1965 show a slight change in average NPRs for the

Table 5.1 Nominal and effective protection indices for import substitutes, 1965 and 1968

Sector	NPI		EPI	
	1965	1968	1965	1968
Agriculture	1.22	1.27	1.44	1.61
Industry	1.45	1.45	1.89	1.96
Mining products	1.35	1.36	1.54	1.62
Food, beverages, tobacco	1.31	1.30	2.46	2.52
Textiles	1.65	1.68	2.52	2.46
Clothing	1.76	1.98	1.92	2.84
Leather and its products	1.53	1.45	2.00	1.60
Wood and its products	1.41	1.36	1.31	1.32
Paper and cardboard	1.37	1.36	1.92	1.90
Rubber products	1.54	1.51	2.38	2.39
Plastic products	1.79	1.68	4.04	2.84
Basic chemicals	1.47	1.54	2.66	3.73
Basic metals	1.36	1.31	2.26	2.42
Metal products	1.31	1.31	1.43	1.40
Machinery	1.33	1.30	1.34	1.30
Electrical equipment	1.42	1.35	1.70	1.67
Electronic equipment	1.57	1.51	2.13	2.41
Motor vehicles	1.57	1.57	2.15	2.89
Miscellaneous	1.75	1.82	4.00	3.84
Total	1.40	1.41	1..74	1.85

NPI, nominal protection index; EPI, effective protection index.
Source: Baruh, 1976

[1] Protection rates were set both at the nominal and at the effective (value-added) level – the latter were based on domestic resource cost estimates for each commodity.

industrial sector, and some increase in the EPR. However, the dispersion of rates decreased, suggesting that manufacturers' decisions on pricing policy could be affected by the expected changes.

Though the effects of the 1962–8 liberalization on resource allocation were minimal, the program did provide the basis for the next stage, which aimed at reducing the protection levels set by the Committee. The evidence suggests that some rates were redundant, a redundancy that could be explained in terms of the safety margins that the Committee allowed when setting the tariff rates.

Data in table 5.2 illustrate the redundancy element in the rates set by the Committee. Nominal and effective rates for industrial output (for 1967) as derived from the Committee's decisions are shown side by side with the corresponding *de facto* rates estimated for 1968. The latter rates were mainly based on price comparisons rather than tariff rates, since tariff rates can be used as proxies for local-to-foreign price differentials only when

Table 5.2 Allowed protection rates in 1967 and actual protection rates in 1968

Subsector	NPR		EPR	
	Allowed (1967)	Actual (1968)	Allowed (1967)	Actual (1968)
Meat, fish, milk products	73	30	104	152
Other food	106		140	
Textiles	92	68	241	146
Clothing	110	98	397	184
Wood and wood products	64	36	77	32
Paper and paper products	56	36	74	90
Leather and leather products	58	45	78	60
Rubber and plastic products	89	62	119	166
Basic chemicals	73	54	133	273
Basic metals	39	31	85	142
Metal products	57	31	104	40
Machinery	56	30	97	30
Electrical equipment	133	43	254	96
Transport equipment	115	57	180	189
Miscellaneous	90	82	143	284
Total	78	45	153	96

Source: Allowed protection rates, Tov, 1972; actual protection rates Baruh, 1976

imports comprise some sizable proportion of the total availability of a given good in the domestic market. The fact that *de facto* nominal rates were systematically lower than the rates based on tariffs set by the Committee points to the existence of tariff redundancy. It stands to reason that the "padding" in the tariffs must have blunted the effectiveness of tariffs cuts introduced after 1968.

Accompanying Policies

Exchange Rate Policy

In February 1962 the formal rate was devalued from IL 1.80 per US dollar to IL 3.00 per dollar, and this rate remained in force until November 1967. The effective devaluation was much smaller, as some import duties were reduced and virtually all export subsidies were eliminated. Consequently, the effective rate for imports rose by 33.4 percent, but that for exports by only 13.5 percent. Whereas the nonformal components of the exchange rate had risen to more than 30 percent of the effective rates in 1961, they were now 16 percent for imports, and virtually zero for exports. Thus, the combined operation eliminated the rate differentials among exports of commodities, and between exports of goods, exports of services, and unilateral and capital transfers; but it increased the differential between the average rates for imports and exports while decreasing the variance among imports.

This basic deficiency in the 1962 effective devaluation led to unequal developments in the use of nonformal components in the later years, to prevent deterioration of real rates of exchange. Their influence is shown in table 5.3. Export subsidies were reintroduced in 1965, rising to 16 percent

Table 5.3 Formal and effective exchange rates, 1961–1969 (Israeli pounds per US dollar)

Year	1 Formal rate	2 Commodity imports	3 Commodity exports[a]	4 Imports	5 Exports
		Average effective rate		*Nonformal component as percentage of effective rate*	
1961	1.80	2.60	2.66	30.9	32.2
1962	3.00	3.47	3.02	16.0	0.1
1963	3.00	3.49	3.04	14.0	1.3
1964	3.00	3.47	3.06	13.3	2.0
1965	3.00	3.55	3.08	15.5	2.7
1966	3.00	3.54	3.27	16.4	8.6
1967	3.00	3.68	3.57	18.5	16.0
1968	3.50	4.13	4.04	15.3	13.7
1969	3.50	4.22	4.05	17.1	13.6

[a] Rates for exports value added in foreign exchange.
Source: Halevi, 1979

of the effective rate in 1967. Import taxes were also raised gradually, but by a much smaller percentage. In November 1967 there was a small formal devaluation, to IL 3.50 per US dollar. This "mini-devaluation" was not combined with large decreases in the nonformal components along the lines of 1962, when a large formal devaluation led to a much smaller effective devaluation.

Export Promotion Policy

Export promotion had two principal components.[2] The most significant was export-biased investment activity, financed mainly via the government budget and government-influenced financial institutions such as the Industrial Development Bank.

EER policy, discussed above, was the second instrument. In 1962–5 it was believed that formal devaluation would be sufficient, and most subsidies were abolished. However, because the February 1962 devaluation for exports raised the average effective rate only slightly, it was very quickly eroded by domestic inflation. Furthermore, the raising of the average rate for imports much more than for exports – import duties were only partially reduced, whereas export subsidies were abolished – again created a bias against exports. Nevertheless the dispersion among rates for various exports was greatly reduced (an important objective of NEP II), though it was still significant in 1965.

Monetary and Fiscal Policy[3]

The 1962 devaluation came at a time of inflationary pressure. The devaluation itself increased the real value of foreign exchange holdings, and large stocks of foreign exchange were converted to local currency. This was the main reason for the 30 percent increase in the money supply (M1) in 1962, and 28 percent in 1963. In an effort to circumvent monetary restrictions a bill brokerage market developed which, according to Heth (1966, p. 117), grew to 24 percent of total bank credit in 1961 and to 42 percent in 1964.

The government tried to curb inflation mainly through the credit market by means of early redemption of mortgages and by floating a short-term loan. But the government expanded its own demand. The Bank of Israel tightened liquidity ratios by granting fewer exemptions, but not by raising ratios. It reduced direct credit to government and to the public, but it did not undertake open-market operations despite the fact that the time was ripe, as witnessed by the development of the bill brokerage market. The

---

[2] There was also extensive export promotion by government assistance in marketing.
[3] Beham (1968) is the main source for this section.

combined actions of the government and the Bank of Israel were inadequate and did not counteract the demand inflation generated by the devaluation. The price control measures merely temporarily repressed some of the inflationary pressure: as shown in table 5.4 the *real* money supply rose in 1962 and 1963. The inadequacies of monetary (and fiscal) policy were what caused the 1962 devaluation to fail in its main objectives (Beham, 1968).

Table 5.4 Changes in the money supply, 1962–1968

Year	Percentage change in money supply		
	Nominal M1	Nominal M2	Real[a] M1
1962	29.7	37.5	20.8
1963	28.1	25.7	20.8
1964	6.1	6.7	1.4
1965	11.2	11.3	1.2
1966	5.7	12.3	− 2.4
1967	25.0	40.3	22.4
1968	11.6	20.3	9.4

[a] Deflated by GNP prices.
Source: computed from data in CBS, *Statistical Abstract of Israel*, 1978

In 1960–4 the average annual growth rate of the money supply was 17.4 percent and that of the monetary base 18.2 percent. Toward the end of 1965 and throughout 1966 and early 1967 a recessionary policy was introduced, mainly for the balance-of-payments reasons. Already in 1964 higher reserve requirements slowed the growth of the money supply. In early 1965 reserve requirements were 69 percent, but 22 percent of reserves were exempted, for directed credit, and in 1965 the money supply grew almost twice as much as in 1964. This reflects the interaction of monetary policy and the effects of a reduced balance-of-payments deficit on the monetary base. There was hardly any real growth since both prices and money grew at similar rates. The government took steps to limit the expansion of the bill brokerage market. Excess liquidity declined towards the end of 1965.

Reduced government financing of investment, particularly of housing, and decreased private housing activity combined to switch the economy from boom to real recession. However, government consumption grew. The main downturn came later in 1966. Decreased private investment activity and curtailment of output growth were accompanied by a switch in the public's asset holdings: the demand for real assets such as real estate and durable consumer goods fell, while monetary asset holdings increased. This intensified the recession.

The unexpected severity of the recession led to a recovery program in 1967, and with the war-induced demand in the latter half of the year economic activity began to pick up. This is reflected in a 25 percent increase in nominal M1, and a 22.4 percent increase in real terms.

Public consumption rose from some 20 percent of GNP in the early 1960s to 30 percent toward the end of the decade. Though civilian public consumption, which fluctuated between 10 and 13 percent of GNP, was somewhat higher in the second half of the decade, the most dramatic increase was in defense expenditure.

Table 5.5 shows the financing of the government deficit. In 1960–4 there was a domestic surplus, and government contribution to money creation

Table 5.5 Financing the government budget, 1960–1967 (percentage of gross national product)

Item	1960–4	1965–7
1 Domestic expenditure[a]	27.0	32.0
2 Net foreign expenditure[b]	1.2	2.8
3 Taxes[c]	28.8	29.6
4 Domestic deficit (row 1 − row 3)	− 1.8	2.4
5 Total deficit (row 4 + row 2)[d]	− 0.6	5.2
6 Base money creation	2.5	2.2
7 Domestic debt finance[e]	− 3.3	0
8 Foreign debt finance	0.3	3.0

[a] Domestic expenditure includes goods and services, subsidies, transfers, and interest on the public debt.
[b] Net foreign expenditure is defined as government expenditure abroad (mainly armaments) plus interest on debt minus unilateral transfers (mainly US government).
[c] Taxes include all direct and indirect taxes and transfers to government.
[d] Row 1 + row 2 − row 3 = row 6 + row 7 + row 8 = total finance of deficit.
[e] Domestic debt finance includes indexed bonds. Figures are net of repayments and of loans to the public sector.
Source: Bruno, 1984, table 2

was negative. In the recessionary period, 1965–7, domestic debt finance was zero; the domestic deficit was small, and was financed by base money creation.

Controls

The process of diminishing overt price controls, continuous from 1952, did not lead to the complete elimination of government efforts to control prices. Many basic commodities were still subject to controls, and subsidies were used to prevent or dampen price increases, particularly for items with significant weight in the CPI. In addition, wide use was made of "moral persuasion" as an indirect price control.

With the devaluation of 1962, great efforts to limit price increases were made by using indirect controls. In September 1962 a special staff was set up to administer these controls; price increases were temporarily dissallowed, and "unreasonable" increases were reversed by threatening to use fiscal measures or to withdraw benefits (and protection), and frequently by a private talk with the Minister of Commerce and Industry. Thus the inflationary forces were at first repressed and gradually released.

In 1963 a law was passed regulating cartel arrangements. Though ostensibly designed to give recourse to those harmed by restraint of trade, it was used officially to sanction cartel arrangements, but in so doing subjected the cartel to direct price control. In later years, controls were generally less significant, though on occasion the same type of indirect controls as those applied in 1962 were resorted to, for limited periods, to dampen the inflationary effects after devaluation.

The controls on foreign capital movements were not changed by NEP II. However, more liberal allowances were gradually given for foreign investments by Israeli firms, and foreign investment in Israel was more actively solicited and encouraged. Transfer abroad of profits from foreign investment in Israel, including those from operation of shipping and airline companies, was liberalized.

6

Economic Performance and Assessment of Policy, 1962–1968

Economic Performance Following Liberalization

The 1962–8 liberalization consisted of macro-policy measures and changes in the form of protection. Both aspects need to be assessed in the light of the economic performance which followed the liberalization.

Prices, Wages, and Relative Prices

After a period of relatively modest rates of inflation (1955–61), when consumer prices rose less than 5 percent a year, the inflation rate in 1962 was over 9 percent and fluctuated between 5 and 7 percent in 1962–3. GDP prices followed a similar pattern, but grew most in 1965, approaching 10 percent. Inflation accelerated because of the devaluation of 1962 and the subsequent monetary expansion, and later because of large wage increases in 1965. In those years, QRs on imports were being replaced by explicit tariffs. Whether this import liberalization restrained price rises in industrial products is an open question. The fact that the volume of competing imports was minimal in those years does not preclude a restraining effect if industrialists felt they would face import competition once they raised their prices beyond the c.i.f. plus tariff level.

Prices continued to rise in 1966, although the economy had entered a recession by the end of 1965. GNP growth rates fell from an average of 10 percent per year in 1962–5 to only 1 percent in 1966, as a result of a slowdown policy aimed at curbing imports. Prices stabilized by mid-1966 and the inflation rates for 1967 and 1968 were very low (1.6 percent and 2.1 percent respectively).

The CPI and indices of nominal and real wage levels for the economy in the period 1961–8 are shown in table 6.1. These indices refer to wages paid by employers.

Table 6.1 Nominal and real wages, 1961–1968

Year	Nominal wage index	CPI	Real wage index	Percentage annual change	
				CPI	Real wages
1961	100.0	100.0	100.0	—	—
1962	115.3	109.4	105.4	9.4	5.4
1963	128.8	116.6	110.5	6.6	4.8
1964	144.8	122.5	118.2	5.1	7.0
1965	170.1	131.9	130.0	7.7	10.0
1966	202.6	142.5	142.2	8.1	9.4
1967	203.4	144.8	140.5	1.6	− 1.2
1968	209.2	144.8	142.0	2.1	1.1

—, not applicable.
Source: CBS, Statistical abstract of Israel, 1974

The subperiod 1962–6 was one in which real wages increased considerably, well beyond the increase in labor productivity. The falling rate of unemployment and the excess demand for workers (both skilled and unskilled) in most branches contributed to this development. Attempts to control prices and wages directly (as in 1963) only briefly improved matters. Only the slackening demand for labor from mid-1965 onward dampened real wage rises, but with a considerable lag. Real wages in 1965 and 1966 continued to rise at rates that were the highest in this period (10 percent and 9 percent respectively) despite decreased labor participation rates and increased numbers of people seeking work. In 1965 public sector employees got a hefty 25 percent increase in nominal wages. In early 1966 wages rose sharply in the entire business sector, as new wage agreements came into force. In 1966 public sector employees received retroactive payments (for 1965), and a general cost-of-living allowance of 9 percent was paid across the board. The effect of the recession was felt on wages in the second half of 1966 and in 1967. In the latter year wages fell by 1 percent, and they increased by only 1 percent in 1968.

Though it had marked effects on the price level, and consequently on nominal and real wages, the 1962 devaluation was intended to bring about a substantial change in the relative prices of tradeables and nontradeables, that is, real devaluation. Data on effective devaluation, nominal and real, are shown in table 6.2.

The immediate effect of the 1962 devaluation was to increase EERs, more for imports than for exports. Various administrative measures and subsidies were used to keep down domestic prices, particularly of basic commodities with importance for the CPI, to which cost-of-living adjustments were linked. These efforts were fairly successful: in each of the four

Table 6.2 Nominal and real devaluation, 1961–1969 (annual rates of change)

Year	1 Effective rates Imports	2 Effective rates Exports	3 GNP prices	4 Effective rates deflated by GNP Imports	5 Effective rates deflated by GNP Exports	6 Relative change in prices[a] Imports	7 Relative change in prices[a] Exports	8 Ratio of price indices of tradeables to nontradeables[b]
1961	1.2	3.1	8.6	− 6.8	− 5.1	− 9.6	− 4.2	1.00
1962	33.4	13.5	7.4	24.2	5.7	21.6	4.7	1.20
1963	0.6	1.0	6.0	− 5.1	− 4.7	− 4.1	− 0.9	1.13
1964	− 0.6	0.3	4.6	− 5.0	− 4.1	− 3.1	− 4.1	1.07
1965	2.3	0.7	9.9	− 6.9	− 8.4	− 5.0	− 4.8	1.05
1966	1.1	6.2	8.3	− 6.6	− 1.9	− 4.8	4.5	1.02
1967	2.6	9.1	2.1	0.5	6.9	0.5	5.0	1.02
1968	12.6	13.2	2.0	10.0	11.0	7.8	9.1	1.02
1969	2.2	0.2	2.3	− 0.1	− 2.1	4.9	2.5	1.00

[a] The relative rates are computed by adding to the effective rates the effective changes in foreign prices before deflation by GNP prices.
[b] Based on a breakdown of items in the CPI into tradeable and nontradeables, carried out by Cukierman and Razin (1976).
Source: Halevi, 1979

quarters of 1962 the CPI rose 2.3–2.7 percent; in 1963 the quarterly increase was 1 percent or less except for the last quarter (when it jumped to 3 percent). However, even though the inflationary effect of the devaluation was drawn out and was not reflected in a large sudden price increase, the cumulative effect was considerable, as discussed above. Since the nominal effective rates for commodity trade remained almost unchanged in 1962–5, that is, after the devaluation (and increased only slightly for exports in 1966), real effective rates – deflated by GNP prices – decreased in 1963–6. Taking changes in the foreign prices of imports and exports into account to compute relative changes in prices for producers of import substitutes and exporters (table 6.2, columns 6 and 7) a similar, though smaller, declining trend emerges in the real effective rates. The prices of tradeable goods rose less than those of nontradeables; thus, the ratio of their relative price indices (column 8) shows a decline from 1962 through 1966. It can be concluded that the dramatic devaluation successfully changed relative prices for only a brief period.

External Transactions

Imports
The NEP II devaluation was not followed by an absolute reduction in imports: both commodity and service imports increased through 1964. As

shown in table 6.3 the higher valuation of imports in current domestic prices raised the ratio of imports to GNP from 0.35 in 1961 to 0.48 in 1962; thereafter, the ratio declined through 1966, and regained the 1963 level in 1968. In constant foreign exchange prices, real imports of commodities increased after the 1962 devaluation, but at much lower rates in 1962 and 1963 than in 1961, and as much in 1964 as in 1961. Thus the effects of NEP II on aggregate imports differed greatly from those of the first NEP.

Table 6.3 Imports, 1961–1968

	1	2	3	4	5
Year	Imports (million current US$)			Imports to GNP[b]	Annual rate of growth in real commodity imports[c]
	Commodities[a]	Services	Total		
1961	521	319	840	0.35	21.7
1962	556	377	933	0.48	8.9
1963	594	423	1,017	0.44	4.9
1964	733	450	1,183	0.45	21.9
1965	730	504	1,234	0.40	− 3.9
1966	855	428	1,283	0.37	− 2.7
1967	965	482	1,447	0.39	− 6.9
1968	1,253	553	1,806	0.49	47.1

[a] Balance-of-payments figures, not trade statistics data.
[b] Current dollar imports were converted by use of EERs.
[c] Nominal dollar values of trade statistics imports deflated by the index of import prices.
Sources: columns 1–4, Halevi, 1983b; column 5, computed from CBS, Statistical Abstract of Israel, 1978, p. 214

In late 1965, recessionary policy was adopted, reflected in no growth of commodity imports (in current foreign exchange prices) in 1965 and a slow growth of total imports in 1965 and 1966. Real commodity imports fell in 1965, 1966, and 1967; they leapt by 47 percent in 1968.

As shown above, the EERM rose more than GNP prices in 1962, but by less in 1963–7. Since the foreign prices of imports fell during this period, the relative change in prices was more moderate; but clearly the "real" devaluation was shortlived, and quickly dissipated.

The price elasticity of commodity imports has been estimated at − 0.35 for 1950–67 (Weinblatt, 1972). Even such low elasticities[1] would have led

[1] These estimates have been criticized by Cukierman and Razin (1976) because they do not allow for a reciprocal relationship between imports and EERs. Their own estimates, based on simultaneous equations, were much higher.

to expectations of more significant decreases in imports had there been real effective devaluation, but, in contrast with the NEP period, imports did not decrease significantly; it follows that relative price policy was not used as a major tool for import limitation. However, the income elasticity, found to be greater than unity (Weinblatt, 1972), explains the stagnation in commodity imports in 1965 and 1966 and general growth when income rose.

The only dramatic change in the structure of imports in this period was the fall in the share of investment goods in the recession. The annual changes in the various subclasses show marked differences. Among consumer goods, durables increased the most in 1963 and 1964, but fell the most in the 1965–67 period as a whole. Investment goods fell in every year except 1964. Inputs showed the least volatility, except for those destined for the construction industry – the most volatile sector in the economy.

In his study on various import classes, Weinblatt (1972) found that consumer goods as a whole were highly price elastic (about − 1.3), with food and current consumption imports being elastic; surprisingly, durables had a relative price elasticity of only − 0.8. However, the EER of durables rose 34 percent in 1962, compared to with only 11 percent and 6 percent for current consumption and food respectively. Thus, even in the one year of real relative devaluation, it was the least price-elastic consumer category that was most affected. Investment goods were found to have an elasticity of − 0.6. They, too, were affected by the devaluation. Inputs, however, the main component of commodity imports, were not found to be responsive to price.

As long as domestic production enjoyed absolute protection, import substitution was a major component of economic growth. Pack (1971, pp. 84–6) found that for 1958–64 exports were a more important source of industrial growth than import substitution, though there was still considerable growth in the latter, whose role was especially significant in wood, paper, printing, chemicals, food, leather, and machinery.

Table 6.4 presents estimates of penetration ratios, that is, the share of "competing imports" in total domestic purchases,[2] for industry in 1965 and 1968. In 1965 the ratio was only 0.16, and in 1968 it had barely changed. In 1968, only four branches (basic metals, machinery, electrical products, and motor vehicles) had penetration indices of over 10 percent. The frequency distribution of the penetration indices with the cumulated percentages based on total domestic purchases show that two thirds of manufacturing output had indices of less than 10 percent in 1965 and 1968.

---

[2] Unlike data showing imports relative to sales in each branch, competing imports are computed by using more disaggregated data to distinguish between products not produced domestically and those which are; only the latter have "competing imports." Domestic purchases are defined as output minus exports plus completing imports.

Table 6.4 Share of competing imports in the
domestic market of the manufacturing sector, 1965
and 1968

Manufacturing sector	1965	1968
Food, beverages	2	4
Textiles	7	10
Clothing and leather products	3	6
Wood products	7	6
Paper products	4	4
Rubber and plastic products	4	7
Chemicals	3	2
Glass and ceramic products	10	13
Basic metals	30	34
Metal products	8	8
Motors and machinery	20	19
Electrical and electronic products	36	46
Motor vehicles	47	45
Total	16	18

Ratio of competing imports (CM) to the domestic market,
defined as the total output (TO) minus exports (X) plus
competing imports (CM), that is $CM/(TO - X + CM)$.
Source: Baruh, 1976

Exports

Exports of goods and services grew continuously; the average rate of
growth (in constant 1968 prices) was 14.1 percent in 1960–5 and 13.0
percent in 1965–70. Even the 1960–70 rate was considerably below the 20
percent average rate for 1955–60. As a percentage of GNP, exports grew
slowly, from 22 percent in 1962 (a jump over 1961 because of higher
valuation) to 29 percent in 1964. Table 6.5 presents annual data for 1961–8.
Real commodity exports rose at a higher-than-average rate in 1962, and
leapt by 20 percent in 1963. After a very moderate increase in 1964, there
were constant rates of growth (11.3–11.7 percent) in 1965–7 and a higher
rate in 1968. There followed wide annual fluctuations in rates of growth.

There were only marginal changes in the share of total commodity
exports during the 1961–8 period. Among commodities, agricultural
exports declined in relative terms, the share of industrial exports increased,
and the share of diamonds fluctuated. The structure of industrial exports
changed over time: from the mid-1950s to about the mid-1960s, the
important export products were mining, cement, plywood, clothing,
textiles, food, tires, chemicals, and transport equipment. Except for the
last two, these were all fairly unsophisticated products. From the mid-
1960s, the trend was to more rapid relative growth of sophisticated
products: transport equipment, machinery, metal products, chemicals, and

Table 6.5 Exports, 1961–1968

Year	1 Exports (million current US$)			4 Ratio of Exports to GNP[b]	5 Growth in real commodity exports[c]
	Commodities[a]	Services	Total		
1961	238	159	397	0.17	10.5
1962	271	201	472	0.22	16.7
1963	337	240	577	0.23	20.4
1964	349	270	619	0.21	5.1
1965	404	307	711	0.20	11.3
1966	476	358	834	0.22	11.6
1967	533	378	911	0.24	11.7
1968	652	498	1,150	0.29	16.3

[a] Balance-of-payments data.
[b] Current dollar exports were converted by use of the EER.
[c] Based on trade statistics.
Sources: columns 1–4, Halevi, 1983b; column 5, computed from CBS, Statistical Abstract of Israel, 1978, p. 214

electrical products. Most of the dramatic changes took place after 1968, however. There is no evidence that skill content contributed to export success before 1965. (Pack, 1971, p. 90, quotes Hirsch on this point.)

Studies of the responsiveness of industrial exports to relative prices have generally found elasticities equal to or greater than unity – higher than for total commodity exports. For the 1955–69 period, Halevi (1972) found an elasticity of 0.87 for export value added; a distributed lag model raised this elasticity to 1.34, with about two thirds of the impact taking place in the first year. The production potential variable (capital stock) had an elasticity of close to 2; clearly, growth was biased in favor of industrial exports.

It was clearly intended that decreased domestic demand in 1965–7 would push producers to more active export activity. Ben-Horin (1972) found that the reduced domestic demand in 1966, compared with 1965 and 1964, did indeed stimulate exports. However, this was not in industries whose output was either predominantly for export nor predominantly for the local market: the former had little output remaining to be switched to exports, and the latter could not switch to export markets quickly but instead reduced output. The recession had few long-term effects. This accords with the conclusions of Beham and Kleiman (1968) that the failure to accompany recessionary demand policy with devaluation prevented long-term structural changes. In other words, "push" and "pull" factors should have been employed together.

Balance of Payments
Import surplus data are shown in table 6.6. Though there were considerable annual fluctuations in the import surplus, as shown by column 2, the
general trend was an increase.

Table 6.6 Absolute and relative import surplus, 1961–1968

Year	1 Import surplus (million current US$)	2 Annual increase in import surplus (%)	3 Ratio of Import surplus to GNP (current prices)	4 Debt- financed import surplus to GNP[a]	5 Direct defense imports to GNP	6 Import surplus to GNP (constant 1955 prices)[b]
1961	443	28.0	0.18	0.04	0.03	16.7
1962	461	4.1	0.26	0.08	0.04	14.5
1963	440	− 4.6	0.21	0.05	0.05	11.9
1964	564	28.2	0.24	0.10	0.04	16.9
1965	523	7.3	0.20	0.08	0.04	13.6
1966	449	− 14.1	0.15	0.05	0.04	10.8
1967	536	19.4	0.15	0.004	0.07	8.3
1968	656	22.4	0.20	0.07	0.06	11.2

[a] Import surplus minus net unilateral transfers.
[b] The conversion to domestic currency was made at the effective rate for 1955.
Sources: columns 1–5, computed from data in Halevi, 1983b; column 6, Michaely,
1971, p. 16

There has been long-standing debate in Israel about whether to compute
the ratio of the import surplus to GNP in current or in constant prices. The
case for using constant prices is strong, particularly when changes in
exchange rates lead to sudden jumps in the evaluation of the deficit, as in
1962. The constant-price figures (column 6) show a decline in this ratio in
1962 and 1963 – when real GNP grew at rates of about 11 percent – and
that is clearly in large part the effect of the devaluation. During the
recessionary period, 1965–7, the relative deficit again fell. This time there
were contrasting movements in GNP: 10 percent growth in 1965 (the
recession started late in the year), and stagnation throughout 1966 and
until late 1967.

Unilateral transfers covered much, but not all, of the import surplus;
consequently, a substantial foreign debt was gradually built up before the
1970s. In all but one year between 1961 and 1965, long-term inflows made
increases possible in net short-term assets. In 1967 short-term assets were

close to US$1 billion compared with US$1.6 billion of longer-term debts and US$300 million of short-term obligations.

Product, Inputs, and Productivity

The 1960s generally followed the growth path of the second half of the 1950s: high rates of investment, GNP, and productivity growth, and low unemployment. But the period was not uniform: as a result of growing balance-of-payments deficits and inflation rates in 1964 and 1965, the government adopted a policy of "dampening" economic activity, from late 1965. The idea was to sacrifice some growth for balance-of-payments improvement and lower inflation rates. Deflationary fiscal and monetary measures combined with unexpected private-market cutbacks, particularly in housing (resulting partly from decreased immigration), to slide the economy into an actual recession. Only in late 1967, after the June war, and with a reversal of policy, did the economy turn around. Data on some relevant macroeconomic variables for the 1962–8 period are presented in table 6.7.

Table 6.7 Some macroeconomic variables, 1962–1968 (annual percentage rates of change)

Variable	1962	1963	1964	1965	1966	1967	1968
1 Real GNP	10.1	11.4	9.8	9.8	1.4	4.6	8.6
2 Real product, business sector	12.4	8.7	9.8	5.1	0.1	− 0.4	21.1
3 Total investment	3.9	6.0	21.2	0.6	− 17.5	− 20.6	41.8
4 Civilian labor force	5.7	2.6	5.4	3.2	3.9	− 2.2	9.6
5 Productivity, business sector	3.8	1.7	2.9	− 0.9	− 3.5	1.0	10.0
6 Unemployment as percent of labor force	3.7	3.6	3.3	3.6	7.4	10.4	6.1
7 Share of investment in GNP[a]	33.5	30.6	34.2	30.0	23.2	17.4	23.5

[a] Calculated from current price data.
Sources: Rows 1, 3, 4, 6, and 7, calculated from data in CBS, *Statistical Abstract of Israel*, variouuuus issues; rows 2 and 5, Gaathon, 1971

Product

Until 1966 real GNP increased at high rates. In 1966 it grew by just a little over 1 percent (a fall of 1.6 percent in per capita terms) – a drastic drop from the previous 10 percent growth rates. Toward the end of 1967 product began to grow again, and a rate of 8.6 percent was achieved in 1968.

Though the recession was induced by policy, it was more severe in the business than in the public sector: the fall in the growth of output was sharper in the former sector and also started earlier – in 1965 – and lasted through 1967. Only in 1968 was there a great leap in output – 21 percent.

The most volatile branch, as usual, was construction: real product fell 13.2 percent in 1966, and 18.5 percent in 1966. Agricultural product fell earlier – in 1965 – but started to rebound in 1966 and was out of the recession in 1967. By contrast, the rate of growth of product in manufacturing was still 10 percent in 1965; it fell to 1.6 percent in 1965, and to – 3.4 percent in 1967, before leaping to 28.7 percent in 1968.

Employment

Unemployment rose rapidly in 1966 and 1967, averaging 7.4 percent in 1967. Thus, a dampening of growth turned into a major, though short-lived, economic recession. This sudden reemergence of unemployment as a serious problem led to grave misgivings as to whether the absorption of earlier mass immigration in employment had been entirely effective. Unemployment was particularly severe in development towns. It also resulted in substantial emigration of skilled workers who could find easy employment abroad.

Whereas the peak in unemployment was reached in 1967, employment in manufacturing fell most – 5 percent – in 1966. Hardest hit were the wood, electrical, metal, and transport product industries. There are no major differences in the employment share of the manufacturing branches between 1961 and 1968.

Capital and Productivity

Real investment barely grew in 1965, fell drastically in 1966–7, and then soared to 42 percent in 1968. Lower investment in construction was a trigger for recession, but housing investment fell less than investment in structures for industry, and rebounded less in 1968. Estimates of capital utilization in the business sector (Metzer, 1983) show a continuous decline from 1962 to 1965, and of another 13 percent from 1965 to 1967, that is, a fall of 20 percent for the entire 1962–7 period. Utilization of capital only gradually increased, but was still below the 1965 level in 1972, after which it again declined.

As would be expected, total factor productivity fell during the recession: whereas productivity in the business sector as a whole grew annually at rates fluctuating between 1.7 and 3.8 percent in 1961–4, it fell by about 1 percent in 1965 and 3.5 percent in 1966. In 1967 there was a slight increase, and in 1968 productivity grew by 10 percent. In manufacturing, reduced use of both capital and labor inputs led to a smaller fall in productivity than in any other branch (in fact, only in 1966 was there a fall, of 1 percent) and in 1968 productivity grew by 15.7 percent.

Assessment of the Liberalization of 1962–1968

Our assessment of the second liberalization episode deals separately with its two components: first, the devaluation, with its "liberalization" aspects which are conceptually similar to but quantitatively different from those of the 1952 NEP, and the accompanying policies; second, the replacement of QR protection of import substitutes by tariffs.

Macro Policy and Liberalization

The macro package of 1962 was less successful than that of 1952 in achieving its desired effects on the balance of payments. Firstly, the formal devaluation was much larger than effective devaluation. The latter was too small, particularly for exports, to create more than temporary real devaluation. Secondly, the deflationary fiscal and monetary policies, which were necessary accompaniments of devaluation under conditions of close to full employment, were not implemented (Barkai and Michaely, 1963). In particular, monetary policy did not compensate for the effects of devaluation on the money suply and financial assets (Beham, 1968).

Figure 6.1 shows quarterly moving averages for exports, imports, and the CPI, from the fourth quarter of 1961 through the last quarter of 1963.

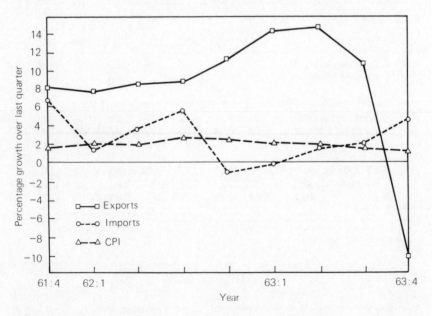

Figure 6.1 Quarterly percentage changes in exports, imports, and consumer prices for 1961:4–1963:4

Export growth increased until mid-1963; the rate then decreased sharply. The rate of change of imports fluctuated, reaching negative levels in only two quarters, and increasing from the second quarter of 1963. The CPI rose a steady 2 percent per quarter throughout this period; this is not a high rate of inflation by Israel's standards, but is sufficient to erode the small real effective devaluation very quickly.

The annual figures show a slight fall in the import surplus in 1963 – resulting from the growth of total exports by US$105 million, while total imports increased by US$84 million – and a jump in the deficit of US$124 million in 1964 when exports rose by only US$42 million. The failure of macro policy led to its replacement in late 1965 by the implementation of (belated) deflationary policy.[3]

The devaluation itself was accompanied by an elimination of almost all export subsidies and decreases in customs duties; thus formal devaluation was in large part a replacement of previous effective devaluation by means of nonformal components of the exchange rate. This step affected the dispersion in effective rates. Table 6.8 presents some ratios of average EERMs to indicate changes in dispersion.

Table 6.8 Ratios of effective exchange rates for commodities, 1961–1967

Ratios of EERs	1961	1962	1963	1964	1965	1966	1967
A Ratio of average EERX to average EERM	1.02	0.87	0.87	0.88	0.87	0.92	0.97
B Ratios of average EERM for types of imports to average for all imports							
1 Consumer goods	1.30	1.18	1.22	1.20	1.25	1.34	1.39
2 Investment goods	0.86	0.94	0.96	0.97	0.97	0.98	0.98
3 Inputs	1.02	1.01	0.97	0.98	0.97	0.95	0.95
C Ratio of lowest average EERM to highest EERM in the category							
1 Consumer goods	0.61	0.77	0.99	0.87	0.92	0.95	0.91
2 Investment goods	0.88	0.86	0.87	0.91	0.87	0.88	0.89
3 Inputs	0.57	0.69	0.63	0.58	0.57	0.56	0.53

Sources: block A, computed from Halevi, 1979; blocks B and C, computed from data in Weinblatt, 1972, table B.8

---

[3] As discussed above, the effects of this policy on balance of payments were significant only in the short run (Ben-Horin, 1972); the main problem was the failure to use devaluation as an accompanying policy (Beham and Kleiman, 1968).

Formal devaluation would have been expected to decrease the difference between the average EERM and EERX. In fact, it did not: the effective devaluation was very small for commodity exports; consequently, the ratio of the EERX to the EERM fell by some 15 percent. This ratio remained constant until the resumption of direct export subsidization in 1966. In this respect, the devaluation had an antiliberalization effect. For exports and imports of services the devaluation did reduce rate disparities in comparison with commodities. (Rate disparities between trade and financial transactions also decreased.)

Among commodity imports, the devaluation reduced the rate disparities for actual imports – the rates are EERMs, not EPRs. In the late 1950s some consumer goods were sold on the "gray" (or "parallel") market at high effective rates. The 1962 devaluation reduced the difference between the average rate for consumer goods and the average total EERM, and also reduced the preference enjoyed by imported capital goods. This reduced disparity was maintained, more or less, for investment goods and material inputs, but not for long for consumer goods: after 1964, consumer goods were taxed much more, on average.

Within each major category, there was considerable rate dispersion. Among consumer goods, the devaluation itself was accompanied by reductions in dispersion, and a much greater reduction was evident in 1963, with some regression in 1964. Among investment goods no trends are evident in this regard, with the ratio between the lowest and highest average rates being fairly close to 0.90. However, the disparities among inputs were very high, and were only slightly, and temporarily, reduced by the NEP II. Agricultural and industrial inputs received preferential rates while inputs for construction and fuel had much higher and relatively rising EERMs. Thus the overall picture of reductions in EERM disparities is one of only partial liberalization.

Changes in Forms of Protection

The hopes that the NEP II would lead to quick sharp reductions in the protection of domestic industry were short lived. As already pointed out in chapter 5, this was not an aborted liberalization because of unexpected economic difficulties or a miscalculation of the economic costs; it was in fact a veto by the Ministry of Commerce and Industry of the approach adopted by the Ministry of Finance.

By 1968 the protracted process of switching from QRs to tariff protection was completed for those items for which this liberalization was intended. However, many products were still excluded. Toren (1976) found that as late as 1975 import competition for specific items was still significantly restricted by QRs, particularly in the subbranches of food, inputs for agriculture and defense, basic metals, machinery, and electronics. However, tariffs were the main protective instrument by the late 1960s.

Table 6.9 presents the ratios of the effective protection indices for import substitutes (EPIMs) for each major branch to the average for all manufacturing industries. Similar ratios are shown for exports (EPIXs), where such estimates are available for the same branches, and of the relative EPIM and EPIX in each branch. The average EPIM was 1.89 for manufacturing as a whole in 1965, and 1.44 for agriculture. That year, the average nonformal component of the exchange rate for commodity imports was only 18 percent of the IL 3.00 per US dollar formal exchange rate. Thus domestic production was receiving substantial additional protection. There was great disparity in the average EPIMs for manufacturing branches: they ranged from as low as 0.7 for machinery and wood products to as high as 2.14 for plastic products.

By 1968 the formal exchange rate had risen from IL 3.00 to IL 3.50 per US dollar, and the average EERM for all commodities had risen to IL 4.13 per dollar, that is, the nonformal component was equal to 18 percent of the

Table 6.9 Ratios of effective protection indices for import substitutes and exports, 1965 and 1968

Manufacturing sector	Ratio of branch to EPIM to average industrial EPIM		Ratio of branch to EPIX to average industrial EPIX		Ratio of branch EPIX to branch EPIM	
	1965	1968	1965	1968	1965	1968
All manufacturing	1.00	1.00	1.00	1.00	0.60	0.59
Mining products	0.81	0.83	0.87	0.99	0.63	0.71
Food	1.30	1.29	0.85	0.94	0.39	0.43
Textiles	1.33	1.26	2.13	1.54	0.96	0.66
Clothing	1.02	1.45	0.76	0.99	0.45	0.30
Wood products	0.69	0.67	1.43	1.63	1.23	1.43
Rubber products	1.26	1.22	0.64	0.95	0.31	0.58
Basic chemicals	1.41	1.90	1.91	1.08	0.39	0.34
Metal products	0.76	0.50	n.a.	0.78	n.a.	0.64
Leather products	1.05	0.82	n.a.	n.a.	n.a.	n.a.
Paper	1.02	0.97	n.a.	n.a.	n.a.	n.a.
Plastic products	2.14	1.45	n.a.	n.a.	n.a.	n.a.
Basic metals	1.20	1.23	n.a.	n.a.	n.a.	n.a.
Machinery	0.71	0.66	n.a.	n.a.	n.a.	n.a.
Electrical equipment	0.90	0.85	n.a.	n.a.	n.a.	n.a.
Electronic equipment	1.27	1.23	n.a.	n.a.	n.a.	n.a.
Motor vehicles	1.14	1.47	n.a.	n.a.	n.a.	n.a.

n.a., not available.
Source: computed from Halevi and Baruh, 1988, appendix tables A.19 and A.21

formal rate, the same as in 1965. Since the EERM for manufacturing barely changed from 1965 to 1968, there was no reduction in the relative protection for import substitutes compared with other imports. The branch EPIMs show little change in relative rates from 1965 to 1968 for most industries, but there are several notable exceptions: clothing, motor vehicles, and basic chemicals received a much higher level of protection – with the last becoming the most-favored branch – while plastic products had a sharp fall in its EPIM (although it remained very high) and machinery, wood products, and particuarly metal products received even lower relative protection.

Industrial exports had an average EPIX of 1.13 in 1965 and 1.16 in 1968; the change in the ratio of the EPIX to the EPIM was negligible: the ratio remained close to 0.6. Clearly in this period there was no change in the anti-export bias of protection. In those branches where EPIMs and EPIXs can be compared, unusually discriminating ratios are found for food, clothing, and basic chemicals in both 1965 and 1968.

Was there any systematic basis for choosing which commodities to examine first, and what level of protection to give? Tov (1972) concluded that the timing of examination of the commodities, their choice over a five-year period, seems to be random. As to the second question, Tov used regression analysis to examine which economic variables, among the information supplied to the liberalization committee, influenced its decisions. The most relevant variable was the pre-liberalization level of nominal protection: the higher this was, the higher the effective protection granted during the shift to tariff protection. Tov found a positive correlation between the cost per US dollar saved in import substitution and the level of protection given. The higher measured cost per dollar saved could reflect either weaker competitive ability or the use of monopoly conditions in the domestic market made possible by protection.

A clearer picture emerges from using later estimates of EPRs in 1965 to examine whether there is any correlation between the level of protection given and the relative efficiency of the industrial subbranches (defined as value added per worker in Israe[1] relative to value added per worker in the same branch in the United States). This was done by Bar-Nathan and Baruh (1986). A significant correlation is found: the relatively weaker subbranches received higher levels of protection. This confirms the conclusion that a basic objective was to prevent injury to industries subject to this liberalization.

Since the less efficient branches also had lower human capital-to-labor ratios, a similar negative correlation was found between the level of protection and the human capital-to-labor ratios. Introducing both variables in a two-stage regression that first estimates the effects of factor ratios and other variables on relative efficiency confirmed that the level of protection given was inversely correlated with both factors, relative efficiency and human capital-to-labor ratio.

About a third of the commodities examined already had some exports before the liberalization. A low protection rate would have pushed output into exports; such lower rates were not set, however, and the EPIX was generally much lower than the EPIM. As shown in table 6.9 there were wide divergences in the branch EPIX-to-EPIM ratios.

In table 6.10 industries are ranked by EPIM in 1968, and this ranking is compared with the ranking by share of competing imports, by export shares in total exports, and by export shares in product; the branches with weaker employment (based on annual changes in employment data) in 1961–5 are also indicated. Clearly, there is no observable relationship between the level of protection existing in 1968 and any other ranking. The industries weakest in employment during the 1961–5 period are all clustered in the lower half of protection ranking. Their clustering seems to be accidental; it certainly does not support the idea that higher protective rates were given to industries with employment problems in order to

Table 6.10 Comparative rankings of industries

Industries ranked in descending EPIM in 1968	By share of			Industries with relatively larger unemployment in 1961–5[b]
	Competing imports in 1968[a]	Total industrial exports in 1970	Exports in branch's revenue in 1970	
Basic chemicals	13	3	4	
Transport equipment	2	10	8	
Clothing	9	7	2	
Rubber and plastic products	12	6	6	
Food	5	2	7	
Textiles	7	1	3	
Basic metals	3	–	11	✓
Electrical and electronic products	1	11	12	✓
Paper products	11	12	13	✓
Mining products	6	4	1	✓
Metal products	8	9	10	✓
Wood products	10	8	9	
Machinery	4	5	5	

–, negligible.
[a] Where the shares of two or more industries were the same in 1968, their shares in 1965 were used to rank them.
[b] Based on changes in employment from year to year, and changes in industry's employment share.

stimulate employment. Tov found no evidence that the employment situation influenced the liberalization decision in the commodity-by-commodity process.

Was there any connection between macroeconomic variables and the liberalization process? The actual increase in competitive imports during the 1962–8 period was small: for the manufacturing sector as a whole, competitive imports were only 16 percent of the domestic market in 1965 and 18 percent in 1968. Thus there was no meaningful substitution for domestic output, nor "unemployment costs" of liberalization. This was obviously the result of replacing QRs with almost absolute tariff protection. The 1965–7 recession was in no way a result of the liberalization process. However, the anti-export bias in the EPRs must have reduced the capacity of the export sector to expand exports quickly during the recession, and to absorb factors of production laid off as a result of the slowdown.

The recession did influence the pace of liberalization. As pointed out by Tov (1972, p. 160), towards the end of 1965 the committee on liberalization appeared to speed up its work. Ironically, the onset of the recession then caused an easing in the liberalization process. Only in 1968 was the process again accelerated and, in the following year, were substantial reductions in protection rates implemented.

7

Liberalization and Accompanying Policies, 1969–1977

There is no clear demarcation line between the second and third liberalization episodes. In fact, the policy announcement of February 1962 contained the provisions for both. We separate the series of events into two episodes because of a change in the nature of the process after 1968. Until 1968 most of the liberalization of imports consisted of switching the form, while only slightly reducing the actual levels, of protection. Thereafter, the main liberalization activity was actual reductions in protection rates. The choice of 1977 as the end of this episode is also somewhat arbitrary. The reductions in protection levels continued after 1977 and, in fact, international agreements called for future reductions to be implemented by the end of the 1980s. However, in late October 1977 a major change in economic policy related to international transactions was adopted, including a change in the exchange rate systems and considerable liberalization of controls on capital transactions. Thus, the post-1977 liberalization should also be regarded as a separate liberalization episode; it is excluded here because this study's concern is with *trade* liberalization.

Introduction of the Liberalization Policy

Economic and Political Circumstances

The economy had almost fully recovered by late 1968; that year real GNP grew by 8.6 percent, average unemployment was 6 percent (and fell to 4.5 percent in 1969), and no new major change in macroeconomic policy was adopted or deemed necessary. The results of the June 1967 war were being assimilated. On the one hand, new territories were under Israeli control – Sinai, the Golan Heights, and the territories on the West Bank of the Jordan river, formerly held by Jordan, and including eastern Jerusalem which was reunited with western Jerusalem. Renewed economic growth now took place in the context of this new territorial reality and with a large potential Arab labor force which could be employed on both sides of the 1967 border. On the other hand, the upsurge in military spending proved to be more than temporary: in 1968 a War of Attrition began, which made heavy economic demands until the cease-fire of August 1970.

There were no changes in the political parties dominating the government coalition, but there were changes in personnel. Of particular importance for liberalization policy was a change in the Ministry of Commerce and Industry; the new minister was more inclined to implement the reduction in protection rates, only partially and sluggishly undertaken before 1969.

These were the circumstances at the beginning of the period. Further dramatic events took place during the 1969–77 period which also influenced the process of liberalization. Chief among these were the Yom Kippur War of 1973 and its aftermath. The economic problems brought about by war (inflation, loss of output, balance-of-payments deficit) were followed by those resulting from the oil crisis of 1973–4, and the worldwide recession. Israel has faced the dual problems of severe inflation and large balance-of-payments deficits ever since, and has resorted to macroeconomic policies to deal with them, marked by drastic sudden changes.

The reductions in protection levels were influenced by macroeconomic developments, but were not viewed as significant economic variables in themselves. Thus there has been little public debate either about the desirability, speed, and timing of liberalization, or about its macroeconomic effects, except for an oft-voiced view that imports should not be encouraged by liberalizing measures when the balance-of-payments deficit is of great concern.

The attitude towards liberalization was strongly influenced by Israel's relations with the EEC. As early as 1958 Israel had expressed a desire to reach agreement with the EEC, and that year Israel established a mission to the EEC Commission. The NEP of 1962 was explained as a necessary step towards developing a competitive position for Israel's industry so that it could fit into the new European order.

In fact, the formal arrangements with the EEC evolved much more slowly than expected: in 1964 a nonpreferential commercial agreement was signed and in 1970 a preferential agreeement, one of a series between the EEC and Mediterranean countries. Not until 1975, some three years after the adoption by the EEC of its global Mediterranean policy, was the free-trade agreement signed. Israel's industrial exports quickly benefitted from EEC tariff reductions; almost all barriers were removed within two years. Israel's tariff concessions were most gradual, with final reductions to be made by 1989. The scheduled reductions took into account Israel's liberalization plans as evolved in earlier years.

Thus most of the liberalization that took place during 1969–77 was not the result of external contractual obligations but rather the implementation of desired Israeli policy, which recognized the advantages for Israel of freer trade. In the words of one analyst (Pomfret, 1984) " . . . the contractual nature of the EEC agreements and the enhanced market access gave Israeli policymakers greater leverage in making import liberalization acceptable to domestic vested interests who had to bear the adjustment costs." Though consultations between government and manufacturers on liberalization referred to arrangements with the EEC in the early 1970s, both policymakers and producers only began to take the implications of greater integration with the EEC seriously as negotiations for the Free Trade Area Agreement proceeded. Serious studies of these implications for Israel's industry were begun in 1973, and various committees were set up in 1975 to assess effects and propose measures to prepare for final integration (Toren, 1973, 1976).

Implementation of the Liberalization Policy

Up to 1968 the few actual reductions in protection rates that did take place were *ad hoc*. In October 1968 there was a 15 percent decrease in all nominal tariffs. A program was announced in August 1969, aimed at reaching a uniform 57 percent rate of effective protection for industrial output by 1976. The program envisaged six annual tariff cuts at the start of each of the six years 1970–5. Because we have estimates for effective protection indices for 1968, 1972, and 1977, we consider separately tariff reductions in 1968–72 and 1972–7. The actual changes made in 1969–72 (as a percentage of tariff level) were as follows:

January 1969 Nominal rates up to 35 percent, unchanged
Rates between 35 and 50 percent, reduced by 10 percent
Rates between 51 and 75 percent, reduced by 15 percent
Rates between 76 and 100 percent, reduced by 20 percent
Rates over 100 percent, reduced by 30 percent
August 1969 Target announced: a uniform 57 percent effective protection for industrial output to be reached gradually by 1975
January 1970 Nominal tariffs were reduced by 5–15 percent
August 1970 A 20 percent levy imposed on all imports (except cut diamonds)
January 1971 Partial reduction in tariff rates
April 1972 5–18 percent reductions in tariff rates
June 1972 5–18 percent reductions in tariff rates

The question is whether the nominal tariff cuts in 1968–72 reduced the level of protection in the industrial sector. The nominal protection index for import substitutes (NPIM) for this sector in 1968 was 45 percent over the IL 3.50 per US dollar formal rate. However, in August 1970 a 20 percent general levy was imposed on practically all imports. Though no official equivalent subsidy was announced for exports, we view this levy as a substitute for devaluation, at least as far as goods are concerned. (Exports received subsidies above 20 percent; therefore, in the computation of effective rates for exports only the portion of the subsidies in excess of 20 percent is included in the calculation.) The nominal protection rate should be calculated in relation to a formal rate including the levy, that is, IL 5.04 per US dollar. This is done in table 7.1. The nominal protection index rate for industrial import substitutes in 1972 can therefore be said to

Table 7.1 Nominal and effective protection indices for import substitution, 1968, 1972, 1977

Branch	1968		1972		1977	
	NPIM	EPIM	NPIM	EPIM	NPIM	EPIM
Agriculture	1.27	1.61	1.09	1.22	1.06	1.25
Industry	1.45	1.96	1.33	1.62	1.16	1.25
Mining products	1.35	1.62	1.21	1.31	1.12	1.16
Food, beverages, tobacco	1.30	2.52	1.23	4.63	1.19	2.64
Textiles	1.68	2.46	1.28	1.40	1.21	1.45
Clothing	1.98	2.84	1.66	1.71	1.24	1.18
Leather products	1.45	1.60	1.41	1.71	1.26	1.38
Wood products	1.36	1.32	1.54	2.12	1.39	1.78
Paper and cardboard products	1.36	1.90	1.37	1.40	1.20	1.31
Rubber products	1.51	2.39	1.40	1.23	1.30	1.48
Plastic products	1.68	2.84	1.75	3.70	1.20	1.27
Basic chemicals	1.54	3.73	1.29	1.65	1.12	1.29
Basic metals	1.31	2.42	1.21	1.53	1.06	1.02
Metal products	1.31	1.40	1.21	1.37	1.07	1.03
Machinery	1.30	1.30	1.26	1.41	1.10	1.07
Electrical equipment	1.35	1.67	1.35	1.66	1.20	1.39
Electronic equipment	1.51	2.41	1.21	1.35	1.07	1.06
Motor vehicles	1.57	2.89	1.44	3.11	1.47	1.45
Miscellaneous	1.82	3.84	1.39	1.74	1.10	1.05
Total	1.41	1.85	1.29	1.52	1.15	1.23

Computed with reference to the following formal rates plus an across-the-board levy on imports: 1968, IL 3.50 per US dollar; 1972, IL 5.04 per US dollar; 1977 IL 13.24 per US dollar.
Sources: Halevi and Baruh, 1988, appendix tables A.20 and A.21

equal 33 percent. Despite the fact that some of the 1968 tariffs were redundant, the 1968–72 tariff cuts were significant enough to bring about a fall in the nominal protection afforded to the industrial sector equal to almost 27 percent of the 1968 level.

The corresponding fall in the EPR was even greater. It fell by 35 percent, from 96 percent in 1968 to 62 percent in 1972. This reduction of the effective rate for the industrial sector meant that the 1975 target rate of 57 percent protection overall was well on its way to achievement.

The fall in the nominal and effective rates from 1968 to 1972 was not accompanied by a fall in the dispersion around the average rates in the two years. The coefficients of variation for the nominal indices (based on data for 42 industrial subbranches) were 0.20 in 1968 and 0.19 in 1972; for the EPIM they were 0.45 in 1968 and 0.43 in 1972.

Furthermore, there is no significant change in the industries' ranking according to their nominal and effective rates. The Spearman correlation coefficients between 1968 and 1972 were 0.53 for the NPIM (64 observations and a significance level of 0.0001) and 0.32 for the EPIM (with a significance level of 0.01).

The tariff cuts in 1972–7 – these continued up to the NEP of November 1977 – were as follows:

January–May 1973	Tariff cuts for some 1,500 imported commodities
January 1974	Tariff cuts for some 1,200 imported commodities making up 12–15 percent of total commodity imports
August 1975	Tariff cuts on some 200 import commodities (cuts of 2.5–5 percent)
January 1967	Tariff cuts on imported commodities whose annual import value was about US$250 million
January 1977	Tariff cuts on 750 imported commodities whose annual import value was about US$175 million

During the later years of implementation of the liberalization program, some reductions were made in tariffs on goods imported from the EEC in accordance with the 1970 preference agreement and in preparation for further integration. After consultation between government officials and a committee representing the manufacturers, agreement was reached in September 1972 on scheduled reductions, over the 1973–6 period, of the difference between the actual protection rate existing in mid-1972 and the ultimate target rate (then set at IL 6.50 per US dollar). Implementation of this program began in 1973, but before the period ended the Free Trade Area Agreement was signed, setting a new schedule for ultimate removal of all protection on industrial imports from the EEC.

The liberalization in 1972–7 halved the level of the industrial sector's nominal protection (from 33 percent in 1972 to 16 percent in 1977). The corresponding fall in the effective protection level was about 60 percent (from 62 percent in 1972 to 25 percent in 1977). It should be pointed out that the tariff cuts in January 1974 were accompanied by the announcement of a new domestic resource cost (DRC) rate for industrial import substitutes: IL 6.50 per US dollar, to be reached by 1976. Given that the relevant rate for computing protection indices was at that date IL 5.04 per dollar (IL 4.20 *plus* a 20 percent general import levy), the 1976 target DRC rate implied a 30 percent effective rate of protection. The effective rate reached in 1977 (25 percent) was thus lower than the 1976 target rate.

The by-branch nominal and effective protection rates in the industrial import-substituting sector – whose averages for each year have been considered in the discussion of the liberalization process – show that in the years for which protection indices are available (1965, 1968, 1972, and 1977) there were generally relatively high EPIMs for the food, textiles, clothing, rubber, and plastic industries, and motor vehicles. In contrast, the protection rates for machinery and metal products were relatively low.

Accompanying Policies

Exchange Rate Policy

Until the mid-1970s there was no basic change in the exchange rate system, which consisted of infrequent formal devaluations and use of nonformal components (subsidies and taxes) to establish higher EERs. The IL 3.50 per US dollar formal rate established in November 1967 held until August 1971, when there was a 20 percent devaluation; a similar "mini-devaluation" took place in November 1974.

In 1975, it became apparent that the rapid rate of domestic inflation could not be adequately compensated for by changes in the nonformal components of the exchange rate and infrequent formal devaluation. A crawling peg was adopted in mid-1975 whereby devaluations of up to 2 percent were permitted within a 30-day period; this was later made more flexible by permitting the 2 percent per month devaluations to be cumulated over quarters. These very small devaluations became commonplace, and devaluation was no longer a dramatic event. The nonformal components were increased in proportion to the devaluations, that is, by 2 percent a month; thus the system maintained the same amount of multiple rate discrimination.

In July 1976, in response to complaints from exporters to Europe that they were being hurt by the strengthening of the US dollar, a basket of currencies was substituted for the dollar in the crawling peg system. (In fact at this time the dollar trend reversed itself.)

Toward the end of 1977 a major change was made: Israel officially switched to a fluctuating rate of exchange, to be determined by "free-market forces." These "market forces" set the immediate rate at IL 15 per US dollar. (In fact, the manipulation of the crawling peg had been transferred to the Bank of Israel, which could use it more flexibly and allow the daily rate to fluctuate; however, the actual operation of the system is outside the framework of this trade liberalization study.)

Table 7.2 presents data on formal and effective exchange rates for 1968–77, and table 7.3 shows annual changes in nominal and "real" exchange rates. The nonformal components were substantial components of the EERM and EERX throughout the period; only in 1975 and 1977 did the nonformal component fall to less than 10 percent of the EERM. The system was not flexible enough, before the switch to the adjustable peg in 1975, to maintain PPP, or to achieve real devaluation for more than very brief periods.

In fact the ratio of tradeable to nontradeable prices never returned to the 1965 level, let alone to earlier levels. The crawling peg gave greater flexibility, made necessary by the high inflation rates (1974–7), but the changes in foreign prices could not be taken into account except with a

Table 7.2 Formal and effective exchange rates, 1968–1977 (Israeli pounds per US dollar)

Year	Formal rate[a]	Average effective rates		Nonformal component as percentage of effective rate		Ratio of tradeable to nontradeable price indices[c]
		Commodity imports	Commodity exports[b]	Imports	Exports	
1968	3.50	4.13	4.04	15.3	13.7	1.02
1969	3.50	4.22	4.05	17.1	13.6	1.00
1970	3.50	4.42	4.49	20.8	22.2	0.98
1971	3.73	4.62	4.57	19.3	18.4	0.99
1972	4.20	5.11	4.78	17.8	12.1	0.97
1973	4.20	4.95	4.89	15.2	14.1	0.95
1974	4.45	5.43	5.45	18.0	18.3	0.95
1975	6.32	7.13	7.50	8.6	15.7	0.96
1976	7.95	9.10	9.42	12.3	15.6	0.96
1977	10.60	12.55	14.30	5.9	25.9	0.98

[a] From 1971, average formal rates are computed to account for devaluations during the course of the year.
[b] Rates for exports value added in foreign exchange.
[c] Based on a breakdown of items in the CPI into tradeables and nontradeables, carried out by Cukierman and Razin (1976); 1961 = 1.
Source: Halevi, 1979, p. 88

Table 7.3 Nominal and real devaluation, 1968–1977 (annual rates of change)

Year	Effective rates		GNP prices	Effective rates deflated by GNP		Relative change in prices[a]	
	Imports	Exports		Imports	Exports	Imports	Exports
1968	12.6	13.2	2.0	10.0	11.0	7.8	9.1
1969	2.2	0.2	2.3	− 0.1	− 2.1	4.9	2.5
1970	4.8	10.8	10.6	− 5.2	0.2	− 4.3	− 4.2
1971	4.5	1.8	12.7	− 7.3	− 10.0	− 4.7	− 6.2
1972	10.6	4.6	17.6	− 6.0	− 11.1	0.1	− 4.5
1973	− 3.1	2.3	17.2	− 17.6	− 13.0	5.5	7.3
1974	9.7	11.5	35.4	− 19.0	− 17.7	11.2	− 3.2
1975	31.3	32.6	35.7	− 3.4	1.3	0.9	6.1
1976	27.6	25.6	25.4	1.8	0.2	3.7	2.4
1977	27.8	51.8	44.4	11.6	5.1	− 4.2	22.0

[a] The relative rates are computed by adding to the effective rates the effective changes in foreign prices before deflation by GNP prices.
Source: computed from data in Halevi, 1979

considerable lag; consequently, there were considerable fluctuations in the annual changes in the relative return to exports and the relative costs of imports.

Export Promotion Policy

The belief that the formal exchange rate would be a sufficient price incentive for exports proved unfounded: in 1966, export subsidization was resumed on a large scale, with different premiums to value-added groups replacing, less efficiently, the pre-1962 subsidization of exports value added. Some exports – textiles, clothing, and plywood – also benefitted from special subsidization schemes based on the use of import tax proceeds within the branch, and cartelization for output allocation between local and foreign markets. In 1972, these branch funds were still substantial components of subsidization, but by 1977 they were being phased out. In that year, exports were subsidized through indirect tax rebates and by means of cheap short-term financing for exports. Table 7.4 shows nominal protection indices for exports (NPIXs) and EPIXs for 1968, 1972, and 1977. In both 1968 and 1972, agricultural exports received higher rates than did manufactured goods; by 1977 the preference was reversed. In the three years examined there was not much difference between the average NPIXs and EPIX but there were large differences for certain commodity classes, and the EPIXs were not always higher than the NPIXs.

Table 7.4 Nominal and effective protection indices for exports, 1968, 1972, 1977

Branch	1968		1972		1977	
	NPIX	EPIX	NPIX	EPIX	NPIX	EPIX
Agriculture	1.13	1.25	1.10	1.16	1.03	1.05
Industry	1.10	1.16	0.98	0.96	1.09	1.16
Mining products	1.12	1.15	1.10	1.16	1.12	1.19
Food, beverages, tobacco	1.11	1.09	1.11	1.33	1.17	1.48
Textiles	1.40	1.79	1.35	1.36	1.19	1.34
Clothing	1.29	1.15	1.32	0.71	1.18	1.04
Wood products	1.41	1.89	1.27	1.27	1.20	1.15
Rubber products	1.13	1.10	1.06	0.61	1.11	0.92
Basic chemicals	1.11	1.25	1.06	0.98	1.10	1.32
Metal products	1.10	0.90	1.09	0.93	1.10	1.15
Machinery	1.10	1.06	1.05	0.95	1.11	1.09
Electrical equipment	n.a.	n.a.	1.07	0.87	1.10	1.08
Electronic equipment	n.a.	n.a.	n.a.	n.a.	1.25	1.51
Ships, aircraft	n.a.	n.a.	n.a.	n.a.	1.03	1.00
Miscellaneous	n.a.	n.a.	n.a.	n.a.	1.08	1.03
Diamonds	1.01	1.00	0.89	0.89	1.04	1.16
Total	1.11	1.19	1.00	1.01	1.08	1.14
Total excluding diamonds	1.18	1.28	1.14	1.06	1.10	1.13

n.a., not available.
Computed with reference to the following formal rates plus an across-the-board levy on imports: 1968, IL 3.50 per US dollar; 1972, IL 5.04 per US dollar; 1977 IL 13.24 per US dollar.
Sources: Halevi and Baruh, 1988, appendix tables A.18 and A.19

Monetary Policy

As shown by the data in table 7.5 the post-recession increases in the money supply ended in 1968. From 1969 there is a trend to a decrease in the real money supply, but the main factor was the rapid inflation rates, particularly after 1973. Efforts to curb monetary expansion were supplemented by the desire of the public to keep smaller cash balances and to switch to inflation-proof financial and real assets.

Bank of Israel monetary policy consisted of measures to affect the total money supply and measures to direct credit to preferred sectors by exemptions from liquidity requirements. Table 7.6 shows the ratio of directed to total credit of the banking system and the rates of interest on various types of credit. Directed credit fell from over 60 percent in 1966 to

Table 7.5 Changes in the money supply, 1968–1977

Year	Percentage change in money supply		
	Nominal M1	Nominal M2	Real[a] M1
1968	11.6	20.3	9.4
1969	1.0	3.0	− 1.3
1970	− 3.9	36.8	− 13.1
1971	8.6	12.1	− 3.6
1972	13.8	12.2	− 3.0
1973	3.8	− 8.3	− 11.8
1974	− 11.5	− 20.4	− 34.7
1975	− 3.5	− 11.9	− 29.0
1976	11.5	4.8	− 11.1
1977	− 4.9	− 6.6	− 34.1

[a] Deflated by GNP prices.
Source: computed from data in *Statistical Abstract of Israel*, 1978

Table 7.6 Ratio of directed to free credit by the banking system, and rates of interest, 1966–1977

Year	1 Ratio of directed to total credit	2 Estimated average interest rate changes					7 Changes in GNP prices
		Market rate for long-term credit	Free credit rate	Subsidized rates for			
		3	4	5 Industry	Housing	6 Exports	
1966	63.6	11.1	10.0	8	–	6	6.2
1967	52.3	4.6	10.0	8	–	6	9.1
1968	46.2	5.7	10.0	8	6.6	6	13.2
1969	40.8	7.5	10.0	9	6.6	6	0.2
1970	37.1	10.0	13.0	9	6.6	6	10.8
1971	37.6	17.2	17.2	9	6.7	6	1.8
1972	36.6	16.4	19.0	9	7.4	6	4.6
1973	37.1	30.4	21.0	9	7.6	6	2.3
1974	32.1	58.9	23.0	10	7.7	6	11.5
1975	33.1	27.1	27.2	14	9.0	6	32.6
1976	34.1	40.9	31.0	17.5	10.3	10	25.6
1977	35.4	48.5	41.0	21	11.5	12	51.8

–, nil.
Sources: column 1, computed from data in Bank of Israel *Annual Reports*; columns 2–6, Sokoler, 1984

some 37 percent in 1970–3, and then to 32–5 percent in 1974–7. The fall in the early years is exaggerated because bill brokerage, which is excluded from credit in the table, still accounted for significant fractions of total credit in 1966, perhaps close to one third, but decreased absolutely and relatively in 1967–9.

Estimates of rates of interest show that there was always a substantial discrepancy between subsidized credit and free credit. The restrictions from the legal interest ceiling of 11 percent led to high free credit rates in the 1970s, reflecting inflationary price increases. Compared with the rise in prices, however, some free rates turned out to be negative in real terms. As interest rates rose, the relative difference between free and subsidized rates increased.

Fiscal Policy

The sharp increase in the ratio of public consumption to GNP in 1967 (a rise from 13.3 to 30.1 percent) reflected war-induced defense expenditures. However, as shown in table 7.7, columns 1 and 2, public consumption fluctuated in a narrow range, while defense expenditures – and consequently total public consumption – fluctuated more widely, generally falling during periods of relative peace but rising to a new plateau with each war episode. Thus the post 1973-war low of 36.5 percent in 1977 was approximately the same as the War of Attrition high in 1970.

Table 7.7 Government fiscal aggregates in percentages of gross national product, 1967–1977

Year	1 Public consumption Total	2 Public consumption Civilian	3 Tax revenue	4 Subsidies	5 Transfers to households	6 Interest on public debt	7 Net taxes[a]
1967	30.1	12.4	31.2	3.5	7.8	3.5	19.5
1968	29.7	11.5	32.4	3.8	7.9	3.6	17.1
1969	31.0	10.8	34.5	3.6	7.9	4.0	19.0
1970	36.3	10.6	37.8	4.1	8.4	4.5	20.8
1971	34.3	10.7	40.8	5.5	8.8	4.7	21.8
1972	31.1	10.3	39.8	4.9	8.8	5.3	20.8
1973	43.8	11.1	42.3	6.4	10.0	5.5	20.4
1974	41.8	10.8	45.0	6.5	12.0	5.9	20.6
1975	45.3	10.7	46.3	15.7	12.4	6.1	12.1
1976	41.7	11.5	56.3	16.3	14.5	7.3	18.2
1977	36.5	12.5	53.0	17.7	15.1	2.7	17.5

[a] Column 3 minus columns 4 plus 5 plus 6.
Source: Berglas, 1983, appendix table

Tax revenue rose almost continuously, from 31.2 percent of GNP in 1967 to 46.3 percent in 1975, and dramatically to 56.3 percent in 1976; it then fell slightly in 1977. This pattern was matched by some rise in the interest on the public debt, more dramatic increases in transfers to households, and a sharp jump in subsidies from 6.5 percent of GNP in 1974 to 15.7 percent in 1975 and to even higher ratios in 1976–77. Net taxes rose during the middle of the period, but were almost back to the 1969 level by 1977.

As shown in table 7.8 there were considerable differences between the 1968–73 and 1974–77 periods with regard to the government budget and its financing. In the latter period there was a marked increase in the ratio of domestic expenditure and taxes to GNP, and in the domestic and total deficits (despite a fall in net foreign expenditure). There was a striking increase in the foreign debt financing of the deficit.

Table 7.8 Financing the government budget, 1968–1977 (percent of gross national product)

Item	1968–73	1974–7
1 Domestic expenditure[a]	41.0	56.4
2 Net foreign expenditure[b]	6.6	3.3
3 Taxes[c]	34.4	42.1
4 Domestic deficit (row 1 − row 3)	6.6	14.3
5 Total deficit (row 4 + row 2)[d]	13.2	17.6
6 Base money creation	3.2	2.6
7 Domestic debt finance[e]	5.4	4.7
8 Foreign debt finance	4.6	10.4

[a] Domestic expenditure includes goods and services, subsidies, transfers, and interest on the public debt.
[b] Net foreign expenditure is defined as government expenditure abroad (mainly armaments) plus interest on debt minus unilateral transfers (mainly US government).
[c] Taxes include all direct and indirect taxes and transfers to government.
[d] Row 1 + row 2 − row 3 = row 6 + row 7 + row 8 = total finance of deficit.
[e] Domestic debt finance incorporates indexed bonds. Figures are net of repayments and of loans to the public sector.
Source: Bruno, 1984, table 2

8

Economic Performance and Assessment of Policy, 1969–1977

Economic Performance Following Liberalization

The liberalizing process of 1968–77 was gradual, extending over the entire period. Consequently, a causal relationship cannot necessarily be inferred for most of the marked changes in macroeconomic performance that characterized the period. We therefore briefly summarize some features of the general macro performance of the economy; we then consider developments in the balance of payments, and examine in greater detail only those developments more closely related to the liberalization.

Major Macroeconomic Developments

Data on some major macro variables are summarized in table 8.1. On coming out of the recession in 1968, the economy attained annual rates of growth in GNP similar to the pre-recession norms. From 1973 there was a major change: GNP grew at much lower rates, in some years (1973, 1976, 1977) being so low as barely to match population growth. Israeli economists are still debating whether this prolonged trend, which was certainly instigated by the Yom Kippur War of 1973 and the ensuing oil crisis and world recession, reflects inability of the economy to cope adequately with those shocks or is normal for an economy that had fully exhausted the factors which had accounted for the abnormally high growth rates of the previous 25 years.

The growth in output in 1968–72 was matched by a two-digit inflation rate. From the end of 1973 this rate doubled, fluctuating between a low of 25.4 percent in 1976 (as a result of drastic deflationary policy) and a (temporary) high of 44.1 percent in 1977. After 1977, much higher inflation rates were the rule.

The Israeli stagflationary experience differed from that of the Organization for Economic Cooperation and Development countries in that

Table 8.1 Some macro variables, 1968–1977

Year	Annual percentage rate of change					Unemployment as percentage of labor force
	Real GNP	GDP prices	Real gross investment	Real wages	Civilian labor force	
1968	8.6	2.0	41.8	1.1	9.6	6.1
1969	12.8	1.7	4.7	3.5	2.1	4.5
1970	8.7	10.6	17.0	2.7	1.1	3.8
1971	10.2	12.7	26.6	3.9	3.2	3.5
1972	13.7	17.6	6.5	1.0	4.2	2.8
1973	2.9	17.2	13.3	6.3	4.4	2.6
1974	5.0	35.4	− 5.2	− 2.5	0.6	3.0
1975	6.9	35.9	− 1.4	− 1.9	1.5	3.1
1976	2.8	25.4	− 10.7	1.1	1.8	3.6
1977	1.8	44.4	− 11.8	10.3	3.2	3.9

Source: calculated from data in CBS, Statistical Abstract of Israel, various issues

unemployment did not attain serious proportions. From a recession high of 10.4 percent in 1967, unemployment fell to a low of 2.6 percent in 1973 and then rose somewhat, but was still less than 4 percent in 1977. Some of the recessionary shocks of the mid-1970s were absorbed by fluctuations in the employment in Israel of Arabs from the occupied territories. For the permanent Israeli labor force, the variations in economic activity and government macro policy are reflected in the changes in real wages: these fell in 1974 and 1975, barely increased in 1972 and 1976, but rose a spectacular 10 percent in 1977.

The effects of anti-inflationary policy are clearly evident in annual variations in investment. Investment fell drastically during the entire recession – some 21 percent in 1967 – and then rebounded an extraordinary 42 percent in 1968. After fluctuating rates of increase in 1969–73, annual investment declined for the next four years. Though the level of gross investment decreased, real net capital sttock continued to grow: at rates between 5.2 and 8.7 percent in 1975–7, compared with 10.5–11.3 percent in 1972–4.

Were these developments a result of the earlier liberalization? Since that liberalization was mainly a change in the form of protection, rather than in its level, it had little immediate effect. The post-1968 liberalization did reduce protection levels, but its effects were more on the structure of activity – discussed below – than on the level of aggregate activity. However, there is reason to believe that the somewhat slower reduction of protection levels in the 1973–7 period, compared with 1968–72, reflects concern with the macro problems of the economy.

Imports and Exports

In this section we consider general developments in imports and exports. The changes in competitive imports, and the role of tariff reductions in the structure of imports and exports, are discussed in the analysis of the effects of liberalization later in the chapter.

Imports of Goods and Services

Table 8.2 presents data on imports of goods and services. Real commodity imports rose tremendously in 1968, when prosperity returned, and grew at varying rates thereafter, falling in only one year (1975) but not increasing

Table 8.2 Imports, 1968–1977

Year	1 2 3 Imports (million current US$)			4 Ratio of imports to GNP	5 Annual rate of growth in real commodity imports[b]
	Commodities[a]	Services	Total		
1968	1,253	553	1,806	0.49	47.1
1969	1,516	659	2,175	0.52	13.0
1970	1,932	732	2,664	0.54	9.7
1971	2,206	890	3,096	0.56	21.0
1972	2,287	1,029	3,316	0.53	2.0
1973	3,966	1,410	5,376	0.69	19.0
1974	4,995	1,759	6,754	0.68	1.7
1975	5,519	2,017	7,536	0.70	− 5.0
1976	5,247	2,222	7,469	0.70	0.9
1977	5,387	2,472	7,859	0.64	7.8

[a] Balance-of-payments figures, not trade statistics data.
[b] Nominal dollar values of trade statistics imports deflated by the index of import prices.
Sources: columns 1–4, Halevi, 1983b; column 5, computed from CBS, Statistical Abstract of Israel, 1978, p. 214

at all in the total 1974–6 period. In current dollars, imports rose fourfold between 1968 and 1977, declining only in 1975. Service imports rose continuously, increasing their relative share in total imports slightly despite higher rates of increase in prices of commodities. The ratio of imports to GNP tended to increase, and was in the 60–70 percent range from 1973; by this criterion, Israel was indeed a very open economy.

Even though higher price elasticities were found for imports in 1968–76 than for earlier periods (0.6, according to Blum, 1983), no trend in imports could be expected from the relative price policy actually implemented.

Since income elasticity for imports is above unity, the considerable fluctuations in imports observed during this period reflect in large measure the variances in demand policy and output growth.

The most noteworthy change in the composition of commodity imports (exclusive of defense imports) in 1968–77 is the jump in the relative share of fuel imports measured in current dollars, owing to the tremendous increase in fuel prices: from about 5 percent in 1969–72 this share rose to 15–16 percent in 1974–7 (and again rose with the 1978–9 price increase). This increase had to be matched by falling shares of other import categories. Whereas the share of final consumer and investment goods was indeed lower in 1974–7 than before (the smaller share of investment goods reflected government policy which decreased relative investment), imports of other inputs did not decline in 1974–7, but remained about 60 percent of commodity imports.

Exports

Exports of goods and services (table 8.3) continued to increase throughout the period, but the average rates of growth were lower in every five-year segment; thus, whereas they were 14.1 percent in 1960–5 and 13.0 percent in 1965–70, they were 10 percent in 1970–5 and only 6.9 percent in 1975–80. Real commodity exports increased every year, but there were much wider annual fluctuations in the 1968–78 period than in the previous decade.

Repetition for the 1970–80 period of the type of regressions run for earlier periods did not give results as clear-cut as those for the earlier

Table 8.3 Exports, 1968–1977

Year	1 Exports (million current US$)			4 Ratio of exports to GNP	5 Annual rate of growth in real commodity exports[b]
	Commodities[a]	Services	Total		
1968	652	498	1,150	0.29	16.3
1969	753	537	1,290	0.28	9.0
1970	807	595	1,402	0.27	7.3
1971	1,003	872	1,875	0.31	17.9
1972	1,220	1,002	2,222	0.32	11.6
1973	1,563	1,249	2,812	0.32	3.0
1974	2,005	1,554	3,559	0.32	5.8
1975	2,181	1,506	3,687	0.33	1.8
1976	2,670	1,930	4,600	0.38	22.5
1977	3,404	2,075	5,479	0.44	11.6

[a] Balance-of-payments data.
[b] Based on trade statistics.
Sources: columns 1–4, Halevi, 1983b; column 5, computed from CBS, Statistical Abstract of Israel, 1978, p. 214

period (Teubal et al., 1986). Running similar regressions for individual industrial branches explains why inconclusive results were obtained for aggregated exports. In general, the more traditional industrial exports continued to show responsiveness to relative prices; the newer more sophisticated branches did not, but they were responsive to variables representing changes in potential output. In other words, changes in the industrial composition of exports must be taken into account.

The shares of major branches in total industrial exports for selected years are shown in table 8.4. The trend from the mid-1960s to more rapid relative growth of the more sophisticated products is quite clear: transport

Table 8.4 Shares in total industrial exports, selected years[a] (percent)

Branch	1966	1970	1975	1980
Mining	14.5	10.8	9.2	5.2
Food	17.2	16.5	13.3	9.8
Textiles	17.6	11.5	5.5	5.0
Clothing	4.6	14.2	11.1	10.3
Wood products	3.7	2.6	1.4	1.4
Rubber products	6.0	6.3	4.8	4.2
Chemicals	15.0	13.9	19.5	21.3
Metal products	2.2	7.3	11.0	11.0
Machinery	7.0	4.6	3.3	5.6
Electrical products	0.7	3.4	10.4	8.7
Transport equipment	1.7	2.4	4.3	12.2
Total[a]	90.2	93.5	93.8	94.7

Computed from current price export data for all major industrial branches exporting at least 5 percent of total industrial exports in any year.
[a] Total of these branches in industrial exports, excluding diamonds.
Source: computed from CBS, *Monthly Bulletin of Statistics*, supplement (various issues)

equipment, machinery, metal products, chemicals, and electrical products all developed into important export industries. Even in some traditional nonsophisticated categories such as clothing, a more detailed breakdown shows that the main growth was the result of a shift to more sophisticated fashion goods. For the more sophisticated exports, an important variable explaining their growth was the accumulation of production and export experience (Teubal et al., 1986).

Whereas Israel evidenced a "Leontieff paradox" in that the capital-to-labor ratio was higher in exports than in imports as late as 1965, and before that year human capital's role in export success was not evident, data on the factor content in industrial imports and exports suggest significant changes after 1965. As shown in table 8.5, the Leontieff paradox with regard to the physical capital-to-labor ratios had disappeared by 1972, and between 1972 and 1975 the relative disadvantage in the production of human capital intensive goods had virtually disappeared.

Table 8.5 Factor content in industrial imports relative to exports

Factor ratio	1965	1972	1975	1977
Ratio of tangible capital to labor	0.65	1.12	1.03	1.10
Ratio of human capital to labor	1.12	1.11	1.03	1.02

The ratio of factor content is estimated for import substitutes and for exports, and the former is divided by the latter.
Source: Baruh, 1986

The Import Surplus and Foreign Indebtedness

The improvements in the balance of payments resulting from the 1966–7 recession were short lived: by 1970 the import surplus had passed the US$1 billion mark. As a result of the Yom Kippur War and its aftermath the import surplus rose rapidly in 1973–5, reaching US$3.8 billion in 1975. The main changes in the import surplus are summarized in table 8.6.

After creeping up slowly in the 1960s, Israel's foreign exchange obligations rose more rapidly from 1969, and even more rapidly from 1973, reaching US$13.6 billion in 1977. Short-term obligations rose faster than long-term obligations and in 1977 were one third of the total gross debt. However, this reflects in large part a growth in the international activity of Israel's banks and matching growth in short-term assets. Nonetheless, from 1972 there has been steady growth in Israel's net indebtedness, and wide annual fluctuations in net short-term assets. At the end of the period, the latter were at about the same absolute level as in the early 1960s, but were obviously a much smaller percentage of annual foreign exchange transactions.

The growing foreign indebtedness created a debt-servicing burden. Though net interest payments as a percentage of exports were no higher during this period than in the early 1960s (in fact they were much lower in 1971–4), the index of debt burden constructed by Liviatan (1982) shows a dramatic increase: from varying within the 0.20–0.30 range from the mid-1960s to the mid-1970s, it rose to 0.70 in 1976 and to 0.84 in 1977.

Table 8.6 Absolute and relative import surplus, 1968–1977

Year	1 Import surplus (million US$)	2 Annual change in import surplus (%)	3 Ratio of Import surplus to GNP	4 Debt-financed import surplus[a] to GNP	5 Direct defense imports to GNP
1968	656	22.4	0.20	0.07	0.06
1969	885	35.0	0.24	0.11	0.08
1970	1,262	42.6	0.27	0.13	0.12
1971	1,221	− 3.2	0.25	0.09	0.09
1972	1,094	− 10.4	0.21	0.01	0.08
1973	2,564	134.4	0.37	0.05	0.16
1974	3,195	24.6	0.36	0.17	0.13
1975	3,849	20.5	0.37	0.20	0.17
1976	3,069	− 20.3	0.32	0.12	0.15
1977	2,380	− 22.5	0.20	0.03	0.08

[a] Import surplus minus net unilateral transfers.
Source: computed from data in Halevi, 1983b

In late 1975, strong deflationary policy was introduced to reduce aggregate demand, and with it both the import surplus and the rate of inflation. This policy was successful for the import surplus: the surplus fell by almost US$1.5 billion in two years. (The rate of inflation also fell in 1976 and early 1977, but reversed before the end of the year.) After 1977 the import surplus rose again.

What explains the jump to new levels of balance-of-payments deficits? Clearly, the Yom Kippur War raised the level of arms procurement – and also provided unilateral transfers from the United States to finance them. In 1973–6 direct defense imports as a percentage of GNP were twice as high as the 1972 level of 8 percent, to which they returned (temporarily) in 1977. A second factor was the sharp increase in the price of oil, and a less dramatic (but substantial) worsening of the terms of trade of other transactions. However, even allowing for defense imports and oil prices, the remaining import surplus in 1975 was twice the level of 1972. Clearly, in the immediate post-war period, balance of payments policy failed to reduce civilian consumption and imports in a manner commensurate with the basic changes that had taken place in the economy's financial resources and requirements.

Because so much of Israel's import surplus is financed by unilateral transfers, which grew absolutely after the 1973 war, it is useful to compare the ratio of import surplus to GNP (table 8.6, column 3) with the ratio of debt-financed import surplus to GNP (column 4), both computed in current prices.[1] In 1977 the ratio of import surplus to GNP was 0.20, that is, back to the 1968 level after gradually rising in the interim to a peak of 0.37 in 1973 and remaining at about that high level until 1976. The debt-financed import surplus fluctuated, reaching a peak of 0.20 in 1975 and then falling sharply, as the import surplus fell, to the levels of the early 1960s.

Although the relative import surplus does not show an increasing trend, but rather temporary growth, the absolute deficits and the absolute level of debt-financed import surpluses rose to new levels, creating substantial changes in Israel's foreign indebtedness.

Output and Productivity

Table 8.7, which presents data on annual changes in product, labor, capital inputs, and total factor productivity for the total business sector and for

Table 8.7 Annual changes in product, inputs, and productivity in agriculture, industry, and the total business sector, 1968–1977 (percent)

Item	1968	1969	1970	1971	1972	1973	1974	1975	1976	1977
Real product										
Total	21.1	13.7	10.4	12.3	12.1	3.7	4.5	2.1	3.1	2.5
Agriculture	0.8	4.4	5.4	10.3	7.2	− 0.3	10.1	8.9	8.0	8.0
Industry	28.7	15.8	9.5	10.5	11.9	4.5	5.1	3.1	5.1	4.3
Labor input										
Total	14.9	7.2	1.6	4.5	8.5	0.3	− 2.7	1.0	0.2	0.9
Agriculture	1.5	− 9.6	− 1.6	1.0	4.8	− 5.5	− 7.2	− 3.4	3.6	− 0.8
Industry	21.1	− 2.4	3.3	2.6	7.8	1.2	4.2	− 0.1	− 0.1	− 1.2
Capital Input										
Total	4.5	7.7	8.4	8.2	10.1	8.3	9.7	9.9	6.3	5.1
Agriculture	2.8	3.1	3.1	3.9	3.7	4.8	4.4	4.9	5.3	5.3
Industry	2.6	7.1	10.4	11.0	10.9	10.8	9.0	8.2	9.1	7.2
Total factor productivity										
Total	10.3	6.3	6.3	6.5	3.0	0.5	2.9	− 1.7	0.5	0.0
Agriculture	− 1.2	8.9	5.0	8.0	2.9	0.0	11.9	8.3	3.6	6.1
Industry	15.0	14.2	3.3	4.4	2.8	− 0.8	− 1.3	− 0.7	1.1	1.5

Source: Metzer, 1983

[1] The massive changes in foreign prices, particularly oil prices, since 1973, which resulted in real changes in world income distribution, make the estimates of these ratios in constant prices of little relevance.

agriculture and industry, clearly shows the marked differences between the 1968–72 and the 1973–9 periods for the business sector. The first period had much higher rates of growth of product, labor input, and productivity then the second. Only capital inputs did not differ substantially in the two periods.

The agricultural sector did not behave like the total business economy: its rates of growth were lower in the first period, and much higher in the second; its changes in labor inputs (generally decreasing) did not match those of the other sectors, and its productivity grew when that of the total economy fell. Its capital inputs were consistently lower than the average. Agriculture received fewer additional inputs, but made the most of them.

A comparison of agriculture with the total manufacturing sector, which had relatively higher product and productivity growth than agriculture in the first period and lower growth in the second, might suggest that industry's poorer performance in the second period reflects the effects of liberalization, which did not apply to agriculture. However, manufacturing was the only sector subject to significant changes in protection levels. Comparison of manufacturing with the total business sector, not only agriculture, shows that output growth in the second period was higher in manufacturing, and productivity changes were not significantly different.

Analysis and Assessment of the Effects of Liberalization

Unlike the earlier liberalization episodes, the essence of the 1969–77 liberalization was a reduction in protection levels for import substitutes resulting from the introduction of across-the-board reductions and the restructuring of the relative protection levels for import substitutes and exports.

In this period, exchange rate policy *per se* was not very important to the liberalization. Our main interest is therefore in the changes in protection levels in the manufacturing sector, and their effects. We first examine differences in the speed and level of reduction in protection levels for import substitutes, and then the possible interrelation between these differences and economic performance in the period before the liberalization. We next attempt to ascertain the effects of liberalization on employment. Finally, some other welfare effects are considered.

Changes in Rates of Protection on Import Substitutes

As we concluded earlier (and as can be seen from the data in table 8.8), for the 1968–77 period as a whole there was indeed liberalization both in the sense of reduced rates of protection for import substitutes (nominal and effective) and in decreased dispersion of protection rates: protection was

Table 8.8 Percentage change in the level of protection for manufacturing import substitutes

Branch	NPIM			EPIM		
	1972 over 1968	1977 over 1972	1977 over 1968	1972 over 1968	1977 over 1972	1977 over 1968
Basic chemicals	− 16	− 13	− 27	− 56	− 22	− 65
Transport equipment	− 8	2	− 6	8	− 53	− 50
Plastics	4	− 31	− 29	30	− 66	− 55
Clothing	− 16	5	− 37	− 40	− 31	− 60
Food	− 6	− 3	− 9	84	− 43	5
Textiles	− 24	− 6	− 28	− 43	+ 4	− 41
Basic metals	− 8	− 12	− 19	− 37	− 33	− 58
Electronic equipment	− 20	− 12	− 29	− 44	− 22	− 58
Rubber products	− 7	− 7	− 14	− 49	+ 20	− 38
Paper products	1	− 12	− 12	− 26	− 6	− 31
Electrical equipment	0	− 11	− 11	− 1	− 16	− 17
Leather products	− 3	− 11	− 13	7	− 19	− 14
Metal products	− 8	− 12	− 18	− 2	− 25	− 26
Wood products	13	− 10	2	61	− 16	35
Machinery	− 3	− 13	− 15	9	− 24	− 18
Rubber and plastics	0	− 24	− 24	− 19	− 39	− 50
Electrical and electronic equipment	− 12	− 11	− 23	− 27	− 21	− 42
Total	− 8	− 13	− 20	− 17	− 23	− 36

Source: computed from Halevi and Baruh, 1988, appendix tables A.20 and A.21

considerably reduced for the industrial branches most highly protected in 1968, and more moderately reduced for the industries less favored in 1968. Although the total reductions in NPIMs were less than in EPIMs, the variations in the NPIM for the initially more protected industries were greater than those in the EPIM; clearly, the ultimate policy objectives framed in terms of effective protection were kept in mind.

The general outcome, however, was not without exceptions. Two branches – electronic equipment and basic metals – which in 1968 had received higher than average protection, but not exceptionally high protection, had their protective rates reduced so much that their ranking by protection rate among 15 branches fell in 1977 to 13 and 15 respectively. For the former, this is mainly a reflection of a change in product mix, to more export-oriented sophisticated products. A more significant exception was food products: though ranking fifth in 1968, its level of protection was raised, rather than lowered, and it ranked first in protection in 1977. This increase in EPIM was not a result of increased NPIM but in spite of a moderate decrease in NPIM. The fact that the decrease in the NPIM for food was even larger than that for motor vehicles, and for the former caused a slight increase in EPIM while for the latter accompanied a 50 percent drop in EPIM, highlights the crucial role of tariffs on inputs, and the difficulties of achieving exact changes in EPIM with limited information. Thus it is not easy to ascertain whether an achieved result was the intended one. However, some indications may be obtained by considering the two subperiods 1968–72 and 1972–7.

Of the five most highly protected branches in 1968, motor vehicles (second), plastics (third), and food (fifth) had their protection rates raised by 1972. Of these, only plastics had an actual increase in the NPIM. Between 1972 and 1977 this trend was reversed: the EPIMs were drastically lowered for motor vehicles and plastics, while for food the decrease was not enough to give an actual decrease in EPIM for the 1968–77 period but did considerably reduce the increased protection given in the first period. The "corrections" were obtained despite great variations in the NPIMs of these three branches, suggesting that changed tariffs on inputs were crucial.

Two other branches – textiles and rubber products – which had substantial reductions in the EPIM between 1968 and 1972, received increased protection in the second period; this mitigated the overall fall in protection by 1977.

Among the branches least favored in 1968, wood products (fourteenth) had a very large increase in EPIM to 1972, via a significant increase in the NPIM. This increased protection was reduced somewhat in the second period, but enabled wood products to rise in the protection scale to second place in 1977.

Cross-section regressions were run showing the level of effective protection given in 1977 as a function of relative efficiency (value added per worker in Israel compared with the United States) and factor intensity. In 1977, as in 1965, the less efficient branches received higher protection. A negative correlation between the protection level and human capital intensity is again observed, but no significant relationship was found between protection and physical capital intensity, and the coefficient for labor intensity is positive and significant.

Influences on Liberalization of Economic Performance

A reasonable hypothesis would be that policymakers would take into account the economic performance of the various branches in the period before the liberalization in deciding on the speed and level of reductions in protection. Both rank correlation and regression analysis failed to show a statistically significant relationship between strength of employment, measured by changes in employment, in the period preceding reductions of protection levels and the size of those reduction (Yashiv, 1985). This does not imply that this factor was ignored in particular instances, however.

Table 8.9 summarizes the changes in employment and product in 1965–8 and 1968–72. A comparison of the economic performance in 1965–8 of

Table 8.9 Percentage change in employment and product, 1965–1968 and 1968–1972

Branch	Employment		Real product	
	1968 over 1965	1972 over 1968	1968 over 1965	1972 over 1968
Chemicals	3	28	47	66
Transport equipment	5	111	25	100
Clothing	27	38	32	135
Food	15	15	28	37
Textiles	6	13	27	38
Basic metals	− 9	19	12	31
Paper products	12	24	41	34
Leather products	14	− 2	5	19
Metal products	4	− 41	12	77
Wood products	− 9	16	35	35
Machinery	− 1	31	16	42
Rubber and plastics	8	35	49	93
Electrical and electronic equipment	4	66	37	93

Sources: Halevi and Baruh, 1988, appendix tables A.7 and A.13

those branches receiving unexpected treatment with regard to reduction of protection in 1968–72 shows the following:

1 The highly protected industries which received additional protection in 1972 – motor vehicles, plastics, and food – were not among the industries with a weak employment record in 1965–8, although motor vehicles were weaker than the average. Food was particularly strong in employment. None of these industries had particularly weak output performance.

2 Two industries having "unexpectedly" large reductions in protection in this period – textiles and rubber products – were not exceptionally impressive either in employment or output performance in 1965–8.

3 Of the four low protection industries in 1968, three received increased protection in 1972: leather products and machinery a modest increase, and wood products a dramatic increase. Both machinery and wood were weak in employment, and leather and machinery were weak in output

performance in 1965–8, with wood strong in output and leather strong in employment.
4 Basic metals received substantially lower protection in 1972 despite an actual reduction in employment between 1965 and 1968.

Clearly, no inference can be drawn that the 1968–72 liberalization was influenced by these major indicators of economic performance in 1965–8.

Comparison of similar data for 1968–72 may cast light on whether the adjustments in liberalization policy made between 1972 and 1977 conformed to or contradicted the economic performance in 1968–72.

The severe reductions in protection rates for motor vehicles were surely made easier by the tremendous performance, in employment and output, in 1968–72. The adjustment of rates for plastics was eased by better than average performance for the plastics and rubber industries taken together; but unless the two subbranches behaved differently there is a contradiction in the increased protection afforded to rubber products. Textiles, too, received increased protection in the second period, despite very strong employment (and fair output performance) in 1968–72. The correction of the overprotection of wood products was made despite mediocre output performance.

Large reductions in protection levels continued for two other industries – clothing and basic metals. Clothing had an exceptional growth in output in the 1968–72 period, and above average growth in employment. However, although there was an improvement in the performance of basic metals, it was hardly exceptional, and does not help to explain the continued high rate of liberalization.

Thus here, too, no general inferences can be drawn about the influence of economic performance on liberalization.

Effects of Liberalization on Employment

A reasonable hypothesis is that branches subject to a greater degree of liberalization, as measured by reduced tariff protection, would face greater import competition and, to the extent that this import competition would lead to reduced output, to decreased employment, at least relative to branches not subjected to import competition. However, while import penetration may decrease production for the domestic market, it may also force producers to more active export activity. We have seen that this "push effect" was evident during the 1966–7 recession. There will also be a "pull effect" arising from a second aspect of liberalization: a decrease in the anti-export bias of protection rates. Thus the effects of liberalization on employment and product are a combination of several components.

Competitive Imports
The share of competitive imports in total domestic sales of manufactured goods was only 18 percent in 1968, just 2 percent more than in 1965. As shown in table 8.10, for most of the 14 industrial branches the share was under 10 percent, and three branches – motor vehicles, basic metals, and electrical and electronic products – had much higher shares.

Table 8.10 Share of competing imports in the domestic market of the manufacturing sector

Branch	Branch share in domestic market, 1977	Share of competing imports		
		1968	1972	1977
Food, beverages	11.8	4	13	20
Textiles	10.5	10	9	23
Clothing and leather products	10.9	6	6	15
Wood products	5.3	6	15	13
Paper products	5.6	4	33	32
Rubber and plastic products	5.5	7	12	16
Chemicals	9.0	2	25	25
Glass and ceramic products	2.4	13	28	28
Basic metals	3.7	34	47	42
Metal products	9.4	8	12	22
Motor and machinery	7.4	19	35	51
Electrical and electronic products	14.3	46	28	32
Motor vehicles	4.2	45	67	60
Total	100.0	18	26	29

Source: computed from data on file at the Bank of Israel and CBS

By 1972 the share of total competitive imports rose to 26 percent. Although there were particularly large increases in the share of two of the branches with large shares in 1968 (motor vehicles and basic metals), increases were substantial in most branches. From 1972 to 1977 the changes were not large, to an overall penetration ratio of 29.

The frequency distributions of the shares of competing imports (table 8.11), based on more detailed breakdowns than the 14-branch industrial classification, show the dramatic decline in branches not faced with significant imports. By 1977 only 14 percent of cumulated output had penetration ratios of less than 10 percent, and 35 percent had penetration ratios of 50 percent or more.

Can we ascribe with certainty the increased import penetration ratios to the liberalization policy? Cross-section regression analysis relating changes

Table 8.11 Frequency distribution of the share of competing imports in the domestic market of the manufacturing sector

CM/ (TO − X + CM)	1965	1968	1972	1977
0–0.099	62	55	36	14
0.10–0.299	15	23	32	51
0.30–0.499	19	17	19	18
0.50–0.750	4	5	13	17
Total	100	100	100	100

Sources: computed from data on file at the Bank of Israel and CBS

in the import penetration ratios to changes in the EPRs suggest the expected relationship, with time lags, but the results are too weak to be more than suggestive. Regressions using changes in the NPRs give much more robust results. This is to be expected since consumers are influenced by the nominal rather than the effective protection. These regressions are summarized in table 8.12. Simultaneous and lagged regressions were run, for various periods, of changes in the dependent variable (import penetration) and the independent variable (NPR), including less reliable penetration ratio estimates for 1979.

For very short periods the simultaneous-period regressions are not significant and are not included in the table. For longer periods there is a clear statistical relationship between lowered protection and import penetration, although, as would be expected in such cross-section regressions, the R^2 values are low. Regressions 6, 9, 11, and 14 all support the conclusion that the relationship is a lagged one: reduction in protection levels increased penetration ratios to a greater extent when given sufficient adjustment time.

Exports

Table 8.13 summarizes developments in the EPIX and the EPIM-to-EPIX ratios. Between 1968 and 1972, only food had significantly increased EPIXs; for most branches EPIX decreased. Between 1972 and 1979 there were decreases in EPIX for food, wood, and textiles (very slight); other EPIXs were increased. For the period as a whole, only three (textiles, clothing, and wood) of the eight branches shown had reduced EPIXs.

More interesting are changes in anti-export bias. In 1968, only wood products had a higher EPIX than EPIM, and many branches had very strong anti-export bias. This was reduced for some by 1972, and by 1977

Table 8.12 Regressions of percentage change in import penetration ratio on percentage change in nominal protection indices

Regressions	Period of change in		Constant	Coefficient of NPI	Number of observations	R^2
	Dependent variable	Independent variable				
1	72–77	72–77	0.46 (1.40)	− 3.74 (− 1.89)	42	0.08
2	72–77	68–77	− 0.03 (− 0.07)	− 4.98 (− 2.13)	42	0.10
3	72–77	65–77	− 0.01 (− 0.02)	− 4.77 (− 2.01)	42	0.09
4	65–77	65–77	0.61 (0.53)	− 10.46 (− 2.01)	31	0.12
5	72–79	72–77	0.31 (0.49)	− 7.45 (− 1.94)	42	0.09
6	72–79	68–77	− 1.07 (− 1.13)	− 11.97 (− 2.71)	42	0.16
7	72–79	65–77	− 0.59 (− 0.59)	− 9.31 (− 2.01)	42	0.09
8	68–77	68–72	2.29 (1.85)	− 17.49 (− 1.84)	36	0.09
9	68–77	65–72	1.82 (1.56)	− 24.90 (− 2.76)	36	0.18
10	68–79	68–72	2.07 (1.41)	− 21.50 (− 1.91)	36	0.10
11	68–79	65–72	1.53 (1.11)	− 29.04 (− 2.80)	36	0.19
12	65–77	65–77	0.61 (0.53)	− 10.46 (− 2.01)	31	0.12
13	65–79	65–72	1.39 (2.21)	− 7.87 (− 2.00)	31	0.12
14	65–79	65–77	− 0.69 (− 0.63)	− 14.20 (− 2.84)	31	0.22

Source: Bar-Nathan and Baruh, 1986

only three branches – food, rubber, and wood – had a significant anti-export bias. These developments should surely have encouraged both exports and the export-to-revenue share.

Export-to-product ratios ("product" being measured by total revenue) for 1965 and 1977, for industries exporting at least 5 percent of their product in 1965, are presented in Halevi and Baruh (1988, appendix table A.38). Some industries that can be classified as "sophisticated" emerged as major exporters mainly for reasons unconnected with changes in relative prices. Others increased their export share as a result of declining anti-export bias, both as pull and as push factors. We had reliable

Table 8.13 Changes in absolute and relative effective protection for manufacturing exports

Branch	Percentage change in EPIX			Ratio of EPIX to EPIM			Percentage change in EPIX to EPIM ratio		
	1972 over 1968	1977 over 1972	1977 over 1968	1968	1972	1977	1972 over 1968	1977 over 1972	1977 over 1968
Food	58	− 10	41	0.43	0.37	0.58	− 14	56	35
Textiles	− 24	− 1	− 25	0.73	0.97	0.92	33	− 5	26
Clothing	− 38	46	− 10	0.40	0.42	0.88	5	110	120
Wood	− 33	− 39	− 61	1.43	0.60	0.64	− 58	7	− 55
Rubber	− 55	51	− 16	0.46	0.50	0.62	9	24	35
Basic chemicals	− 22	35	6	0.34	0.59	1.02	75	73	200
Metal products	3	24	28	0.64	0.68	1.12	6	65	75
Machinery	− 10	15	3	0.82	0.73	1.02	− 11	40	24

Source: computed from Halevi and Baruh, 1968, appendix tables A.19 and A.21

comparable data for 1965 and 1977 on export share (export-to-product ratios) and on EPIM-to-EPIX ratios for only 14 subbranches.

Regressing the percentage change in the export-to-product ratio between 1965 and 1977 and the percentage change in the EPIM-to-EPIX ratio in the same period gave surprisingly strong results: the coefficient (elasticity) of the change in the EPIM-to-EPIX ratio was negative, as expected, high (− 2.14), with a t value of 2.95 and an adjusted R^2 of 0.37. Clearly, the decrease in anti-export bias, mainly due to the lowering of protection levels for import substitutes, did push (or pull) many branches into export markets.

The smallness of our sample resulted from a paucity of EPIX estimates for industries which became important exporters by 1977 but exported very little in 1965. If we make the not unreasonable assumption that the effective protection levels allowed them in 1965 were equal to the average allowed to other exporting industries, excluding the most highly subsidized exceptions such as textiles and plywood, we can increase our sample considerably (up to 29 industries). For this sample, we regress the change $D(X/TO)$ in export shares in output from 1965 to 1977 on the change in EPIM/EPIX. The result is as follows:

$$D(X/TO) = 0.303 - 0.270 \; D(\text{EPIM/EPIX})$$
$$(6.31) \qquad (4.02)$$

$$R^2 = 0.35$$

This supports the conclusion that reduction in anti-export bias stimulated exports.

Combined Effects on Employment
We thus find that the two aspects of liberalization – reduced protection levels for import substitutes and reduced anti-export bias – work in opposite directions on employment. We can summarize our findings in three additional regressions for 1965–77, for a cross-section of 29 industries. The first relates changes, $D(E)$ in employment measure in mandays, to changes in exports $(D(X))$ and in competitive imports $(D(CM))$:

$$D(E) = 1.48 + 0.020D(X) - 0.069D(CM)$$
$$(3.89)\quad(4.05)\qquad\quad(5.78)$$
$$R^2 = 0.62$$

The expected results are obtained. Whether employment will go up or down depends on whether exports compensate for increased imports. Calling the difference between the increase in exports and the increase in competitive imports "net exports" (NX), we regress changes in employment on changes in NX:

$$D(E) = 1.05 + 0.025D(NX)$$
$$(2.30)\quad(4.06)$$
$$R^2 = 0.38$$

The relationship here, too, is clear and statistically significant.
   Finally, to relate the changes in net exports to changes in the reduction of anti-export bias, we regress changes in the former on changes in the latter:

$$D(NX) = 88.77 - 69.26D(EPIM/EPIX)$$
$$(3.80)\qquad(-2.12)$$
$$R^2 = 0.14$$

The expected sign is obtained, and it is statistically significant. However, the R^2 is quite low. This is to be expected considering that these changes in protection levels were taking place over an extended period of time during which other – perhaps more basic – economic developments were also taking place, which could "swamp" the influence of liberalization.

Simulation of Effects of Liberalization on Employment
Because our data do not make possible meaningful econometric analysis of the effects of liberalization by isolating the effects of the various factors operating on the economy, it may be suggestive to attempt simulations that measure the effects which could have been expected from the reduced EPIM and reduced EPIM-to-EPIX ratios in the 1968–77 period had there been no change in any other relevant variables. Such exercises would be possible if we had reliable price elasticities of supply for Israel's manufacturing branches. Unfortunately, such estimates are not available.

For the purposes of this exercise, we make the heroic assumption that we can apply estimates of supply elasticities made for the United States (Stern et al., 1982).[2] Using these estimates of price elasticities of competitive imports (e_m) and of domestic supply (e_s) for identifiable subbranches and Israeli data on value added ratios, we computed the price elasticity of supply of value added (E).[3] The change in domestic production of import substitutes would then be equal to $E_j V_j T_j$, for each branch j where V_j is the value added in the production of the final product and T_j is the percentage change in the EPIM.

Using input–output coefficients for 1968 and industrial survey data, we arrive at an estimate of the percentage change in 1968 employment which would have resulted from the decrease in EPIM between 1968 and 1977. This has an element of underestimation because not all industry is included, and it does not allow for the positive effects of efficiency. The figures are summarized in table 8.14, columns 1 and 2.

However, export activity was stimulated by increasing the EPIX-to-EPIM ratio. As a second step of our exercise, we use estimates of the relative price elasticity for export value added in 1970–80 (Teubal et al., 1986), for only those branches where a relationship between these variables was found, to estimate how the change in the EPIX-to-EPIM ratio alone would have increased exports. Again using input–output coefficients and industrial survey data, we get a (minimum) estimate of changes in employment. These are shown in column 3.

The results of this simulation are that there could have been a decline in employment for production of import substitutes equal to 14 percent of total industrial employment for that purpose in 1968 had the 1977 EPIM rates prevailed. This was about 11 percent of total industrial employment. The increase in employment for exports would counteract this: our estimate, surely a very minimal estimate, is that employment would have increased some 2 percent. Thus the net (partial equilibrium) sum of employment effects is a fall in employment of 9 percent as an upper limit.

Considering all the shortcomings of this exercise, no hard conclusions should be drawn from it. However, it does support the general contention that the liberalization, because it spread over a long period of time, did not have very large negative effects on employment. The time that elapsed permitted general growth factors to swamp the negative employment effect. However, the interbranch differences could have been important: clothing, rubber, and plastics would have been hard hit. Basic metals and electrical goods, too, would have been hit by the fall in production of

---

[2] The idea for using these elasticities, and some data, came from Joseph Pelzman, who used them in a different manner for his study of the US–Israel Free Trade Area Agreement (Pelzman, 1985).

[3] E is equal to value added divided by total consumption of product (e_s).

Table 8.14 Simulation estimates of the employment[a] effect in manufacturing of reducing the 1968 protection levels to those prevailing in 1977

Branch	Decrease in employment as percentage of		Increase in employment for exports, as percentage of total branch employment
	Employment in production of import substitutes	Total branch employment	
Food	0	0	14
Textiles	14	9	n.a.
Clothing	23	19	4
Leather products	5	4	n.a.
Wood products	2	2	− 1
Paper products	4	4	n.a.
Chemicals	13	10	n.a.
Rubber and plastics	22	18	n.a.
Nonmetallic mineral products	14	13	[b]
Basic metals	39	36	2
Metal products	9	8	n.a.
Machinery	19	18	n.a.
Electrical and electronic equipment	27	24	2
Transport equipment	2	2	n.a.
Total	14	11	2

n.a., not available.
[a] Employment effects calculated on the basis of mandays per unit of output coefficients.
[b] This branch was found to have high export price elasticity, but it is excluded because its EPIX estimates are not separated from the larger mining section, not included here.

import substitutes, but these branches expanded export, although the electrical products branch did so not primarily as a result of relative price changes and with considerable intrabranch substitution in production.

Welfare Effects

The type of simulation used to estimate changes in employment can also be used to give some measure of increased welfare that arises from the increased consumption resulting from reduced tariffs and from the saving in costs obtained from producing fewer import substitutes. This is a partial equilibrium analysis, using the Johnson triangulation method based on assumed linear curves (Johnson, 1969).

Multiplying our estimated decreased domestic production resulting from more competitive imports by one half of the change in EPIM, we arrive at an estimate of the welfare gain due to the production effect. The estimated increase in consumption is found by using the American elasticity estimates of demand.[4] From the demand for imports elasticities (e_m), we can compute own-price elasticity of demand for final commodities (e_d).[5] These

Table 8.15 Simulation estimates of the welfare effects of reducing the 1968 protection levels to those prevalent in 1977

Branch	Percentage change in			Welfare gain	
	NPIM[a]	EPIM[a]	Competitive imports	From consumption percentage of total availability	From production as percentage of value added
Food	9.7	2.2	1	0	0
Textiles	28.0	40.2	68	8	7
Clothing	37.4	58.5	36	21	19
Leather products	16.0	47.2	29	2	8
Footwear	10.3	2.7	42	2	1
Wood products	14.5	14.5	24	1	1
Furniture	7.1	− 1.2	− 5	–	–
Paper products	11.8	31.1	14	1	2
Chemicals	27.3	65.4	55	6	12
Rubber products	13.9	38.1	53	3	8
Plastic products	28.6	55.3	95	10	18
Pottery, ceramics	21.7	35.0	42	3	7
Other nonmetallic goods	19.1	31.4	43	3	4
Basic metals	25.9	70.5	62	5	33
Metal products	14.5	23.6	26	1	2
Machinery	15.4	17.7	67	4	3
Electrical and electronics equipment	22.4	41.8	42	3	10
Transport equipment	7.0	49.8	3	0	2
Total	20.0	40.0	50	5	7.5

−, negligible.

[a] The branches had to be regrouped to fit the classification for the US elasticities. Therefore in some cases the changes in average protection indices do not match those used in the rest of this study.

[4] This is probably a more defensible assumption than using American supply elasticities.
[5] The formula is as follows: import penetration index $\times$ $(e_m - e_s) + e_s$.

are used to give estimates for each branch of total increased imports due to increased competition. In fact, of the total increase in imports from consumption and substitution effects, some three quarters were estimated to arise from the consumption effect.

Multiplying these consumption effects on imports by one half of the change in NPIM gives an estimate of this welfare gain. The results of this exercise are summarized in table 8.15. The welfare gain due to the consumption effect amounted to some 5 percent of total availabilities of industrial importables. The welfare gain due to the production effect amounted to some 7.5 percent of the total value added generated in the production of industrial import substitutes.

9

Summary and Concluding Inferences

The story of Israel's experience with liberalization is peculiar to that country's specific economic, social, and political conditions; nevertheless, discussion and analysis of the Israeli experience has suggested some conclusions about the timing and sequencing of liberalization which may be applicable to other countries. This chapter's brief recapitulation of the principal elements of the process attempts to provide a basis from which such inferences may, with caution, be drawn.[1]

Trade liberalization policy in Israel in 1952–77 was a continuous process, with changing stresses but no major reversals. From a rigid system of controls in the early years, a much more open-market economy emerged. Government intervention decreased not only in foreign trade but in all areas. Even at the end of the period covered, however, government control of the economy (much of it indirect) remained considerable, and "non-liberalized" trade was still significant. Although liberalization has been continuous, no complete ideological shift toward reliance on market forces has taken place.

Because liberalization was so protracted, its division into discrete episodes is somewhat arbitrary. To facilitate international comparison, however, three episodes have been distinguished, the choices being based on differences in the nature of the liberalization measures taken in each.

The first episode (1952–5) was essentially a switch from almost complete reliance on direct controls to use of the price mechanism: EERs were used to influence trade that was not competitive with domestic production. The reforms were undertaken as part of a macroeconomic policy package during a severe crisis in the balance of payments. We believe the crisis situation probably stimulated the strong departure from the hitherto prevalent ideological convictions of the dominant political forces. Those

---

[1] The general inferences which the authors have drawn from this study were presented in several versions in previous drafts, benefitting from discussions in several conferences. Particular thanks must be given to Stephen Guisinger, Oli Havrylyshyn, and Martin Wolf, who made extremely helpful and penetrating comments at the final June 1986 Conference.

who took the first major step probably did not foresee its inevitable consequences. Nonetheless, we are convinced that the first liberalization was a necessary condition for all future liberalization, and we therefore gave it extended coverage even though it contained so few of the "classic" elements of liberalization.

The second episode (1962–8) was primarily a change in the form of protection, but because it was accompanied by devaluation it repeated some of the elements of the first episode. The third episode (1969–77) can be distinguished from the second in its progress to an actual reduction in protection levels for import substitutes and accompanying (consequent) reduction of anti-export bias.

The summary table (table 9.1) outlines the economic conditions preceding and following the liberalization measures taken in the three episodes.

The Israeli experience can be looked at from different points of view and, indeed, opposing opinions have been voiced by discussants of various drafts of this study. One view is influenced by the fact that at the end of the period covered (and even some eight years later) there were still many restrictions on trade, within a general context of still significant government intervention in the economy. It concludes that our liberalization story has been greatly exaggerated. Another view compares the situation in 1977 with the initial situation (1952) and concludes that very considerable liberalization has taken place. The authors share the latter view. In fact, considering the original socialist and interventionist convictions of the political elite, the fact that so much liberalization has actually taken place has been viewed as puzzling. One explanation offered is that trade policy must have been considered as less essential than other policies, and consequently economics technicians were allowed more freedom than elsewhere to impose, in a gradual and often sporadic manner, their market-oriented views. This very interesting point seems to be contradicted by several basic facts: Israel is highly reliant on trade, and all politicians have known this; trade policy has been considered so important that influential politicians have eagerly sought to control it; and finally promotion of exports and import substitutes has been a cornerstone of development policy for the entire period discussed.

However, while rejecting the idea that trade policy was not considered vital, we cannot ignore the fact that it was a leading sector in liberalization despite the ideological climate. Our explanation is that the development of industry, to begin with, was less locked-in ideologically and most subject to pragmatic considerations. The focus of Israel's original socialist ideology was the development of agriculture. In the 1950s it became evident that agriculture's role in Israel's economic growth was limited, and new industries were the branches of the future. Here the socialist labor ideology had less vested interest, and the original desire to develop industry through government or Histadrut enterprises was replaced by a pragmatic

Table 9.1 Israel: a summary

	Episode I 1952–5	Episode II 1962–8	Episode III 1969–77
Broad nature	Greater reliance on price mechanism	Change in form of price mechanism	Reduced protection levels
Main tools	Formal exchange rates and monetary policy	Switch from QRs to tariffs	Reduced tariffs
Duration	Relatively brief	Protracted	Protracted
Stages	None	Episode III is delayed stage of episode II	Gradual approach to target rates, slowdown in second stage 1973–7
Economic circumstances			
Dramatic changes in continuing balance-of-payments deficits	Yes	Yes	No
Inflation	Yes	Yes	Yes
Rate of growth	No	High	High first stage, low second stage
Openness of economy	Low	High	Higher
Shock	Yes	No	Yes, in middle of period
Political circumstances			
Stable government	No	Yes	Yes, until middle of period
Ideological shift	Yes	Partial	Partial
Public perception and debate	Yes	Slight	No
Administering arm	Ministry of Finance	Ministry of Commerce and Industry	Ministry of Commerce and Industry
International influence	Partial	Supporting	Indirect
Accompanying policies			
Exchange rate	Multiple formal rates, devaluations	Devaluations, rate unification	Several rate adjustments, crawling peg
Exchange control	Stringent, with black markets	Retained, but eased	Retained, but eased
Export promotion	Higher formal rates, subsidies	Exchange rate, subsidies renewed 1966, development budget aid	Subsidies, tax, and credit aid

Monetary policy	Stringent	Inadequate	Unrelated to liberalization
Fiscal policy	Partial contraction	Expanded	Fluctuating with general increase in public sector
Controls	Greatly relaxed	More use of indirect controls	Use of indirect controls

Implementation

Stages	Main change ended by 1955, general easing of controls thereafter	Gradual, more protracted than anticipated	Faster pace until 1973 shocks, slower thereafter

Economic performance

Growth	Immediate fall, then very healthy upsurge in GNP and productivity	Rapid growth, with recession in 1966–7	Poor growth after 1973 shocks
Employment	Short period of sharp unemployment	Rise in unemployment in middle of period, but unrelated to liberalization	Low unemployment but change is unrelated to liberalization
Inflation	Lower rates	Low rates with post-devaluation upsurges	Very high from 1973 shocks
Balance-of-payments deficit	Improvement short lived, returned to higher levels	General increase except for recession years	Major jump from 1973
Foreign indebtedness	Relatively slight	Gradually increasing	Rapid increases from 1973
Imports	Temporary fall	Generally increasing, recessionary variations	Growing, with large fluctuations due to macro policy
Exports	Rapid growth	Rapid growth	Slower growth, relative increase in sophisticated industrial products
Real wages	Temporary fall, resumed gradually	Recessionary impacts on general growth	Macro-policy-induced fluctuations

approach: whatever worked would be encouraged. Thus a more liberal trade policy was adopted when it was deemed appropriate in the light of changing economic circumstances, in particular the need to be able to compete with Europe. The Israeli economy in the 1960s and 1970s was far more developed and sophisticated than in the early 1950s. Some ideological predilections were rendered obsolete by actual developments. Significantly, however, the liberalization measures of the second and third episodes excluded the agricultural sector.

In attempting to draw inferences from this liberalization process for the timing and sequencing of liberalization, the authors' conclusions result from a mixture of analysis of the data presented in the study and personal intuition arising from protracted exposure to the discussions, opinions, and studies in Israel related to these issues.

Single-stage versus Multistage Liberalization

Was such a prolonged process of liberalization, with separate episodes or stages, really necessary? Two factors, and their interaction, support an affirmative answer: political–ideological orientation and economic conditions. Israel could not switch immediately from the tightly controlled distorted economy of 1952 to considerable trade liberalization. The political–ideological conditions were not ready for such a move, and even the more influential "free-traders" of the time (who were a minority) generally believed that a major complete switch in trade regimes could be catastrophic under existing economic circumstances.

In 1962, after a decade of ever increasing reliance on the price mechanism and significant reduction in public control of the economy in general, it was still not politically feasible to merge the measures of the second and third episodes. In fact, the Treasury actually visualized such a liberalization, but the ministry directly responsible for trade and industrial policy, supported by industrialists in both the private and the Histadrut sectors of the economy, was adamantly opposed to haste in exposing Israel's industry to world competition, and these forces prevailed. Clearly, the Israeli case strongly supports the concept that gradual multistage liberalization may have greater feasibility and sustainability than a drastic one-stage shift.

Sequencing

Sequencing involves both ordering and the desirability of having separate stages. We believe that, in terms of ordering, the sequence chosen was essentially correct. First, it was necessary to adopt measures to create the basis for a more market-oriented economy, where the price mechanism in general, and the rate of exchange in particular, have a major impact on economic decision making. Second, switching from QRs to tariff protection, and thereby establishing more visible and measurable levels of protection, was a prerequisite for significant lowering of protection levels.

The question whether or not a separate stage concerned with export promotion is desirable remains ambiguous. Israeli policymakers operated for many years under the assumption – supported by some economists – that economic growth is best served by starting with import substitution and then switching to exports. In Israel, exports were encouraged in many ways throughout the period; but since there was a strong anti-export bias in protection rates until the mid-1970s it can be argued that the export promotion stage, in the sense of the elimination of disadvantageous rates, came late. There is no evidence to contradict the view, shared by most Israeli economists, that it would have been better to reduce the anti-export bias much earlier, avoiding any semblance of a separate stage. As shown in chapter 8, the reduction in anti-export bias was mainly the result of lowering EPIMs. Reducing the bias earlier would have required raising EPIXs or making greater use of exchange rate policy. This would both have increased exports and have reduced misallocation of resources. Increased export earnings would also have eased balance-of-payments problems, which at times held back liberalization.

Speed of Implementation

The time elapsed between completion of the main components of the first episode (1955) and the beginning of the second episode (1962) could certainly have been reduced, though elements of liberalization continued in the interim. There is no doubt that the slow process of switching forms of protection and reduction of protection levels in the second and third episodes prevented negative public reactions, but we believe that these processes were somewhat overcautious: the switch in form of protection could have been completed earlier, and the actual reductions in protection levels could have been speeded up.

These conclusions obviously depend on the analysis of the relationship between liberalization and employment because, if lowering of protection levels had been believed to be the cause of severe unemployment, a reversal would have been likely. The analysis in chapter 8 shows that negative import substitution reduced employment and that stimulation of exports as a result of eliminating anti-export bias increased employment, but the net effect could have been negative. Our simulations suggest a *ceteris paribus* reduction in industrial employment of some 9 percent although, since they ignore the influence of liberalization on the efficiency of factor allocation and understate the growth of exports, this estimate is probably exaggerated. However, if the time taken had been too brief, an "employment-reducing effect" anywhere near this figure would have been unacceptable. Prolonging the process of reducing protection meant that other factors, in particular the general growth of the economy, could eclipse the employment-reducing effects. However, more convincing signals to producers coupled with more active promotion of exports could have led to more rational development policy and to greater export growth. Our analysis is inadequate for suggesting an alternative timing and leads us only to the weaker conclusion, presented above, that the process need not have been quite so prolonged.

In retrospect, the delay in actual reductions in protection levels may have been fortuitous. Success in liberalization may sometimes be a matter of luck. In late 1965 Israel entered a recessionary period, for reasons quite unrelated to protection policy. Had there been significant reductions in protection levels in 1964–5, they could have been identified in the public's, and perhaps policymakers', mind with the recession, which could easily have led to a reversal in liberalization policy. As it was, the recession merely postponed the next stage.

Discriminatory Treatment

Israeli policymakers have tended to support discriminatory treatment, either on ideological grounds (for example, pro-agriculture or pro-import substitution) or for political and bureaucratic reasons. In fact, despite a long process of liberalization, there is still considerable government intervention in the economy, much of it discriminatory.

During the second episode products were chosen for "liberalization consideration" in a manner not statistically explicable by any economic factor. Since the levels of protection given to "chosen" products were clearly intended to prevent almost every industry from being hurt, it may be inferred that such considerations were also behind the choice of which products to consider first. Special-interest and pressure groups were influential both in the switch from QRs to tariffs and in the early stages of tariff reductions. From 1969, across-the-board reductions became the norm, but there is no doubt that special interests were still important and have led to discriminatory treatment even to the present. The fact that not all QRs were abolished supports this conclusion.

The speed and extent of liberalization, and the degree of discrimination in the process, are inexorably linked to "political considerations," a term we use to include all pressures from special-interest groups. Our study has focused on one direction in a two-directional process; for instance, we have found that the negative employment effects of liberalization have so far not been large, but we could not determine to what extent this is the result of discriminatory treatment which diligently prevented or slowed down liberalization in subbranches where such negative effects (even if temporary) were more likely to appear.

Appropriate Circumstances for Liberalization

The idea of appropriate circumstances includes both those relevant to the adoption of a liberalization policy and those necessary for sustaining it.

The first liberalization episode differs from later ones in this respect. It was adopted in a period of balance-of-payments crisis severe enough to convince policymakers that a drastic revision of the entire foreign exchange regime was necessary and that the painful short-run effects on employment and output were a necessary price to pay. The foreign aid received in 1954 from the "consolidation loan" taken by the philanthropic institutions helped Israel weather the crisis years. The second episode contained two elements: the first, a devaluation, could also have been undertaken in a more serious immediate balance-of-payments situation than existed in 1962, but the second, the announcement of a commitment to import liberalization and actual change in the form of protection, could not have been undertaken in a severe balance-of-payments crisis or in a serious unemployment situation. This is certainly true for the third episode, which consisted of lowering protection levels.

Employment and balance-of-payments situations are important for sustainability. Since Israel is a nation of immigrants strongly committed to continuous immigration, Israeli society is strongly averse to heavy unemployment, which is viewed as a threat to the basic social fabric. If liberalization had led to serious unemployment, or was believed to have caused it, there would be strong political pressure for its reversal.

Balance-of-payments deficits are the norm in Israel; a balance-of-payments "crisis" is therefore a situation in which the deficit seem to have got out of hand relative to sources of external finance. The role of foreign aid was extremely important: on the one hand, it may have delayed action by alleviating a difficult balance-of-payments situation; on the other hand, the availability of external sources of funds gave Israel more time for adjustment. Therefore temporary balance-of-payments setbacks and resulting increases in foreign indebtedness were not sufficiently alarming in Israel to warrant abandoning liberalization. Thus, despite a very drastic increase in the balance-of-payments deficits following 1973, there was no major reversal of liberalization, but only a slowing down of the process. However, the deficits in the early 1980s – a period not covered in our study – elicited calls for curbing imports and a return to antiliberalization techniques. Some, in fact, were adopted in the 1984–5 anti-inflationary policy. It is not possible to be sure that had Israel not received massive additional US aid during these years more serious reversals would not have taken place. So far, however, Israel's commitment to liberalization has stood up well in the face of balance-of-payments problems. Israel's experience suggests that, of the two dangers to sustainability of liberalization, unemployment is perhaps a more serious threat than the balance of payments. This differs from the experience of some other countries studied in this project.

Has Israel reached the stage of an irreversible commitment to liberalization? There are those who maintain that the memory of the chaos resulting from the severe controls of 1949–51 is strong enough to counteract any drastic antiliberalization designs. However, the present and future generations of technocrats (and even political leaders) "knew not Joseph," and there is no guarantee that past mistakes will not be repeated.

Foreign pressures have always played a role in the liberalization process. The importance of American Jewry in aiding Israel in the early years helped make the first serious inroads in the prevailing ideology. US aid added to this. IMF pressure was important in consolidating formal exchange rates in 1962.

The emergence of the EEC played a dual role. It was crucial in convincing some policymakers that, like it or not, Israel would have to become competitive, and that this would entail reduced protection. For many, even those who fought a rearguard action against real liberalization, this external force was a useful excuse and helped to overcome domestic pressure groups. The actual signing of free-trade area agreements with the EEC (restricted to industrial goods), and more recently with the United States, has drastically changed the role of external commitments on trade policy. These necessitate a faster pace of import liberalization within the next few years. More important, they will strongly restrict Israel's freedom to reverse its liberalization process.

Relationship to Other Policy Measures

Liberalization policy is a composite of measures relating to foreign trade, whose effect is largely determined by various accompanying policies. Israel's early steps toward liberalization, in the first episode, were in fact the manifestations of a major change in the general economic regime. Furthermore, the success of the first episode hung on devaluation being real, not just nominal. This was achieved by accompanying monetary and fiscal policies.

The second episode contained a devaluation component, which failed for lack of adequate monetary and fiscal restraint. This is a clear example of deficient accompanying macroeconomic policy. The other aspects of that episode, and the reductions in protection in the third episode, are less directly related to accompanying macro policy; however, as discussed above, speed and sustainability depend on circumstances which are influenced by macro policy. For example, the failure to use devaluation as part of the macro package in 1965 led to a more severe recession in 1966–7 and a consequent slowing down of the liberalization process. Similar interactions were observed in 1974–80.

More generally, there are strong indications that liberalization cannot be carried out forcefully, nor sustained, in periods of severe economic crisis, even though Israel had greatly benefitted from massive foreign aid as a buffer. In fact liberalization can be the scapegoat for economic crisis (although this has not been true so far in Israel). The major macroeconomic policies – fiscal, monetary, and exchange rate measures – are responsible for crisis avoidance and crisis management. Liberalization cannot substitute for correct macro policy, yet its success often depends on the appropriateness of accompanying policy.

Liberalization and Economic Performance

The impetus for examining the timing and sequencing of trade liberalization is the assumption that such liberalization is intrinsically a "good thing." Implicit is the belief that a liberal trade regime will lead to greater efficiency, less distortion, and, in general, superior economic performance. Our discussion of economic performance after liberalization may at times have seemed to be at odds with this basic assumption.

The liberalization of 1952–5 led to an immediate temporary downturn in economic performance when measured by output and employment. By 1954 these indicators had already turned dramatically upward, and the economy grew rapidly for a long time. Obviously, many factors contribute to this success story, but there can be no doubt that the change in the trade regime, commencing with the NEP of 1952 and specifically the new role assigned to the EER, were instrumental in fostering a new more rational economic development.

Since the second liberalization episode was essentially only a change in the form of protection it could not be expected to have a dramatic effect on economic performance. The third episode, however, during which protection levels were reduced, was accompanied by an overall economic performance which seems puzzling: the period of greatest liberalization was one of poor macroeconomic performance. This may lead to two inferences: first, that the basic assumption may be mistaken, or second, that liberalization was in fact rather insignificant. Both inferences are inappropriate, in our judgment.

From 1969 the reduction both in protection levels and in anti-export bias was significant. These measures could be expected to increase efficiency, but certainly not without a period of adjustment. From 1973 the entire economic situation of Israel changed: war, tremendous increases in defense expenditures, the oil crises, domestic inflation, and worldwide recession. These forces swamped the influence of liberalization on overall economic performance, both shorter-run negative and longer-run positive influences. Furthermore, the liberalization was restricted to the industrial sector. As late as 1965 industrial product was less than a quarter of total NDP, with trade, finance, and private and public services accounting for half of product. Thus the influences of liberalization on the industrial sector, both negative and positive, could not be expected to be properly reflected in overall performance.

An examination of the data on industrial composition and growth, however, (as in chapter 8) certainly supports the idea that liberalization led to greater efficiency, relative to what would have happened under the same circumstances in the absence of liberalization. The estimates of welfare gains (summarized in table 8.15), though substantial, may be deemed unacceptable because of the questionable assumptions on which they are based. However, the findings that (a) reduced anti-export bias led to greater export growth, coupled with (b) the fact that the growth of industrial exports, though insufficient to pull the entire economy to levels of rapid overall growth rates, was much higher than the average growth rates are strong evidence that the liberalization of 1969–77 did indeed have definite positive effects.

The process of liberalization is not as yet complete; toward the end of the 1980s a final stage of trade liberalization is due to take place in accordance with the free-trade area agreements. The conclusions regarding the effects of liberalization in the years covered by this study support the cause of further liberalization.

References

Bahral, U. (1965) *The Effects of Mass Immigration on Wages in Israel*. Jerusalem: Falk Project.

Bank of Israel *Annual Report*, various issues.

Barkai, Haim (1964) "The public, Histadrut and private sectors in the Israeli economy." In *The Falk Institute Sixth Annual Report, 1961–1963*. Jerusalem: Falk Institute.

Barkai, Haim and Michael Michaely (1963) "The new economic policy after one year" (in Hebrew). *Economic Quarterly*, March–August, 23–37.

Bar-Nathan, M. and Joseph Baruh (1986) "Determinants of the Tariff Structure of the Israeli Industrial Sector 1965–1977," Bank of Israel Research Department, Jerusalem (forthcoming in *Journal of Development Economics*).

Baruh, Joseph (1976) *The Structure of Protection in Israel, 1965 and 1968*. Jerusalem: Bank of Israel Research Department.

Baruh, Joseph (1979) "Protection levels in Israel, 1968 and 1972–1974." *Bank of Israel Economic Review*, nos 45–6, 1–22.

Baruh, Joseph (1980) "The new economic policy and protection levels on industrial import substitutes and exports." *Bank of Israel Economic Review*, nos 48–9, 84–91.

Baruh, Joseph (1986) "Factor proportions in Israel's trade in manufactures, 1965–1980." Jerusalem: Bank of Israel Research Department, Discussion Paper 83.11, in *Journal of Development Economics*, 24 (1988), 131–9.

Beham, M. (1968) *Monetary Aspects of the 1962 Devaluation*. Jerusalem: Falk Institute.

Beham, M. and Epharaim Kleiman (1968) "The cost of a slowdown" (in Hebrew). *Quarterly Banking Review*, 29, 31–42.

Ben-Horin, M. (1972) "The effect of the slowdown on exports" (in Hebrew). In Nadav Halevi and Michael Michaely, eds, *Studies in Israel's Foreign Trade*. Jerusalem: Falk Institute.

Ben-Porath, Yoram (1985) "Changes and ethnic diversity in population and the labor force." Jerusalem: Falk Institute, Discussion Paper 85.02.

Ben-Porath, Yoram, ed. (1986) *The Economy of Israel: Maturing Through Crises*. Cambridge, MA: Harvard University Press.

Ben-Shahar, Haim (1965) *Interest Rates and the Cost of Capital in Israel, 1950–1962*. Basel and Tubingen: Kyklos Verlag and J. C. B. Mohr.

Ben-Shahar, Haim, S. Bronfeld and A. Cukierman (1971) "The capital market in Israel." In P. Uri, ed., *Israel and the Common Market*. Jerusalem: Weidenfeld and Nicholson.

* Berglas, Eitan (1983) "Defense and the economy: the Israeli experience." Jerusalem: Falk Institute, Discussion Paper 83.01.

Blum, Leora (1983) "Israel's demand function for imports of goods, 1968–1976." *Bank of Israel Economic Review*, 55.

Bruno, Michael (1962) "Interdependence, resource use and structural change in Israel." Jerusalem: Bank of Israel Research Department, Special Studies No. 2.

* Bruno, Michael (1984) "External shocks and domestic responses: macroeconomic performance, 1968–1982." Jerusalem: Falk Institute, Discussion Paper 84.01.

CBS (Central Bureau of Statistics), *Gross Domestic Capital Formation in Israel, 1950–1978*. Special Series, no. 635.

CBS (Central Bureau of Statistics), *Monthly Bulletin of Statistics*, various issues.

CBS (Central Bureau of Statistics), *Statistical Abstract of Israel*, various issues.

Chenery, Hollis Burnley (1983) "Interaction between theory and observations in development." *World Development*, 11, 853–61.

Citron, Z. and A. Kessler (1958) "Investment in manufacturing made through the investment center." Jerusalem: Falk Project, Research Paper no. 2.

Cukierman, Alex and Assaf Razin (1976) "The reciprocal relationship between exchange rate policy and exports and imports" (in Hebrew). In Nadav Halevi and Yaccov Kop, eds, *Israel Economic Papers*. Jerusalem: Falk Institute.

Fishelson, Gideon, Arye L. Hillman, and Zeev Hirsch (1979) "The economic integration of Israel in the EEC: the factor content of Israel's trade in a multilateral setting." The David Horowitz Institution for Research of Developing Countries, Paper no. 2/79.

Gaathon, Arie Ludwig (1959) *"Survey of Israel's economy in 1951."* Jerusalem: Arie Ludwig, Central Bureau of Statistics, Technical Paper no. 1

Gaathon, Arie Ludwig (1961) *Capital Stock, Employment and Output in Israel, 1950–1959*, Jerusalem: Bank of Israel Research Department.

Gaathon, Arie Ludwig (1971) *Productivity in Israel*. New York: Praeger.

Gafni, Arnon, Nadav Halevi, and Giora Hanoch (1963) "Classification of tariffs by function." *Kyklos* 16(2), 303–18.

Genihowski, Dov (1965) "The first decade of Bank of Israel" (in Hebrew). *Economic Quarterly*, 44, 329–40.

Gottlieb, S. (1957) "Government subsidies in Israel: 1954 and 1955." In *Falk Project Third Annual Report 1956*. Jerusalem: Falk Project.

Halevi, Nadav (1956) *Estimates of Israel's International Transactions: 1952–1954*. Jerusalem: Falk Project.

Halevi, Nadav (1971) "Exchange control in Israel." In P. Uri, ed., *Israel and the Common Market*. Jerusalem: Weidenfeld and Nicholson, pp. 29–65.

Halevi, Nadav (1972) "Devaluation, relative prices and exports in Israel" (in Hebrew). In Nadav Halevi and Michael Michaely, ed. *Studies in Israel's Foreign Trade*. Jerusalem: Falk Institute. (An English version appeared in *Economica*, August 1972.)

Halevi, Nadav (1979) "The exchange rate in Israel: policy and opinion." *Revue Economique*, 30 (1), 10–30.

Halevi, Nadav (1983a) "The political economy of absorptive capacity: growth and cycles in Jewish Palestine under the British mandate." *Middle Eastern Studies*, 19 (4), October, 456–69.

* Halevi, Nadav (1983b) "The structure and development of Israel's balance of payments." Jerusalem: Falk Institute, Discussion Paper 83.02.

Halevi, Nadav and Joseph Baruh (1988) "The Timing and Sequencing of Trade Liberalization Policy: Israel, Statistical Appendix." Available from the Brazil Department, World Bank, Washington, DC.

Halevi, Nadav and Ruth Klinov-Malul (1968) *The Economic Development of Israel*. Jerusalem and New York: Bank of Israel and Praeger.

Hanoch, Giora (1961) "Income differentials in Israel." *Falk Project Fifth Report 1959 and 1960*. Jerusalem: Falk Project.

Heth, Meir (1966) *Banking Institutions in Israel*. Jerusalem: Falk Institute.

Hovne, A. (1961) *The Labor Force in Israel*. Jerusalem: Falk Project.

Israel Economist, October 1953, p. 213.

The Jerusalem Post, February 18, 1952; April 8, 1952; April 18, 1952.

Johnson, Harry Gordon (1969) "The theory of effective protection and preferences." *Economica, New Series*, 36, (142), May, 119–38.

* Klinov, R. (1984) "Israel's changing industrial structure: years of growth and years of slowdown." Jerusalem: Falk Institute, Discussion Paper 84.10.

Landsberger, M. (1963) "Changes in the consumer price indices of different income, origin, and family-size groups, 1954–62." *Bank of Israel Bulletin*, 19, 64–74.

Liviatan, O. (1982) "Estimation of the extent of Israel's balance of payments problems" (in Hebrew). *Economic Quarterly*, 112, 12–24.

* Mayshar, J. (1984) "Investment patterns in Israel." Jerusalem: Falk Institute, Discussion Paper 84.07.

Metzer, J. (1982) "Fiscal incidence and resource transfer between Jews and Arabs in mandatory Palestine." *Research in Economic History*, 7, 87–132.

* Metzer, J. (1983) "The slowdown of economic growth: a passing phase or the end of the big spurt?" Jerusalem: Falk Institute, Discussion Paper 83.03.

Michaely, M. (1963) *Foreign Trade and Capital Imports in Israel* (in Hebrew). Tel Aviv: Am Oved.

Michaely, M. (1971) *Israel's Foreign Exchange Rate System*. Jerusalem: Falk Institute.

Michaely, M. (1975) *Foreign Trade Regimes and Economic Development in Israel*. New York: National Bureau of Economic Research.

Ofer, G. (1967) *The Service Industries in a Developing Economy: Israel as a Case Study*. Jerusalem and New York: Praeger and Bank of Israel.

Ofer, G. (1976) "A cross-country comparison of industrial structure" (in Hebrew). Nadev Halevi and Yaccov Kop, eds, *Issues in the Economy of Israel*. Jerusalem: Falk Institute and Israel Economic Association.

Pack, H. (1971) *Structural Change and Economic Policy in Israel*. New Haven, CT: Yale University Press.

Patinkin, D. (1956) "Monetary and price developments in Israel: 1949–53." In Roberto Bachi, ed., *Scripta Hierosolymitana*, Vol. III: *Studies in Economic and Social Sciences*. Jerusalem: The Magnes Press, pp. 20–52.

Patinkin, D. (1967) *The Israel Economy: The First Decade*. Jerusalem: Falk Institute.

Pelzman, J. (1985) "The impact of the US–Israel free trade area agreement on Israeli trade and employment." Jerusalem: Falk Institute, Discussion Paper 85.08.

Pines, D. (1963) *Direct Export Premiums in Israel: 1952–1958* (in Hebrew). Jerusalem: Falk Project.

Pomfret, R. W. J. (1984) "Main economic trends in EC–Israel economic relations since the creation of the common market." Paper presented at International Conference in Israel, May.

Rubner, A. (1961) *The Economy of Israel*. London: Frank Cass.

Sicron, M. (1957) *Immigration to Israel*. Jerusalem: Falk Project and CBS.

Sokoler, M. (1984) "The inflation tax on the monetary base, the inflation subsidy implicit in cheap credit and their effects on the inflationary process in Israel." Jerusalem: Bank of Israel Research Department, Discussion Paper 84.05.

Stern, R. M., A. V. Deardoff, and C. R. Shiells (1982) *Estimates of the Elasticities of Substitution Between Imports and Home Goods for the US*, Washington, DC: US Department of Labor, Office of Economic Research.

* Syrquin, M. (1984) "Economic growth and structural change: an international perspective." Jerusalem: Falk Institute, Discussion Paper 84.08.

Teubal, M., N. Halevi, and D. Tsiddon (1986) "Learning and the rise of Israel's exports of sophisticated products." *World Development*, 14 (11), 1397–1410.

Toren, B. (1973) *The Effects of the Free Trade Area Agreement with the EC on Manufacturing Products* (in Hebrew). Jerusalem: World Institute.

Toren, B. (1976) *The Redeployment of Manufacturing as a Result of Formation of the Free Trade Area with the EC* (in Hebrew). Jerusalem: Van Leer Institute.

Tov, I. (1972) "The exposure of Israel's domestic production to import competition: 1962–1967" (in Hebrew). In Nadav Halevi and Michael Michaely, eds, *Studies in Israel's Foreign Trade*. Jerusalem: Falk Institute.

Weinblatt, J. (1972) "The effects of the effective exchange rate on imports: 1950–1969" (in Hebrew). In Nadav Halevi and Michael Michaely, eds, *Studies in Israel's Foreign Trade*. Jerusalem: Falk Institute.

Weiss, U. (1964) "Price control in Israel, 1939–1963" (in Hebrew). M. A. thesis, The Hebrew University of Jerusalem (unpublished). (Condensed English version published in *Bank of Israel Economic Review*, 37, March 1971.)

Yashiv, E. (1985) "The effects of import liberalization on employment in Israel's manufacturing, 1962–1979" (in Hebrew). Unpublished Hebrew University Seminar Paper, Jerusalem.

Zanbar, M., and S. Bronfeld (1973) "Monetary Thinking, Policy and Development, 1948–1972" (in Hebrew). *Economic Quarterly*, 77, 3–16.

* Versions of these papers appeared as chapters in Ben-Porath (1986).

Part II

Yugoslavia

Oli Havrylyshyn
George Washington University
Washington, D.C.

Contents

List of Figures

List of Tables

Acknowledgments

This study was funded and supported by the World Bank under its project "The Timing and Sequencing of Trade Liberalization Policies: RPO 67331" (see the Preface to the volume). I am grateful for this support and for the invaluable guidance provided by Armeane M. Choksi, Michael Michaely, and Demetris Papageorgiou, the coordinators of the project. While often provocative, their suggestions were always helpful and finally never obtrusive. Two colleagues in Yugoslavia were especially helpful: Vladimir Pertot with his deep and learned insights, and Lojse Socan who with his staff willingly provided volumes of information for the study. I am also grateful for comments from all the project participants, in particular those with explicit comments at various meetings: Mario Blejer, Charles Blitzer, Tercan Baysan, Jacob Frenkel, George C. Kottis, Mark M. Pitt, and Martin Wolf. Able research assistance was provided by Ken Cobb and Nidal Shaar and priceless typing efficiency was forthcoming from Loretta Alessandrini. I wish to thank Mme Muggerli of Chesières, Switzerland, for every morning's fresh ham, cheese, and encouraging smiling, all of which imparted to the arduous task of writing a sustaining measure of enjoyment. Finally, I thank my wife, Tamara, and our children, Alexandra and Andre, for their patience and encouragement during the research and writing of this work.

1

Introduction

The Yugoslav economic experiment has attracted many observers with theoretical as well as policy interests. Attention has been primarily directed to the unique middle-of-the-road approach of workers' management, intended to combine the efficiency advantages of capitalist profit incentives and the equity advantages of socialist ownership. However, another important economic experiment took place in Yugoslavia in the mid-1960s: an attempt to liberalize trade relations. The objectives were increased international competitiveness, balance-of-payments stability, and full convertibility of the dinar. At that time Yugoslavia had a considerable and typical array of trade intervention policies; hence its experiment with trade liberalization may provide some lessons for policy-making in developing countries today. In this study we aim to analyze the trade liberalization experiment, and to draw from it some inferences for trade policy in developing countries.

After World War II, the Yugoslav economy was modeled closely on Soviet central planning, which included a state trading monopoly. With its break from the Soviet camp in 1948 and the consequent "turning to the West," trade policy became increasingly more liberal. However, it was not until the 1960s that a major reform of the trade regime took place. A unification of the exchange rate and the establishment of a tariff regime in 1961–2 allowed Yugoslavia associate member status in the General Agreement on Tariffs and Trade (GATT) and set the stage for the true liberalization steps taken in 1965–7. These steps consisted of reductions in tariffs, quotas, and restrictions, a realignment of domestically controlled prices, removal of export subsidies, and a concomitant devaluation of the dinar.

The opening up of the economy was part of a general economic reform aimed at greater liberalization of economic decision-making power and increased influence of market forces. The reform was to achieve greater productive efficiency and full implementation of workers' self-management principles. Most observers agree that the reform was in general not successful; nor indeed was the trade liberalization. The changes in trade policy which were to be implemented over five to ten years soon began to be modified, reversed, or postponed. While the trading regime of the late 1970s was certainly more open than that of the 1950s or early 1960s, this period saw a series of revivals and reversals in which liberalization made limited progress. Perhaps the clearest sign that the experiment was largely unsuccessful was the introduction in 1983 of another broadly similar reform known as the Economic Stabilization Program. The focus of this study is on the earlier experiments before the 1980s, particularly the major episode of trade liberalization of 1965–7 and its first reversals in 1967–70.

The Methodological Approach

As one of a series of studies of related countries (see the Preface to this volume), the present work may contribute to a better understanding of the policy problems attendant on trade liberalization in two ways. First, it provides, in a systematic format, information on the economic background, the trade liberalization measures, and the performance of the economy, thus facilitating cross-country comparisons which may lead to some generalized lessons for policymaking. Second, the more detailed analysis specific to a single country permits us to make judgments in the context of a full local background.

The general purpose of this series of country studies is to draw lessons for policy from actual trade liberalization experience in developing countries. Common themes are the timing of liberalization, its extent and duration, its relation to other economic policies (especially macrostabilization), its economic and sociopolitical impacts, and finally, of course, the reactions to these impacts which determined the continuation or curtailment of the liberalization process. The broad nature of these objectives, as well as the strongly policy-oriented approach they dictate, means that the analysis puts more emphasis on political economy than is typical of present-day economic research, characterized as it is by theoretical and quantitative rigor. This "softer" approach has made the task of the researcher (and reader) both easier and harder – exactly in the sense that outside economics the word "softer" has both a pejorative and a commendable connotation. It is pejorative to the extent that it implies lack of rigor, and permits the researcher to use quantitative precision when it works well and to ignore it otherwise. The commendable connotation of "softer" (subtler, more sensitive to nuances) implies here that the research task is neither bound by statistical-probabilistic rigor nor precluded from investigating important but unquantifiable phenomena.[1]

Yugoslavia's Uniqueness and Similarity

So much for the methodological approach. Given the study's role as a link in a chain of comparable studies, it also seems useful to note briefly the uniqueness of Yugoslavia on the one hand and its similarity to other developing countries on the other.

First, we consider its singularity. While many countries are described as a crossroads between cultures or continents, Yugoslavia is plainly unique in being in the middle of several spectra. Its political and economic institutions cover the middle ground between the capitalist market-oriented and Soviet-style socialist economies. Yugoslavia's stage of economic development puts it midway between industrialized and developing countries. Its progress in economic development, while enough to merit inclusion in the newly industrialized countries (NICs) club, has been (especially of late) far less impressive than that of the East Asian miracles, though probably a little better than that of some Latin American countries. Finally, its historical and cultural legacy is a mix of eastern (Turkish) and western (Austrian and Italian) colonial status, and eastern and western religious affiliations (Muslim and Orthodox Christian on the one hand, and Catholic on the other). The mixture manifests itself today in, among other things, a great regional diversity: several republics in a federal state, a number of different ethnic groups and religions, and several distinct, albeit related, languages.

This great diversity, which has been glued together into a demonstrably functioning polity, gives rise to fluidity in perceptions, philosophy and ideology, and, of course, institutions. While critics see in this fluidity a persistent "identity crisis," sympathizers consider it a reflection of the dynamism of a society seeking ever better ways to organize itself. The central phenomenon in which this fluidity is observed is the system of economic decision making. In the central-planning period, enterprises simply acted as in the Soviet economy. The political break in 1948 occasioned rethinking of economic institutions, and in 1952 the new era of self-management was proclaimed. Workers, rather than the state or a capitalist, now owned and controlled their enterprise. Each enterprise

---

[1] The paradox of easier and harder economics is captured in the (apocryphal) story of the reasons Whitehead and Planck are said to have given for not studying economics. The former, finding the level of mathematics (then very limited) extremely crude for a mathematician, said economics was too easy. The latter, finding himself perplexed by the irregularities of real-life human behavior, said that economics was too hard compared with physics.

acted in the open market; hence a worker had the same incentive to maximize profits as a capitalist. However, owing to the inadequate implementation of this system, the power of the workers tended to pass into the hands of a managerial–administrative elite operating both inside the enterprises and in the remaining governmental power centers. A major reform of the system aimed at decentralizing decision making was consequently undertaken in 1975 by the Communist leadership. This time indiscipline by workers' councils, manifested in excessive wages and poor investments, was blamed for economic deterioration, and yet another set of general reforms was needed in the 1970s.

In short, the recent history of Yugoslavia is checkered with social experimentation. In this context, trade liberalization was influenced by three forces. First, one of the many polarities of the society was the split, fostered by the intellectual and historical background, between etatist and more market-oriented ideologues. Second, trade liberalization, as the opposite of state-regulated trade, is inherently a candidate for experimentation, given Yugoslavia's penchant for being different from others and even different from its previous self. Third, economic liberalization policies happened to coincide with the nationalist regional autonomy objectives of certain groups and thus to be politically expedient (Rusinow, 1977, ch. 5).

Such characteristics are relatively unique, but equally Yugoslavia's economy shows many fundamental similarities to those of other developing countries. First, with few exceptions, all developing countries are on a "capitalist–socialist" spectrum: essentially mixed economies embodying a market mechanism modified by considerable government intervention. More specifically, since the mid-1950s the bulk of Yugoslav trade has *not* been in the form of balanced bilateral exchange, as in most socialist countries; the near automaticity of imports and exports has been replaced by a situation common to developing countries – the potential for chronic balance-of-payments deficits. As in many other countries studied, these have played an important double role in trade liberalization; often one reason to attempt liberalization was a worsening external deficit but, just as often, the inability to ameliorate this deficit contributed to a reversal of trade liberalization.

As in most developing countries, most trading is done by individual enterprises and not by a state trading agency. However, this autonomy is subject to various government regulations such as tariffs, quotas, foreign exchange allocation, and the like, with the important result that there exists in Yugoslavia, as in other developing countries (but *not* in centrally planned economies), a large "market" for political economy privileges.

Yugoslavia's unique system of workers' management has been widely analyzed by economists, both Yugoslav and "Western." A principal, though not universal, contention has been that such a system, with profit maximization per worker and no portability of asset shares, restricts the mobility of both labor and capital. As resource reallocation is clearly central to the success of trade liberalization, this characteristic would seem to make Yugoslavia very different from other countries. However, such a view exaggerates factor immobility in Yugoslavia and mobility elsewhere. For one thing, most resource reallocation tends, in practice, to occur at the growth margin. For another, a more important issue than factor mobility turns out to have been something very similar to that found in many developing countries – a "soft budget" for weak enterprises, be they public or private. That is, a typical government response to the difficulties of weak enterprises or sectors has been to supply budgetary support, in the name of conserving jobs, rather than to introduce mechanisms to ease mobility and adjustment. The independence of Yugoslav enterprises has in this respect been neither greater nor smaller than those of other developing mixed economies.

The complementary effect of macrostabilization policies during episodes of trade liberalization has been a recurrent theme in this series of studies; it is so also for Yugoslavia. Since the inception of workers' management in the 1950s, stabilization tools comprised much the same fiscal and monetary elements as elsewhere.[2] A specific example is the similarity of the Yugoslavian experience to that of many Latin American countries in the late 1970s, where attempts at liberalization were evident in a period of high inflation (unmanageable external deficits) and large public deficits. These circumstances necessitated a deflationary policy, which made short-run adjustment to any disemployment caused by trade liberalization all the more difficult. In Yugoslavia's major attempt at liberalization in 1965, a deflationary policy was followed for much the same reasons, although the magnitudes of inflation and external and public deficit were far less dramatic. Another element common to many of the case studies is the external influence of international institutions (especially the International Monetary Fund (IMF) and the World Bank).

Most country studies of liberalization have emphasized exchange rate adjustments. Unlike the centrally planned socialist economies, and more like the mixed economies of the developing world, Yugoslavia's policy on exchange rates can best be characterized as irregular lagged adjustments of official exchange rates. (In the late 1970s, adjustment became more regularly related to inflation, as in many other developing countries.) Since bilateral state trading has not been used to force external balance, exchange rates have mattered. Any unfavorable movement of the real

---

[2] With the surprising peculiarity that, in this socialist country, fiscal tools have been largely lost by federalist devolution of powers and macromanagement has relied far more on monetary policy. This is more fully described in chapter 6.

exchange rate for extended periods (as happened in the period after liberalization) obstructed the success of trade liberalization, reducing exports and increasing imports. However, the inability to close these external gaps through state trading also meant that the exchange rate eventually had to be readjusted. In such cases (as happened at the outset of the liberalization efforts) the exchange rate policy could enhance the trade liberalization objectives by increasing exports, thus reducing the scarcity value of restricted imports.

Finally, we should note a fundamental similarity between industrialization policies in Yugoslavia and other developing countries in both orientation and the types of tools used. Infant industry attitudes, by no means unknown in the socialist world, were, if anything, fostered by security arguments. Nor was the Yugoslav historical background lacking in such attitudes; the etatism typical of both the Ottoman and Austrian empires was far more prominent in the *Weltanschauung* of the intelligentsia than was Anglo-Saxon liberalism. The early central-planning period (mid-1940s to mid-1950s) was characterized by forced Soviet industrialization with the establishment at high cost of many heavy industries such as steel, chemicals, machinery, shipbuilding, and vehicles. Thus by the 1960s the industrial structure was largely indistinguishable from that seen in many other developing countries pursuing industrialization.

From the mid-1950s even the policy tools used in Yugoslavia began to resemble those of other developing countries, as central planning was replaced by a range of indirect incentives including government funding, tax incentives, sector discrimination, import restrictions, and export incentives. One example among many was the widespread use of export subsidies for industries such as shipbuilding and machinery. The dismantling, or at least judicious rearrangement, of such a package of policy measures has in all countries been the "brass tacks" of trade liberalization.

In conclusion, despite Yugoslavia's unique socialist character, it is important to emphasize the many points of similarity in the *mechanisms* of economic policy. Thus Yugoslavia is like other developing countries not merely because it has been undergoing structural change and may have developed a somewhat distorted pattern of resource allotment, nor only because its problems of balance of payments, debt, inflation, and lack of adjustment flexibility resembles those in other countries. What is most important in drawing lessons from the Yugoslav experience for other countries is that many of the mechanisms of the economy – stabilization policy tools, governmental support for enterprises, import restrictions, export incentives, exchange rate adjustments, and so on – are quite similar.

Perhaps it comes down to the following simple points. On the one hand Yugoslavia, while socialist in one sense – at the level of enterprise decisions – is not socialist in another sense – the use of strong central planning. The government policy must take the forms common in mixed economies: fiscal, monetary, and trade policies. On the other hand, many developing countries of a mixed-economy type are characterized by considerable public ownership at the enterprise level, or at least considerable dependence by private enterprise upon direct and indirect public support. Thus Yugoslavia and most developing countries converge within some middle ground of economic policy.

Plan of the Study

This study is divided into five parts. An overview and a descriptive background are provided in chapters 1–3, the steps taken to liberalize trade in the post-war period are recounted in chapters 4–6, and the evolution of the economy during the major liberalization episode of 1965–70 is described in chapters 7–9. In chapters 10–12 an attempt is made to evaluate the effects of trade liberalization upon the economy, and finally in chapters 13 and 14 the conclusions of the analysis for Yugoslavia are summarized and the policy lessons that can be drawn from the Yugoslav experience are indicated.

Considerable overlapping of issues and repetition in different chapters is inevitable, because the economic phenomena studied are interrelated over time and hence there is no natural compartmentalization. To tell the story chronologically in full statistical-analytical detail would be prolix and even, perhaps, impossible in view of the circular cause and effect between trade liberalization and economic performance. The interplay was complex, both in the circularity of economic relations and in the dynamics of time effects. Hence any structure of the study would necessarily involve some repetition to insure coherence in each part of the story.

2

The Yugoslav Economy

Evolution and Structural Change, 1950–1975

Long-term Performance

In the three and a half decades since Yugoslavia broke with the Soviet bloc and embarked on its unique road to a westward-looking socialism, its economic performance has been impressive (tables 2.1 and 2.2). The gross domestic product (GDP) grew at rates of well over 6 percent until 1965 and

Table 2.1 Basic indicators of Yugoslav economic performance, 1952–1983 (percent)

Annual growth of selected indicators	1952–9	1960–4	1965–9	1970–82
GDP	6.7	6.2	4.8	5.5
Consumption	4.8	4.7	6.3	5.2
Gross fixed investment	9.7	7.5	6.3	8.2
Exports (goods and services)	12.5	12.0	8.2	11.1
Imports (goods and services)	8.4	8.3	11.7	9.8
Cost of living	6.4	13.7	11.4	20.0

Sources: Dubey, 1975; World Bank, 1983; Federal Institute of Statistics, *Statistical Yearbook of Yugoslavia*, various issues

continued to grow thereafter at abated, but nevertheless creditable, rates of about 5 percent. With a sharp decline in population growth to less than 1 percent by 1970, this has meant a substantial increase in per capita income and hence in living standards. Though Yugoslavia is still a "poor" country on the periphery of Europe, just as it was before World War II, the absolute gains and structural changes undeniably transformed it from a backward agricultural economy to an industrial country ranking in the upper middle income range of the developing world. With a per capita

Table 2.2 Structural indicators for Yugoslavia (percentage share)

Share of selected structural indicators	1952	1960	1965	1970	1982
Investment in GDP	22.0	30.6	34.7	32.8	29.8
Agriculture in GDP	37.9	29.8	23.8	20.7	13.0
Manufacturing in GDP	16.3	24.5	30.2	32.2	32.0
Labor force in agriculture	68.3	56.3	n.a.	48.0	29.0
Urban population	22.0	28.0	n.a.	35.0	44.0
Manufactured exports	n.a.	37.0	n.a.	n.a.	80.0
Current account (% GDP)	− 4.0	− 3.3	0.7	− 5.9	− 4.5
Population growth (% per annum)	1/6	1.4	1.2	0.9	0.8

n.a., not available.
Sources: Dubey, 1985; World Bank, 1983; Federal Institute of Statistics, *Statistical Yearbook of Yugoslavia*, various issues

income of US$2,800 in 1982, it is well below the leading developing countries (Singapore, Hong Kong, Israel, and Greece) but above many newly industrialized countries (Argentina, Portugal, Mexico, Brazil, and even South Korea) and of course far above the levels of most developing countries in Asia, Africa, and Latin America.

The most remarkable point about GDP growth is the sharp slowdown in the years 1965–9, coinciding with the implementation of trade liberalization. Although the inference that trade liberalization was the cause is shown to be fallacious, the reality of cause and effect may not have mattered as much as the perceptions. Indeed, the sharp slowdown – including nearly two years of employment decline in industry – was pivotal in the decision to reverse liberalization. In chapter 8 we explain how other policies resulted in poor performance. The crucial connection between trade and macro policies is a principal theme of this study.

Further, before 1965, consumption growth was much lower than that of gross national product (GNP) while in 1965–9 the reverse was true. However, gross fixed investment continued to grow more quickly than GDP. Closer analysis in chapters 7–9 will elaborate on this, but the main lines of the explanation are worth noting here. The greater freedom of workers to make decisions after 1965 resulted in a surge of wages and consumption, but investment volume remained high because the lower savings of enterprises were balanced by increased bank financing. Unfortunately, this was too often done with inadequate financial discipline, and poor investments contributed to later weaknesses of the economy.

On the trade side, three broad tendencies stand out. First, with exports and imports growing far more rapidly than GDP, the economy was clearly becoming more open and trade oriented. Second, while before the trade liberalization year of 1965 export growth was higher than import growth, this was reversed after 1965. Third, the current account deficit, which had been declining as a percentage of GDP from 1952 to 1965, worsened continuously thereafter.

Finally, prices increased steadily over the three and a half decades. The magnitudes were not high in the 1960s, but this was in general not a decade known for inflation. The issue of macro policy *vis-à-vis* inflation is a key issue in this study. Whether inflation rates of just over 10 percent were a real problem for the economy or not, policymakers in Yugoslavia clearly thought them so and took strong monetary restrictive measures to control inflation. The consequent deflationary impact on the economy occurred in conjunction with trade liberalization and, as shown in chapters 7–9, contributed a great deal to its reversal.

Returning to the country's rapid growth in the long run, it seems evident that this was fed by a high rate of investment (over 30 percent of GDP before 1965, and only slightly less afterwards) and a shift of resources from agricultural to industrial activities. Agriculture employed 68.3 percent of the labor force in 1952 and contributed 37.9 percent to value added. By 1970, only 48 percent of labor remained in this sector, which produced only 20.7 percent of GDP. The importance of the agricultural sector continued to decline after 1970. Manufacturing (excluding construction) asserted itself very early with 24.5 percent of GDP in 1960, reaching by the 1970s levels at which international experience shows it tends to peak, 33–5 percent. The same dramatic structural transformation is visible in exports, 37 percent of which were manufactures as early as 1960, with that figure reaching 80 percent by 1982.

Urbanization proceeded (perhaps fortunately) at a less dramatic pace. In the early 1950s, about a fifth of the population (22 percent) was urbanized; this doubled to 44 percent in 1982, still well below the rates found in many developing countries (61 percent in South Korea, 69 percent in Brazil and 82 percent in Chile). This share of urbanized population, plus the socialist regime's inclination to offer widespread social services at low cost and, of course, the fact of "socialist" ownership of capital, have meant that living conditions and their distribution may be somewhat better than the per capita income comparisons would indicate. Thus, for example, life expectancy is 71 years compared with 65 years for all upper middle income countries (1982 GDP per capita US$1,600–6,000), infant mortality is 34 per 1,000 (cf. 58), the daily calorie supply is 1,440 (cf. 117), the population per physician is 550 (cf. 2,021; the average for industrial economies is only 554!), the enrollment ratios are 83 for secondary and 22 for higher education (cf. 51 and 14), and the income share of the poorest 20 percent is 66 percent – higher than any country in the comparable group (World Bank, 1984, data annex).

Population and Labor Force

Yugoslavia, a medium-sized country with a population of 17 million in 1953, already had a relatively low population growth, due in part to the huge gap in the population pyramid in the young adult groups, the result of enormous losses in World War II. The 50–64 age group constituted 18 percent of the labor force in 1953, and declined steadily thereafter. The natural rate of increase fell very steadily with development, especially in the more developed regions of the west and north. The continuing high rates of population growth in the south and east (Kosovo and, to a lesser extent, Macedonia and Bosnia-Herzegovina) reflect the problem of wide regional disparities of development.

Although employment creation has always been an important issue in Yugoslavia, population pressures have not been overwhelming by developing country norms. As a result of migration and declining participation rates owing to increased education, the growth in the labor force has been even lower than the population growth, ranging from about 0.8 percent in the 1950s to less than 0.7 percent in the 1970s. Migration abroad (guest workers in Europe) leapt from 100,000 in 1961 to about 900,000, or about 10 percent of the labor force, ten years later.[1]

Since economic activity outside agriculture is largely socialized in Yugoslavia, only a small portion (1 percent) of the labor force is in private nonagricultural activities. In agriculture, the opposite holds true, with private preponderating over socialized activity.

Regional Differences in Development

There were wide differences in per capita income between the poorest political unit of the Yugoslav federation (Kosovo) and the richest (Slovenia) (Havrylyshyn, 1988, appendix table 2.1). In fact the gap widened from 1955 to 1964 (just before the trade liberalization) and continued to widen in the subsequent decade. Since part of the 1965 reform involved reduced federal budgetary power, fewer direct transfers could be made to the poorer regions. Furthermore, trade liberalization was more likely to harm industries in poorer regions – at least at first – because these were generally far less efficient having been more often formed as an outcome of political expediency (Fisher, 1966, p. 9).

However, as chapter 8 demonstrates, while direct federal assistance for poorer regions did decline, indirect inflows (bank credit) permitted these regions to continue enjoying investment-to-GDP ratios far higher than

---

[1] *One* manifestation of Yugoslavia's uniqueness in the Socialist group is that it does not follow policies of closed border for its citizens.

those in developed regions. Furthermore, while output after liberalization declined more in the underdeveloped regions, employment declined less. The political economy pressures of job creation led to continued rapid growth of capacity (new investments) despite output tendencies.

Structural Changes

The principal structural changes of the domestic economy in 1950–75 were (a) rapid, but not necessarily efficient, industrialization, (b) a shift of the labor force out of agriculture, (c) moderate urbanization, (d) a decline in the role of activities based on natural resources, and (e) substantial upgrading of the education and skill levels of the labor force.

The broad outlines of these changes, which are presented in table 2.2, have already been discussed. Here, those aspects of structural changes most relevant to the issues of trade liberalization will be highlighted.

Industrialization: Not Necessarily Efficient

The share of manufacturing, which excludes the "industrial" activities of transport and construction, nearly doubled in the period 1952–65, so that on the eve of liberalization it was already 30.2 percent, close to the peak in cross-national comparison. This high share of activity, however, masked several underlying phenomena.[2] As has been documented in several studies (Pertot, 1972; Dubey, 1975; Chittle, 1977), the basic strategy of industrialization was import substitution. The resulting industrial capacity established by the high investment regimen was excessively oriented to large capital-intensive projects and, as in the Soviet economies, strongly weighted towards heavy capital goods industries rather than light consumer goods.

Furthermore, the use of quasi-centralist planning methods and the strong restrictions on imports had engendered poor quality and unsophisticated product lines. All in all, though an extensive manufacturing base had been established, it was ripe for rationalization of product quality, diversity, micro level productivity, and sectoral allocation. Reforms aimed at promoting a phase of "intensive growth" evolved out of this situation.

Labor Force in Agriculture: Continued Dualism

Given the high share of manufactures and the low share of agriculture in value added (30.2 and 23.8 percent respectively in 1965) and approximately 50 percent of the labor force in agriculture, it is clear that there was a continuing dualism in the economy. The simple output-to-labor ratio

---

[2] A technical point is that the controlled price structure for 1965 was biased in favor of manufactures and against agriculture; hence the 30.2 percent may be somewhat of an overestimate.

implied by these shares shows that in 1965 agricultural labor was less than half as "productive" as the economy average and about one fourth as productive as manufacturing. Although some of this low productivity reflects the statistical bias of underpriced agricultural output, much of it is a statement of the relative productivity of labor, skills, capitalization, and technological sophistication. In this respect Yugoslavia was not unlike many developing countries in transition.

Thus, despite rapid industrialization, about half the labor force was still employed in agriculture at the time of liberalization. There remained a substantial backlog of agricultural labor to be absorbed in the "modern" sector, whether industry or modernized agriculture. The employment goal, while less critical than in some countries because population growth was very low, nevertheless tended to overshadow the objective of liberalization.

Urbanization: Not an Intense Pressure Point
Typically, the structural imbalance of agriculture and labor is accompanied by an apparent imbalance between the rural and urban populations. Though pressures of rapid urban growth existed and were thought by Yugoslav policymakers to be important,[3] these were far less intense than in Latin America or even Asia. The rate of urbanization was much lower in Yugoslavia, and the distribution of urban population among cities was much more even. In 1960 only one city had over 500,000 inhabitants, and it contained only 11 percent of the population. Even in 1960 it was not uncommon for developing countries to have 20–50 percent of their population concentrated in the largest city. The relatively low degree of urbanization and continuing high ratio of agricultural labor – related but not identical phenomena – are attributed by Horvat (1976) to an extremely equitable distribution of land ownership, with a Gini coefficient of about 0.2. The importance of medium-sized cities and small towns is less easy to explain, though it may have a historical basis. Until World War I, Yugoslavia had been under three different political, and hence economic, regimes with limited transport and trading facilities. The rather broken terrain of mountains and rivers in all but the northeast Pannonian Plain made for economic fragmentation of regions and therefore encouraged the establishment of a large number of local urban centers.

Declining Role of Activities Based on Natural Resources
Yugoslavia is relatively well endowed with natural resources, not only in agriculture and fishing but also in forestry and mining. Before World War II only about 20 percent or less of exports were manufactures, about

---

[3] In the late 1960s the Belgrade authorities deliberated requiring "passports" to live in the city (Havrylyshyn, 1977).

40–50 percent were agricultural goods, and 15–20 percent were timber products, and by 1939 as much as 15 percent were minerals, almost entirely unprocessed beyond a concentrate stage (Pertot, 1971). Copper, lead, and zinc were the major minerals. While it was a "hewer of wood and drawer of water," Yugoslavia did not suffer from a high export concentration. In the late 1930s the three major products (timber, livestock, and wheat) accounted for only about one third of exports.

Industrialization after 1950 led to a marked decline in the importance of natural resources in the economy, with a clear shift to more processing in agriculture and mining (Havrylyshyn, 1988, appendix table 2.2). While agriculture's share of GNP declined sharply, the shares of food processing and metallurgy rose. The same phenomenon is seen in the employment share but not in exports. In the export sphere, food processing declined sharply and metallurgy was variable but unchanged between 1960 and 1975.

Although alternative explanations for these trends in export shares abound, it may be useful to consider some of the more prevalent. The sharp decline in agricultural goods and processed food is often attributed to protection in the European Economic Community (EEC) markets since the 1960s. An alternative explanation is that, even after the price readjustments of 1965, Yugoslavia maintained classical import substitution policies biased against agriculture.

Another hypothesis concerns raw material inputs in general. There is a perception in Yugoslavia that, since 1965, import dependence has increased, and that a structural imbalance exists between the output of finished products and the local production of raw materials and semi-finished inputs. The *ex post* measure of total import content in production shows an increase for every branch of production. Because the line between "dependence" and "increased integration" is not easy to discern, judgment as to whether this increase was a bad thing will be postponed. Import dependence is seen as having increased, and this is closely related to the view that production of raw materials as well as of semi-finished goods was lower than it might have been.

Increased Education
Finally, the fifth main structural shift took place in the area of education and skills. Students as a percentage of population increased from 12.4 percent in 1953 to 17.6 percent in 1961. By 1960, Yugoslavia's primary school enrollment was virtually 100 percent, for secondary schools it was 58 percent (compared with 20 percent for all upper middle income developing countries), and for higher education it was 9 percent (compared with 4 percent) (World Bank, 1984).

This educational dynamic is reflected in the skill composition of the labor force shown in table 2.3. A rapid and consistent upgrading of the

Table 2.3 Skill structure of employed in social sector (percentage of total)

Skill type	1957	1961	1965	1968	1970	1972
Nonprofessional	69.3	69.8	77.5	69.4	69.0	67.2
Unskilled	22.0	28.8	30.9	23.8	24.4	13.2
Semiskilled	16.7	12.5	14.8	13.4	12.7	14.8
Skilled	24.9	23.6	26.2	25.5	25.3	29.5
Highly skilled	5.7	4.9	5.6	6.7	6.6	9.7
Professional	30.4	29.9	22.5	30.6	31.0	32.8
Some training	13.0	14.4	9.0	8.9	7.9	4.2
Intermediate training	12.2	10.5	9.3	13.5	14.2	16.6
Higher training	5.2	5.0	1.6	3.3	3.8	5.3
Highest-level training			2.6	4.9	5.1	6.7

Source: Federal Institute of Statistics, *Statistical Yearbook of Yugoslavia*, various issues

employed labor force from less to more skilled categories took place, although in the period 1957–65 the number of unskilled workers increased substantially (from 22.0 to 30.9 percent); this increased the nonprofessional share compared with the professional share from 69.3 to 77.5 percent. While this is somewhat puzzling, it may turn out to be attributable to the stress laid on infrastructure and large industrial projects in the early 1950s and the shift to a somewhat more diversified industrial structure after about 1955.

In any event, the skill structure of labor was clearly considerably improved in the period before liberalization and continued to improve afterwards. Even as a general indicator of labor mobility, this suggests increased potential for structural adjustment, unless of course the skills developed were sector specific.

Trade and Balance of Payments

The major aggregate trends of exports and imports have been outlined earlier. The focus here will be on principal structural changes.

1 Yugoslav export shares in world trade rose until about 1965 and then declined.
2 The structure of exports shifted sharply away from agriculture and toward manufactured products.
3 The dependence of the economy on imports increased after liberalization.
4 The current account situation was reasonably stable in the 1950s but grew steadily worse after 1965, despite large increases in foreign exchange receipts from tourism and worker's remittances.

5 Trade with countries in the Council for Mutual Economic Aid (Comecon) fell sharply after the 1948 political break, but has since generally tended to increase – more slowly in periods of liberalization and more rapidly in restrictive periods.

The deterioration of world shares for Yugoslav exports after 1965 is indicated in figure 2.1. It is also described in several studies of Yugoslav

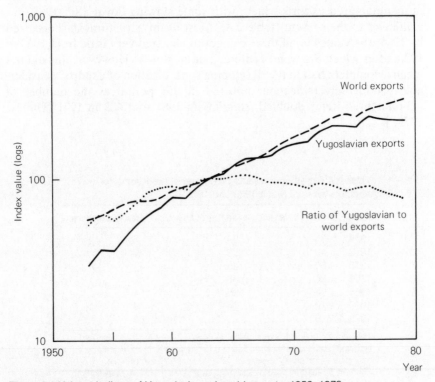

Figure 2.1 Volume indices of Yugoslavia and world exports, 1953–1979
Source: IMF, International Financial Statistics

export performance using constant-market-share analysis or other indicators. For example, Schrenk et al. (1979) estimate the percentage of export growth not explained by growth of the Yugoslav markets, which is sometimes called the competitive or residual effect. For 1961–5 this amounted to 59 percent of the growth of exports, while for 1965–70 and 1970–5 the residual was actually negative, with values of − 1 percent and − 8 percent respectively. Similar results were found by Chittle (1977) and in a World Bank study of exports (World Bank, 1980). Not all agree. For example, Dubey (1975, p. 280) suggests that the export performance for 1965–70 was not nearly as bad as it appears. While exports to all destinations grew more slowly than world imports (9.0 percent versus 10.2 percent), this reflected a particularly poor performance in developing country markets and hid a creditable performance in industrial countries. In those markets, Yugoslav exports increased their market share, growing at 15.4 percent compared with 12.0 percent for total imports. Yugoslavia even increased its market share in the EEC, despite increased protection of agricultural goods.

The second important structural tendency was the rapid rate of increase in manufactured exports which, with some slowing down after 1965, has continued to the present (table 2.4). Most of this structural shift occurred by 1965; the values in all three categories changed very little from 1965 to 1970, after which the trend continued more slowly. However, this did not mean a complete halt in the developing sophistication of exports: considerable product diversification occurred in this period as the number of manufactured items doubled from 737 in 1961 to 1,483 in 1971 (Dubey, 1975, p. 276).[4]

Table 2.4 Export composition by degree of processing for selected years between 1939 and 1975

Year	Raw materials	Semiprocessed	Highly processed
1939	35	39	6
1952	40	50	10
1955	36	45	17
1960	26	38	36
1965	14	35	51
1970	12	34	54
1975	9	28	63

The data for "manufacturers' share" in table 2.2 are based on Standard Industrial Trade Classification 5–9 and correspond to the third category here plus a portion of the second. They are not fully comparable.
Sources: Federal Institute of Statistics, Yugoslavia 1945–64; Statistical Yearbook of Yugoslavia, various issues

On the negative side, the capital goods share rose from 2.7 percent in 1954 to 18.3 percent in 1966 and then declined sharply to about 13–14 percent in 1975. This probably reflects the role of direct and indirect subsidies, which were considerable before 1965, sharply reduced with liberalization, and then reinstituted in the 1970s. Thus, while the share of capital goods exports was very high for a developing country, especially in the 1960s, it

[4] The calculations are redone at the seven-digit level of the Standard International Trade Classification (SITC).

reflected not only an increasing sophistication of manufactures production but also the use of "artificial" supports for exports.

On the import side, the only significant structural change is the increased share of raw materials and intermediate imports, which rose from 52 percent in 1954 to 64 percent in 1971 while the dependence upon imports for all raw material and intermediate imports increased from 12.0 percent in 1960 to 16.4 percent in 1971. Many Yugoslav analysts have noted this as a structural problem of excessive import dependence. However, a greater role of imports was surely to be expected when the economy was opened up, in particular after a period of relatively restricted trading.

Consider the much simpler macro indicators of trade orientation – import and export shares of GDP – given in table 2.5. The gradual opening up is evident, even during the period of regulated trading before 1965. The values after 1965 seem about normal for a country of Yugoslavia's size and per capita income. Chenery and Syrquin (1975) indicate that a country of 20 million should have an export ratio of about 20 percent. More to the point, it is evident from the figures that Yugoslavia was far below the norm before 1965.

Table 2.5 Trade orientation ratios 1950–1980 (selected years)

	1950	1955	1960	1965	1970	1975	1980
Exports (% GDP)	8.3	9.9	14.3	18.3	21.3	18.3	17.5
Imports (% GDP)	12.3	13.9	17.6	17.6	27.3	24.2	20.2

Source: Federal Institute of Statistics, Statistical Yearbook of Yugoslavia, various issues

However, the opening-up tendency does not explain the increased share of raw materials imports. Two hypotheses suggest themselves. First, the increases may be a typical effect of import substitution policies: reduced imports of final highly protected goods, but increased import requirements for less protected upstream products. Note that this share increased very slightly after 1965, most of the change occurring in the earlier period which is generally regarded as one of import substitution. As we will show in chapters 4–6, many of the import substitution biases that were reduced in 1965–7 were reintroduced after 1967; thus the effect of bad policy reasserted itself. The second hypothesis is more kind to policymakers: with industrialization, investment, and skill formation, Yugoslavia's comparative advantage progressed from natural resources to manufactures. However, this last possibility is inconsistent with the evidence of lagging export competitiveness (figure 2.1).

The phenomenal surge in the import ratio from 17.6 in 1965 to 27.2 in 1971 is especially noteworthy. While the indicators in table 2.6 show

Table 2.6 Indicators of import "dependence" (percent)

Indicator	1954	1960	1965	1971
Ratio of imports to GDP	14.1	17.6	17.6	27.2
Import content of gross output	n.a.	11.0	11.4	13.4
Share of raw materials and intermediates in imports	52	57	62	64
Share of imports in total use of raw materials and intermediates	n.a.	12.0	13.6	16.4

n.a., not available.
Source: Dubey, 1975, pp. 280–1

increases that may be altogether reasonable for an economy which is opening up, there was nevertheless cause for concern, especially since the increase on the export side was much smaller than for imports.

An increased flow of workers' remittances permitted a large and growing gap between imports and exports. However, by all accounts (see for instance OECD *Economic Surveys*; Dubey, 1975) remittances after 1968–9 were not enough to permit the continued widening of this gap, and a critical balance-of-payments pressure developed and persisted throughout the 1970s. Increasing recourse was made to foreign borrowing, including occasional IMF borrowing. From 1964 to 1972, Yugoslavia's debt rose by 18 percent a year, and from 14 to 29 percent of GDP; its structure shifted from long-term public loans toward short-term suppliers' credits. If the story sounds familiar, it is to be recalled that the years in question are the late 1960s, a decade before such trends became typical in most developing countries. The debt pressure on the balance of payments grew rapidly, with the debt service ratio rising from a modest 13.0 percent in 1966 (already higher than before) to a worrisome 18.0 percent by 1971. To some extent this underestimates the problem, since most of the debt was with the West in convertible currency, while a large part of export earnings was in nonconvertible currencies of the Comecon.

This brings us to the last major structural movement in foreign trade – the gradually increased share of trade (especially exports) with the Eastern bloc countries. Before Yugoslavia was expelled from the Communist bloc by Stalin in 1948, over half its trade was with the Soviet bloc (Havrylyshyn, 1988, appendix figure 2.1). This dropped immediately and sharply to virtually zero in the early 1950s, but by 1954 rose to approximately 23 percent in a balanced trade. Looking westward for funding, Yugoslavia continued to import proportionately more from the West and less from the Comecon in the period of its most rapid industrialization from the mid-1950s to 1961. While the import share fell to 19 percent, on the export side, in contrast, it rose to 32 percent. Since the mid-1950s, Yugoslavia has had a large surplus in its merchandise trade with the Eastern economies, but unfortunately this has been of little help to the balance of payments and debt servicing because of the convertibility problem.

While the pattern of these trade shares after 1961 is somewhat volatile, a moderate upward tendency is evident, especially for exports. Perhaps even more relevant to the liberalization issues, the shares declined sharply during the period of liberalization, 1965–70. In the case of imports this is not surprising: as restrictions were lifted on imports and on access to convertible currency financing (via bank or supplier credits arranged directly by purchasers), there was naturally a rush to buy from the West. However, exports also shifted to the West, suggesting some combination of the effects of devaluation and perhaps a rationalization of industries' ability to improve their export competitiveness in Western markets. When the reversals of liberalization came in the 1970s, trade shifted once again toward the Comecon. In the case of exports this was further pushed in 1974–5 by the OECD recession and the consequent retardation of these markets for Yugoslav exports. However, we should not underestimate the importance of political influences in drawing Yugoslav trade into the Soviet orbit. Anecdotal evidence reveals the following pattern. When convenient, Soviet (or East European) buyers come to Yugoslav producers with open order books. These exports are of low quality goods, which are perhaps not even price competitive. The production experience plus the difficulty of shifting from Western to Eastern markets bodes ill for competitiveness in non-Comecon markets in the long run.

Factor Mobility and Flexibility to Adjust

As is now becoming better understood in industrialized countries facing adjustment to import competition, slow growth is itself inimical to factor mobility, hence the significance of the 1965–70 downturn. Yugoslavia experienced a turning point after 1965, attributable not so much to trade liberalization as to other aspects of the reforms (decentralization, promotion of consumption, capitalization) and to a restrictive macromonetary policy. It is probably fair to conclude that the macro-environment was not the most conducive to the factor mobility that should accompany trade liberalization.

Employment expansion, though only one ingredient in the mix, succinctly reflects the situation. When employment growth stagnates or even becomes negative for a period of three to four years after a trade liberalization, labor is likely strongly to resist moving out of existing "inefficient" jobs. As Comisso (1979, p. 87) put it: "The new dynamic [after 1965] was of enterprises meddling in government as firms hit hard by the new competition ran to political bodies for bail-outs in the form of subsidies, protective tariffs, special laws, and price increases."

Capital Mobility

The Yugoslav system of self-management, which has been described and theorized on at length by Western authors (Domar, Ward, Vanek, and Horvat; reviewed by Wachtel, 1973), is said in itself to impede capital mobility. Workers in an enterprise have usufructuary rights in the capital but not liquidation rights. Outsiders cannot buy shares in a successful enterprise, nor can workers of a successful enterprise invest their surplus directly in another. While the laws have on occasion been designed to evade this restriction (including most recently an attempt to encourage profitable and efficient Slovenian enterprises to invest in less developed republics), this weakness of self-management has remained.

Several other factors may have been more important than this in reducing capital mobility. Overall, interest rates were set too low almost throughout the post-war period,[5] encouraging excessive capital intensity and overborrowing. More relevant to mobility was the lack of adequate incentives to savers, including highly profitable enterprises, which meant fewer funds for financial intermediation.

Before 1965, reallocation of capital was strongly dependent upon central government decisions; taxes extracted enterprise surpluses and these funds were redistributed for investment. Credit creation was also fully centralized. The 1965 reforms reduced these direct allocations sharply and gave increased autonomy to banks. However, most banks are founded by enterprises and local governments, so that, as Dimitrijevic (1973) aptly stated, "credit conditions are determined by the users themselves." Not surprisingly, banks will do little lending outside the group of founders, thus reducing geographic capital mobility, and even within the group will not allocate resources efficiently.

Another element reducing capital mobility has been the absence of bankruptcy or similar discipline. Banks and the local, republic, and federal governments eventually step in to provide support and some *ad hoc* tightening, but have almost never applied bankruptcy laws.

In such an environment, not only was financial intermediation greatly curtailed, but inefficiency was encouraged for there was no "bottom line." "In Yugoslavia anybody could order goods, invest, distribute, and consume, without paying for it. The guilty persons were not punished by being

---

[5] Dubey (1975) discusses the relevant 1965–70 period. Interest rates to depositors were almost always negative; those to borrowers were occasionally positive but barely so. Bery et al. (World Bank, 1983) make it clear that this continued through the 1970s.

deprived, through bankruptcy, of the right to manage social property"
(*Ekonomska Politika*, January 8, 1969). This was done in two ways. Banks
became essentially a "Treasury Department" for their founding enterprises, and they extended credit on request as long as it was available.
When this failed, enterprises postponed or ceased paying their suppliers
and creditors, that is, inter-enterprise payable–receivable accounts became
a credit instrument. Sirc (1979), citing a 1969 study by Vukman, presents
evidence to this effect, showing that interfirm credit increased about
fivefold between 1964 and 1969.

In conclusion, it seems clear that capital mobility was hindered not only
by self-management behavior but equally, if not more, by macro policies.
Most important were negative interest rates and a financial system too
weak to make good initial choices or impose discipline on bad investments.
While the self-management system may have contributed to capital
immobility, given the very high share of investment in GDP, incremental
capital formation surely mattered more.

Labor Mobility: Geographic

An old saying in Croatian, "*trbuhom za kruhom*," loosely translated as
"follow your stomach and earn your daily bread," encapsulates the
fundamental willingness of Yugoslavs to move around in search of better
economic opportunities. The rapid increase in the migration of Yugoslav
guest workers from virtually none at the end of the 1950s to nearly a
million by the early 1970s illustrates the same economic wanderlust.
However, internally, the movements of labor geographically or from one
enterprise to another may not be nearly as dynamic.

There is a strong consensus among scholars that inter-regional migration
is less than the large economic disparities would be expected to generate.
Breznik (1969) and Dubey (1975) both note that language differences,
among other things, are obstacles to such migration. Except for the
Albanians of Kosovo, however, language differences, while real, are very
small in practice; greater impediments may be ethnic and religious.
Havrylyshyn (1977) shows that these important ethnic differences result in
a migration pattern in which people migrate primarily within ethnically
similar regions. While this is a proclivity and not a categorical phenomenon, it clearly reduces the degree of inter-regional mobility.

Despite these impediments, migration rates are quite large. A net total
of 265,000 migrants moved from less developed to more developed regions
in the decade 1961–71. This is about 4–5 percent of the total population in
the poor regions and about 19 percent of their natural increase. Gross
inter-republic migration was over a million, or about 5 percent of the
population. Gross external migration covered an almost equal number of
people. Though this is not exceptionally high, nevertheless a substantial

proportion of the population has expressed a willingness to move over medium to long distances.

Migration is much higher over short distances, much of it rural to urban. Thus in 1961 (reflecting 1953–61 movements) domestic migration ranged from 24 percent of population in Bosnia-Herzegovina and Vojvodina (a rich agricultural zone) to 42 percent in Slovenia, averaging almost 30 percent for Yuggoslavia as a whole (Havrylyshyn, 1977, p. 101). As migrants tend to have fewer than average family dependents, it seems safe to say that, adding domestic and external migration, perhaps nearly half of Yugoslavia's labor force had migrated – no trifling figure, particularly as the below-normal rate of urbanization means that much of this migration was inter-urban.

Indeed, the relatively low inter-regional migration is less important for economic adjustment than the high short-distance migration. Since urban centers and industrial activity are quite dispersed, economically effective labor reallocation needs only high mobility over short rather than long distances.

Intersector and Interfirm Mobility

The increasing education and skill acquisition of the labor force further enhanced the potential mobility of labor, since skilled workers tend to be more mobile. However, the large differences in skill mix among sectors and industrial branches probably work in the opposite direction, at least in the short run: if certain sectors or industries are forced to cut back and adjust to competition, the skill mix of the released labor does not immediately conform to that of growing sectors. Such "structural unemployment" issues would have been exacerbated by the macro features noted: growth stalled in Yugoslavia after the reform and employment actually fell. There was no increment to make good the mismatching.

The conventional theoretical interpretation of Yugoslav self-management concludes that workers maximize profits per employee and therefore tend to restrict employment opportunities. Sirc (1979, p. 203) and most analysts suggest that, though they will not actually dismiss those already in place (especially in hard times such as 1965–70), new hires will be restricted. Horvat (1976 and elsewhere) disagrees on theoretical grounds, suggesting that a neoclassical objective of total profit obtains, and Schrenk et al. (1979) support this on empirical grounds. Schrenk et al. note that, apart from the "once-and-for-all adjustment to the 1965 reforms" (p. 259), there was a continual high rate of employment generation given the output growth. The calculated "employment to output elasticity before 1965 and 1968 was virtually the same at about 0.7 as for all Latin American countries, between 1960 and 1969 it was 0.6" (Schrenk et al., 1979, p. 259).

The pure theory of self-management (Vanek 1970) suggests that workers will not want to move because they have "invested" capital which they cannot liquidate, and workers in another enterprise will be generally unwilling to allow new workers to share in the value of accumulated investment. This discourages labor mobility by, apparently, a quasi-fixity of labor and capital. However, if in fact industrialization and growth overall are so rapid that new hires are welcomed, even those with jobs will move. Indeed, since they already have industrial skills and experience, they may be more welcome than rural migrants. Horvat (1976 and elsewhere) argues strongly in favor of expansionary policies, perhaps because rapid growth overcomes many of the "theoretical" weaknesses of the system, such as its tendency to reduce factor mobility. Estrin (1983) shows that income disparities across sectors, within sectors, and within occupations across sectors were much larger than in other countries and increased in the self-management era. While this appears to display strong evidence of labor immobility, there is a fallacy, for in the self-management context employee income necessarily contains the payment to labor *plus* a profit share, whereas in the countries compared there is no profit share. Higher labor skills may be associated with higher capitalization and hence "profits" per worker; therefore a higher dispersion of labor income would be observed in Yugoslavia than in other countries.

Unemployment played a very important role in mobility. Official unemployment rates for registered work applicants of between 7 and 8 percent throughout the 1960s considerably underestimate the excess supply of labor. First, external migration took nearly 10 percent of the labor force out of Yugoslavia. Second, not all openly unemployed were registered. Dubey (1975) notes that the Employment Institute (where unemployed persons register) estimates that only half the jobs are obtained through the reporting system. Third, considerable disguised unemployment existed in the rural sector; Dubey gives an illustrative figure of a million, and Schrenk et al. (1979) parenthetically mention 20–30 percent of the agricultural labor force. In either case this amounts to about 10–12 percent of the total labor force. Fourth, and most contentiously, "unproductive employment" was present in the nonagricultural sector. Sirc (1979, p. 92) quotes the newspaper *Ekonomska Politika* to the effect that in 1964 between 250,000 and 400,000 workers (8–12 percent of the social sector) were employed "without justification."

Clearly, unemployment in Yugoslavia before and during the trade liberalization episode was very high (Havrylyshyn, 1988, appendix table 2.3). Such a situation is not conducive to the success of a policy experiment aimed at "shaking out" inefficient or inappropriate economic activity and displacing workers. While the potential unemployment shocks of trade liberalization can be softened by compensation, the Yugoslav system offers very little scope for this. About a tenth of those registered as unemployed and seeking work received money, which amounted to about 25–30 percent of average labor income in industry (Havrylyshyn, 1988, appendix table 2.4).

The labor mobility issue can be summarized as follows. First, the significance of reduced mobility is not clear; many analysts have argued its unimportance. Second, geographic mobility was very high, and where it was impeded, this was due as much to noneconomic factors related to nationality differences as to the system's workings. Third, economic expansion in all but the 1965–70 period was so rapid that, just as for capital, new additions to the industrial–urban labor force probably obscured any immobility effects of self-management.

3

The Political Context

In this chapter we briefly review the salient features of the political background against which the experiment of trade liberalization was set. Three features, historical and political, seemed to play the largest roles in the political economy of trade liberalization: Yugoslavia's middle-of-the-road international politics; its singular version of Marxist ideology, namely workers' management; and its federalist structure, comprising several republics corresponding broadly to the different nationalities making up the country. In the final section of the chapter we describe how these features combined to produce a strong liberalizing tendency, partly manifested in the trade liberalization which is our principal interest in this study.

International Politics of Yugoslavia

Even the most skeptical Western observers of Eastern Europe agree that the communist regime established in Yugoslavia in 1945 had more autonomous legitimacy and was far less dependent on the support of the Soviet Army for its existence than was the case for other countries in the region. The relatively greater acceptability among the populace of the communist regime has been attributed to its antecedents as a resistance movement against the Nazi occupiers, which succeeded, at least until 1945, in subordinating nationalist (particularly Serbo-Croat) antagonisms, as well as the purely communist ideology, to the principal objective of liberation.

Perhaps because of this popular acceptance, the communist regime in 1945 began to implement a Soviet policy which was more Stalinist than Stalinism. On the political front this meant strong and harsh consolidation of power, and an almost virulent anti-Western position internationally. On the economic front it meant a thorough coverage of centralized planning, forced industrialization, and of course a state trading monopoly.

However, quickly as this policy was first implemented, it was equally sharply turned around in the years 1949–52. Perhaps again because the regime sensed itself to be relatively popular, it was the first to defy openly the string-pulling of the Moscow masters in the areas of economic exploitation in trade and of Soviet spying and subversion inside Yugoslavia. The reaction from Moscow was expulsion of Yugoslavia in 1948 from the Soviet camp, that is, from the political body of the Communist International, the military alliance, and Comecon.

After a brief period of shock during which futile entreaties were made to Moscow to reverse this dramatic division, the Yugoslav regime decided, in a bold display of one-upmanship, to go it alone along a path claimed to be closer to true socialism than that followed by the Soviets themselves. While the Soviets were mired in the state monopoly phase of socialism, the Yugoslavs announced that they would leap ahead to the stage where the power of the state "withered away" and was truly handed over directly to the people.

International relations had also changed radically by 1952. The break in economic relations with the East in 1948 left a vacuum which was quickly filled by mutual agreement with Western aid and reopening of trade flows. The Western orientation was reconciled with socialist ideology through the formula of nonalignment. As is well known, Tito, along with Nehru and Nasser, was one of the principal founders of the nonaligned movement.

Political nonalignment has been a reality to this day. The Western orientation since 1948 has certainly not been complete, and, indeed, less than a decade later Soviet–Yugoslav diplomatic relations were reestablished. While formally this middle-of-the-road position has also been maintained for economic relations, in practice Yugoslav trade has been largely oriented to the West. An important related feature is Yugoslavia's open-exit policy since the early 1960s. Substantial, though largely temporary, emigration followed the paths of other Southern European laborers to the labor-short economies of Europe. The liberal attitude behind such a policy was self-perpetuating. It provided via remittances the foreign exchange which would pay for the influx of Western imports after trade liberalization, and it reinforced the Western linkages through the personal exposures of Yugoslavs.

Economic Ideology

The break with Stalinism in 1948 made it imperative for the regime to legitimize itself by undermining the legitimacy of the Soviet regime. Consequently, while Stalin was entrenching the institutions of state capitalism and hence allegedly working against the ultimate aims of the revolution, the Yugoslav regime announced that it would do what was correct and truly give power to the people. Thus was born the Yugoslav concept of self-management of economic enterprises by the workers, a notion entirely consistent with the theoretical writings of Marx, Engels, and Lenin.

The institutional form of this power was to be like Marx's free association of producers. Although in the phase of state capitalism workers "owned" their means of production, the state acted as a trustee and made all the decisions on their use. Yugoslav self-management gave the workers in each operating unit not only legal ownership but also freedom to make economic production decisions. The first legal step was taken in June 1950 when the National Assembly passed the law on workers' self-management. Implementation was not to be immediate, but even when it was fully legally in place, its functioning was not as successful as planned. Indeed, attempts at reforming the system to make it function properly have recurred with remarkable regularity since 1950. The 1965 trade liberalization studied here was but a part of a general reform intended to make workers' management finally a reality.

The essential features of the system are simple enough. In a given unit such as a factory or a section of a large enterprise, workers elect members of a workers' council, which in turn appoints a director, possibly from outside. While the director is responsible for day-to-day managerial responsibility, his role is confined to implementing the major decisions taken by the council. The council decides on investment plans, production, marketing, hiring, and wages. One important limit to these powers differentiates Yugoslav self-management from worker-owned companies in capitalist economies: workers cannot liquidate the assets of the enterprise and take their share in cash. The workers as a group are still in essence "trustees" of the producing assets. Indeed, this limitation applies not only to the group as a whole, but to each individual. A worker "owns" a share in the factory only as long as he or she remains there; leaving the group means giving up the share, and joining another group means being given an "ownership" share in the new group. This implies reduced labor mobility. In such an environment, trade liberalization starts out with a considerable handicap. However, as we have already argued in chapter 2, mobility may not have been as restricted as the theory implies. First, even in theory, it follows that a worker has an incentive to leave a weak factory where the value of his or her share is low and go to a dynamic one where it would be high. The workers in the new factory will not refuse new workers if expansion means, as it can, greater income per worker. This is true even while the workers follow the rule of maximizing profit per worker because, of course, expansion via investment and greater market shares means that the average product curve is shifted outward and upward by new technology embodied in the investment.

Second, the practice of workers' management has not entirely fulfilled the theoretical intentions, as is evidenced by the continued series of reforms and modifications. Two principal shortcomings have plagued successful implementation: directors have been much more powerful than intended, especially on all nonwage issues and workers' councils have been too free with allocating revenues to wages instead of investments.

Another feature of workers' management relevant to trade liberalization is the necessary dismantling of central planning. The decentralization of economic decisions need not be complete, and it does not automatically follow that with workers' management the market will replace central planning. In Oskar Lange's well-known theory of market socialism (to which the Yugoslav system has been likened), central planners set prices in imitation of the market. We could envisage a similar situation in Yugoslavia, and in fact the first decade of workers' management saw, rather than the demise of central planning, a reduction of its roles to two main activities: allocating new investments and setting prices. In such a context, foreign trade is not only likely to be regulated but indeed *must* be regulated as long as centrally determined prices differ from world prices.

While economic logic implies that trade will be regulated as long as prices are not set freely by the market, the decentralized power that workers' management created fed upon itself and pressed for increased decentralization, including a greater role for the market. As is described more precisely in the final section of this chapter, this decentralizing tendency of workers' management combined with a number of other forces to push the Yugoslav regime into a major liberalization of the economy in the 1960s.

Regional and National Differences

Yugoslavia comprises six republics – Bosnia-Herzegovina, Croatia, Macedonia, Montenegro, Serbia, and Slovenia – and in all but the first the majority of the population is ethnically distinct. While all but the Albanians are Slavs, to different degrees they have, or perceive themselves to have, a separate national identity with a distinct history, language, and even religion. The Albanians are concentrated in the autonomous region of Kosovo within Serbia.

Before World War I, a Yugoslav nation did not exist and each of these regions was under different foreign dominance: Ottoman, Austrian, and Italian. An autonomous Serbian state was in existence for a few decades before the war. After World War I, the Kingdom of Serbs, Croats, and Slovenes came into being as an expression of self-determination for South Slavs (the word Jugoslav means South Slav). However, this experience was not happy, as Serbian domination of political power resulted in considerable bloodletting among the southern Slav brothers, especially the two major groups, Serbs and Croats.

The communist regime of 1945 saw itself as a healer of these old wounds, reemphasizing the common interests of the nationalities. Its success in building up a leadership of diverse national backgrounds during and after the war is unquestioned. Further, the violence of nationalist clashes almost entirely disappeared save for manifestations in Kosovo. However, the differences have remained and play an important role. Perhaps the best evidence for this is the nature of the so-called Presidency which has ruled the country since Tito's death. This is a body with two representatives from each republic (hence, each nationality), among whom a titular head is chosen in rotation for a short term.

Since 1945 the conflict of nationalities has not gone away but – until very recently – has taken less violent forms, particularly in the allocation of economic powers or privileges. All republics, since the gradual decentralization of power in 1950, have continued to press for more power. This centrifugal force has motives other than nationalism, but has often been strengthened by it. Because nationalism is frequently not explicit – in fact, it was part of the communist discipline to curtail explicit expression of nationalism – it is nearly impossible to identify its influence in specific political discussions and decisions. One exception is described below: the strong liberal tendencies in Croatia and Slovenia, the rich republics. But perhaps the most important influence of national particularism in the context of trade liberalization is its contribution as a decentralizing (and hence often liberalizing) force.

Economic as well as nationality differences distinguish the republics and autonomous regions. The disparity between the richest (Slovenia) and the poorest (Kosovo) remains substantial, with a per capita income ratio of about 5 to 1. Industrialization in Slovenia first began at the turn of the century under the Austrian empire, and in Croatia only slightly later. Even by 1960 the southern and eastern regions were still largely agricultural and only slightly touched by developments such as road and rail systems, mechanization in agriculture, and industrial build-up. Perhaps worse, where industrialization did come in these areas, it was more often than not inefficient and in need of assistance. The development strategy of the central-planning period to about 1950 and the transition period to 1960 included special efforts to industrialize the backward regions, including many parts of Serbia. Considerable funds were channeled from Belgrade to these regions, establishing vested economic and political interests that would prove important in the future.

Liberal Tendencies Leading to the 1965 Reforms

While the period since workers' management was formally instituted experienced considerable political ferment in one sense, in another it was one of political stability. The socialist government under the leadership of the League of Communists and the strong personality of President Tito was able, after the 1948 expulsion from the Cominform, to find a secure and stable equilibrium between East and West. Substantial domestic stability was attained by a combination of political control and popularity far surpassing anything in Eastern Europe. Admittedly, the above centripetal forces were in constant tug-of-war with the ideological push to decentralization of power, and the regional cum ethnic pressures for greater autonomy, but nevertheless the resultant political tensions at no time threatened immediate disruption or sharp political changes of regime in the period before the reform. In the implementation period of the reform (and some political analysts argue because of the reform) a crisis did occur in 1968, but was eventually resolved and stability, at least political stability, returned. The politics culminating in the liberalization policies were in fact played out in this arena of opposing forces, most openly and visibly in the debates prior to the Eighth Congress of the League of Communists in December 1964, such as those in the press, in the Federal Assembly, and among academics (see Rusinow, 1977, ch. 4, for an excellent and incisive account).

Though the lines cannot be drawn too precisely, we can speak of two sides in the debate. The "conservatives" – one of the leading characters was Rankovic – tended to be centralist, to worry about retaining power and influence of the League of Communists, to be cautious of too great a Western orientation (though rarely and certainly not openly pro-Soviet), to favor a more centralized economic system, and to oppose both internal and external market liberalization. They included among others the political and economic bureaucracy at the federal level, the army, and the representatives of less developed regions which favored a continuation of a strong economic center redistributing funds from the more developed to the less developed regions and supporting nascent but economically weak industries in the central and southern regions. On the other side were the "liberals" who, like the Croatian party leader Bakaric and the Slovenian Kardelj, favored greater delegation of political power to the republics (the early implementation of which was supposed to be consistent with the fundamental Yugoslav philosophy of workers' management and the withering away of the state), a liberalization of domestic markets leading to economic rationalization, and a liberalization of external markets. The liberals were most likely to find support from the technocrats in enterprises, academics, and the more developed regions, especially Croatia, Slovenia, and, to a lesser extent, northern parts of Serbia and Bosnia-Herzegovina.

These ideological differences were intensified by an (infrequently admitted) element of nationalist–ethnic differences: the regional geographic split noted above coincided dangerously closely with ethnic groupings. For our purposes, the relative importance of ideology and nationalism is less relevant than the outcome: economic liberalism was strongest in the economically advanced Croatian and Slovenian Republics, while economic administrative-centralism was strongest in the more backward republics.

The result of the "great debate" in Yugoslavia (expressed in the pronouncements of the Eighth Congress of the League of Communists in December 1964) was that the liberal view prevailed. The victory was not complete by any means, and for the most part did not mean a removal of the conservatives from power; certainly, the change in "regime" was absolutely nonviolent. The general reform, of which trade liberalization in 1965 was only a part, included delegation of fiscal power to republics, decentralization of the banking system, greater power of decision making by the worker-managed enterprises on production investment and labor incomes, considerable reduction in central-planning activities including gradual decontrol of prices, and a realignment of prices to reflect market forces more closely. As such, trade liberalization was not the central focus of the ideological shift, but merely a natural component.

However, trade liberalization was not only justified ideologically, it was also a pragmatic reaction to the growing evidence of difficulties in external trade relations. While the balance-of-payments situation was not critical by the norms of the 1980s' debt crisis, it was critical enough to lead both internal analysts and outside institutions such as the IMF to recommend that action be taken to rationalize the system. More explicitly, the Western orientation of Yugoslavia led along the natural path to GATT membership (IMF and World Bank membership had already come in the 1950s) and necessarily pushed in the direction of uniform exchange rates, replacement of a quantitative restriction (QR) regime by tariffs, and eventually reduction of those tariffs.

It is difficult to determine how these outside influences affected the timing of the liberalization, but one had the sense that they led many politicians simply to accept the need for opening up without paying much attention to *how* it was to be done, concentrating instead on the other aspects of the reform. This is in essence the view that Fabinc (1969) espouses: trade liberalization was viewed (by policymakers, not by economic analysts) in too simple a way, as a panacea for the economic irrationalities such as excessive reliance on imports for raw materials or inadequate export performance needing subsidy support.

The public was not as interested in commercial policy as in the liberalization of enterprise decision making (especially concerning the greater freedom to set personal incomes) and in the intra-republic economic issues. Burg (1983, pp. 43–51) discusses the various public opinion polls taken in this period and notes that two broad issues dominated: relations among the nationalities and inter-republic economic relations. However, as later discussion will show, once the effects of trade liberalization began to be felt by individual enterprises or regions, there was no lack of expression of dissatisfaction and of lobbying attempts to help affected industries and regions. The initial lack of interest in commercial policy was by no means due to lack of awareness, as the debate was fairly public throughout, and the press, while not completely free, was not unduly controlled by the government and hence revealed substantial differences of opinion. For example, while the newspaper *Komunist* was the official organ of the League, others such as *Borba*, *Vjesnik*, and the important *Ekonomska Politika* were relatively more open (Rusinow, 1977, ch. 3, nn. 36–45).

Was the policy widely regarded as likely to be implemented? The answer in a narrow sense is in the affirmative, but skepticism abounded as to whether it would accomplish the intended results. This was not because the government was considered too weak or only mildly committed. Indeed, the strong commitment of the government was clearly reflected in three elements: that the "debate" was eventually resolved in favor of the liberalizing tendency, that it was made open and explicitly announced in political pronouncements as well as official government documents such as laws, resolutions, and plans, and that the ideological shift was accompanied by some shift of political power from conservatives to liberals.

However, elements of doubt remained. Many academics, especially more "liberal" economists, argued that too many compromises were made and that not enough attention was given to fundamental realignments of prices, investment priorities, and allocation mechanisms. (Horvat, (1976, pp. 200–3) reviews some of these criticisms by Fabinc, Mrkusic, Cicin-Sain, Kovac, Pertot, and others.) As concerns external liberalizations, some of the skepticism was based on the failure of two earlier attempts (1952 and 1961) and possibly on a perception that this was because the government was not in fact willing to carry the program through if things began to go badly.

The last point addressed in this section concerns the administrative loci of power to implement the trade liberalization policies. There were three or four principal loci of such power (and responsibility, one might add!). The Federal Assembly (and in particular the so-called "Economic Chambers" of that Assembly) had legislative power in such matters as the amendment of customs laws, as well as the basic regulations on retention quotas for exporters and the import control systems in broad outline. A more direct power of implementation was in the hands of the Ministry of Foreign Trade, whose analyses in principle led to the choice of tariff levels by sector, to the inclusion of product-specific import-control categories, and to the *changes* in such inclusions. The Ministry also enjoyed a considerable latitude in the application of temporary tariffs or surcharges of certain types. The third important actor was the Central Bank which controlled the foreign exchange allocations and supervised the working of the retention quota. Finally a fourth (indirect) actor was the Federal Price Bureau which controlled prices: domestic prices could be set relatively independently of world prices for many goods because quotas remained explicitly or implicitly, noncompetitive markets existed domestically, and finally price wedges not consistent with tariff or other import restrictions could be supported by budgetary coverage via subsidies, taxes, commissions, and so on.

4

Long-term Trends in Trade Policy

Identifying Liberalization Episodes, 1948–1986

Yugoslavia, like most developing countries, has conducted a more restrictive than liberal commercial policy throughout the last three and a half decades. Nevertheless, the long-term trend has been towards liberalization, or at least there has been a "continuing effort, after 1952, to reduce the multiplicity in the exchange and trade systems and to liberalize and simplify them with the ultimate goal of integrating the Yugoslav economy with the world economy" (Dubey, 1975, p. 263). However, it is widely agreed that this was not achieved, as evidenced by the introduction of yet another major reform and liberalization effort in 1983.[1]

Commercial policy tools went far beyond nominal tariffs or explicit trade-related subsidies. Foreign exchange retention quotas, QRs or licensing of imports, foreign exchange allocation quotas, *ad hoc* or temporary customs surcharges (or exemptions), and many other nontrade taxes and subsidies which indirectly affected the ratio of domestic to world prices for tradeables have been extensively used. The net effects of such measures should be reflected in effective protection rates (EPRs), effective exchange rates (EERs), or domestic resource costs. However, only two EPR estimates exist for Yugoslavia, both for 1970 and covering only nominal tariffs (Ekonomski Institut, Pravne Fakultete, 1972; Fabinc and Lazic-Djerdj, 1973). With nontariff barriers playing such a large role, EPRs can be calculated only by using price comparisons; this precludes making such calculations for the past, not only because of the size of the task but also because historical price comparison data are lacking. Direct price comparisons have been used by Pertot (1973) to calculate what he calls "parity ratios" for 1962 and 1965; except for the omission of subsidies and other production assistance, parity ratios are the same as what Western literature

---

[1] The current program of liberalization is linked to IMF standby credit arrangements and a World Bank Structural Adjustment Loan (World Bank, 1983; Yugoslavia, 1983).

labels EERs.[2] Unfortunately, data for later periods permitted Pertot to calculate only price index adjustments to these ratios. Comparisons over time of the degree of protection for different sectors are therefore questionable, although for lack of other information they are attempted later in this study.

Despite the shortcomings of these data, the major liberalization trends of the period are quite easy to identify. These are depicted in figure 4.1, which uses an index of 1 (least liberal) to 20 (most liberal) to reflect the degree of openness in trade policy. Because of substantial nontariff elements and the lack of previous quantitative studies of protection, the index is constructed qualitatively and reflects the judgment of the author. It is based on a combination of two "hard" measures (nominal tariffs and coverage of imports by regimes of varying liberality) and a variety of qualitative information in the relevant analytical literature, newspaper and

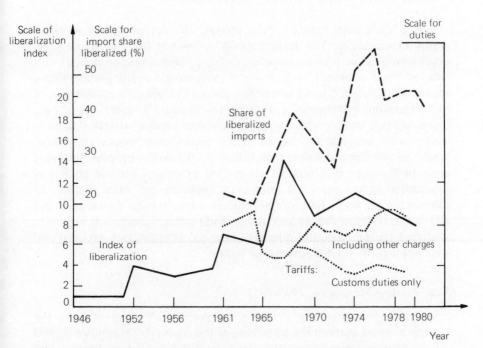

Figure 4.1 Index of liberalization in Yugoslav trade policy, 1946–1980

[2] In fact, Pertot's work did include calculating various production benefits in separate computations. Unfortunately, this was not done for export- and import-substituting production separately as was the case for the direct price comparison calculations. Given the importance of the export bias issue, it was the latter that was used in this study.

other accounts, as well as numerous discussions with Yugoslav and foreign experts. The evolution of export promotion policies and their interpretation for the liberalization index are considered separately below. The index and the trends of commercial policy it reflects will be discussed more fully by describing the six major phases of trade policy:

1946–51, state trading monopoly (central control and high protection);
1952–60, administered trade regime with multiple exchange rates (indirect but high intervention and high protection);
1961–5, uniform exchange rate and tariff regime (reduced intervention, continued high protection);
1965–74, major liberalization (reduced restrictions, tariff, intervention);
1975–83, decentralized interventionism regime (increased *ad hoc* intervention, possibly also increased protection);
1983–6, structural adjustment liberalization (reduction of anti-export bias as part of IMF/World Bank adjustment lending).

Before discussing each of these phases, the notion of liberalization merits examination. The term "liberal" is widely used in writings on development as well as trade policy (as in a "liberal pricing policy" or a "liberal trade regime") to connote a movement toward getting prices economically "right." More often than not, no distinction is made between two dimensions of "liberal:" (a) the degree to which economic agents are free to act in a market without government intervention; (b) the degree to which, with intervention, actual prices approximate opportunity cost. While the two dimensions are closely linked, they do not necessarily always move in the same direction.[3] Thus in 1961 interventionism in trade was substantially reduced, while protection probably fell only slightly. In contrast, in the mid-1970s formal protection may not have increased, but *ad hoc* intervention did. In fact understanding this distinction is crucial to analyzing the fundamental question: how did liberalization proceed and what explains its relative success or failure?

State Trading Monopoly, 1946–1952

While 1948 witnessed the dramatic expulsion of Yugoslavia from the Cominform and marked the beginning of the country's divergence from a central-planning regime, several years passed before new mechanisms were established. All international trade was handled by a state trade ministry or state-owned firms with trading rights (Amacher, 1972). Tariffs and exchange rates that had existed before World War II were considered

---

[3] An elaboration of this point in a different context concerns domestic price policy (Havrylyshyn, 1985).

unnecessary and were abolished. The state set internal prices at which the foreign trade agency bought or sold exports or imports, and in the world markets its transactions were at world prices. A reserve of funds for foreign transactions was used to fill (or absorb) the space between domestic and world prices. The official exchange rate of 50 dinars per US dollar was largely an accounting device or was used for limited transactions such as foreign travel. The period is of only indirect interest for the issue at hand: the experience and familiarity with a highly centralized system of trade management may have affected the political economy of liberalization, in the sense that a bureaucracy with an interest and knowledge of administered rather than free trade was built up and continued until 1961.

Administered Trade Regime, 1952–1960

The first of what Horvat (1976, p. 194) calls "three steps towards free trade" was taken in 1952. In the spirit of the general economic reform of the time,[4] centralized control was eased. In addition to the shift away from direct control and state trading, four changes were implemented: the dinar was devalued from 50 to 300 per US dollar; exporting enterprises were given a retention quota, initially 45 percent; a limited foreign exchange market was set up to mediate these retentions; and finally a set of "exchange coefficients" (multiple exchange rates) was established for different categories of goods.

The 1952 liberalization was limited in scope and even more limited in results. The foreign exchange market experiment lasted about a year; retention quotas were sharply reduced and the official exchange rate quickly became unrealistic. By 1954, an exchange rate for actual settlements was established at 632 dinars per US dollar. Perhaps most damaging was the lack of realism in controlled domestic prices. The "coefficients of trade" acted to shield distorted domestic prices relative to world prices rather than to force them into closer correspondence.

The effective exchange rate for traded goods was established by multiplying the official exchange rate of 300 (the settlement rate after 1957) by the appropriate coefficient, which provided either a protective or a subsidy effect. The number of categories ranged from 12 to 35, and the coefficient values ranged from 0.5 to 6.0 for exports and from 0.5 to 10.0 for imports. Although it is in principle possible to derive tariff protection equivalents from such coefficients, this has never been done in a manner compatible with post-1961 categories. Hence tables in this study do not show tariff values before 1961. However, a study by Frkovic (1957) does give the

---

[4] The year 1952 marked the formal beginning of a turn away from Soviet style planning to the Yugoslav middle-of-the-road socialist system of workers' management; that is, the 1950 law began to be implemented at this time.

following broad picture. Protection was over 100 percent for consumer goods but was negative for other goods. Other qualitative evidence clearly suggests that, at least until the mid-1950s, import substitution prevailed, implying that the overall protective effect was high. Development policy essentially aimed at industrialization. Therefore the coefficients for agricultural exports were low, while those for industry were high. On the import side, capital goods and inputs faced low coefficients; other goods faced high coefficients. While at first the policies had an overall anti-export bias, by 1957 this had shifted to a pro-export bias. However, the system was complex, uncertain, and doubtless inefficient. Horvat (1976, p. 197) cites several Yugoslav writers to the effect that export enterprises were induced "to press for an increase in coefficients, not to compete on the world market." Rent-seeking activity was already in evidence.

Unified Exchange Rate and Tariff Regime, 1961–1965

While formally the administered regime continued until 1961, the groundwork for liberalization began earlier. Pertot (1973, p. 196) identifies 1956 as the start of a more realistic view of trade policies, though noting that until 1961 this was more a matter of changing attitudes and political declarations than actual policy implementation. Nevertheless, in 1956 Yugoslavia became an observer at GATT, in 1959 an associate member, in 1962 a provisional member, and finally in 1966 a full member.

A second step toward freer trade was taken in 1961. The dinar was devalued to 750 per US dollar but, unlike 1952, a substantial supply of foreign exchange was obtained by borrowing and no attempt was made to establish a foreign exchange market. More important, the system of multiple exchange rates (coefficients) was replaced by a uniform exchange rate and tariffs (18.8 percent on average) plus export premiums. A retention quota of 7 percent was allowed for exporters. Finally, about 20–5 percent of imports (by value) were liberalized in the sense that they could be imported without special license or quota restrictions, and, in principle at least, foreign exchange for such imports could be purchased at will. Another 20 percent of import value was subjected to a foreign exchange availability quota, while the rest fell under quota or similar restrictions.

As figure 4.1 suggests, this liberalization began to erode almost immediately. A rising trade deficit in 1962–4 led to restrictive measures. Tariffs increased to 23.3 percent in 1964 (table 4.1); tighter import controls were imposed, with the liberalized group falling to below 20 percent (table 4.2). Export premiums and subsidies were increased sharply in 1964 to as much as 45 percent. Various other tax rebates added to all these changes and finally resulted in a return to a system of multiple exchange rates, in fact if not in name. The reversal of liberalization was not complete, however, and

Table 4.1 Average rates of duty and other import charges, 1961–1979 (percent)

Year	Average effective customs duties	Import surcharges	Tax equalization charge	Customs evidence tax	Total	Effective rates of additional charges	Average effective import charges
1961	18.8	—	—	—	—	—	18.8
1964	23.3	—	—	—	—	—	23.3
1965	10.3	—	—	—	—	—	10.3
1966	12.3	—	—	—	—	—	12.3
1967	12.3	—	—	—	—	—	12.3
1968	13.8	—	—	—	—	—	13.8
1969	13.9	—	3	1	4	n.a.	17.9
1970	13.3	5	3	1	9	n.a.	21.3
1971	12.1	6	3	1	10	7.2	19.3
1972	10.4	6	3	1	10	8.7	19.1
1973	9.1	6	3	1	10	8.9	18.0
1974	8.5	6	3	1	10	10.8	19.3
1975	9.4	10	3	1	14	9.1	18.5
1976	10.1	10	5	1	16	12.4	22.5
1977	10.1	10	6	1	17	13.2	23.3
1978	9.8	10	6	1	17	13.4	23.1
1979	8.9	10	6	1	17	13.9	21.8

—, not applicable; n.a., not available.
Sources: 1961 data, Chittle, 1977, p. 49; 1964–7 data, Ivanovic, 1968; 1968–79 data, World Bank, 1980

Table 4.2 Coverage of imports by degree of liberalization 1961 and 1964–1980

Year	1 Fully liberal	2 Conditional liberal	3 Foreign exchange quota	4 Value quota	5 Quantity quota	6 License	Total restricted (columns 3–6)
	LB	LBO	GDK	DK	RR K	D	
1961	20–25	—	—	(——50–55——)		20	75–80
1964	20–						80 +
1965	(——25——)		(——————75——————)				75
1967	16.9	24.0	54.4	(—— 4.3——)		0.4	59.1
1969	20.8	14.2	44.8	(——12.9——)		7.3	65.0
1971	28.7	—	45.7	(——20.3——)		5.3	71.3
1973	51.6	—	21.2	(——20.6——)		6.5	49.3
1975	54.3	—	17.2	4.0	17.5	7.0	45.7
1976	43.7	—	17.4	4.3	16.9	17.7	56.3
1977	45.0	—	18.8	4.4	14.7	17.1	55.0
1978	46.3	—	0	18.2	21.8	13.7	53.7
1979	42.5	—	0	18.5	23.3	15.7	57.5
1980	42.4	—	0	16.2	20.2	21.3	57.6

Parentheses indicate that available data cover several categories; —, category not active.
Sources: 1961–65 data, Dubey, 1975, p. 264; Horvat, 1976, pp. 194–200; 1967–73 data, World Bank, 1980, p. 51; 1975–80 data, World Bank, 1983, p. 69

by all accounts the "score" on the liberalization index was still higher in 1964 after three years of restrictionism than it had been before the 1961 liberalization.

The Major Liberalization Phase, 1965–1974

Yugoslavia cannot truly be regarded as undertaking significant liberalization until the third step in 1965. In several respects the 1965–7 policies were a repetition of 1961. The dinar was again devalued, IMF credits were obtained to help the adjustment, tariffs were reduced more sharply to 10.5 percent, and the coverage of liberalized imports was increased. Liberalized imports accounted for 25 percent of value in 1965, 41 percent in 1966, and 35 percent in 1967 (table 4.2). In addition to being much more far-reaching than in 1961, the 1965 liberalization measures also differed on the export side, as virtually all subsidies were abolished. Retention quotas of 7 percent, however, were maintained.

The context also differed. While the 1961 program was mostly a trade policy reform, trade policies were only one aspect of the 1965 reforms, which are widely considered a major step in the evolution of Yugoslav self-management. Although the basic mechanisms of such a system were established by 1952, the central power remained dominant. The reforms of 1965 (see chapters 1–3) were intended to decentralize power: resource-allocation decisions were to be made increasingly by workers, and domestic price setting was to be decontrolled and made more subject to market influence. Trade liberalization, while clearly consonant with the overall philosophy of the reforms, was only one element.

The entire reform package was very explicitly announced through various channels: Five-Year Plan documents, writings and statements by public officials; newspaper coverage of the reforms; specific details of legislation, and so on. The broad orientation and objectives were stated in *Yugoslavia, Five Year Plan for 1965–70*. Indeed, wide public discussion of the possible directions of reforms well before the official reform regulations were passed constituted, in effect, a "pre-announcement" that trade liberalization was likely to occur.

In 1967 the system of import categories by degree of restrictiveness which had been informally applied since 1961 became formalized. The evolution of trade policy is to some extent reflected in the allocation of goods to the different categories shown in table 4.2 and figure 4.1. The percentage of imports in a given category is an *ex post* value; goods were put on one or another list and this resulted in the percentage attributions of import values as shown in the table.

The main categories of imports by degree of liberality were as follows: LB, fully liberalized imports – free access for anyone to buy foreign exchange from the bank up to the value of the imports of such goods;

LBO, conditionally liberalized imports – imports of these goods from the nonconvertible area entitled the buyer to import additional amounts from the convertible area; GDK, goods for which enterprises could use retention quotas on foreign exchange earnings; DK and RK, quotas in dinar value or unit quantity with separate quotas for convertible and nonconvertible areas; D, goods subject to licensing on an *ad hoc* administrative basis.

The import categories help trace the degree of liberalization to some extent, and (as seen in figure 4.1) the major directional movements are certainly reflected in the share of imports that is liberalized. However, the figures do hide something; as noted earlier, Pertot (1973) emphasized the continuing administrative and therefore inconstant nature of even these categories. First, coverage of each category could be (and was) frequently changed. Second, the LB category could still mean informal limitations – foreign exchange credits would simply be delayed. Third, the number of subcategories very quickly expanded after 1967; Pertot (1973, pp. 294–8) finds a total of 19 categories. The very fact of such complexity indicates nonliberality in the first sense discussed above – that is, the degree of interventionism as opposed to the extent of tariff-equivalent protection. Finally, it is never possible to know how much weight to give to any category when constructing the liberalization index, for two reasons. A license, universally listed by all analysts as if it were the least liberal, may, in times of foreign exchange crises, be *less* restrictive than foreign exchange quotas! Thus in 1969–71 when, as is widely agreed, the regime became less liberal, there was only a modest reduction in the coverage of fully liberalized imports (35–28.7 percent) and an actual decline in licensing coverage. By all accounts, restrictionism operated more subtly, with administrators applying the quotas in categories GDK, DK, and RK much more stringently. In contrast, the next balance-of-payments crisis (1974–5) saw extensive use of licensing with coverage rising from 7.0 to 17.7 percent (see table 4.2).

Somewhat similar qualifications apply to tariffs, although to a much lesser degree. Customs duties alone show a very decided and largely uninterrupted downward trend since 1965. After 1970 (table 4.1) there was an accelerating trend toward the imposition of additional charges under different headings: temporary surcharges, stamp taxes, "statistical" taxes, and so on. Not only did this mean a proliferation of regulations with consequent interventionist effects, but it effectively raised the true tariff levels. These are approximated by the values in the last column of table 4.1 and the upper fork of the "tariffs" line in figure 4.1. The sharp rise in these values from 1967 to 1970, and a smaller one after 1974, help to identify the turning point of the liberalization index. The tariff movements in 1967–70 are also evidence that the sharp increase in the share of liberalized imports after 1971 did not mean a return of the liberalization index to its 1967 peak. The continued rise of tariffs after 1974, taken together with evidence of the declining share of liberalized imports and other qualitative information, forms a basis for the judgment on the index of liberalization: after 1974 there was a return to restrictionism of about the same degree as before the 1965–7 reforms.

Because of the strongly administrative character of trade policy after 1969 (and before 1965), EPR measures that use only tariffs are unreliable. EPRs seem to be very low by developing country norms, nor is the variability by sector very large. Though the formal nature of the 1965–7 liberalization made a clean sweep of most aspects of protection and considerably reduced both dimensions of liberalism (the degree of administrative intervention as well as the level of protection), 1968–9 saw a reversal, particularly with respect to administrative interventionism. Thus, the indications of the EPR values may have been reasonably valid even as late as 1970, though they became increasingly meaningless later.

While it is impossible to be precise about the actual degree of restrictiveness in the applications of licensing or foreign exchange allocation, we might gain some insight into the degree of liberality in the system by analyzing what sort of commodities figure on the different lists and how this changes. Thus an increase in the share of raw materials in a more liberal category (LB or LBO in table 4.2), could mean increased effective protection for finished goods, a movement perhaps to be interpreted as restrictive and not liberalizing. While it has not been possible to obtain detailed lists of this sort, some broad indications can be gained from the figures of table 4.3 which show the percentage of imports of raw materials in liberal categories and the same as a proportion of total imports.

If we take these figures at face value, some questions may arise about the liberalization tendencies shown in figure 4.1 after 1970. There is no obvious problem for the 1965 liberalization; before 1965 raw materials were afforded the lowest protection, and this clearly continued after 1968. As the 1967 data in table 4.3 show, a higher percentage of raw materials were "liberalized" (59.1 percent) than was the case for all imports (40.9 percent). Tariff levels also indicate the same situation, at least so far as the direction of movement is concerned.

The picture is clouded for the 1970s, however, as the gap between all goods and raw materials closed (see table 4.3). That is, for 1971 and 1975, the percentage of liberalized raw materials was only slightly higher than the percentage for all goods, and from 1976 on the difference was insignificant. Other things being equal, this would suggest a reduction in effective protection in the 1970s resulting from a reduced dispersion of protective levels.

If this were so, the index of figure 4.1 should not show a decline in the early 1970s. However, it does show a decline for several reasons. First, while the dispersion of protection may have been slightly lowered in the early 1970s with the tendency toward an equalized percentage of liberal-

Table 4.3 Percentage of liberalized
imports: all goods and raw materials,
1967–1979

Year	All goods	Raw materials
1967	40.9	59.1
1971	38.7	40.1
1975	56.3	60.7
1976	45.7	46.5
1977	45.0	48.1
1978	46.3	46.7
1979	42.5	41.8

These calculations are not applicable to the
period before 1965, but available EER
calculations, tariffs, and qualitative
information suggest low and even negative
protection for raw materials.
Sources: All goods, table 4.2; raw materials,
Dubey, 1975, p. 264, for 1967 and 1971, and
World Bank, 1980, p. 53, for other years

ized imports for all goods and raw materials noted in table 4.3, such
dispersion remained a strong factor in the nominal tariffs until 1976.
Second, the figures of tables 4.2 and 4.3 cannot be taken at face value for,
as Pertot (1971) emphasized, liberalized imports may be less restricted in a
formal sense but could easily be more restricted at the final step of
receiving foreign exchange allocations, which in practice were not automatic. It is then necessary to fall back upon more qualitative judgments,
and the consensus seems to be strong that after 1967 the liberalization
index fell.

The slight resurgence of the liberalization index from 1971 to 1974 is not
inconsistent wth the tendency shown in table 4.3, but its decline after 1974
is. An explanation can be found in the fact that after 1974 nominal tariffs
increased, products were shifted out of liberal categories, the amount of
discretionary control of foreign exchange grew (although this was reversed
in the late 1970s as discussed below), interventionism was on the rise in
general, frequent changes in regulations took place, and so on. Thus, while
all the indirect tools combined may have outweighed the tariff and
licensing effects and resulted in lower effective protection, its extent is at
best unknown, and unfortunately no estimates exist to help the analysis.
What is known is that tariff and quota-like systems did become more
restrictive, so that, with respect to the second dimension of liberalism – divergence of prices from opportunity costs – the economy seems to
have become less liberal. It is also known that the degree of interventionism increased. Hence, with respect to the first dimension of liberalism, the
economy clearly became less liberal.

Decentralized Interventionism, 1975–1983

It is difficult to choose an appropriate label for the character of commercial policy after 1974, just as it is difficult to categorize the Yugoslav system in general. The 1974 Constitution and economic reforms saw, paradoxically, both some centralization of power and a continued devolution of power to microunits. The latter came in the form of a break-up of enterprises into so-called Basic Organizations of Associated Labor (BOALs) and a constitutional amalgamation of these as the focus of power in Yugoslavia's workers' self-management system. Power was recentralized partly by restoring some federal taxation and fiscal powers, but most importantly (and, alas, least transparently) in the myriad of rules, regulations, and procedures which circumscribe the exercise of BOAL authority. The central government (and the party) exercised more indirect but probably more influential power after 1974, although by no means as much as before 1961.

In relation to trade policies, intervention was expressed in several ways, some already noted in discussing the reversal of liberalization. First, control of tariffs, taxes, categorizations, and foreign exchange allocations remained more federal than decentralized. Second, changes in regulations were more frequent. Third, indirect coercion and moral suasion were more often applied in the context of the new system. All BOALs with an interest in foreign trade were "free" to make decisions subject to the "social compact" to which they all subscribed. That is, they had to belong to a group called a Community of Interest for Foreign Exchange Relations (CIFER), within which subgroups of BOALs had to reach "self-management agreements" on foreign transactions. In such agreements, all who contribute to export earnings (final sellers, suppliers) are jointly allowed a certain retention quota (far higher than the old 7 percent) but must agree to share it, or sell it to the bank, or exchange it somehow with yet other groups of BOALs.

The potential for implicit arbitrage of foreign exchange thus introduced by letting those who need it informally bid up its price may have led to something of a competitive market. However, it also created strong anticompetitive pressure. The requirement to associate is obviously a formalization of collusive groupings, while the requirement that many BOALs together must make agreements leaves ample room for central authorities (federal and republic governments, party) to intervene and apply moral suasion.

The system is decidedly more complex than the one in force either in the pre-1961 centralized administrative period or in the liberalized period 1965–70. Certainly, the fact of continued decentralization *per se* did not mean trade liberalization because restrictions and distortions were merely applied by regional governments in collusion with the BOALs. However, for both the 1961 and the 1965–7 reforms, a general decentralizing tendency was closely linked (in circular causation) with a tendency to liberalize both domestic and foreign trade markets. Both these trends were considered positive steps in the direction of creating the Yugoslav ideal: a microsocialism wherein the state has withered away.

Since 1974, the perception has been that the costs of too much decentralization and liberalization threaten the nation-state's viability. Political costs such as excessive nationalism or social disturbances (student and workers' strikes) may come from excessive decentralization. Economic costs (balance-of-payments crises) are perceived to follow liberalization. Both, paradoxically, are thought to threaten the very purpose of the policies by risking an explosion or weakening the state. This paradox is thought by the Yugoslav authorities to have been resolved in the post-1974 arrangements. On the one hand, devolution of power to the very core of workers' groupings (BOALs) was a continued step in the desired direction. On the other hand, some retention of power at the center improved the state's ability to manage crises and correct any "errors" of decentralized decisions. Also, the requirement of BOALs to associate and reach microlevel social compacts which fit into the broader nationwide social compacts provides a system of checks and balances to control decentralized action.

Structural Adjustment Liberalization, 1983

On the surface, attitudes appear to have changed yet again under the newest phase of reforms. Partly in reaction to the economic difficulties of the early 1980s and partly because of continued internal influences favoring a more open economy, but also largely because of pressure from the IMF and the World Bank from which Yugoslavia was requesting large short-term adjustment loans, a renewed effort at liberalization was introduced in 1983. The Economic Stabilization Program of course included various other policy directions. On the international relations side, it echoes very much the statements of 1964–5. The broad aims are to achieve a more open economy, alignment of internal with world prices, and eventual convertibility of the dinar. Specific instruments are to be maintenance of a realistic exchange rate and reunification of the exchange rate, reduction of protection via tariffs and QRs, duty drawbacks, and selected incentives for exports.

However, there is something new in the 1983 program. First, the importance of a realistic exchange rate is more explicitly recognized. (At least, regular adjustments are being made to domestic inflation; see, for example, United Nations, 1985.) Second, and perhaps more important, there is a recognition that exports must be encouraged, not by excessive widespread subsidies as before, but by permanently removing the biases

Table 4.4 Some indications of anti-export bias in Yugoslav policy

Indicators	1953	1957	1959	1962	1964	1965–70	1970–80	1980
(a) EER Exports	375	858	1,044	1,178	1,055	Semifab. 12[a] Finished 22[a]	n.a.	14–30[b]
(dinars per US$) Imports	588	719	839	1,029	924	Semifab. 12[a] Finished 25[a]	n.a.	30–63[b]
(b) Sectoral biases			Industrial exports highly subsidized, consumer goods highly protected, agriculture and services faced relative disincentives, negative protection, low export EER, but bias allowed to be pro-export nevertheless			Export subsidies almost eliminated, import tariffs cascading	Reappearance of export subsidies, but also increased tariffs, quotas, and foreign exchange allocations favoring industrial goods but increasingly raw materials	
(c) Overall character of regime	Anti-export		Pro-export for non-consumer industries, modern pro-export for agriculture?			Anti-export or neutral?	Growing anti-export bias with sporadic corrections	Anti-export bias particularly strongly favoring all industrial goods

n.a., not available.

[a] 1968 percent protection.

[b] Domestic resource cost by sector.

Sources: (a) 1953, 1959 and 1962 data, Pertot, 1971, table 8.9, median values; 1964 data, Pertot, 1984, table 8; 1957 data, Chittle, 1977 table 9; 1964 data, Chittle, 1977, table 10; 1980 data, World Bank, 1983, table 4.10, p. 81; DRC values at market prices by sector, expressed in dinars per US dollar.

(b) See discussion in text for various references

(c) Author's qualitative assessment

favoring production for domestic markets and applying only limited export incentives such as duty drawbacks. Clearly, some lessons from the past unsuccessful episodes of liberalization have been incorporated in the latest attempt to revive the movement toward a more open economy. It remains to be seen whether the post-1983 liberalization policies will be any more successful than the 1965 episode.

A Review of Export Promotion Policies

The period of the administered trade regime (1952–60) was at first one of anti-export biases, with the EER for exports (375 dinars per US dollar, table 4.4) being far below that for imports (588 dinars per dollar, table 4.4). However, as the Western orientation of the economy manifested itself, the need to earn foreign exchange led to changes in the coefficients applied so as to favor exports. Thus, by 1957 the EER for exports had been devalued to 858 dinars per dollar, while that of imports had reached only 719 dinars per dollar. There were important sectoral variations. In conformance with the industrialization objectives of policy, industrial goods exports benefitted from a substantial effective subsidy of 35 percent (Havrylyshyn, 1988, appendix table 4.1) while exports of agriculture, forestry, and services were effectively taxed between 16 and 21 percent. Nevertheless, the fragmentary evidence suggests that, for food at least, the EER was slightly in favor of export activities.

Pertot (1971) shows the following parity ratios for exports and domestic production in 1962: food, 1,084 and 819; tobacco, 1,530 and 1,066; wood industry, 955 and 926; paper, 1,145 and 1,244; metallurgy, 942 and 1,175; nonmetallic minerals, 1,055 and 1,094. The incentives for consumer goods industries would appear to have been on the side of import substitution, with a protective effect of over 100 percent.

Export incentives continued to provide a pro-export bias after the 1961 reforms. While a unified exchange rate was introduced, export premiums and subsidies replaced the favorable export coefficients, and indeed may have reached levels as high as 45 percent (Chittle, 1977, p. 30) in 1964. Of course, the devaluation of the dinar in general encouraged exports. The existence of export coefficients before 1961 and of subsidies afterwards makes the overall real exchange rate movements irrelevant, if not actually misleading. What matters is the net impact of all trade policy instruments, as evidenced by any change in the EER for exports. Thus, while the official rate devaluation from 632 to 750 dinars per US dollar seems to be a 15.7 percent devaluation, the effective export exchange rate moved from 981 dinars per dollar in 1960 to 1,021 dinars per dollar in 1961, a mere 3.9 percent devaluation. What this means is that the export subsidy system after 1961 was slightly less favorable than the export coefficient system before that time. This was the first small step toward reducing relative export incentives.

With the 1965 reforms, there may have been a sharp switch of orientation with the removal of most export subsidies. Whether this was enough to change the system to an anti-export or neutral one is unfortunately not easy to establish since, for this period of time, almost no quantitative estimates have been made of the relevant measures such as EERs for exports versus imports. For example, the existing estimates of effective protection for 1970 (besides not making direct price comparisons) do not differentiate between exports and imports. Qualitatively, we "know" three facts: export subsidies were eliminated and then slowly reintroduced; tariffs, first cut sharply but then increased, remained largely escalating in pattern (low for raw materials, medium for semifinished goods, and high for finished goods); nontariff restrictions on imports, though perhaps at first reduced, were also gradually increased. While the first fact would in general reduce pro-export incentives, the other two could compensate by lowering incentives for import substitution and, in an effective protection sense, by lowering the costs of raw material imports for exporters. (Recall that the data of table 4.3 show in 1967 a greater proportion of raw materials on the liberal list than of all goods in general.)

A 1968 calculation by Pertot (1971) for the level of protection afforded exports versus domestic producers (see table 4.4) suggests that, overall, incentive policies were balanced or neutral. Qualitative interpretations by most authors who address this question suggest a stronger change in policy to an anti-export bias, at least for the early part of the reform.

That an anti-export bias developed in the 1970s seems more certain. Bery et al. (World Bank, 1983, p. 68), for example, note that "a substantial anti-export bias existed, generated through the operation of informal rather than formal mechanisms of commercial policy." For 1980, they show the extent of this bias using domestic resource cost (DRC) calculations (see table 4.4). Thus, in the 1970s, despite increased export subsidization (table 4.5), the lagging value of the dinar, increased tariffs, and, in particular, increased nontariff protection of domestic industry via quota licenses and foreign exchange allocations seem to have caused the strong anti-export bias which is so typical of complex trade regimes. The best piece of evidence of this tendency toward growing anti-export bias since the mid-1960s may be, somewhat circularly, the export performance of Yugoslavia. As described earlier, the pre-1965 period was one of rapidly growing exports, increased competitiveness, and controlled balance of payments. After 1965, the tendency reversed: export growth slowed (though it was by no means low); world market shares declined, especially after 1970; and balance-of-payments problems became a regular feature of the economy.

Table 4.5 Export subsidies as a percentage of exports

Year	Export subsidies (% exports)
1960	15.0
1962	24.0
1964(a)	45.0
1964(b)	20.0
1965	20.6
1966	6.3
1967	4.4
1968	7.3
1969	13.6
1976	24.4
1977	19.9
1978	25.9
1979	28.9
1980	17.4

Sources:1960, 1962 data, Sirc, 1979, p. 24; 1964(a) data, Chittle, 1977, p. 30; 1964(b) data, Dubey, 1975, p. 38; 1965–9 data, Mrkusic, 1972, p. 43; 1976–80 data, World Bank, 1983, p. 79

How does the evolution of export promotion policy affect the interpretation of the liberalization index? We have chosen to leave the liberalization index as shown in figure 4.1, basing it largely on the degree and level of interventionism with regard to imports. If favorable or neutral export bias were to be considered as signifying a more liberal regime, the index would be much higher in the period 1955–65 and much lower in the period 1970–80. However, this is surely not the interpretation that should be given to export biases. A strong pro-export bias may be as harmful as its opposite. In the Yugoslav case, a more plausible and useful reading of the situation would be as follows.

The high pro-export incentives before 1965 doubtless resulted in the commendable export performance observed, but this may have been a false competitiveness. When the subsidy props were removed rather abruptly in 1965 and import restrictions of various sorts were liberalized, the underlying weakness of the export industries became plain and not even the huge nominal devaluation of 65 percent sufficed to prevent the decline in export performance. Thus, while the pre-1961 policy was somewhat outward or export oriented as a result of strong subsidization to counter import substitution, it was nevertheless fundamentally distortionist. The only period that was truly liberal on all three counts – a relatively low degree of import restrictions, neutral export–import incentives, and a low degree of government intervention – was the period 1965–70. After 1970, the distortion illiberality was again substantial and growing, and by then even the export–import orientations had reversed to an anti-export bias.

Focus of the Study: the 1965–1967 Liberalization

The long-term tendency of trade policies in Yugoslavia can be roughly characterized as a generally liberalizing trend, punctuated by several sharp liberalization upswings of one to two years followed by reversals lasting three to four years. Four distinct attempts at liberalization can be identified: in 1952, 1961, 1965–7 , and 1983–6. A fifth upswing in 1971–3 is better regarded as a limited attempt to resume the major liberalization movement of 1965–7 and will be treated as such in this study. The first liberalization of 1952 is not analyzed here for two reasons: it was very short lived, and it retained a very high degree of protection plus interventionism in the form of multiple exchange rates. The latest liberalization of 1983–6 is too recent to permit analysis of its effects. While the 1961 liberalization was far less substantial than that of 1965, it was nevertheless important in taking two major steps which paved the way for 1965: replacement of multiple exchange rates by a uniform rate, and institution of a customs tariff to replace the implicit protection of earlier years; it is reviewed briefly in the next chapter. The attempt at freer trade in 1965–7 and its sequel through to 1974 is without question the major effort and the one to be analyzed in depth in this study.

5

Implementation and Reversal of the Major Liberalization, 1965–1974

In this chapter we focus upon the trade policy actions taken in the decade 1965–1974, following a brief review of the preceding phase (1961–4), and the continuation of restrictive tendencies to 1983. The story is essentially of an abortive attempt at trade liberalization, as the strong steps taken to open up the economy in 1965–7 were quickly curtailed and reversed. More modest attempts were made to restart the liberalization process in 1971 and again in 1978, but to little avail.

The policy actions taken in each important stage of the liberalization are recounted in the first section, and the visible political economy reactions which resulted in the reversal of liberalization are described in the second section. The latter is a partial analysis of the political economy process, describing briefly *how* it operated. Evaluation of *why* political reactions were what they were and how they were stimulated by actual or perceived effects of liberalization upon economy will be dealt with in chapters 10–12.

Trade Policy Actions

The Path of Implementation 1961–1983

Figure 5.1 reproduces the index of liberalization (see figure 4.1) and for the period of 1965–74 adds a notional estimate of the *intended* degree of liberalization in each episode or subepisode. This is a strictly judgmental indication serving only to represent graphically the text discussion on implementation. Table 5.1 summarizes the nature of each liberalization episode.

In broad terms, the evolution of intended and actual liberalization can be characterized as first a *nearly full* early implementation (1965–7), then a

Table 5.1 Chronology of liberalization, Yugoslavia, 1961–1983

1 *Pre-liberalization changes, 1961–4*
   Jan 1961   Dinar devaluation of 16%
   1961–2   Tariffs replace export and import coefficients
                      "Temporary" export subsidies introduced

2 *Major liberalization, 1965–7*
   Jul 1965   Dinar devaluation of 40%
   From mid-1965 to   Tariffs reduced from 23% to 10.5% average
     end 1967   Shift of products from restricted to liberal "lists"
                      Export subsidies abolished
                      Foreign exchange retention quotas of 7–12% for
                        exporters
                      Some realignment of internal administered prices
                        lessening the disparity of effective exchange rates

3 *Reversal, 1967–70*   Reintroduction of export subsidies
                      Increase of tariffs to average 13% by 1970 plus
                        selective surcharges of up to 7% in 1970
                      Shift of products from liberal to restricted lists

4 *Renewed liberalization 1971–4*
   Jan 1971   Dinar devaluation of about 17%
   During 1971   Reduction of tariffs but increase of products in
   Dec 1971   restricted list
   1972–3   Dinar devaluation of about 20%
                      Further limited tariff reductions
                      Reduction of products in restricted list
                      Exporter retention quotas raised from 7% to 20% and
                        eased credit for exporters
                      Dinar put on a managed float

5 *Second reversal 1974–78*
   1975–8   Import restrictions in form of increased surcharges;
                        tightened administrative use of foreign exchange
                        quotas
                      Fluctuating and *ad hoc* directions of policy; growing
                        administrative intervention

6 *Entrenchment of administered protectionism*
   1978–83   Continued intervention with various and frequent
                        changes in temporary import restrictions via QRs,
                        regional production agreements, foreign exchange
                        allocation mechanisms, export subsidies via
                        premiums, credits, etc.

7 *Liberalization for structural adjustment*
   1983–present   Goals
                        Maintenance of a realistic exchange rate
                        Unification of exchange rates
                        Reduction of tariffs and QRs
                        Selective export incentives such as retention quotas
                          and duty drawbacks
                        Achievement of dinar convertibility

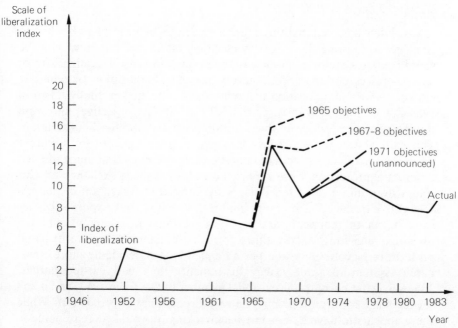

Figure 5.1 Intended and actual values of trade liberalization index, and goals of Yugoslav trade policy, 1946–1983

reversal rather than a delay in the program (1967–70), and finally a series of announced and unannounced efforts at *partial re-liberalization* in 1971–4 and 1978–9. However, these renewed efforts at continued liberalization were much weaker than the original 1965 program and never regained the level achieved in 1967. It must be emphasized that (as discussed in chapter 4 and described in more detail by Pertot, 1984) the reappearance of restrictiveness in trade policy took increasingly informal and subtle forms of *ad hoc* administrative protection. Thus the degree of reversal shown in the index (from 14 in early 1967 to below 10 after 1974) is much stronger than may be suggested by "hard" data such as tariffs, percentage of items on restricted lists, and so on (see chapter 4).

The ups and downs of liberalization policy can be divided into seven subperiods, with four episodes of progress in liberalization (1961, 1965, 1971, 1983) and four reversals, the last subdivided into two periods (1974–8 and 1978–83). The period 1978–83 was essentially a continuation of the growing administrative interventionism of 1974–8, with many isolated instances of both apparently liberal and apparently restrictive moves but no major reorientation until the 1983 Economic Stabilization Program.

Setting the Stage in 1961–1962

It was widely believed that three broad objectives of long-run policy had to be achieved to bring the Yugoslav economy into closer harmony with the world trading system: adherence of Yugoslavia to GATT, realignment of internal prices closer to world levels through liberalization of domestic markets, and a liberalization of trade policy. The steps actually taken in 1961–2 were limited with respect to all but the first objective, and were primarily intended to set up the institutions needed for later liberalization. The earlier system of varying exchange rate coefficients for different products – in effect a system of multiple exchange rates containing implicit differential protection – was replaced by a formal single exchange rate for transactions and a tariff schedule. Some limited liberalization of imports was also introduced. However, import restrictions and export subsidies soon began to reappear, and by 1964 an implicit system of multiple exchange rates functioned within a formalized system of open tariff-based protection. Nevertheless, the period ended with a decidedly more transparent system of trade policy instruments than had existed earlier, Yugoslavia did become a provisional member of GATT in 1962, and it had set the stage for a more comprehensive dismantling of protection. While there appears to have been some backtracking, it would be reasonable to characterize implementation in this episode as close to full.[1]

The Major Liberalization and Reversals, 1965–74

The First Stage, 1965–1967
Trade liberalization elements of the 1965 reforms were meant to be implemented over the period 1965–7 and to continue gradually thereafter. However, no specific timetable or determination of magnitude was announced either for the first stage (which is arbitrarily defined in this study as the period 1965–7) or for subsequent stages. Hence it is not possible to compare actual with planned achievements in anything but a rough qualitative way.

The major economic reform of 1965 went far beyond the trade regime to various domestic reforms aimed at decentralization of economic (and sociopolitical) power and a gradual liberalization of internal markets. The central idea was that worker-owned and self-managed enterprises should

---

[1] Pertot (1984), in a background paper for the project, had independently estimated the value for a trade liberalization index. His judgment of the 1961–4 period suggests a less dramatic but continued liberalization. With this exception, Pertot's index and that constructed by the present author in chapter 4 are nearly identical not only in turning points but even in magnitudes.

be free to act within a basically market-oriented system with only minimal interference. In order to attain international competitiveness and dinar convertibility, external liberalization was also necessary. While a full schedule for trade liberalization was not announced in advance, a broad set of targets was indicated.

The short-run goals (by 1967) were as follows:

1 substantial but unspecified reductions in tariffs;
2 creation of a transparent system of import controls with some increase in liberalized imports;
3 removal of export subsidies leaving foreign exchange retention quotas as the only export incentive;
4 realignment of internal administered prices towards parity with world prices.

The long-run goals (early to mid-1970s) were as follows:

1 continued liberalization of both domestic and external markets;
2 full convertibility of the dinar and elimination of the balance-of-payments deficit.

Four liberalization tools were to be used: reduction of tariffs, reduction of coverage of imports by QRs, removal of export subsidies, and adjustment of controlled prices. Tables 4.1, 4.2, and 4.5 provide information on the first three. Tariffs were lowered immediately from an average of 23.3 percent in 1964 to 10.3 percent in 1965, and although there was some regression in 1966, with tariffs raised slightly to 12.3 percent, they remained low until surcharges began to be added in 1969.

Reduction of QR coverage was introduced, as planned, a little later, with the new law of 1967 establishing six major categories and reducing the coverage of restricted imports from about 75–80 percent before 1967 to about 59 percent in 1967 (table 4.2). There is little doubt that in this first stage the incidence of QRs was substantially reduced – though it was far from being completely removed.

Export subsidies were cut sharply from about 20.6 percent of the value of exports in 1965 to 6.3 percent in 1966, and even further to 4.4 percent in 1967. On this score also, government intervention clearly decreased significantly. Finally, we may recall that in mid-1965 a substantial devaluation occurred from 750 dinars per US dollar to 1,250 dinars per dollar.

By mid-1967 many of the objectives of trade policy had been implemented. Tariffs were cut to a very low average of 10.3 percent. Import controls were made more explicit, liberalized imports increased from about 20–25 percent to 40 percent, and almost all export premiums were abolished.

Furthermore, controlled domestic prices were sharply readjusted with agricultural goods, intermediate inputs, and light consumer goods subjected to much sharper increases than the other categories (Havrylyshyn, 1988, appendix table 6.2). The combined effect of these policies was probably[2] to reduce considerably the variation in EERs for imports from a range of 1–8 in 1964 to a range of 1–5 by 1967, and to reduce the biases of earlier policy favoring heavy industry against primary goods and light manufactures. In chapters 10, 11, and 12 we look more closely at the fragmentary evidence on sectoral differences in liberalization; the conclusion reached is that the stated goals were largely achieved. The 1965 reforms were intended to reduce the biases favoring heavy industries via investment, production, and export subsidies, high controlled prices, and high protection. While it is not clear what happened to the first type of support, the movements of controlled prices and tariffs were generally in accordance with intentions, at least until 1967.

All in all, the first stage of liberalization was implemented quite successfully, inducing a considerable change in the level of nominal protection, a reduction of sectoral distortions, and a reduction of interventionism in external trade.

Reversal, 1967–1970

By the latter half of 1967, however, the achievements began to be reversed, with some (at first modest) increases in tariffs, administrative restrictions on imports, and (to compensate on the export side) a reintroduction of export subsidies. By 1970 average tariffs had been raised to a level of nearly 20 percent inclusive of surcharges, similar to 1964 levels. Liberalization of imports was also eroded as the coverage of the liberalized list fell to 35 percent in 1969 and 29 percent by 1971. By 1969 export subsidies were 14 percent (table 4.5) and, though data are not available for 1970, clearly continued into the 1970s. Qualitative evidence (to be discussed later) also suggests that the same heavy industry and capital goods sectors as before were favored with export subsidies. That is, the pro-export compensation policy was detrimental in the long run because it buttressed the position of comparatively disadvantaged industries already helped by import protection.

Perhaps the most pernicious change in this period was the increased use of *ad hoc* administrative charges in response to perceived short-term and localized difficulties of sectors or firms. Before 1961, of course, trade

---

[2] The statement about EERs is qualified by the word "probably" for the reasons discussed in chapter 4. Pertot's (1971) calculations of parity ratios are in principle equivalent to EERs, but do not always include subsidy and tax treatment effects for the export–import categories. In his 1984 background paper, however, he does interpret the 1965 liberalization cum price adjustment actions as lessening distortions.

policy had been very protectionist and clearly set by the central authority. The pattern of the 1961 and 1965 episodes was that of the government applying formal and explicit rules to trade and then adopting a "hands off" posture. Starting in 1967,[3] the earlier pattern of administrative intervention returned, not so much by way of dismantling the new institutions as by resorting to "temporary" changes in the new rules, or by informally undermining the letter of the rules by withholding permits, complicating paperwork, or by delaying credits on legally allowable foreign exchange.

As Pertot (1984) suggests, in reaction to the pleas of enterprises (or sectors, or regions) hard hit by the new competition of liberalized imports or affected by the removal of previous subsidy support, the old protectionist mentality quickly returned and was adapted to operate within a framework of superficially liberal institutions. The newly free worker-managed enterprises learned during 1967–70 that their economic difficulties could be successfully presented to the authorities as special cases; in a word, rent seeking in a formally liberalized environment was discovered.

Renewed Liberalization Attempt, 1971–1974
While worsened economic performance coincided with the 1965–7 liberalization, output, employment, and prices improved during the reversal period. (See chapter 10 for a discussion of the combination of policies that account for the poor performance and of the purely temporary and superficial efficacy of restrictionist remedies.) This amelioration was short-lived, and by late 1969–70 slower growth, higher inflation, and a worsening trade deficit led to a renewed effort to achieve the original aims of the 1965 liberalization. Two devaluations in 1971 were followed by a managed float of the dinar by mid-1973. Commitment to continue the liberalization begun in 1965 was manifested by some gradual reductions in tariffs and import controls. With exports, however, the policy this time was different. Not only were export subsidies untouched; they may have been raised. No data are available for the years 1970–5, but certainly by 1976 subsidies amounted to nearly 25 percent of export value. The exporters' retention quota was definitely increased in 1971 from a base level of 7 percent to 20 percent, and more for some sectors (construction, tourism) and large exporters.

The Slide to Administered Protectionism

Second Reversal, 1975–1978
Continued difficulties of slow growth, high inflation, and a marked

---

[3] Or perhaps even earlier: tariffs on paper products, textiles, and clothing, which had been dramatically lowered in 1965, had already begun to increase in 1966.

worsening of the trade deficit, especially in 1974, contributed to the second reversal of liberalization. Import restrictions began to be reimposed in 1974 both informally (tightened access to foreign exchange) and formally. There were increases in tariff rates (table 4.1) and by 1976 in QRs (table 4.2). This, plus increased support for exports in the form of subsidies (table 4.5), increased credit, and other measures, quickly stemmed the external deficit. Price controls plus restrictive growth policies curbed inflation as intended. However, this success was again short lived. While output growth improved, inflationary and external deficit problems worsened by 1977–8.

Entrenchment of Administered Protection, 1978–1983
The year 1978 is considered by Yugoslav authorities as introducing an important liberalization of foreign trade operations. In this year there was a full implementation of various new laws supposedly decentralizing decision making with respect to foreign trade, foreign exchange allocations, and so on. The system is far from explicit, but its principal idea is that all producing units must belong to a Community of Interest for Foreign Exchange Relations (CIFER), within which agreements are reached on trade balances, administration of export subsidies, foreign exchange allocations, and external borrowing rights (World Bank, 1983).

While some effects of this decentralization may have been liberalizing (informal markets for foreign exchange within CIFER led to premiums which doubtless improved allocation efficiency), others were restrictive (CIFER could restrict import rights of members), and certainly the collusive nature of such a system could not but hamper competitive actions by exporters and importers. Perhaps most important, the system entrenched the arbitrariness and obscurity of the rules of the game. Despite the intended decentralization of power, administrative intervention was not necessarily reduced. Local and regional governments became even more involved than before and federal authorities were by no means loath to step in to take care of problems as they arose.

Thus this period saw a hardening of administrative intervention and very little, if any, reduction in the formal levels of protection, since tariffs remained at the same level as in the mid-1960s, import controls were, if anything, more restricted, and export subsidies remained very high. Indeed, far from a renewed attempt at broad-scale liberalization, 1981–2 saw a sharp tightening via price controls, import controls, and export subsidy measures. This was in reaction to the drying up of new credits globally, and for Eastern Europe in particular, after the Polish debt crisis.

The Political Economy of the Reversal

Overall Political Instability

Internal political phenomena created the liberalizing tendencies described in chapter 3. They also brought about its reversal. However, the reversal in trade liberalization did not arise from a change of actors or attitudes in the political arena; rather, economic slowdown coinciding with, though not resulting from (see chapter 10), the first stage of liberalization combined with independent political developments in 1968 in the form of a federalism crisis to put both political and economic pressures on the central authorities to resort to special treatment. As far as trade policies were concerned, these measures to constrain centrifugal forces took the form of general increased protection, *ad hoc* exemptions, direct support of investment activities, renewed export subsidies, and indirect support for continued production and employment of weak factories via financial infusions by supposedly autonomous banks.

Though the macroeconomic details will be discussed later, a brief statement may be useful here. Output and employment growth fell in 1965 despite rapid growth of exports, but inflation worsened somewhat. Monetary policy became increasingly restrictive from 1965 to 1967 causing a sharp slowdown in GDP in 1967 and a successful reduction of inflation from over 10 percent in 1965–6 to about 2 percent (for producer prices). In the meantime, labor income continued to grow at a rate of 5–10 percent in real terms despite the recession. By 1967 the favorable effects of devaluation upon exports and imports had been eroded by inflation, and the fuller implementation of import liberalization began to be reflected in an import growth far exceeding that of exports. The double pressure of lagging employment and a worsening trade balance would perhaps have been enough to lead any government to the first refuge of policy in such circumstances: trade restrictions. Added to this was a new environment of political economy in which regional and local governments combined with producer interests to put pressure on the central authorities for assistance.

Throughout the liberalization period (1965–70) the political situation, while never seriously threatened by a change of government, was nevertheless in considerable ferment, which was partly intentional as policy was shifting (as planned by the 1965 reform) from a very strongly centralized system with federal representation at the center to a more strongly federalist system with decision-making power (as well as budgetary power) devolved to the republic and local entities. Rusinow (1977, p. 62) refers to the period 1967–9 as the phase of "federalization of the party, state, and government." This in general occurred without unusual public disruption or open dissension until 1968–9, when the political situation dramatically worsened. This, the unintended part of the ferment, came in the form of open regionalism and nationalism, with a substantial component of demands for economic "fairness" in the federation. One sign of political conflict, largely noneconomic in nature, was the publication on March 17, 1967, by leading Croatian cultural organizations of a "Declaration on the name and position of the Croatian literary language," asserting the uniqueness of Croatian as a language different from Serbian or the lingua franca Serbo-Croat. This broke the unspoken agreement to eschew the provocative assertion of ethnic differences, and initiated a dangerous nationalities crisis which developed until 1971–2.

A year later, political problems became more open and explicit and more directly tied to the economic situation. In June 1968 students at Belgrade University staged a strike focusing on the problems of growing unemployment, increasing economic inequalities, growing materialism of Yugoslav society, and so on. A student strike in the year 1968 was not exactly unique to Yugoslavia, but in Eastern Europe, for a socialist country with a strong unitary government, it was an event profoundly disturbing to the authorities. Paradoxically, the August 1968 Soviet invasion of Czechoslovakia at first contributed to stabilizing the situation, because of fear of Soviet action spreading to Yugoslavia.

Meanwhile, the economic situation continued to deteriorate, and the simmering ethnic problem brought into the open by the Croatian declaration of March 1967 erupted in July 1969, this time with a purely economic character, in the so-called Slovenian road-building crisis. Certain road projects that Slovenia proposed for inclusion in a loan request to the World Bank were excluded, a fact received in Slovenia "with criticism and protests the like of which cannot be remembered in post-war Yugoslavia" (*Politika*, July 31, 1969). The discussion quickly took on nationalistic overtones. The Ljubljana newspaper *Delo* (August 4, 1969) pointedly noted that the disagreement went beyond the roads, and was "primarily about the material–financial relationship between Slovenia and the Federation."

This situation was soon calmed, with the Slovenians essentially accepting the federal decision, but a much more serious Croatian crisis developed in 1970–1: the nationalist issue first raised publicly in the March 1967 declaration developed into open nationalism in Croatia that was increasingly injected into all social, political, cultural, and economic issues. The threat to the existing political power and the federation was substantial. Though little if any open action was taken, the federal party leadership resolved to stem this movement and exhorted local leaders to act.

The crisis surfaced in November 1971 with a strike called by Zagreb University students "because of problems connected with the foreign exchange and foreign trade systems." While the initial declaration suggested economic motives, the demands were much more focused on nationalist matters such as making Croatian an official language. The regime survived this crisis partly by resorting to strong action – demanding resignations and even forcing the removal of many people in leading positions – and partly by accepting some of the Croatian demands, among them a raising of export retention quotas from 7 to 20 percent and the institution of a "floating" dinar. Both these economic changes were likely to favor Croatian (and incidentally Slovenian) enterprises which were stronger and more export oriented than those in other republics.

Can the political instability be attributed to the liberalization? Despite the public statements pointing to economic conditions, the answer would seem to be "not really." First, student strikes in 1968 and after were likely to have happened, liberalization or not. Second, most of the instability was nationalist and not strictly (if at all) economic. Third, where an economic element was included, it was generally neither for nor against liberalization. The economic demands of the Croatian crisis, for example, were if anything for more trade liberalization, at least in the form of foreign exchange retention by exporters and a fully floating dinar; however, the strong Croatian industry was as quick as any other to request temporary protection where it had special interests, for instance in the metal products sector.

It might have been expected that the negative short-run effects of trade liberalization would be greatest in the economically backward republics where the most inefficient "political" factories were concentrated. Fragmentary evidence (unfortunately only for production and employment by republic and not for exports or competitive imports) seems to counter this expectation, as the greatest absolute as well as relative decline in employment occurred in Slovenia and Croatia. However, these data reflect as much the regional political will to allow adjustments as they do the need to adjust. That is, the richer republics were perhaps more willing (and certainly more able) to absorb any labor displaced by liberalization – at least at first. In contrast, in the weaker republics the competitive effect was perhaps simply not allowed to evolve. Existing firms were supported by "persuading" banks to continue extending lines of credit despite the build-up of inventories, and new factories continued to be established at a rate far higher than in the richer republics. The ratio of investment to GNP in 1965–9 (see chapter 10) was 32.1 in the underdeveloped republics compared with 25.4 in the developed republics.

Political instability therefore seems to have been greatest in the developed republics where the liberalization was being allowed to occur, perhaps because of a perception that the other regions were not paying the necessary adjustment costs. To that extent, trade liberalization may have contributed to political instability. However, an alternative explanation is that decentralization of power to republics allowed greater expression of local discontent. The generally deteriorating economic situation (not due simply to liberalization) was a catalyst that led to more open expression of dissatisfaction. Of course, the international contagion of student strikes in 1968 helped this along, and local politicians either rode and exploited the waves or were simply carried along by them.

Nevertheless, there was a perception that trade liberalization, foreign exchange crises, and the role of Western financing were indeed to blame for the economic difficulties. Thus student strikers' demands (not always notable for their internal consistency) included both "liberal" changes – greater freedom of (Croatian) exporters to retain foreign exchange – and some diametrically opposed demands – reduced dependence on foreign goods and greater stimulus to domestic producers.

The New Lobbying Power of Enterprises and Local Governments

A factor of great importance in the political economy of the reversal was the increased power of enterprises and local governments. Enterprises or their representatives played little direct part in the debate preceding the 1965 reforms. After 1965 this changed substantially. In the spirit of decentralization and de-etatization which was to justify the phrase "workers' management," enterprises began to express their interests much more vocally. Comisso (1979, p. 87) has put it aptly:

> Whereas prior to the reforms, the pattern had been one of political "meddling" in the affairs of the enterprises, the new dynamic can be more aptly characterized as enterprises meddling in the government, as firms hit hard by the new competition ran to political bodies for bail-outs in the form of subsidies, protective tariffs, special loans and price increases.

Given the decentralization of government and budgets, these appeals were likely to be addressed to local or republic governments, not just to Belgrade. However, despite decentralization, there was a limit to the economic policy powers of local governments. Certainly, their increased budgets allowed some use of funds to support existing enterprises or for new investments. Also, the decentralization of banking activity allowed local governments to apply political pressure on banks to grant loans to local enterprises. When this power was exhausted, the governments and the enterprises had a common interest (local jobs, economic activity, local tax base) in asking for help higher up. Bank regulations limited lending activities, but these could be extended by relaxation of rules at the center or infusion of funds from the still larger "national" banks. Assistance in the form of direct federal funds was still available, albeit in reduced amounts. Most important, control over import and export regulations was of course still federal. Thus, "temporary" tariff or quota protection as well as export support came essentially from the federal government.

Enterprise lobbying had occurred before; in the administrative trade regime of 1952–60 considerable economic benefits could be obtained by pressing the officials of the Foreign Trade Ministry to increase the relevant exchange coefficient. What was new after 1965 was the increase in local power and the encouragement given by the prevalent climate of reform.

Two additional institutional changes strengthened and expedited such economic lobbying. First, central planning of the top-down variety was essentially replaced by indicative planning of the bottom-up type. The process and obligation of passing information up from the enterprise to the planning authorities facilitated lobbying. Second, the reform of 1965 stressed the need for modernization and rationalization of industry, and saw as one mechanism to achieve this a movement toward concentration and mergers of enterprises in enterprise associations – similar to a characteristic of French planning. Such concentration is clearly likely to encourage noncompetitive activity and political lobbying. It is well attested that a good deal of concentration did occur after 1965: between 1962 and 1970 concentration increased, often substantially, in all but one of 19 sectors (Petrin, 1981).

It was of course presumed that the privilege of increased decentralized power carried obligations with it. Two such obligations prominent in the debate and the reform statements were the obligation of workers to limit the labor income they awarded themselves and to leave a reasonable amount for investment and the obligation to suffer the consequences of competition in the market.

As we will describe in chapters 7–9, the freedom to determine one's own income resulted in an unsurprising tendency to increase this income sharply. Had the second obligation been allowed to work its way through, this splurge in personal income might have been quickly curbed. Instead, enterprises in difficulty, as a first recourse, sought government assistance. As the various levels of government yielded to these requests, the signal became even clearer: the authorities were prepared to make special concessions to bend the rules, and it was worth the effort to try. In a word, rent seeking became widespread, resulting in the sharp reversals of liberalization observable in the period from 1969 to 1971 and after 1974.

6

Economic Policies Accompanying the 1965 Trade Liberalization

It has already been emphasized that trade liberalization was only part of a program of long-term institutional policy changes – the 1965 reforms. In this chapter we consider short- and medium-term macroeconomic policies, such as exchange rates, fiscal and monetary stabilization, income and price controls, capital flows, and public investment and banking policies. Some of these, such as devaluation and selective adjustment of controlled prices, were formulated as part of the liberalization package. Others were based on considerations not directly related to trade liberalization, such as the use of monetary restrictiveness in 1965–7 to control inflation. However, all the policies applied at the time liberalization was being implemented had some effect on the performance of the economy and hence upon the outcome of liberalization. Therefore it is of critical importance to understand the various policy measures taken in the period, whether they "accompanied" trade liberalization organically or merely coincidentally.

A brief review of the economic circumstances at the time of liberalization follows, to help illuminate the rationale behind some of the policies.

Economic Circumstances

The economy of Yugoslavia in the 1950s had a record of strong growth, rapid structural shift toward industrial activity, and a negative but manageable balance-of-payments situation, with export growth exceeding import growth, a debt-to-GNP ratio in 1960 of about 17 percent, a debt service ratio of about 15 percent (counting only convertible currency exports), and low inflation rates.

For a year or two before the 1961 liberalization the trade and current accounts deteriorated and inflation grew (table 6.1). The balance of payments improved again by 1962, only to begin to deteriorate immediately in the next year. Thus, both the 1961 and the 1965 policies came on

Table 6.1 Some measures of economic circumstances at the time of liberalization

	1959	1960	1961	1962	1963	1964	1965	1966	1967	1968
External										
Trade balance (million dinars)	− 660	− 810	− 1,040	− 602	− 2,106	− 3,282	− 2,527	− 4,442	− 5,687	− 6,650
Current account (million dinars)	− 466	− 574	− 803	− 255	− 885	− 1,772	+ 291	− 865	− 1,025	− 1,325
Current account (% GNP)	− 1.9	− 2.0	− 2.3	− 0.7	− 1.9	− 2.9	+ 0.3	− 0.9	− 1.0	− 1.1
Export growth (volume) (%)	11.0	15.0	0.0	17.0	12.0	5.0	12.0	9.0	2.5	3.1
Export price index (1961 = 100)	97	100	100	104	106	113	121	125	127	124
Import price index	98	99	100	102	106	110	117	117	117	117
Terms of trade	99	101	100	102	100	103	103	107	109	109
Industrial growth EEC (%)	n.a.	n.a.	4.6	9.6	4.3	7.3	4.1	3.9	n.a.	n.a.
Domestic										
GNP Growth	16.5	6.1	5.7	3.8	11.8	13.0	13.4	8.5	1.8	4.5
Open unemployment rate	5.6	5.1	5.6	6.7	6.4	5.6	6.1	6.7	7.1	8.0
Inflation (CPI)	1.5	9.6	8.1	9.9	5.7	11.8	34.5	22.8	7.0	4.9
Agricultural output growth	+ 32.2	− 12.2	− 2.0	+ 1.5	+ 6.1	+ 5.7	− 7.2	+ 19.4	− 0.5	− 3.3

n.a., not available; CPI, consumer price index.
Sources: Dubey, 1975; Federal Institute of Statistics, *Statistical Yearbook of Yugoslavia*, various issues

the heels of a balance-of-payments crisis and both entailed devaluations which helped correct the problems.

Export performance for the period 1960–4 remained as strong as it had been earlier and showed only brief setbacks in the years 1961 and 1964. The first was partly due to a poor harvest in 1960 and 1961, while the second is attributed to strong internal demand; note that GNP growth in the years 1963 and 1965 was very strong.[1] External price movements were on the whole favorable in this period, as the indices for prices of exports, imports, and terms of trade in table 6.1 make clear.

The growth rates of Yugoslavia's major trading partners (Europe, 40 percent; Comecon countries, 30 percent) were high in the first half of the 1960s, but the period 1965–7, when trade liberalization was implemented, saw slightly slower growth. Perhaps even more important than the level of economic activity in the export markets was the fact of increasing barriers to Yugoslav exports into the EEC, especially for agricultural goods.

The availability and terms of long-term capital inflows were largely unchanged in this period. In fact development assistance was becoming increasingly available at below-market terms, and Yugoslavia had no difficulty in obtaining short- or long-term credit. In both the 1961 and 1965 liberalizations the IMF extended credits of US$75 million and US$110 million respectively (equal to about a tenth of annual imports), and equal amounts were obtained from associated bilateral arrangements.

No major economic or political shocks occurred at the time of the liberalization, with the exception of a very poor harvest in 1960–1 and a very good one in 1966.

The years immediately preceding liberalization (1963–4) saw a worsening of inflation and of the external balance. The first stage of liberalization (1965–7) coincided with a cyclical downturn, alleviated somewhat by healthy growth in 1968. Unemployment worsened steadily, a situation probably underestimated by the values in table 6.1 which show registered work seekers as a percentage of the labor force; furthermore, the actual pressures of underemployment were temporarily relieved by a surge in short-term migration of guest workers to Europe. Inflationary pressures, felt for the first time before and during the 1961 liberalization, were barely contained for about a year in 1963 before emerging again even more strongly, reaching levels of 25–30 percent in 1965–6. They were sharply curtailed in 1967–8 by a very tight monetary policy. Finally, the balance-of-payments situation moved in much the same way as inflation. It deteriorated before the 1961 devaluation and improved briefly afterwards, only

---

[1] These assumptions, as well as other points of interpretation in this section, are based on OECD *Economic Surveys* of various years. However, different interpretations are possible. In the next section we see that there was an appreciation of the real exchange rate from 1961 to 1964, which may have been a factor behind the slowdown of export growth.

to deteriorate again in 1963–4. The 1965 devaluation brought another improvement for a year or two which was followed by a new worsening, though this last is seen clearly only in the trade balance.

Exchange Rate Policy

The nature of the exchange rate regime changed most dramatically in 1961, as already described. The system of coefficients by product which was in effect a system of multiple exchange rates was replaced by a uniform exchange rate. Though differentials in effective exchange rates remained with export premiums on one side and tariffs on the other, the 1961 move was significant. The new fixed-rate system remained in force until July 1972 with very restrictive controls over actual transactions, although the system of allocations of foreign exchange was slightly looser.

Thus, while all transactions had to pass through the National Bank, foreign exchange earnings did not have to be automatically surrendered by exporters, or by others who earned foreign exchange such as migrant workers, but could be held in foreign currency accounts. The disposition of the funds was nevertheless subject to the permission of the Bank under a variety of rules, the most important of which was the range of retention quotas for exporters, which in 1961 were set at 3 percent for agriculture, 7 percent for industry and services, and 25 percent for printing and publishing. These were later revised for some products in 1965–7 and raised to a 20 percent minimum in 1972, and to as much as 45 percent for tourism and 100 percent for construction enterprises operating abroad.

The dinar was devalued several times in this period (see table 6.2), and in mid-1972 it was put on a managed float. Until then the movements in the real exchange rate (RER1 and RER2 in table 6.2) followed a pattern of depreciation with the nominal devaluation, and then a period of appreciation as domestic inflation exceeded world levels. The real appreciation was particularly sharp after the 1965 nominal devaluation, and was in fact not fully reversed by the devaluation of 1971.

Details of export promotion policies described in the previous chapter need not be repeated here, but it is important to note some of the connections between export promotion and exchange rate policies.

The devaluation in general encouraged exports, but the existence of export coefficients before 1961 and of subsidies afterwards may make a consideration of the overall real exchange movements misleading. What matters is the net impact of all trade policy instruments as evidenced in any change in the effective exchange rate for exports. Thus, while the 1961 devaluation from 632 to 750 dinars per US dollar was in theory a 15.7 percent devaluation, the effective export exchange rate moved from 993 dinars per dollar in 1960 to 1,040 dinars per dollar in 1961 (Pertot,

Table 6.2 Exchange rates and price movements (1961 = 100)

Year	Dinars per US$	NERI	YWPI	WWPI	RER1	PTR	PNTR	RER2
1960	6.32	84.3	94.8	99.0	80.7	99.5	91.7	91.5
1961	7.50	100.0	100.0	100.0	100.0	100.0	100.0	100.0
1962	7.50	100.0	101.7	101.7	100.0	100.3	105.9	97.3
1963	7.50	100.0	103.4	103.2	99.8	106.0	109.7	96.6
1964	7.50	100.0	108.6	105.4	97.0	112.0	117.5	95.3
1965	12.50	166.7	127.6	107.6	140.6	118.0	156.8	125.4
1966	12.50	166.7	151.7	110.0	120.8	120.5	200.9	99.9
1967	12.50	166.7	172.4	110.2	106.5	120.5	229.4	87.5
1968	12.50	166.7	181.0	111.4	102.6	120.0	249.5	80.2
1969	12.50	166.7	190.5	115.3	100.9	125.4	278.0	75.2
1970	12.50	166.7	206.4	121.8	98.3	137.2	303.6	75.4
1971	15.00	200.0	239.0	127.1	108.2	142.3	344.0	82.7
1972	17.00	226.6	273.1	132.2	101.2	150.1	382.4	88.9
1973	15.50	206.6	317.5	146.8	95.5	180.0	447.7	83.6

Calculations shown for the real exchange rate: NERI, nominal exchange rate indexed at 1961 = 100.0; RER1, using wholesale prices of Yugoslavia (YWPI) and six major partners (WWPI); RER2, using an index of tradeables' prices PTR (weighting by exports and imports) and an index of nontradeables' prices (housing, health, education, culture, recreation, services) PNTR.
Source: Federal Institute of Statistics, *Statistical Yearbook of Yugoslavia*, various issues

1971), a mere 3.9 percent devaluation. Clearly, the export subsidy system post-1961 was slightly less favorable than the export coefficient system pre-1961. This was the first small step toward reduction of relative export incentives.

However, the direction of movements in the real exchange rate and the real effective exchange rate for exports (when the later are available) are consistent. The 1965 devaluation had a sharp pro-export effect at first, despite the removal of export subsidies, with the effective exchange rate increasing from 1,029 in 1964 to 1,244 in 1965 (22 percent).

Monetary Policy

After the 1961 reforms, and even more so after those of 1965, monetary policy became the most important macro policy tool of the federal government, since fiscal revenues were considerably decentralized and budgetary policy coordination became difficult if not impossible. Although the banking system was also decentralized beginning in 1961, by 1967 the National Bank of Yugoslavia had regained a wide variety of powerful tools to control monetary aggregates.

The Bank could use rediscount rates, undertake central bank lending, change reserve requirements, and change credit ceilings. Open-market operations in the usual sense were not relevant, since few if any financial instruments used in such operations existed. Furthermore, the rediscount rate, and hence in effect the on-lending interest rates, were *not* changed from the value of 6 percent throughout the period 1965–72, largely reflecting the aversion of the socialist government to putting a high price on capital, but also of course typical of the government of a developing country wishing to stimulate growth. Consequently, for most of this period, real rates of interest were negative, given the inflation rates of over 10 percent (table 6.3). Real rates of interest on foreign debt were considerably higher and rose somewhat over the period.

Table 6.3 Interest rates (percent)

Bank accounts	1966	1967	1968	1969	1970	1971
Sight savings	5.0	6.0	6.0	16.0	6.0	6.0
Time savings	6.0	7.0	7.0	7.5	7.5	7.5
Bank credits	8.0	8.0	10.0	8.0	8.0	8.0

Source: Dubey, 1975, p. 228

The major policy tools that did change in the course of the reform were the quantity of rediscounting operations, the reserve requirements, and credit ceilings.

The basic direction of monetary policy is fairly evident from the data of table 6.4, columns 5 and 6. In the second half of 1964 and the first half of 1965, reserve requirements were raised to the legal limit of 35 percent, largely with the intention of suppressing inflationary pressures, and a money supply crunch set in. A slight easing in 1966 was quickly followed by a return to restrictiveness by the third quarter, when the National Bank considered that there was excess liquidity and decided to absorb it by a further reduction of credits and the imposition of credit ceilings on banks in the system. As a result, credits to enterprises fell sharply and continuously from 4.2 billion dinars in 1964 to 2.5 billion dinars in 1967 (column 2), and the money supply declined in 1967 by 5.6 percent. Only the continued rise in consumer and housing credits (largely the latter) kept the decline from being even sharper. This discriminatory policy favoring consumption was in line with the general aim of the 1965 reform to allow greater income gains for workers and increased consumption opportunities.

Attempts to discriminate by credit policy in favor of exports and thus at least to achieve the balance-of-payments objectives of the 1965–7 policies

Table 6.4 Monetary aggregates, 1963–1972 (billion dinars)

Year	1 Total money supply	2 Enterprise credits	3 Housing and consumer credits	4 Ratio of MS to transactions	5 Inflation CPI (per-cent)	6 MS growth rate (percent)	7 Implicit rates of in-terest, foreign debt
1963	19.3	3.1	1.0	19.4	5.7	n.a.	3.6
1964	21.1	4.2	1.2	18.3	11.8	9.4	3.8
1965	22.2	3.8	1.6	14.9	34.5	5.0	4.2
1966	23.2	3.2	2.0	12.3	22.8	4.5	4.4
1967	21.9	2.5	2.5	11.4	7.0	− 5.6	4.0
1968	27.6	4.2	3.5	13.1	4.9	25.8	3.8
1969	30.8	4.8	4.4	n.a.	8.3	11.6	4.0
1970	38.5	6.8	6.6	n.a.	10.3	25.0	5.1
1971	43.3	6.9	8.9	n.a.	16.0	12.5	3.9
1972	60.5	6.2	11.4	n.a.	17.2	39.7	n.a.

n.a., not available; MS, money supply.
Sources: column 1, Schrenk et al., 1979, p. 323; columns 2, 3, and 5, Federal Institute of Statistics, Statistical Yearbook of Yugoslavia, various issues; column 4, Horvat, 1976, p. 229; column 7, calculated from Dubey, 1975, tables 42 and 43, Annex, as ratio of interest payments to disbursements

were unsuccessful but did seem to cause a sharp diminution in economic activity. In 1968, when inflation also seemed to be under control, this was recognized and the policy was reversed, beginning a period of almost annual "stop–go" policies (table 6.4, column 6).

Fiscal Policy and Investment Funding

Decentralization in the 1960s reduced the flexibility of fiscal policy as a stabilization tool. This was not because the relative value of government revenues or expenditures fell but rather because of the devolution of both taxing and expenditure power from the center to the republics and local governments. While the ratio of public expenditure to GDP remained fairly stable at about 32–3 percent, the actual deficit situation (in a macromanagement sense) was not a meaningful measure, as it could not easily be determined by coordinated policy. Furthermore, the deficit–surplus operations were in general very insubstantial. For budgetary accounts alone, the surplus in most years was typically very small; this was also true of total public expenditure shown for the years 1967–70 (Havrylyshyn, 1988, appendix table 6.1).

What was very significant in this period was the decline in federal power over the budget (the figures in fact overestimate the decline since part of federal expenditure included transfers to republic budgets). A considerable reduction of the government's role in investment funding reflected the decline. Before 1964, state-financed investments were considerable, as table 6.5 shows.

Table 6.5 Domestic sources of funding for fixed investment[a] (percent)

Sources	1960–3	1964	1965	1966	1969	1970	1971	1972
Economic organizations	30	26	29	39	28	27	27	30
Other social organizations	7	6	8	7	6	6	7	8
State finance	60	36	27	15	16	16	15	20
Federal	(33)	(7)	(3)	(6)	(9)	(9)	(7)	(2)
Republic	(8)	(8)	(4)	(3)	(3)	(2)	(4)	(14)
Communes	(19)	(21)	(20)	(6)	(4)	(4)	(4)	(4)
Banks	3	32	36	39	49	51	51	42
Total	100	100	100	100	100	100	100	100

( ), estimated.
[a] Includes all investments financed out of social resources, plus private investment financed through bank credit.
Source: Dubey, 1975, p. 221

The pattern changed, however, and the government's direct role declined sharply from 1960–3 (60 percent) to 1965 (27 percent) and continued to decline (to between 15 and 20 percent). The role of the banks increased, and the influence of government became only indirect. Indeed, the decentralization of the banks meant that republic and local governments had more indirect influence than the federal government on investment decisions by banks.

There was no restriction of investment or access to capital (banks or government funds were the only sources), though interest rates were indeed regulated, as the earlier discussion on monetary policy and table 6.3 indicate. The rate was essentially negative in real terms throughout both liberalization periods.

Both the low interest rates and the operation of direct government investment funds implicitly acted as capital subsidy elements, but there were no explicit schemes for subsidizing investment beyond this.

International Capital Movements

Little need be said on this aspect of the Yugoslav economy, for such movements were (and continue to be) essentially restricted. As the dinar was not convertible at any time, outflow of capital was not permitted and, except for repayment of debts, was irrelevant. Inflow was only permitted in the form of loans; foreign direct investment was not permitted until 1967. This timing seems to be related to the initiation of liberalization. The 1967 law permitting joint ventures was another indication of increasing openness. However, the size of foreign investment was quite small, rising from US$2.5 million in 1968 to US$39.7 million in 1973 – only about 4–5 percent of gross capital inflow, and a minuscule proportion of total domestic investment.

Official borrowing was of course permitted, and increased considerably in volume. An indication of orders of magnitude may be useful at this point. First, the extent of indebtedness increased sharply from US$941 million in 1965 to US$2,706 million in 1971 (from 12 to 24 percent of GDP).

Second, the structure of outstanding debt began to shift away from official sources to private sources (30 percent in 1965 and 62 percent in 1971). This unfavorable tendency, by now so familiar from analysis of the debt crisis in the 1980s, occurred far earlier in Yugoslavia than in developing countries in general.

Domestic Controls

Price

Since 1965 the Federal Price Bureau has been responsible for a system of administered price controls in Yugoslavia. As in any system of price controls, it is difficult to judge the effective degree of control or liberality, as coverage statistics do not always indicate how much market forces lie behind the decisions of the pricing authorities. Nevertheless, it seems clear from the figures in table 6.6, which shows the extent of price control coverage, that the degree of intervention in prices was reduced substantially during liberalization.

The system of price controls was not complicated on the surface. Fixed prices were set for some essential goods (electricity, transport, cigarettes, sugar, oil, salt); ceiling prices were set for key raw materials (metallurgical products, coal, petroleum); guaranteed or minimum prices were set for agricultural goods; industrial goods prices were set by acceding or not acceding to requests of producers supported by cost documentation.

Table 6.6 Price controls coverage of industrial
goods (percent)

1962	1962–5	1965	1968	1970
67.0	60.0	70.0	46.0	43.0

Source: Horvat, 1976

The general policy orientation underlying the pattern of prices before 1965 has been noted in chapter 4; raw materials, agricultural goods, and intermediate inputs were low priced; consumer goods, capital goods, and other export-intended goods had high prices. Where the domestic structure of prices differed from world prices, a variety of mechanisms were used to close the gaps. Before 1961 the trade coefficients, in effect a system of multiple exchange rates that were very product specific, were used. After the 1961 reform introduced a uniform exchange rate, four forms of "wedging" were used. First, QRs were retained for many products explicitly (or implicitly in the form of foreign exchange allocation limits), in effect obviating the need for a wedge at all. Second, some minor realignment of prices *did* occur, following, at least in spirit, the notion of world prices as a benchmark. Third, differentiated tariffs were instituted. Fourth, export subsidies and premiums of various sorts were used as a replacement for the differentiated coefficients.

With the 1965–7 liberalization, the initial removal of export subsidies, the sharp reduction of tariff rates, and the increase in liberalized imports put the onus on the second mechanism: a major realignment of the administered prices, with a strong boost in prices of agricultural goods, inputs, and raw materials, and a much lower increase in prices of capital goods (Havrylyshyn, 1988, appendix table 6.2). That a major realignment of prices occurred in the 1965–7 period is without doubt, and it continued in the case of producer prices even after 1967. Pertot (1984) has shown that the range of relative disparity between world and domestic prices (in effect the range of EERs) narrowed sharply in 1965–7 from 1–8 to 1–5. However, despite this major realignment of prices, other wedges were soon reintroduced, and the 1965 reforms were characterized by Pertot (1984, p. 54) as an important missed opportunity for correcting the distorted price structure developed over the 1950s under the regime of administered prices and multiple exchange coefficients.

Labor Income (Wages)

Under self-management, workers decide how the operating surplus (after costs such as raw materials and inputs plus any capital charges and tax obligations) is divided between personal income and investment. Before 1965 there were several limitations on the workers' freedom to allocate themselves personal incomes. Not only was the system far from being "self-managed" in reality, there were rules and regulations tying the increases in personal incomes to productivity growth, or other rules requiring minima for investment allocations.

In 1965 greater power was given to enterprises to make this decision, releasing it from productivity growth and investment "plans" imposed from the center. Part of the motivation was simply to allow consumption growth to catch up. The results (which are discussed again in chapters 7–9) were dramatic (table 6.7). Labor incomes in real terms leapt forward in 1964–8

Table 6.7 Indices of development of labor income (1971 = 100)

Year	Labor income in real terms	Labor productivity	Investment-to-GNP ratio
1960	50	56	30.1
1961	50	57	31.7
1962	52	60	32.4
1963	57	66	31.3
1964	64	71	32.2
1965	67	74	28.0
1966	75	78	27.9
1967	80	79	27.8
1968	83	84	29.2
1969	88	90	28.2
1970	95	95	30.7
1971	100	100	30.2
Increase, four-year periods (%)			
1960–4	28	27	+ 7
1964–8	30	13	− 10
1968–71	20	23	+ 3

Source: Dubey, 1975

at a rate nearly three times the growth in labor productivity, having grown at a rate equal to productivity in the preceding period. This led to a decline in the investment-to-GNP ratio.

There was somewhat of a reversal in policy after 1968 through a variety of new taxes and calls on enterprises for contributions to central investment funds, such as the fund for less developed regions. There was no formal announcement of restriction of the freedom of enterprises to determine their own allocations until the so-called Incomes Agreements in 1971. A constitutional amendment in that year required each republic to establish an incomes policy, in effect regulating the growth of real income per worker.

7

Output and Price Movements

Aggregate Tendencies in Output, Inputs, and Productivity

Output

The period immediately following the start of liberalization in mid-1965 turned out to be one of a deep recession, as has already been noted in chapter 2. Partly because of a poor harvest, GDP growth fell dramatically from nearly 10 percent in 1964 to 5.0 percent in 1965 (table 7.1). A moderate recovery in 1966 (6.6 percent) was largely due to an agricultural rebound, with industrial activity coming to a halt in 1966, quarter I, remaining almost stagnant for the next year and a half, and picking up only in 1967, quarter IV. Unfortunately, the recovery of industrial production in 1968 – which at about 6.4 percent a year was still weak by Yugoslav historical norms – was offset by another poor year in agriculture, so that GDP growth rose to only 4.0 percent. Strong growth was not resumed until 1969, and then unevenly (agriculture led while industrial output slowed *vis-à-vis* 1968) and intermittently, with a slowdown in 1970 followed by a resurgence in 1971.

Employment

While output growth, except for two quarters in 1967, was always positive albeit slow, employment in industry declined from mid-1965 to 1968, quarter I and only fully regained its 1965 level in 1969, quarter IV. Starting in 1965, quarter III, output slowed, though with some continuing expansion, while in the following year employment fell substantially. Apart from minor recoveries in mid-1966 and mid-1967, employment continued to decline and hit bottom in 1968, quarter I, two quarters after the industrial production index had touched bottom. This lag of employment behind output was perhaps most important in manufacturing, for this was of course the tradeables part of the economy potentially most affected by liberalization. While agriculture was also a tradeables producer, a decline

Table 7.1 Evolution of aggregate product, 1964–1971

| Quarter | Quarterly data | | Annual data | | |
	Index of industrial product	Index of employment (industry)	GDP growth (%)	% change in ratio of output-to-labor (%)	Index of agricultural output (1964 = 100)
1964	100	100	9.9	8.8	100
1965 I	105	102			
II	107	103			
III	108	101			
IV	109	96	5.0	2.5	91
1966 I	109	94			
II	110	97			
III	111	98			
IV	112	96	6.6	5.2	105
1967 I	113	94			
II	110	96			
III	109	97			
IV	112	95	1.0	0.7	104
1968 I	114	93			
II	117	96			
III	119	98			
IV	123	98	4.0	6.0	100
1969 I	125	96			
II	131	100			
III	134	101			
IV	131	101	9.8	7.1	110
1970	137	104	5.7	6.4	105
1971	148	109	7.8	5.2	112

Sources: Federal Institute of Statistics, *Indeks*; *Statistical Yearbook of Yugoslavia*, various issues

in employment there would be less significant politically, as declining agricultural employment is appropriate for a developing economy. However, the lag in employment growth should be interpreted with care, since productivity improvements would always entail such a lag. We return to this issue in the section on productivity changes below. First, however, it is useful to observe that unemployment rates, shown in table 7.2, increased steadily from 5.56 percent in 1964 to 8.19 percent in 1969. Also important was the fact that employment levels actually fell from 1965 to 1968 (Havrylyshyn, 1988, appendix figure 7.1).

While these rates may be somewhat of an underestimate, as they exclude the discouraged workers who did not register as seeking work, the numbers concerned are probably not very significant. What kept pressures in the labor market relatively low was the increased emigration to the European

Table 7.2 Registered job applicants (annual average) and unemployment rates[a] in Yugoslavia, 1960–1975

Year	No. of persons seeking work (thousands)	Annual unemployment rate (%)
1960	159.2	5.08
1961	191.3	5.57
1962	236.6	6.66
1963	230.3	6.36
1964	212.5	5.56
1965	237.0	6.08
1966	257.6	6.71
1967	269.1	7.03
1968	311.0	7.98
1969	330.6	8.19
1970	319.6	7.67
1971	291.3	6.73
1972	315.3	6.97
1973	381.6	8.14
1974	448.6	9.04
1975	540.1	10.19

[a] Annual unemployment rates are calculated on the basis of the number of persons seeking work compared with the number of employed (in both the social and private sectors) plus the number of persons seeking work.
Source: Federal Institute of Statistics, Statistical Yearbook of Yugoslavia, 1970, 1977

labor markets. Although annual data are not readily available, the trend was strong. Schrenk et al. (1979) show about 100,000 "temporary" migrants working abroad in 1961, and about 913,000 or approximately 10 percent of the labor force in 1971. Had it not been for this safety valve the unemployment problem in the liberalization period might have been far worse.

Capital and Investments

Despite the recession, investment continued to increase, although very slightly, so that the ratio to GNP fell (table 6.7). With their new-found freedom, workers increased the share of incomes and reduced that of investment. Since employment fell from its peak in 1965, the capital-to-labor ratio rose sharply. However, in the years 1966–7, when output and employment were experiencing the deepest part of the recession, investment levels nevertheless grew at rates of 9.5 percent and 4.4 percent compared with output growth of 6.6 percent and 1.0 percent (Havrylyshyn, 1988, appendix table 7.1).

What happened was that government reacted to the tendency of workers to reduce allocations to investment from enterprise from income. The federal authorities used persuasion as well as direct funding or tax incentives (low capital tax) to increase investment via both bank financing and enterprise allocations. Republic and local governments became more active in establishing new enterprises or creating new capacity in old ones or both. Thus, new enterprises were established while old establishments were liquidated, despite the slow growth (Havrylyshyn, 1988, appendix table 7.2). No precise figures are available to compare the frequency of new establishments and liquidations, but an approximation can be made. Suppose that the share of output attributed to new establishments is taken as a proxy for the share of employment. With over a million employed in industry in the mid-1960s, this implies that 2 percent, or over 20,000 jobs, were created by new enterprises in 1967, while only at most a few thousand jobs were lost through liquidation of old ones. Of course, the *total* number of jobs lost must have been far larger, as employment fell by nearly 40,000 (Havrylyshyn, 1988, appendix table 7.1). The point is not that workers were not being dismissed, but that not enough inefficient enterprises were being liquidated to achieve rationalization. Sirc (1979) describes the situation as follows:

The first panic reactions to the reform were claims that up to 50 percent of enterprises would not be able to adjust (*EP* 12.6.65). *Ekonomska politika* accused the opponents of the reform of spreading such rumours and asked them whether they were afraid of their own incompetence. Later estimates reported in the *Economist* (London, 3 and 31.12.66) put the percentage of enterprises that should be closed down to achieve consistency in the economy at 30 percent. This sounded realistic in view of a report by the Social Accountancy Service in 1965, when there were still many subsidies, that one enterprise out of seven was working at a loss and that these enterprises employed 584,000 workers (about 20 percent of the industrial labour force) (Vukovic, *B* 23.6.65).

Ekonomska politika (*EP* 15.10.66) stressed that there could not be a new structure without bankruptcies and disappearance of organisations, but nothing much happened so that the paper repeated the same request for liquidations almost a year later (*EP* 29.7.67). Between July 1964 and July 1966 a total of 150,000 people lost their jobs in business organisations (*EP* 22.10.65) but of these only about 8,300 in 1965 and 4,600 in 1966 were because of the liquidation of their enterprises (*SG* 68, p.104). Later on, the number of workers losing jobs because of liquidation dwindled to about 2,000 in 1975 and 1976 (*SG* 77, p. 127). Mijalko Todorovic [a politician who played a large role in the reforms] warned (*B* 18.6.65) that in order to achieve distribution according to work it was also necessary "to stop finally the practice of adjusting policy and economic instruments to particular conditions and thus saving everything and everybody from failure, including the most irrational production." His admonitions went unheeded.

Consistent capacity utilization series are not readily available, but a few estimates have been made and are shown in table 7.3. Puljic (1982) used various indices of equipment usage to construct his index which, though it seems on the high side, nevertheless clearly shows the downturn of the recession. The timing in 1965–6 is confirmed by Sirc's selected sectoral estimates. What is interesting beyond this unsurprising decline is the continued decline in capacity utilization after 1967 despite the upturn in production. This is entirely consistent with the rebound of investment activity in 1968–70 and the pace of new establishments. Thus, for example, while output (GNP) grew at 6 percent, 8 percent, and 9.5 percent in each of the years 1968, 1969, and 1970, fixed assets expanded faster, at rates of 7.4 percent, 9.5 percent, and 9.0 percent.

Table 7.3 Some estimates of capacity utilization (percent)

	1964	1965	1966	1967	1968	1969	1970
Industry	91.5	90	90.5	87.5	87	89	87.5
Selected sectors							
Metals	60	55	57	n.a.	n.a.	n.a.	65
Electric	68	58	58	n.a.	n.a.	n.a.	71
Textile	75	63	74	n.a.	n.a.	n.a.	55

n.a., not available.
Sources: industry, Puljic, 1980, p. 187; selected sectors, Sirc, 1979, p. 80

Productivity Changes

Consider first the simple measure of partial labor productivity – the ratio of output to labor. The observed lag of employment growth behind output growth implies a certain amount of increase in partial labor productivity. While in 1960–5 this grew at 5.6, during the first stage of liberalization (1965–7) it increased much more slowly and during the second (reversal) stage it increased more rapidly. However, for the period 1965–70 as a whole, the increase in the output-to-employment ratio was the same as for the preceding five years.

For total manufacturing, the second half of the decade had a lower growth rate in the output-to-labor ratio: 5.2 percent compared with 5.7 percent. The decline was especially marked in basic metals, chemicals, textiles, clothing and shoes, and processed food. All but chemicals in this group were industries which were candidates for correction of previous disincentives. Nevertheless, the overall tendency must be regarded as one of little or no change in partial labor productivity.

Many authors have emphasized that the productivity of the Yugoslav economy deteriorated considerably after the 1965 reforms and liberalization. Thus, for example, Dubey (1975, pp. 61ff) describes the slowdown of investment effort (investment-to-GDP ratio) and, more important, the steady rise in aggregate (incremental capital-to-output ratio (ICOR) from 2.4 in 1953–9 to 2.7 in 1960–4 and 2.9 in 1965–70. Much the same is noted by Vukina (1982) who calculates ICOR using a regression analysis and finds it rises steadily from 1952 to 1977. Thus there seems to be an inconsistency between the worsening of ICOR and the stability of output-to-labor ratios.

However, both the output-to-labor ratio and ICOR are partial measures which tell at once too little and too much. It is important therefore to consider measures of total factor productivity. One of the earliest studies was by Horvat (1969). Using a Cobb–Douglas estimation he found the rate of technical progress throughout the period 1956–67 to be steady at about 4.5–5.8 percent, except in 1967 when it fell to 3.2 percent. However, since the growth of output averaged around 10 percent in 1956–64 and only 4–5 percent in 1965–7, this means that the contribution of technological progress as a source of growth rose sharply after 1965 (table 7.4).

A fuller picture was provided by Puljic (1980), whose estimates took into account semiskilled labor and were adjusted for capacity utilization. However, the basic conclusion is very similar to Horvat's: the rate of technical progress declined slightly, but its contribution to output growth increased. Averaging annual values from the calculation of Puljic, the following picture emerges of liberalization (1965–7), retrenchment (1960–70), and an attempt at revival (1971–4). In the first stage of liberalization (1965–7) technical progress falls substantially to 3.0 percent from the value of 4.5 percent in the period 1955–64, but its share in output growth rises to 90 percent. Thus, as the recession develops most of the growth observed is attributable to technical progress. With the macrorecovery in the reversal period (1967–70), growth rebounds; technical progress does also, but now accounts for a more reasonable 55 percent of output growth. In the 1971–4 attempt at renewing liberalization, technological progress falls off even more sharply, and its share in output declines to pre-1965 levels. Puljic concluded from this that the post-reform retardation is attributable more to slower growth of factor inputs (capital and labor) than to reduced productivity. (Discussion of capital and labor movements below will confirm this conclusion.)

Sapir's (1980) picture of the changing pattern of technological progress is similar, but is ascribed to a somewhat different cause. As table 7.4

Table 7.4 Some estimates of technical progress

Estimates	Rate of technical progress (%)	Share in explanation of GDP growth (%)	
Horvat 1969			
1956–64	4.9	47	
1964–7	4.6	85	
Puljic 1980			
1955–64	4.5	38	
1964–74	3.7	50	
(Our calculations)			
1965–7	3.0	90	
1968–70	5.0	55	
1971–4	2.5	40	
Sapir 1980			
1955–65	4.8	38	
1966–79	4.8	63	
This study[a]			
(1) Total economy 1961–5	2.4	26	
1966–70	2.0	34	
Manufacturing 1961–5	3.3	30	
1966–74	1.5	26	
(2) Translog efficiency frontier	Technical progress	Technical efficiency	Total
1961–5	5.0	− 10	− 5
1966–70	2.0	9	− 11

[a] Calculations made by the author in collaboration with Ivan Kebric, Ekonomski Institut, Ljubljana.

summarizes, technological progress in Sapir's study accounts for a higher percentage of output growth after 1965, although his results do not show any decline in the annual rate of technical progress. He concludes that the reason for this new pattern after 1965 is a strong capital intensity bias in the economy, which is attributable to the inherent theoretical tendency of workers' management to maximize income per worker (and hence maximize capital-to-labor ratios). That is, Sapir concludes that the nature of self-management was the cause of the slowdown in performance.

On the face of it the evidence supports this explanation: capital-to-labor ratios did grow much faster after 1965, and fastest in the three to four years before new restrictions on enterprise freedom were reintroduced. However, several counterpoints are apposite. First, it was a stated policy intention to make growth after 1965 more capital intensive, and much was done to this end. Second, there is considerable doubt whether workers were genuinely free to decide what to do with enterprise revenue, except for a few years after 1965 – and then they tended to sharply increase their incomes and reduce reinvestment funds. Investment fell behind and needed a policy push. The observed sharp increases in capital-to-labor ratios in these years (approximately 1964–8) are of course overstated by the cyclical downturn of employment. Third, the most plausible explanation for capital bias (recognized by Sapir) is not the one that differentiates theoretically between Yugoslavia and other developing countries, but the one that considers Yugoslavia in the same way as any other developing country. Various factor price distortion policies (negative interest, high labor costs) are common, and go a long way toward explaining the capital bias. Note again that Sapir does *not* find the rate of technical progress declining, but just output growth declining, which is to say – along with Puljic – that what happened during the liberalization was not a matter of slowdown in productivity but a slowdown in growth of factor inputs.

In a recent study of factor productivity growth in Yugoslavia, Nishimizu and Page (1982) used a translog production function to estimate efficiency frontier movements in different sectors, and were thus able to separate technical efficiency (a movement of producers to an isoquant) from "pure" technological progress (a shift of the isoquant). They concluded that the period 1965–70 was "characterized by improving levels of technical efficiency," and that "change in technical efficiency dominated technological progress in their relative importance in sectoral total factor productivity growth" (Nishimizu and Page, 1982, p. 928). Unfortunately they did not estimate these changes for the pre-reform period.

In an analysis performed by the author in collaboration with the Institut Ekonomski Raziskovanja, Ljubljana, as part of this project, the translog methodology was used to compare the periods 1960–5 and 1965–70. The results are summarized in table 7.4. First, a conventional source-of-growth calculation is made using the coefficients estimated. For the total economy, technical progress is found to be 2.36 percent in 1961–5 and falls to 2.06 percent in 1965–70, but its contribution to output growth rises. As the data base and method differ from all preceding studies cited, the fact of lower absolute values need not distract us, particularly as the trends are exactly the same. Thus, with a different data set (industrial and republic cross-section pooled over time) and a very different econometric approach, we conclude, as did most others, that technical progress slowed a little after 1965 but far less than output, and hence it became a more important explanatory component in growth.

However, the story does change for manufacturing: technical progress falls more sharply, while its contribution to output growth declines rather than rises. This is consistent with the earlier finding on partial labor productivity, which declined after 1965 despite a rise in the economy as a whole. Some anomalies clearly remain.

The breakdown of "total" factor productivity change between technical efficiency (movements toward the efficiency frontier) and technological progress (movements of the efficiency frontier) is shown in row 2 of table 7.4. Though the results contain some inconsistencies, the pattern confirms the finding of Nishimizu and Page (1982) that after 1965 technical efficiency improvements dominated technical progress. The results suggest that the liberalization period was one of increased microefficiency, or rationalization in factor utilization – conclusions similar to those found in the World Bank's Southern Cone Liberalization project described by Condon et al. (1985).

To summarize, available studies of factor productivity conclude that the slowing down of output growth is more to be explained by a factor input slowdown than by a productivity slowdown. Total factor productivity did not slow down very much while technical efficiency improvements (movements toward the efficiency frontier) increased substantially. The increase of output-to-labor ratios and the decline in ICOR are consistent with the stated slight decline in total factor productivity and are explained by the sharp increase in capital-to-labor ratios – judged by most analysts to have been excessive.

Price Movements

General Price Level of Goods

In the early period of liberalization (mid-1965 to 1966) there was a sharp price increase which in effect was a continuation of the price readjustments started even earlier (figure 7.1; Havrylyshyn, 1988, appendix table 7.3). As intended, price increases were highest for agricultural goods and raw materials, and lowest for machinery, capital goods, and other industrial goods. The cost of living rose even faster than producer prices of consumer goods for two reasons: service tariffs of various sorts (electricity, transport) were increased, and the mid-1965 devaluation increased domestic prices of imported goods. Given the system of controlled prices, this increase had to be "legitimized" either by decontrol or by formal increases of fixed prices by the Federal Price Bureau.

In the remaining two years of the first stage (1966–7) no further major readjustments were made by the Federal Price Bureau, but inflation continued at a slower rate and less evenly. Consumer price rises were the strongest (probably fueled by the demand for increased real wages – see below), while the pace slowed for other goods. Indeed, for agricultural goods there was a reversal of price levels starting in the second half of 1966, coinciding with a good harvest in that year.

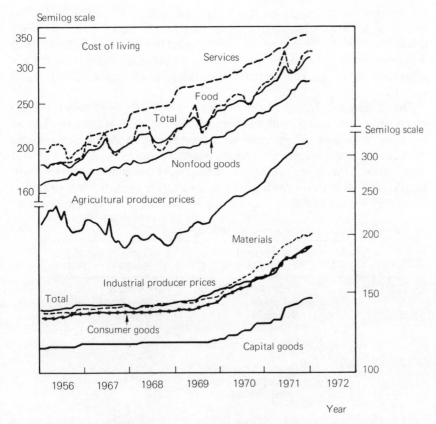

Figure 7.1 Prices, 1958–1977
Sources: OECD, *Economic Surveys, Yugoslavia*, 1973; Federal Institute of Statistics, *statisticki bilten*, various issues

In the liberalization reversal period (1967–70) inflation began to accelerate, especially after 1968.

Wages or Labor Income

Since the self-management system permits workers to determine their own level of income by deciding how to allocate net revenue between reinvestment and personal income, the term "wages" is not altogether correct. In this study we therefore follow Yugoslav convention in using the term "personal income" (which includes a wage component as well as a profit component).

As can be seen in table 6.7, real wages rose sharply in the first years of the liberalization but the trend was stemmed equally sharply after 1968. Some industries experienced higher increases than did others, but there is no obvious pattern relating these variations to the liberalization (Havrylyshyn, 1988, appendix table 7.4). Except for the initial burst of "wage taking" in 1965–6, there is no reason to expect liberalization differences to influence differences in wage increases by sector as the basic reason was a relaxation of the workers' management rules, which was applicable to all sectors.

The government reacted, as noted earlier, by increasing direct financing and pushing for greater bank financing. Secondly, they pressed workers to be more conscious of investment requirements. A likely response of workers to such government urgings would be requests, as a reward for cooperation, for other forms of government assistance: tax or tariff exemptions, protection from imports, credits for exports, and so on. In

Table 7.5 Relative sectoral evolution, 1965–1969

Rate of growth	First stage of liberalization 1965–67	Retrenchment of liberalization 1968–9
High	Electricity Petroleum Shipbuilding Chemicals Paper Rubber Food processing Printing and publishing Miscellaneous	Electricity Nonmetallic minerals Shipbuilding Electrical Chemicals Construction materials Metals
Average	Iron and steel Nonferrous Nonmetallic Electrical Construction materials Textiles	Petroleum Iron and steel Nonferrous Paper products Rubber Printing and publishing
Below average	n.a.	Coal Nonferrous Rubber Food processing Textiles Wood Leather and footwear Miscellaneous
Negative	Coal Metals Leather and footwear Tobacco	Tobacco

n.a., not available.

view of the great publicity attached to the decentralization, authorities could not easily backtrack on the concept and force enterprises to behave "properly." They had to have recourse to other means of persuasion, including measures which reversed trade liberalization.

Sectoral Output Tendencies

A brief overview of the output tendencies by sector is given here and will be elaborated in chapters 10, 11, and 12.

The basic movements of production by sector (table 7.5) show responses that are extremely varied, suggesting that incentives changed considerably. More significant, perhaps, is the apparent instability of responses in the first stage (1965–7) and in the second or reversal stage (1967–70). Of 20 sectors, 13 change categories. Only three stay in the high or low categories: electricity generation, shipbuilding, and chemicals remain high growth sectors in both periods, while wood products, leather and footwear, and tobacco remain low growth sectors.

While earlier discussion in chapter 4 indicated some correction of the pre-1965 biases against comparative advantage industries (resource-based and relatively labor-intensive industries), this finer sectoral detail reveals that the correction was neither substantial nor long lived.

Furthermore, the instability of sectoral restructuring is significant for assessing the liberalization inasmuch as it suggests incentives. Indeed, the description of the reversals starting in 1968 has already noted that most of the liberalization ground gained in 1965–7 was lost by raising tariffs, reintroducing QRs implicitly or explicitly, reintroducing export subsidies, and reversing some of the price-adjustment corrections made in 1965.

8

International Trade and Finance

Imports

Imports grew much more rapidly than domestic production after liberalization (see table 8.1). The ratio of imports to GDP jumped from 17–18 percent in the first half of the 1960s, to 20.5 percent by 1966, and continued to increase rapidly, peaking at 26–7 percent by the early 1970s. During the 1970s, de-liberalization gradually reduced this ratio to about 21–2 percent by the early 1980s. Despite the reversal, however, the economy was clearly more open at the start of the 1980s than it had been before the 1965 liberalization.

With the long-run tendency of the import-to-GDP ratio closely related to the degree of liberalization, the short-run movements were affected by other factors. In particular, in 1965, the first year of liberalization, imports actually fell, as did the import-to-GDP ratio (table 8.1). The explanation is simple. The sharp devaluation in mid-1965 preceded the implementation of import liberalization. While tariffs were reduced immediately, quota restrictions and related measures were not reduced much until 1967 (see figure 4.1). Thus the first effect on imports was to increase the dinar price of imported goods via devaluation, and it was only over the next two years that a reduction of imported goods prices was felt via liberalization. The latter effect was made stronger by the sharp erosion of the real exchange rate owing to inflation.

The upshot of these effects was that imports fell sharply in 1965, but then grew very rapidly in 1966–7. In 1968 the first effects of liberalization reversal began to be felt and import expansion slowed, so that the ratio of imports to GDP stabilized briefly before rising dramatically in 1970 to 27.2 percent. This sharp increase in import dependence can be reconciled with the reversal of liberalization by reference to two phenomena. First is the continued appreciation of the *real* exchange rate, which in 1970 reached a

Table 8.1 Total imports and exports (million 1966 dinars)

	1960	1961	1962	1963	1964	1965	1966	1967	1968	1969	1970	1971
Net exports of goods and nonfactor services	− 2,462	− 3,451	− 924	− 901	− 2,517	635	− 1,100	− 1,855	− 2,203	− 2,886	− 7,686	− 9,359
Exports of goods and nonfactor services	10,961	11,585	13,459	15,474	16,778	18,635	20,988	22,070	23,160	25,745	27,654	30,291
Imports of goods and nonfactor services	13,423	14,956	14,383	16,375	19,295	18,000	22,088	23,925	25,363	28,631	35,340	39,650
GDP at market prices	76,628	80,670	83,544	92,039	101,131	102,505	107,662	108,631	112,379	122,853	129,849	139,822
Export-to-GDP ratio	0.142	0.141	0.163	0.171	0.168	0.187	0.195	0.203	0.206	0.210	0.213	0.197
Import-to-GDP ratio	0.175	0.185	0.172	0.178	0.190	0.176	0.205	0.220	0.226	0.233	0.272	0.262
Aggregate trade ratio[a]	0.317	0.326	0.335	0.349	0.358	0.363	0.400	0.423	0.423	0.433	0.485	0.459
Trade deficit/GNP (%)	3.2	4.2	1.1	1.0	2.5	(0.6)	1.0	1.7	2.0	2.4	5.9	6.7

[a] Sum of export-to-GDP ratio and import-to-GDP ratio.
Source: Havrylyshyn. 1984–6, table 15, Part I

level of 60.1 *vis-à-vis* 1965.[1] The second phenomenon was the manifestation of the classical paradox of an import substitution regime: increased
import dependence particularly focused upon raw materials and intermediate inputs. For this to have happened, however, it was necessary to have
facilitating sources of foreign exchange. Since export performance was
lagging behind, the facilitating sources lay elsewhere: growing remittances
of temporary migrants, and increased borrowing.

The increased import dependence on raw materials and intermediate
inputs is first seen in the structure of imports, which changed quite rapidly
in the years 1965–70. Raw materials and inputs fell from 62.1 percent of the
total in 1965 to about 57 percent for each of the next three years (table
8.2). Also, food imports fell from a high of 12.8 percent in 1965–6 (inflated
by a poor harvest) to a low of 4–5 percent. Recall that these two categories
of goods had been discriminated against before 1965, in both price setting
and protection. Evidently the correction of these biases led to some
desirable import substitution activity. In contrast, the highly protected
sectors (investment goods and consumer goods) became more open, and
consequently imports of these goods increased their share of the total.

Table 8.2 Structure of imports, selected years (percentage
share)

Year	Raw materials and inputs	Food	Investment goods	Consumer goods
1954	51.9	23.8	22.2	2.1
1960	56.8	8.1	28.5	6.6
1965	62.1	12.8	4.7	5.3
1968	56.9	4.7	24.9	13.5
1971	63.7	5.3	21.0	10.0

Source: Federal Institute of Statistics, *Foreign Trade Statistics*,
various years

---

[1] See table 6.2: RER2 1965 = 125.0 and RER2 1970 = 7.5 implies RER2 1970 = 60.1 with a
1965 base. If RER1 is used, appreciation is somewhat less (69.9) but still substantial. The
effect on imports of devaluation compared with liberalization is hard to estimate because
meaningful elasticities cannot be derived since quantitative and administrative import
restrictions were widespread (except, perhaps, in 1965–8). Burkett (1983b) summarizes some
attempts at estimation, noting numerous cases of positive or at best negative but insignificant
coefficients. One of the significant negative elasticity estimates (Tyson and Neuberger, 1979)
yields a short-run elasticity (quarterly) of 0.33 and long-run elasticity of 0.94. That is, proper
devaluation should, with such values, work to dampen imports. The estimate includes an
attempt to capture the effects of QRs with a proxy variable: trade deficit as a ratio of imports.
The variable is negative, as expected, and highly significant. Unfortunately, the
Tyson–Neuberger estimate excludes the first three years of liberalization – in effect the first
and strongest stage.

Thus investment goods rose from 19.7 percent in 1965 to 24.9 percent in 1968, and consumer goods rose from 6.1 percent to 13.5 percent.

The import-substituting nature of the Yugoslav trade regime biased the import structure in the direction of a greater share of "reproduction goods" (a concise Yugoslav term for "raw materials and intermediate inputs"). The period of liberalization, 1965–8, saw some short-lived reversal of this bias; the only more permanent correction of the tendency was for food. Apparently, the biases against domestic agriculture were effectively reduced.

The phenomenon was even stronger at the sectoral level. Total (direct plus indirect) import shows only the effect of the reversal of liberalization after 1967. With only one exception, import content increased sharply for all sectors from 1966 to 1970 and continued to increase in 1972. Even in the

Table 8.3 Trade production ratios 1965–1970

	Imports/production		Exports/production	
Sector	1965	1970	1965	1970
Total industry	26.6	32.7	21.8	17.8
Coal	23.4	18.1	0.6	3.4[a]
Petroleum	26.6	28.4	7.7	3.4
Iron and steel	60.7	72.2	10.0	14.3[a]
Nonferrous	25.2	50.1	53.1	52.5
Nonmetallic	32.3	54.8	38.2	26.1
Metals	46.6	62.3	23.2	14.1
Shipbuilding	12.4	22.9	82.6	76.0
Electrical	26.8	28.4	26.4	19.8
Chemicals	42.7	49.2	18.1	15.1
Construction materials	0.1	2.9	1.6	1.1
Wood	3.1	8.5	39.3	24.7
Paper	17.7	36.8	19.1	16.6
Textiles	28.3	25.9	17.8	19.2[a]
Leather	2.9	18.2	35.6	37.1[a]
Rubber	53.9	46.9	4.5	6.7[a]
Food processing	13.9	11.8	17.0	11.2
Printing	5.4	3.4	1.7	1.8
Tobacco	0.1	2.2	32.1	24.3
Agriculture	9.4	5.9	8.7	6.2
Forestry	1.7	12.1	14.7	11.2

Production was defined as value added plus materials costs. Thus the ratios here measure only the direct content, unlike those shown in table 8.4.
[a] Export-to-production ratio increased.
Source: Calculated from data in Federal Institute of Statistics, *Statistical Yearbook of Yugoslavia*, various issues

case of the exception (rubber and rubber products) the decline from 1966 to 1970 was fully reversed by 1972 (Havrylyshyn, 1988, appendix table 8.1).

Since, in the aggregate, liberalization necessarily implies a more open economy and hence a higher trade-to-output ratio, it need not be surprising or disappointing to find that import-to-output ratios are also higher at sectoral levels. What is surprising and perhaps a "bad" sign is that import-to-output ratios rose in *all* sectors and that export-to-output ratios declined overall, for surely those sectors that had previously been facing disincentives would experience efficient import substitution and we would expect export-to-output ratios to increase both in aggregate and for many individual sectors. Table 8.3 clearly demonstrates that such was not the outcome. Not only did the export-to-production ratio fall for industry, agriculture, and forestry, but this ratio increased – and by not very much – in only five of 18 industrial sectors. To some extent time lags occurred on the export side, but by 1975 the export-to-GDP ratio had declined to its 1965 level (see table 2.5). Perhaps the clearest indication of the phenomenon of increased dependence on reproduction goods characterizing an import substitution regime can be seen in table 8.4.

Table 8.4 Intermediate input indicators

Indicator	1965	1970
Ratio of value added to production		
Total economy	52	50
Agriculture	57	53
Industry	44	40
Index of intermediate input[a]		
Production	100	123
Imports	100	280
Exports	100	230
Index of total industry output	100	140

For intermediate input we take the category "reproduction materials."
[a] Volume index = value price index.
Source: Federal Institute of Statistics, *Statistical Yearbook of Yugoslavia*, various issues

Note that while the export-to-GDP ratio increased (table 8.1), the export-to-gross production ratio fell (table 8.3). This was because the ratio of value added to gross production declined, as seen in table 8.4:

$$\frac{\text{exports}}{\text{GDP}} = \frac{\text{exports/production}}{\text{value added/production}}$$

An increased reliance on reproduction goods is typical of import substitution, as the increase in production of certain products requires greater
inputs, but the inefficiency generated by distortions makes local production less competitive with imports. Table 8.4 supports the common view
that the corrections of 1965 were not sufficient to reverse this trend.

The problem of import dependence was much written about by Yugoslav
analysts in the 1970s, a common theme being that this was a "structural"
problem. The clearest perceptions of what this really meant were those
which spoke of the distorted structure of prices (Pertot, 1971, 1984;
Horvat, 1976; Sirc, 1979). Unfortunately, many writings on the matter fell
prey to a "fallacy of composition:" the sectoral increase in import
dependence was used as evidence favoring protectionist or interventionist
(read distortionist) policies, such as restriction of imports and support for
exporters.

Exports

Unlike imports, exports were growing faster than GDP before liberalization, and although this continued after liberalization the pace was much
reduced. Thus, while the export-to-GDP ratio increased considerably from
about 14 percent in 1960–1 to 18.7 percent in 1965 (table 8.1), its increase
through 1970 was very modest, to 21.3 percent. In the 1970s export
performance became even worse: while 1972 and 1973 saw a brief spurt of
export growth in reaction to devaluation (see table 6.2 for the depreciation
effect on the real exchange rate), from 1974 through 1978 export growth
slumped, so that by the end of the decade the export-to-GDP ratio had
fallen back to about the same levels as in the early 1960s – 16–17 percent.
As will be discussed in more detail in the next section, this tendency of
exports, given what was happening to imports, meant a deteriorating
balance of payments.

The weakening of aggregate export performance is visible in such
measures as market share, or the value of the residual in a constant-
market-share analysis, as shown in table 8.5. Clearly, export performance
grew dramatically worse after 1965 with a considerable loss in market
shares, compared with a substantial gain in the period 1960–5. Some of this
is due to external factors (closing of EEC markets), but the strong decline
in export performance (see figure 2.1) cannot be ascribed to outside
phenomena alone. The export engine stalled, and this contributed not only
to an immediate reversal of liberalization (in 1968) but doubtless bears
some part of the responsibility for the economic problems of the 1970s.
The stalling of exports cannot be attributed to reallocation in the direction
of efficient import substitution – this did not occur (table 8.3).

The share of raw materials in exports (one of the previously disfavored
areas, to be resuscitated by the 1965 reform) rose briskly after liberaliza-

Table 8.5 Constant-market-shares analysis of Yugoslav export growth, 1961–1965, 1965–1972

Indicator	Yugoslav exports		
	1961	1965	1972
Total (million US$)	568.8	1,091.3	2,237.3
	1961–5 million US$ (%))		1965–1972 (million US$ (%))
Increase in exports	522.5 (100.0)		1,146.0 (100.0)
Increase due to			
World trade effect	233.5 (42.8)		1,322.7 (115.4)
Commodity composition effect	– 10.4 (– 2.0)		– 44.2 (– 3.8)
Market distribution effect	2.3 (0.4)		– 100.8 (– 8.8)
Competitive effect	307.1 (58.8)		– 31.7 (– 2.8)

Source: Chittle, 1977

tion, after a decade of decline. In contrast, capital goods shares fell after 1966 – again in conformance with the planned realignment of incentives. We also observe a slight decline for "other" consumer goods (Havrylyshyn, 1988, appendix table 8.2). Food was one of the product groups considered to have been unfavorably treated and inviting encouragement in the 1965 reform (in the form of rapid price increases most importantly, and less tariff reduction than the average or even a rise in tariffs). In this case, however, the export share continued to fall sharply. This is probably partly due to an underlying movement in comparative advantage toward manu-factured goods, and partly to the closing of EEC markets, though a World Bank (1980) study applying a constant-market-share analysis suggests that EEC closure had a strong effect only after 1970. From 1963 to 1970, while EEC imports of primary commodities from all sources grew at 8.1 percent, those of Yugoslavia grew at 7.4 percent – a lower rate, but not by much. From 1970 to 1977, however, while EEC imports expanded at 17.9 percent a year, their imports from Yugoslavia expanded at a fraction of this – 5.3 percent.

Finally, we consider the change in industry export structure in Pertot's (1971) categories: resource industries, newly created industries, and others (table 8.6). Resource industries can be classified as traditional exporters, and newly created industries can be classified as import substituting; the third category is less easy to classify, although, with textiles and leather dominating, it could reasonably be described as import substituting in early years but, with strengthening comparative advantage, as a "traditional exporter" from about 1960, at least potentially. Chittle (1977, p. 90) ranks these two sectors (textiles, and leather and footwear) as 1 and 6 in a

Table 8.6 Structure of industrial exports by sector[a] (percent)

Industry	1952	1960	1965	1970
Domestic resource industries	84.0	49.6	38.5	38.9
Nonferrous metals	28.0	12.4	11.1	15.9
Nonmetallic minerals	4.0	3.2	3.2	2.9
Wood products	42.9	15.8	11.5	9.4
Pulp and paper	0.4	1.3	2.0	2.5
Food processing	4.7	12.1	7.3	6.3
Tobacco manufacturing	4.0	4.8	3.4	1.9
Newly created industries	6.8	39.3	45.6	42.5
Petroleum	1.1	0.9	1.7	0.9
Iron and steel	2.8	3.8	2.5	3.2
Metal products	0.4	16.3	18.1	13.6
Shipbuilding	–	8.0	9.5	10.0
Electrical equipment	0.2	7.2	7.9	8.2
Chemicals	2.3	3.1	5.9	6.6
Other	9.2	11.1	15.9	18.6
Textiles and clothing	3.3	7.2	10.2	12.1
Leather and footwear	0.7	3.3	5.4	5.9
Other	5.2	0.6	0.3	0.6
Total industry	100.0	100.0	100.0	100.0

[a] Exports in constant 1969 prices: 1952 = average 1951–3; 1960 = average 1959–61; 1965 = average 1964–6; 1970 = average 1969–70.
Sources: Pertot, 1971, vol. II; Federal Institute of Statistics, Statistical Yearbook of Yugoslavia, various issues

hypothetical comparative advantage ranking. In any event, before 1965 the import-substituting (newly created) industries clearly tended increasingly to dominate Yugoslav exports. After 1965, coinciding with liberalization, devaluation, and some reduction of price distortions, the trend was reversed or virtually halted. Traditional industries stopped losing ground, the textiles and leather and footwear industries gained ground,[2] and the newly created (import-substituting) industries lost some ground.

The reform and liberalization thus appear to have had some limited success in readjusting the relative incentives and biases against traditional and labor-intensive goods. However, this must be put in the context of the poor aggregate export performance. What appears to have happened is the

---

[2] That these were import-substituting sectors in the 1950s is in little doubt. Chittle calculates that overall import substitution for 1952–61 was 26.9 percent of total growth. The six industries assigned to this category by Havrylyshyn (1988, appendix table 8.2) have considerably higher percentages.

following. Before 1965 the great export success of Yugoslavia was based on various forms of export support for the very same industries that had been protected via import substitution policies. The correction of distortions from 1965 modified relative export performance, but removal of export subsidies led to worsening cost competitiveness in general and a poor aggregate performance. In short, not enough time or flexibility of adjustment was allowed to offset the "artificial" export success to 1965.

That some outward success was achieved in exports is unquestioned. The degree of export diversification in Yugoslavia is substantial even in comparison with advanced industrial countries. For example, the number of three-digit UN Standard International Trade Classification (SITC) products exported by Yugoslavia is 1976 was 159; only the United States, West Germany, and Spain were higher (Havrylyshyn, 1988, appendix table 8.3). While similar calculations for earlier years are not available, diversification undoubtedly increased considerably in the 1950s and 1960s. Havrylyshyn (1988, appendix table 2.2) shows that the percentage of highly processed goods in exports rose from a mere 10 percent in 1951–3 to 36 percent in 1959–61 and 51 percent in 1964–6.

Balance of Payments

Trade Deficit and Remittances

Figure 8.1 presents the basic data on balance-of-payments movements (Havrylyshyn, 1988, appendix table 8.4). It is clear that the trade balance deteriorated almost immediately after the reform and became much worse by 1970–1. This does not necessarily mean that the widening deficit was "caused" by liberalization (we return to this matter in chapter 10). The current account balance, though worsening, was not nearly as bad until 1969, principally because of three items on the invisible side: transportation, tourism, and workers' remittances (Havrylyshyn, 1988, appendix table 8.4). However, the substantial growth in these sectors, especially the last, did not suffice to avert another balance-of-payments crisis in 1971. This was dealt with in the short term by devaluation and monetary restraint. Longer-term policies were, as in 1961 and 1966, liberalization and restructuring, supported by an influx of credits from the IMF and other sources.

The growing remittances, which doubled from US$59 million in 1965 to US$118 million in 1967, doubled again in 1969, and more than doubled by 1971, provided an inflow of foreign exchange which was already, in the mid-1960s, enough to cover 25–30 percent of the trade deficit; by 1969 it covered 37 percent and by 1971, 48 percent.

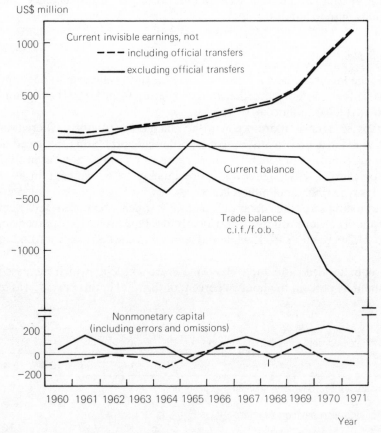

US$ million

Figure 8.1 Balance of payments, 1960–1971
Negative values of monetary movements indicate deterioration of the gold and foreign exchange position of the monetary sector
Source: OECD, *Economic Surveys, Yugoslavia*, 1973

Taken together with the positive net balance for transportation and tourism, both sectors of recognized comparative advantage for Yugoslavia, these constituted a considerable inflow of foreign exchange during 1965–70, which widened the gap between imports and exports. Thus, after five years of substantial current account deficits (1960–4), averaging about 3 percent of GDP, the liberalization period was on the whole one of eased pressure, since the current deficit for the years 1965–9 did not rise much above 1 percent. This reduced pressure induced an unfortunate illusion, akin to the complacency that often accompanies "Dutch disease" circumstances. The surge of foreign exchange inflow permitted the authorities to ignore the hard question: was the large and growing trade deficit justified by this inflow, or were there problems of inefficiency and distortions in merchandise trade?[3]

External Debt

Despite the favorable development of service exports and remittances, the volume of foreign debt nevertheless rose sharply from US$941 million in 1965 to US$2,706 million in 1971.

Perhaps of equal importance was the change in structure. There was increased reliance on private sources (substantially pre-dating this trend in developing countries in general), whose share rose from 32 percent in 1963 to 41 percent in 1967 and even more quickly to 62 percent in 1971 (Havrylyshyn, 1988, appendix table 8.5).

More telling are the data of table 8.7 which show selected debt indicators. The debt-to-GDP ratio nearly doubled from 13.0 percent in 1966 to 24.2 percent in 1971, while the debt service ratio rose from 13.2 to 18.0.

The debt service ratio for convertible currency debt, which increased from about 84 percent to about 94 percent of the total in this period, was in

Table 8.7 Selected debt indicators (percent)

Indicator	1966	1967	1968	1969	1970	1971
Ratio of debt service payments to debt outstanding[a]	20.6	19.2	16.4	18.6	22.8	23.1
Ratio of amortization payments to debt outstanding[a]	6.2	12.6	12.6	14.0	17.9	19.3
Ratio of debt service payments to exports of goods and services including factor income	13.2	12.3	13.2	14.2	16.2	18.0
(Debt service ratio in convertible currency)	(17.0)	n.a.	n.a.	n.a.	n.a.	(23.0)
Ratio of debt outstanding[a] to GDP at constant 1966 market prices	13.0	15.6	17.2	18.2	19.8	24.2
Ratio of debt service payments to GDP at current market prices	8.3	8.3	9.0	10.3	13.9	17.6

n.a., not available.
[a] Disbursed only.
Source: Dubey, 1975

[3] A related effect may have been to push the exchange rate up, but only after 1970 when remittances reached a level equal to 25–30 percent of exports. Before 1970 the appreciation of the real exchange rate cannot have been justified by remittances, which ranged from 10–15 percent of exports.

fact much worse: already 17 percent in 1966 and 23 percent in 1971. However, if the ratio is calculated in relation to total foreign exchange earnings inclusive of workers' remittances, it is of course somewhat lower and the deterioration is far less: the adjusted numbers are 16 percent and 18.6 percent.

In summary, the external situation was one of very brief improvement in 1965–6 as the devaluation boosted exports and restricted imports. However, from 1966 on the tendency was toward increasing external deficits. Most dramatic was the worsening of the trade balance, which until 1969 had been almost completely offset by the favorable movements in invisibles plus remittances. Nevertheless, the volume of increased external transactions was great enough, as the Yugoslav economy opened up, for the growth of external debt to continue quite high even in the years 1965–9. After 1969 the deterioration in the trade balance became so severe that the offsetting inflow was not enough to prevent a sharp rise in the current account deficit, which of course occasioned an acceleration of external indebtedness. This reached 24 percent of GDP by 1971, while the debt service ratio was 25 percent in convertible currency.

9

Income Distribution

Distribution among Factors of Production

Overtime, and particularly after the 1965 reform, both the actual measured "share" of capital rentals (table 9.1) and marginal productivity of capital (MPK) tended to decline. The measured "share" of capital versus that of

Table 9.1 Estimates of capital shares and productivity: industry

Year	Actual share (Horvat) (%)	Imputed share (Sapir) (%)	Imputed MPK (%)
1955	74	33	11.3
1960	62	31	13.0
1961	54	27	10.8
1962	53	24	9.1
1963	53	25	10.6
1964	50	25	11.5
1965	48	22	9.9
1966	56	19	8.3
1967	45	15	6.2
1968	—	14	5.8
1969	—	14	6.1
1970	—	12	5.3
1971	—	11	4.9
1972	—	10	4.4
1973	—	9	3.7
1974	—	9	3.9

—, not applicable.
Actual share in Horvat is the sum of amortization, interest, capital taxes, and net profit. Sapir's estimates are imputation using estimated parameters of a constant elasticity of substitution production function.
Sources: Horvat, 1969, p. 41; Sapir, 1980, p. 301

labor is a less clear concept in Yugoslavia than in either a capitalist or a centrally planned socialist economy. The income a worker receives is, at least in principle, a combination of the worker's labor contribution to production and a share in the return on capital. However, in practice, workers probably never attained complete freedom to determine their personal income.[1] Before the 1965 reform, personal incomes were doubtless close to market concept of wages. After 1965 this was less true, but the explosion of personal income that worker managers granted themselves in the early years of this freedom led to various legal and indirect limitations in the 1970s.[2] One was a ceiling on the increase of personal income equal to labor productivity increases; another was a minimum of savings and reinvestment; a third was a set of "voluntary" contributions to various capital funds.

While these legal limitations were ostensibly based on the notion of social "agreement" between enterprise and various authorities, there was obviously much room for authorities to impose their will. Parenthetically, it should be noted that the proliferation of such regulations on income distribution paralleled developments in the trade regime. In principle liberal, the complexity of regulations, their frequent changes, and hence their obscurity actually meant increased *ad hoc* administrative interventionism (Sirc, 1979, pp. 137–40).

As far as labor versus capital shares of income are concerned, this meant that by the 1970s personal incomes were once more directly and indirectly regulated, and could therefore be considered as labor income. The decline of the capital share is attributable to the institutional tendency already noted: greater freedom for worker managers resulting in decisions to increase personal incomes substantially in the period 1965–8. The decline in imputed shares of capital and its marginal productivity, as Sapir (1980) finds, is explained by the rising capital-to-labor ratio in a circumstance of an elasticity of substitution that is well below unity, not only in aggregate but also for individual sectors. In a word, as capital deepening accelerated after 1965, perhaps even resulting in excessive capital intensity, the marginal productivity of capital naturally declined and its imputed share in output fell.

These are the tendencies of actual or imputed shares. What happened to the costs of factors in factor markets was probably different, although solid data are impossible to obtain. The movements of the real interest rate are

---

[1] The motive for strikes furnishes the best indication that personal incomes were not freely set by workers; the most important motive, according to surveys, was inadequate incomes (Canapa, 1971, p. 147).

[2] The first limitation on these freedoms came in the 1968 Fundamental Act on the Establishment and Distribution of Income which contained a provision authorizing sociopolitical organizations (federal and local governments) to restrain unwarranted distribution. Progressive taxation of "excess" incomes was its principal tool.

described in chapter 6: with nominal rates below inflation and largely unchanged, real rates were essentially negative. Since a capital market never existed and external capital flows were at first entirely restricted to loans through official channels, and only slightly loosened to allow joint ventures, it is not hard to conclude that capital was underpriced at a price which remained more or less stable. Any rationing that was done would of course imply selective cases of very high costs, but the qualitative evidence indicates not only a continuing willingness to finance investment by the authorities (albeit indirectly via banks after 1965) but even, after the incomes surge of 1965–8, an effort to encourage it. (Note that the investment-to-GDP ratio fell only slightly in 1965–8.)

As to labor costs, there were two opposing tendencies. On the one hand emigration to the EEC must inevitably have driven up labor costs, especially for semiskilled and skilled labor. On the other hand, long-term underemployment persisted, and in the immediate post-liberalization period open unemployment increased, putting downward pressure on wages, at least for unskilled labor. However, labor markets are also limited in Yugoslavia, both in the sense that firms cannot "hire" workers at a contracted wage but must give all a share in their proceeds, and in the sense that layoffs are very uncommon and that redundant workers are kept on somehow or other.

It is likely that labor costs went up relative to capital costs, perhaps much in excess of underlying opportunity costs – at least in the formal part of the dual factor markets. Two phenomena in addition to rural–urban duality provide a barrier between markets. First is the propensity, in workers' management, for the employed to attempt to maximize income per worker, and hence to restrict new employment and to stress capital deepening. While this seems a unique characteristic of Yugoslavia, it is but another version of the common phenomenon found in less developed countries of the segmented labor markets: an informal low wage segment, and a unionized modern formal segment with higher wages. Second, the capital market in (socialist) Yugoslavia inevitably imparts a bias in credit and financing availability favoring the socialist against the private sector (which in 1965 still employed half the labor force and produced over one fifth of national income). Though this duality of capital markets is declining, it was certainly (and remains) an element that cannot be ignored. Again, the appearance of uniqueness to Yugoslavia (or at least to socialist regimes) is deceptive: the duality closely resembles that of the capital markets in less developed countries between the more favored sectors (modern, capital intensive, industrial, and often public) and those less favored. While a socialist economy, almost by definition, will involve strong government influence on capitalist allocations, it is equally obvious that strong government influence on capital allocations is common to most developing countries. Yugoslavia uses somewhat different institutions, but exhibits the same phenomenon.

Distribution by Income Levels

General Tendencies During Liberalization

Duality in labor markets is further reflected in the trends of personal income distribution, for which several indicators are summarized in table 9.2. As the first two panels show, distribution of income became slightly less equal in the period immediately after liberalization. Gini coefficients

Table 9.2 Indicators of size distribution of income

I *Standardized households: Gini coefficients for income*

	1963	1968
All households	0.22	0.24
Nonagricultural households	0.22	0.25
Agricultural households	0.17	0.18
Workers' households	0.22	0.24

II *Growth rate of income 1963–8 by household category and percentile*

	Top 10%	Average	Mid-50%	Bottom 40%
All households	6.9	4.8	4.8	3.2
Nonagricultural households	9.7	6.1	5.1	3.2
Agricultural households	4.6	3.2	3.2	3.3
Workers' households	9.8	5.9	4.2	5.3

III *Indicators of earnings distribution (employed only)*

	Ratio of high to low		Gini coefficient
	Total	Industry	Total economy
1962	—	—	0.257
1963	2.74	2.73	—
1964	2.68	2.65	—
1965	—	—	0.251
1966	—	—	—
1967	2.73	2.62	0.250
1968	2.58	2.39	—
1969	2.75	2.70	0.244
1970	—	—	—
1971	—	—	0.235
1972	—	—	0.226

—, not applicable.
Source: I, II, Dubey, 1975, pp. 103 105; III, ratios from Dubey 1975, p. 109 and Gini coefficients calculated by IER Ljubljana for the project

increased slightly, especially for nonagricultural households (panel I), and the growth rates of income for all categories of households (panel II) showed the same pattern of above average growth for the top 10 percent and below average for the bottom 40 percent of households.

However, the distribution of earnings for those who were employed shows an exactly opposite pattern in this period, as differentials tended to narrow. The ratio of high to low earnings (in industry as well as all the social sectors) fell substantially between 1964 and 1968, but regained its earlier levels in 1969.

The Impact on Adjustment to Liberalization

The narrowing of differentials for those who were employed in the face of widening differentials overall is consistent with the situation described earlier of worsening unemployment and growing differentiation or duality of labor markets. Unemployment pressures and recessionary problems led enterprises to narrow the gap between high and low earnings rather than cut wages. The self-interest of those who were employed was clearly to keep their jobs and to seek the highest possible incomes, particularly in the face of double-digit inflation. Formal sector labor is able to achieve this in a typical developing country with dual labor markets. In Yugoslavia the formal sector was much larger, and was moreover given increased powers in 1965.

This situation is linked with trade liberalization to the extent that liberalization aimed at a reallocation in order to stimulate production. This would argue for flexibility of adjustment but, in Yugoslavia, whatever the fundamental theoretical implications of workers' management may be for mobility, it seems clear that flexibility of adjustment was reduced rather than increased at the very time when trade liberalization was being attempted.

This was not simply due to the increased freedom of workers to decide on various production and income matters. Their interests were, as noted above, to keep their jobs and raise their incomes, something they achieved in 1965–8. The real fault lay not here – such self-interest is a fact of life – but in the failure of the authorities with respect to the second freedom of worker managers: the "freedom" to suffer the consequences of changed market conditions. Excessive exercise of the rights to determine income and continue production in the context of a liberalized economy created numerous problems. Accounting losses mounted sharply from 340 million dinars in 1966 to 1,252 million dinars the next year and 1,600 million dinars in 1968. In that year, the 1,724 enterprises suffering losses employed 14.6 percent of the labor force (Sirc, 1979, p. 156).[3]

---

[3] Unfortunately more systematic time series data on this phenomenon are not readily available.

However, the stated intentions of forcing economic discipline via greater application of bankruptcy regulations and liquidating remained no more than intentions. We have already noted in chapter 7 how few jobs were lost in enterprise liquidations. Another illustrative statistic is the number of bankruptcies. The peak year for bankruptcy procedures was 1967 when 86 were started, mainly for very small enterprises. In 1968, when over 1,700 enterprises suffered losses, only 57 were liquidated (Sirc, 1979, p. 157).

Special Adjustment-Compensation Policies

The lack of will to enforce the harsh discipline of labor (and enterprise) adjustment may have been connected with the absence of explicit adjustment-compensation mechanisms. There was absolutely no indication in the statements of the 1965 reform of measures for adjusting to new lines of production by enterprises, or retraining for workers, or even direct unemployment compensation for redundancy. General compensation for unemployment was available but minimal. The number of people covered, though increasing sharply from about 20,000 in 1964–5 to over 30,000 in 1966–8, was a mere 10 percent of registered unemployed (265,000–325,000), itself an underestimate of actual unemployment. Further, the level of compensation was limited to about 200–280 dinars per month or less than one third of average income (700–900 dinars per month), and was limited in duration to 25 days (Havrylyshyn, 1988, appendix table 9.1). Only about 20 percent were unemployed for so short a time, and over 50 percent were unemployed for more than three months – although even these are probably underestimates as they include only registered job applicants.

Support for individual firms was extensive, especially after 1968, but its nature is not easily discernible in available statistics. Much of it, for example, consisted in delays in payments of tax obligations and moral pressure on banks or other firms to extend credit to enterprises in difficulty, plus special concessions on duties, extension of export subsidies, and so on. Explicit subsidy payments became less important after 1965, though they began to reappear in 1968. Even those, however, are hard to trace in financial accounts.

Agricultural versus Nonagricultural Activities

In chapter 2 we described the strong bias against agriculture and the policies in the mid-1960s aimed at correcting this. To what extent they were effective is unclear, as various indicators point in opposite directions. It would appear, however, that the bias was strongly corrected, since the terms-of-trade index (PA/PI in table 9.3) immediately moves in favor of

Table 9.3 Indicators of rural–urban differences

	Terms of trade	Protection levels				Index of personal income in social sector	
		Wheat		Maize			
	PA/PI	NRP	ERP	NRP	ERP	Agriculture	Total
1964	100	—	—	—	—	100	100
1965	123	—	—	—	—	109	105
1966	130	1.02	1.07	0.76	0.58	130	117
1967	115	1.01	1.07	0.84	0.59	142	1225
1968	112	1.08	1.24	0.90	0.59	142	130
1969	128	1.23	1.90	0.90	0.59	153	138
1970	131	1.06	1.16	0.83	0.34	162	148
1971	143	1.21	1.95	0.69	0.94	179	156
1972	160	0.79	0.63	0.97	0.54	185	156
1973	177	0.45	0.29	0.75	0.25	185	153
1974	156	0.79	0.69	0.54	0.72	198	186
1975	144	0.89	0.80	0.97	0.91	—	—

—, not applicable; PA, price index for agricultural goods; PI, price index for industrial goods; NRP, nominal rate of protection; ERP, effective rate of protection.
Sources: Terms of trade, Federal Institute of Statistics, Statistical Yearbook of Yugoslavia, producer price indices; protection levels, ULG Economic Consultants Ltd, 1977; index of personal incomes, calculated

agriculture in 1965, swings back somewhat in 1967–8 (as weakened industries request and obtain price increases?), but revives and continues to improve through the early 1970s.

These trends notwithstanding, in 1963–8 incomes in agricultural households grew much more slowly (3.2 percent) than in nonagricultural households (6.1 percent) (table 9.2, panel II). However, table 9.3 shows that real personal incomes in the socialized agricultural sector increased much more rapidly than in the economy as a whole. The contradiction is illusory: the former indicators relate to all agriculture while the latter relate to a small proportion (10 percent) of agricultural laborers. This disparity is another reflection of the duality in labor markets discussed earlier, and the disequilibrium in this market.

On balance, protection of the agricultural sector seems to have increased somewhat after 1965 (chapter 11) but, as table 9.4 shows, not in all sectors; in any case the increase seems to have been eroded in the 1970s. However, in the short and medium term the anti-agricultural bias was, if not eliminated, significantly reduced.

Regional Differences

It was mentioned in chapter 3 that in general the rich republics (especially Croatia and Slovenia, far less so Serbia) were more inclined to liberalization, and the poorer republics were against it. The effect of the liberalization on individual republics is not easy to trace except in a simple *ex post facto* review of some economic indicators. Two major difficulties in the interpretation deserve mention. First, export and import data by republic are not published; in any event these would be difficult to interpret unless export data were in direct and indirect content terms, and import data were in production-competing rather than consumption categories.[4] Second, the difference among republics in trends of output, employment, investment, capital-to-labor ratios, and so on include any responses to problems by local authorities, central government, or enterprises lacking the economic discipline of bankruptcy. In short, the *ex post* economic indicators measure the net effect of trade liberalization impacts set against government countermeasures.

With this in mind let us consider some basic indicators, as in table 9.4. The first, which is an index of regional income inequality (higher values mean greater inequality), shows a long-term worsening trend for poor regions. But in the short run the liberalization period, the opposite occurs, that is, the relative position of poorer republics improves. The inequality trend resumes after 1969.

Economic growth in aggregate, however, slows more in the underdeveloped regions after 1965 than it does in the developed regions, as block 2 of the table shows.[5] This is largely attributable to the much sharper decline in investment-to-GNP ratios in the underdeveloped compared with the developed regions (block 3). This last set of data shows the effect of decentralization on investment efforts in underdeveloped regions. Central funds for this purpose were sharply reduced, and investment in those regions suffered immediately.

Yet despite the decline in the investment ratio and the growth of unemployment in underdeveloped regions (exacerbated by rising popula-

---

[4] In the early 1970s there was considerable public discussion about how much foreign exchange each republic earned (*Ekonomska Politika*, March 2, 1970). In 1971 the Croat Institute of Economic Planning calculated that Croatia and Montenegro were the only republics with a balance-of-payments surplus. However, neither this nor any other calculation incorporated the indirect content effect arising from inter-republic transactions.

[5] This is not necessarily inconsistent with the narrowing of inequality as the index measures variance among all republics, and not simply the difference between averages in developed and underdeveloped. Also, population growth rates in developed regions continued to decline, while they actually increased in some underdeveloped republics.

Table 9.4 Some indicators of regional differences

1 Index of regional inequality (higher is less equal)		2	Growth rate of GNP	
			Developed	Underdeveloped
1952	0.260	1953–9	8.3	6.4
1955	0.297	1960–4	6.9	7.2
1960	0.319	1965–9	6.4	6.0
1965	0.359			
1966	0.330	3	Investment-to-GNP ratios (%)	
1967	0.339		Developed	Underdeveloped
1968	0.351			
1969	0.355	1953–9	17.2	32.9
1970	0.370	1960–4	29.0	41.2
1971	0.380	1965–9	25.4	32.1

4	Capital-to-labor ratio (industry) (thousand 1966 dinars per worker)		5	Capital stock and output shares (industry) (%)	
	Developed	Underde-veloped		Developed	Underdeveloped
			Capital stock		
1960	36.3	35.8	1962	82	18
1965	45.9	46.9	1970	72	28
1970	64.1	64.6			
			Output		
			1962	82	18
			1970	79	21

Sources: Dubey, 1975 (block 1, p. 194; block 2, p. 199; block 3, p. 199; block 4, p. 202; block 5, p. 191)

tion growth rates), capital-to-labor ratios – which were already higher than in developed regions – continued to increase as fast. Consequently, we observe a substantial imbalance developing in capital allocations and output shares. While in 1962 the underdeveloped regions accounted for about 19 percent of capital stock and only slightly less output (18 percent), by 1970 the capital stock share climbed to 28 percent but output share rose to only 21 percent – a clear sign of inefficiency of allocation of capital by regions. The higher capital-to-labor ratios in the underdeveloped regions (item 4) also indicate misallocation; it is of interest to note that the excessive capital-deepening and capital intensity biases of Yugoslavia after 1965 (Sapir, 1980) are particularly strong in the underdeveloped regions.

Finally, consider the movements of industrial employment and production by republic. While production did not decline in any republic in the first (recessionary) stage of liberalization, the average for underdeveloped regions was much below that for the developed regions (6.2 percent versus

11.3 percent), though some developed regions were below the national average (Serbia) and some underdeveloped regions were above (Macedonia, Kosovo) (see Havrylyshyn, 1988, appendix table 9.2, for details).

However, the picture for employment differs somewhat, especially if individual republics are considered. While industrial production growth in Croatia considerably exceeded the national average (15.2 percent versus 10.7 percent), employment fell more sharply than the national average. The reverse was true for Serbia: production gains were below average, and employment decline was much below the national average. In this instance, the patterns for total developed versus underdeveloped regions are not as interesting.

The recovery phase (1968–71) also shows the difference for Croatia and Serbia. Croatia expands production at only slightly below the national average, but employment expansion is much slower. In Serbia production expansion is well below average but employment expansion is above average. Slovenia, even more than Croatia, exhibits an increased output-to-employment ratio, with growth of output exceeding the national average substantially and growth in employment being well below average.

The underdeveloped regions as a group tend to have employment and production rising at about the national average, and an output-to-employment growth ratio at about the national average. Montenegro is an exception which exhibits the same tendency as Serbia: below average growth of production and above average growth of employment. The upshot of all this "elevator economics" is that the burden of adjustment does not seem to have been uniformly spread either between developed and underdeveloped regions or between the two largest republics, Croatia and Serbia. In the first shock period (1965–8) Croatia absorbed the greatest amount of disemployment (44 percent of industrial disemployment), although its output was above the national average. In contrast, Slovenia's employment increased, while that of Serbia declined only marginally even though its output growth was low. Of course, taking Croatia as an illustration, this may reflect good or bad adjustment. A rationalization of industry might at first entail a decline in employment with a simultaneous rise in output by the newly efficient sectors. However, a decline in the employment-to-output ratio should not be occurring in an economy with some surplus labor; these movements may reflect a worsening rigidity of labor markets and an excessive capital bias.

The Slovenian experience indicates that it was possible to expand both output and employment at high rates. Indeed year-by-year data (Federal Institute of Statistics, *Statistical Yearbook of Yugoslavia*, 1973) display a pattern even more favorable than might be expected from efficient adjustment. The years 1966 and 1967 saw a decline in employment with output growing above the national average. Then in 1968 there was a sharp increase in employment with output continuing to grow above the national average. Slovenians might justly claim (as they did in the road-building crisis described earlier) that they had achieved the adjustment expected from the liberalization.

In any event, there is little doubt that in each of these developments there was cause enough for regional disenchantment. Croatians could feel that they were absorbing most of the labor adjustment problem while still contributing their share to output growth. Slovenians could point to their efficiency and speed of adjustment to liberalization and expect a fair share of federal "action" such as loans for road building. Underdeveloped regions could and did note that investment to promote their catching up was no longer available. All in all, enough disparity in adjustments existed to ensure plenty of opportunity for local authorities to plead special interests and need for special treatment.

10

The Relationship between Trade Liberalization and Economic Deterioration

The deterioration of the economy's macroperformance after 1965, particularly the sharp recession during the first stage of liberalization (1965–7), is evidently a key factor in evaluating the liberalization experiment. An obvious line of reasoning seems to present itself: trade liberalization which generated import competition led to the recession and an understandable political reaction in favor of slowing and eventually reversing the liberalization. This simplistic *post hoc ergo propter hoc* logic is invalid. Closer examination reveals that factors other than trade liberalization led to the recession which "caused" a reversal of liberalization.

In a nutshell, the timing of policies and economic movements was as follows: liberalization was implemented gradually (1965–7), monetary restriction took place during implementation, and the worst part of the recession came before liberalization reached its peak at the end of 1967 and began to be reversed. Thus, if any *post hoc* logic is applicable here, it should be reasoning by exclusion: *post hoc, ergo non propter hoc.* Significant liberalization came after the recession, and hence the recession could not have been its cause.

While this summary account may suffice to justify the cause–effect conclusion, the importance of potential policy lessons about the process of trade liberalization calls for fuller treatment. That is the first purpose of this chapter, and is dealt with in the first section. A second purpose is to address the longer-term effect. While liberalization never reached its stated aims and underwent considerable reversal, post-1965 Yugoslavia was nevertheless more open than pre-1965 Yugoslavia. As economic performance, variously measured, continued to be relatively worse after 1970 than it had been pre-1965, the possibility should be considered that the limited liberalization achieved was somehow responsible for this. Therefore the factors behind the longer-term deterioration of economic performance are discussed in the second section of this chapter.

Short-run Fluctuations 1964–1975

The first years of liberalization (1965–7) were also years of a sharp recession with output growth falling to 3.2 percent, or half its level in the preceding period. Employment actually declined (table 10.1). The explanation for this lies in a combination of five policies. In approximate order of importance these were a very tight monetary policy; the policy of decentralizing economic powers to workers' councils and in particular the determination of income; policies to stimulate modernization and hence intensification of capital; the implicit real exchange rate policy after 1965,

Table 10.1 Evolution of major economic variables by liberalization period (annual growth rate unless indicated otherwise)

Economic variable	1960–4	1965–7	1968–70	1971–4
1 GDP	6.2	3.2	6.0	6.5
2 Employment	4.6	− 1.2	2.6	4.0
3 Rate of open unemployment (%)	5.9	6.6	8.0	7.7
4 Export volume	12.0	9.6	7.8	6.4
5 Import volume	9.5	7.4	10.1	7.6
6 Ratio of trade balance to GDP	− 2.4	− 0.7	− 3.4	− 6.1
7 Reserves in months of imports	0.7	1.6	2.0	n.a.
8 Debt service ratio (%)	10.1	13.4	14.5	17.7
8a Growth of debt	22.5	18.5	14.9	23.6
9 Export prices	3.2	2.6	3.6	15.0
10 Import prices	3.6	2.0	4.5	17.5
11 Terms of trade	+ 1.8	+ 4.8	− 2.6	− 8.4
12 CPI	8.6	23.5	8.0	19.0
13 Industrial producers' prices	2.6	9.4	4.2	17.1
14 Real exchange rate[a] (value at beginning/end of period)	80/88	100/100	97/92	102/85
15 Real rate of interest[b]	− 4	− 2	+ 1	− 6

[a] Nominal exchange rate divided by ratio of Yugoslav to weighted industrial countries' wholesale price index.
[b] Nominal lending rate – industrial producer price changes.
Sources: Dubey, 1975; Federal Institute of Statistics, Statistical Yearbook of Yugoslavia, various issues

that is, its appreciation through inflation; and the policy to cut the bulk of export subsidies almost immediately. These policies led to the critical economic situation of 1967–8 and its attendant political repercussions, including a reversal of the trade liberalization program.

Consider first the policy of decentralizing decisions on personal incomes. As has already been shown (chapter 6), 1965 and 1966 saw an explosion of labor income. The cost–push inflation that this occasioned[1] was given a one-time boost by the sharp devaluation of mid-1965, and the accommodating adjustments of controlled prices (table 10.2). An important point about the liberalization–recession sequence follows immediately from this. Import liberalization lagged behind the devaluation, and hence the potential price-reduction effects of liberalization did not come until much later.

Table 10.2 Key indicators of domestic and foreign trade activity 1965–1969 (percentage growth per annum, current prices)

Indicator	1965	1966	1967	1968	1969
Labor income	37.8	38.3	13.6	9.5	14.8
GDP (constant prices)	5.0	6.6	1.0	4.0	9.8
Producer prices	14.5	11.8	2.1	0.5	3.0
CPI	32.9	22.4	7.3	5.7	7.5
Money supply	5.0	4.5	− 5.6	25.8	11.6
Export growth	11.1	12.6	5.2	4.9	11.2
Import growth	− 6.7	22.7	8.3	6.0	12.9
Trade balance as percentage of GDP	10.6	− 1.0	− 1.7	− 2.0	− 2.3

Source: OECD, Economic Surveys, Yugoslavia, various years

The consequence of strong inflationary pressures in the first stage of the reform should not be underestimated. The primary objective of macrostabilization policy was to stem inflation. Since 1965, and largely up to the present, the only major macrostabilization tool available to the federal government was monetary policy, for decentralization had reduced central taxing power and revenues. World Bank analysts (Dubey, Schrenk, and Bery) as well as OECD annual reviews stress the loss of fiscal policy tools as a major policy problem in Yugoslavia. As federal budgets have become relatively smaller in total and as the law requires both federal and local budgets to be balanced, fiscal stabilization has become virtually

---

[1] While there are dissenters, most analysts agree that Yugoslav inflation is very much a cost–push phenomenon which starts with enterprises trying to raise wages and then attempting to pass these on in the form of higher prices, with part of the process requiring government to permit higher prices by price controls and the requisite protection. See, for example, Bajt (1969), Horvat (1971b), and Sirc (1979). This explanation is further used to explain the paradox of a negative relation between output and inflation.

impossible. Consequently, monetary policy was extremely restrictive during trade liberalization (table 10.2). Money supply, which had grown at 9.4 percent in 1964, slowed considerably.

There is little doubt that the aim of curbing inflation was largely achieved, since the consumer price index (CPI) fell from 32.9 percent in 1965 to 22.4 percent and then 7.3 percent. However, the cost in output and employment terms was very large. The employment situation was exacerbated by a tendency to capital intensity in the economy. As chapter 7 showed, capital-to-labor ratios rose sharply in the years 1965–7 as the various policies designed to modernize and improve industrial productivity began to be implemented through new investments.

Finally, as to external transactions, the first stage of liberalization saw a brief improvement followed by a continuation of the worsening trend of the trade balance (see table 10.2). For one year only, 1965, export growth exceeded import growth, and then it fell behind. Consequently, the trade balance was positive in one year only, worsening consistently thereafter. The reason is simple: in 1965, devaluation boosted exports while imports were curtailed by a combination of devaluation and slowed output growth. As the real exchange rate appreciated considerably by 1966 with high inflation, these effects were ameliorated.

Note, however, that the growth of exports in 1965–7 was lower than in 1960–4 (table 10.1), doubtless owing to the removal of export subsidies and the reduced availability of credit. While the intention was good (to reduce the high "artificial" support for exports in heavy industry in particular and hence to correct EER distortions), the short-term impact must have been to curb export expansion. Since positive reactions to such rationalization by newly favored sectors were not immediately forthcoming, export growth was probably lower than it would have been had a policy of some export promotion continued.

Such export promotion should not have been – as it had been before 1965 – via simple direct subsidies but by the offsetting of import substitution by such means as import duty drawbacks for exporters. Moreover, the industries earlier selected for export support were on the face of it obviously bad candidates: heavy industry, capital goods, and capital-intensive industries.

Nevertheless, it may still have been better for the general macro conditions in which liberalization was being implemented to continue even with inappropriate export promotion tools, at least for a year or two. This relates to the follow-up to trade liberalization measures. If "wrong" export supports had not been removed immediately but only as imports came to be progressively liberalized, at least the macro conditions would have been better, for export volume could have grown enough to avoid the deteriorating trade balance situation.

As it was, macroperformance provided little encouraging evidence of the positive effects of liberalization. While subsequent chapters will demonstrate that import liberalization did have many of the expected positive effects, such as increased productive efficiency, such subleties were neither immediately evident nor would they have provided very effective arguments in the face of a widespread worsening of the economic situation.

These circumstances encouraged policymakers to take actions to expand employment, output, and exports while trying to control prices and at the same time reinforcing their receptivity to pressures from below to help individual industries or sectors. The coincidental resurgence of centrifugal nationalist forces strengthened the lobbying power of local units (enterprises and/or governments), and these pressures together brought a change in policies which slowed and eventually reversed the liberalization. On the macro side, monetary policy in 1968 became expansionary to stimulate growth while controls on administered prices were used to curb inflation. Inflation was also helped by policies to slow somewhat the growth in real incomes and hence consumer purchasing power; this had the added desirable effect of raising the investment-to-GDP ratio and contributing to output expansion. In reaction to the many cries for help from industries losing ground to imports or exporters deprived of former large subsidies, import restrictions were increased in various forms and export supports began to be reintroduced.

However, the success of this policy was short lived, at least in some important aspects of the economy. The positive elements were, on the surface, output and employment. Output expanded at a high rate in response to monetary policy and increased investment demand; employment also rebounded strongly, partly in response to output, but also to policies designed expressly to set up many new enterprises and moral suasion to induce existing enterprises to absorb more labor.

On the negative side, the external balance worsened considerably. Despite the reintroduction of export subsidies and favorable credit, export growth slowed as the effect of reintroducing import-substituting incentives overwhelmed the effect of direct export supports, especially since the export support went, as before, to capital-intensive heavy industries which had an inherent comparative disadvantage. Import growth also increased despite the growing selective across-the-board restrictions. The trade deficit opened up to reach 3.4 percent of GDP. While some of this was sustained by rapid growth of remittances, part was financed by increased indebtedness. Starting already in 1960, debt grew throughout the period far faster than GDP or exports, causing the debt service ratio to rise steadily from 10.1 percent in the first period (1960–4) to 14.5 percent in 1967–70. In fact the problem was worse than this, for in terms of convertible currency the debt service ratio was already 23 percent in 1969.

Long-term Growth: Tendencies and Sources

We can begin the discussion of the 1965–70 economic performance with investment financing. Following decentralization of investment powers in 1965, workers (as mentioned earlier) naturally increased the revenue allocation to personal income, it growth (RPGI in table 10.3) rising after 1965 despite the fall in growth of GDP (RGY). Most critical is the fact that before 1965 personal income growth was slightly below output growth, while this relationship was reversed in the post-1965 cyclical downturn. This rise in personal consumption after 1965 was compensated for by a simultaneous sharp decline in the share of the government consumption, as intended, plus an unintended rise in the foreign deficit.

Table 10.3 Indicators of development efforts and effectiveness, 1952–1969

Indicator	1952–9	1960–4	1965–9
RGPI (rate of growth of personal income)	6.5	5.9	7.0
GFI/Y (gross fixed investment as percentage of GDP)	24.0	32.0	30.0
K/L (capital-to-labor ratio, social sector) (thousand dinars per laborer)	45.0	50.0	70.0
ICLR (incremental capital-to-labor ratio, social sector)	65.0	149.0	438.0
ICOR (incremental capital-to-output ratio)	3.6	4.2	5.4
RGY (rate of growth of GDP)	6.7	6.2	4.8
RGY/L (rate of growth of labor productivity)	4.5	3.9	4.9
RGTP (rate of growth of technical progress)	4.8	4.3[a]	4.0
C/Y (ratio of consumption to GDP (%)	54.0	51.0	56.0
RGCPI (rate of growth of CPI)	6.4	13.7	11.4
RGM (rate of growth of imports)	8.4	8.3	11.7
RGX (rate of growth of exports)	12.5	12.0	8.2

[a] Technical progress data from Puljic (1980) as in table 7.4.
Source: Calculated from data in Havrylyshyn (1984–6)

The declining role of government sources for investment financing is noted in chapter 6. State finance, which accounted for as much as 60 percent of investment financing up to the early 1960s, fell sharply to 36 percent in 1964 and to 15 percent in 1966. Banks became the principal channel for these funds, raising their share from an insignificant 3 percent before 1964 to something between 40 and 50 percent. Enterprises themselves ("economic organizations") maintained a fixed share (except in one year) reflecting the sharp increase in allocation to personal income of net enterprise revenues. (Direct foreign investment was allowed but remained at very low levels, as discussed in chapter 7.)

However, despite the smaller role of government, high investment levels were maintained, essentially by monetary and credit policies, using the newly important banks as the channel for allocations. That is, enterprises with greater freedom to make their own investment decisions borrowed from banks at low interest rates rather than from government agencies. The low, usually negative, rates of real interest generated excess demand for investable resources (Dubey, 1975, p. 216) and consequently, despite the increase in the ratio of personal consumption to GDP (C/Y) the ratio of gross fixed investment to GDP (GFI/Y) remained high.

The reforms also included a drive toward "intensive" development via increased capitalization, and a consequent rise in output-to-labor ratios. The capital-to-labor ratio (K/L) and especially the incremental capital-to-labor ratio (ICLR) rose sharply in this period. As a result, the simple measure of partial labor productivity did increase dramatically (see figure 10.1): its growth rate (RGY/L) rose to 4.9 percent compared with 3.9 percent in 1960–4 and 4.5 percent in 1952–60. However, this "success" in productivity gains was illusory, as two other measures of productivity deteriorated ICOR increased substantially to 5.4 percent, continuing the trend of 1960–4 when it was already high by comparison with norms of 4.2 percent prevailing in developing countries. (Vukina, 1982, has shown that the deterioration of ICOR occurred across most sectors and persisted in the 1970s.) Most importantly, the total factor productivity also showed a declining tendency, described in chapter 7 (see data from Puljic, 1980, in tables 7.6 and 10.3).

Thus output growth slowed despite the rise in K/L ratios as capital if not labor productivity declined sharply. This phenomenon was described in chapter 9 (the tendency of the marginal productivity of capital to decline). With increased K/L ratios, as Dubey (1975) and Schrenk et al. (1979) emphasize, the effect on employment growth was dramatic – it came to a virtual halt in this period. As seen earlier, it fell in 1966 and 1967 and only regained its 1965 level by mid-1968, as the strategy of intensive development succeeded in raising growth in the output-to-labor ratio RGY/L from already high growth levels before 1965 (4.5 before 1960 and 3.9 in 1960–4) to 4.9 a year after the reforms.

However, the negative consequences[2] did not end with a slowdown in employment generation. The sharp rise in personal income growth already noted generated excess demand for consumer goods at a time when investment was also being maintained, reflected in price pressures plus

---

[2] Reduced savings and investment was not in itself necessarily a bad thing for economic welfare. If pre-1965 levels determined by government had unduly restricted consumption given workers' time preferences, the increased consumption after 1965 might be considered optimal. However, we would then expect improvements in efficiency of investment which did not occur.

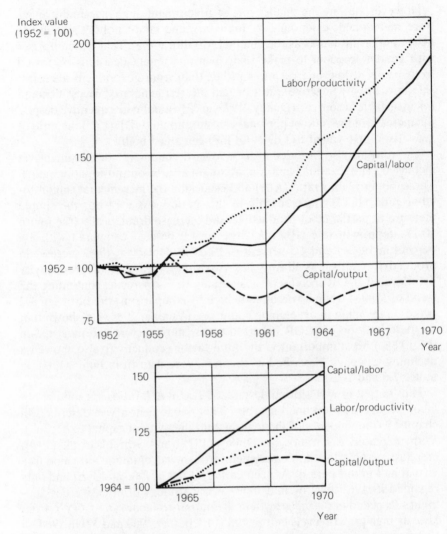

Figure 10.1 Growth in capital-to-output, capital-to-labor, and labor-to-productivity ratios, social sector, 1952–1970

Source: Federal Institute of Statistics, *Statistical Yearbook of Yugoslavia*, various issues

import demand (RGCPI and RGM in table 10.3). To the extent that a cost–push mechanism operated, the effect on prices was even more direct. The rise in prices was in fact strongest in 1965–6 (33 percent and 29 percent respectively for the CPI), which is explained to a large extent by the one-time increase in import costs after the 50 percent devaluation in mid-1965 and the related lifting of domestic price controls and price control ceilings. Credit policy was at the same time, at least throughout 1967, very restrictive; all this goes a long way to explain the economic slowdown. Horvat (1976) puts great emphasis on this confused policy to explain the failures in the reform period.[3] Certainly, the second negative consequence of this policy mix was the exacerbation of inflation and trade imbalances.

One more loose end needs to be tied up: how could enterprises sustain themselves in circumstances of such poor economic performance? The answer is to be found in a unique version of "soft" budgeting: illiquidity financed by expanding bank credits and intrafirm credits, and uncontrolled by bankruptcy discipline.

This problem was described in great detail by an outside critic (Sirc, 1979) and was widely recognized by Yugoslav analysts. Thus, for example, Madzar (1979) concluded: "the fundamental cause of illiquidity is the high propensity of working collectives to increase wages at the expense of capital accumulation . . . and . . . the virtual absence of the institution of bankruptcy."

Macro Tendencies and Liberalization Attitudes in the 1970s

The growing external imbalance plus resumed inflationary pressures in 1969 paradoxically renewed interest in liberalization as a solution. This was partly due to the influence of external creditors such as the IMF and the International Bank for Reconstruction and Development (IBRD), and partly a reflection of the continued strength of the "liberal" view among policymakers; the 1968–70 reversal was said to be only temporary. Thus an effort to resume liberalization was made in the period 1971–4.

By this time, however, two new policy attitudes had developed which were to make the implementation of liberalization more difficult: the demonstrated willingness in 1968–70 to use *ad hoc* measures for "temporary" import restrictions and/or export support and the growing view that inflation must be combated by short-term stabilization measures. Thus, when the 1971 rate of GDP growth reached 8 percent and the trade balance worsened dramatically, deflation policies were initiated at the same time as liberalization. As this began to slow GDP growth to 4 and 5 percent in the next two years, employment was also affected and demands for selective relief were renewed. In fact even in advance of such demands, the government applied restrictions to imports in order to combat the external imbalance problem. The underlying weakness of subsidized Yugoslav exports, and the inevitable dynamics of growing import requirements for inputs and capital attributable to the long-standing import substitution

---

[3] Rusinow (1977, pp. 229–31) gives an excellent account of the open public debate on the lack of economic knowledge in policymaking, in which Horvat was a principal.

orientation, ensured a worsening external balance. Correction of such biases and internal price distortions had been part of the intended 1965 reforms but, as Pertot (1984) shows, only a limited narrowing of distortions in effective exchange rates was achieved in 1965–7, and the reversal of 1968 put an end to this trend.

Despite the managed float of the dinar since 1973, the real exchange rate appreciated over the period (see table 6.2). Moreover, external factors made the trade balance even worse. EEC agricultural import restrictions continued to affect Yugoslavia. The oil price shock directly damaged the terms of trade, and by 1974 indirectly affected Yugoslav export markets in Europe.

In summary, the period 1971–4, though superficially one of high average growth, saw a series of "stop–go" policy actions that at best hampered the implementation of liberalization and at worst required "temporary" and often *ad hoc* restrictions on imports plus export incentives. While output and employment grew rapidly on average, export growth continued to decline, falling well below that of imports and resulting in a ratio of trade deficit to GDP of 6.4 percent and a sharp increase in the debt service ratio. Inflation intensified (17.1 percent for producer prices) despite all attempts to control it. By mid-1974 the overwhelming importance of inflation and short-term trade balance corrections finally resulted in the second reversal of liberalization which lasted until 1978.

While the trade balance and inflation continued to worsen throughout the decade and export performance was continually deteriorating (see chapter 8), the global availability of commercial credit permitted economic expansion to continue without the necessity of correcting the underlying price distortions. That is, solving the problem of noncompetitiveness could be postponed by foreign borrowing. Therefore liberalization was not seen as an immediate policy objective.

It was not until the debt crisis period of the early 1980s, and the curtailment of commercial credit globally, that Yugoslavia was forced once again to give serious consideration to trade reforms. To a considerable extent the return to liberalization ideas came in response to IMF and World Bank pressures, as these were the only institutions willing to lend (or to persuade others to lend). However, it was also recognized by domestic policymakers – and even more so by academic critics – that the opening up of the Yugoslav economy had never been achieved, that distortions between domestic and world prices continued to be large, and that these conditions were what lay behind the continuing external imbalance. Hence, once again as in the period preceding the 1965 reforms, much discussion at government and public levels took place, and finally a new economic reform package including both domestic and external liberalization was introduced in 1983.

11

Sectoral Effects of Liberalization

Sectoral Differences in Liberalization

Precise and reliable sectoral estimates of changes in protection and the degree of protection afforded are not available. The analysis performed here evaluates sectoral effects by identifying two broad groups of sectors – favored and disfavored – and by considering for each of these groups changes in major economic characteristics. The distinction between favored (group A) and disfavored (group B) sectors is based on the measured changes in the best available estimate of EERs – Pertot's parity ratios.

Using direct price comparisons from 1958 to 1962 for over 1,000 products, Pertot (1971) estimates for each sector, and for the whole economy, the ratio of domestic dinar prices to world prices in US dollars. His price parity ratios are in principle equivalent to EERs. For other years, detailed price indices were applied to estimate the ratios; the quantitative results for the changes over time generally bear out the qualitative judgment that policy was directed to reducing earlier biases in favor of heavy capital goods industries (group A) and against agriculture, raw material, and light consumer goods (group B) (see chapter 4).

Table 11.1 summarizes the changes in EERs for these two groups of sectors. Taking Pertot's EER values, the extent of relative protection is measured as the ratio of a sector's EER to total industry EER. The absolute change in this ratio indicates the policy effects for 1964–7, 1967–70, and over the entire period 1964–70.

With three exceptions – wood, iron and steel, and metal products – table 11.1 confirms the direction of policy noted: reduced bias favoring group A. There is no obvious reason for the case of wood, and the discrepancy may simply result from inaccuracies in the EER computations. The case of metal products may be a problem of disaggregation: the sector includes both heavy goods such as machinery and light consumer goods. The relative values of EER close to unity, and the small changes in these, suggest that heavy goods may belong to group A and the lighter ones to

Table 11.1 Indicators of sectoral protection levels and changes

Sector	Relative EER imports[a]			Change in EER		
	1964	1967	1970	1964–7	1967–70	1964–70
Total industry	1,151.00	1,430.00	1,536.00	—	—	—
A Favored sectors						
Wood products	1.42	0.97	0.94	– 0.45	– 0.03	– 0.48
Electrical products	1.22	1.18	1.15	– 0.04	– 0.03	– 0.07
Chemicals	1.49	1.10	0.81	– 0.39	– 0.29	– 0.68
Shipbuilding	3.05	1.28	1.02	1.77	– 0.26	– 2.03
Average (simple) A	1.80	1.13	0.98	– 0.67	– 0.15	– 0.82
B Disfavored sectors						
Agriculture	0.81	0.97	1.01	0.16	0.04	0.20
Industry						
Coal	0.80	1.07	1.27	0.27	0.20	0.47
Tobacco	1.09	0.42	1.25	– 0.67	0.83	0.16
Food products	0.89	1.43	1.00	0.54	– 0.43	0.11
Nonferrous metals	0.61	0.86	0.83	0.25	– 0.03	0.22
Nonmetallic minerals	0.81	1.16	1.03	0.35	– 0.13	0.22
Building materials	0.69	0.95	0.90	0.27	– 0.05	0.22
Iron and steel	0.72	0.95	0.87	0.23	– 0.08	0.15
Metal products[b]	1.01	1.03	1.07	0.02	0.04	0.06
Textiles	0.83	1.01	0.98	0.18	– 0.03	0.15
Footwear	0.86	1.04	1.27	0.18	– 0.23	0.41
Average B	0.83	0.95	1.05	0.12	0.10	0.22

—, not applicable.
[a] Ratio of sector EER to total industry EER.
[b] Includes machinery and transport equipment other than ships.
Source: Pertot, 1984, figure 8

group B (nominal tariffs in 1964 for machinery were 42.0 percent while those for metal products excluding transport goods were 17.7 percent (Havrylyshyn, 1984–6, part I, appendix table 28). There is also some overlapping in the case of iron and steel: while it is clearly a heavy industry, it never had high protection because it was considered a raw material important primarily as an intermediate input. However, the EER may be misleading, as support for the industry came through substantial injections of developmental capital in the 1950s and early 1960s; that is, the effective protection of value added was probably high. (Indeed, the effective protection for iron and steel in 1972 was 69 percent, compared with 11.2 percent for all metallurgy (Fabinc et al., 1976).

Thus, on balance, the liberalization of 1965, even with the 1968–70 reversal, succeeded in reducing the favorable treatment of group A sectors and improved the relative position of group B sectors. In the post-1967 reversal, however, while the position of the heavy industries continued to decline, the improvements for most group B sectors were also undermined. That is, the sectoral impact of the reversal was even more selective than had been the 1965 liberalization, a fact consistent with increased *ad hoc* and arbitrary administrative reactions.

The major characteristics and economic development before 1965 of each sector in these two groups are summarized in table 11.2. An unweighted average value is calculated for each of the two groups.

The relative importance of a sector in terms of protection and special treatment is probably better measured by employment than by value added, and also by the share of a sector in external trade. Table 11.2, columns 1–3, shows these values for 1964. The four favored sectors together accounted for 31.9 percent of 1964 employment and only one of these had a substantial share at 10.1 percent. There were, in fact, two sectors in the disfavored group with much larger shares – metal products and textiles – but given the aggregation problem in metal products this sector's high share of 18.4 percent is not so meaningful. In total, the disfavored sectors accounted for a much higher share of employment, 67.9 percent.

The relative importance of these two groups in exports and imports was somewhat different. The disfavored sectors provided only 41.9 percent of exports in 1964 – well below their employment share – while the favored sectors provided 23.3 percent – above their employment share. Thus the sectors that had been favored before 1965 were relatively more export oriented. Also, they were subject to less import penetration. While their total share of employment in 1964 was 21.9 percent, their share of imports was lower at 17.5 percent. These trade characteristics are also reflected in the trade ratios of columns 11–14. In 1965, the import-to-production ratio was slightly lower (21 versus 23) and the export-to-production ratio was markedly higher (37 versus 23) in the favored sectors of group A.

With the exception of shipbuilding and iron and steel, there was little geographic concentration of industries. Shipbuilding is highly concentrated in two coastal cities (Rijeka and Split), and the Republic of Croatia accounted for about 85 percent of employment in the sector. Iron and steel was traditionally concentrated in Bosnia-Herzegovina (Zenica Works) and the north of Slovenia (Jesenice). Beginning in the late 1950s, diversification was planned with major mills in Skopje, Smederevo in Serbia, and Sisak in Croatia. At least some of these (Skopje) were considered inefficient, and certainly the diversification in general was considered to result in "grave diseconomies of scale" (Dubey, 1975, pp. 114, 135).

Even with the diversification, in 1965 the two traditional areas in Bosnia-Herzegovina and Slovenia still accounted for a major part of employment, 41 percent and 23.4 percent respectively. Furthermore, at

Table 11.2 Characteristics of sectors with favorable and unfavorable treatment before liberalization

	1 Share of total exports 1964	2 Share of total imports 1964	3 Share of total employment 1964	4 Four-firm concentration Ratio 1965	5 1969	6 1960–4 growth rate Employment	7 Output	8 Exports	9 Imports	10 Import-to-production ratio 1965	11 1970	12 Export-to-production ratio 1965	13 1970	14 Average labor income (dinars per month) 1965	15 1968	16 1970
A Favorable treatment																
Wood products	10.7	0.8	10.1	49	53	5.5	11.9	8.4	43.0	3	9	39	25	401	659	988
Electrical products	4.3	5.1	5.7	84	84	12.8	17.0	12.3	14.3	43	49	18	15	477	880	1,155
Chemicals	3.7	11.2	4.6	76	76	8.4	18.3	18.7	10.2	27	28	26	20	570	977	1,248
Shipbuilding	4.6	0.4	1.5	86	87	-0.5	11.0	21.0	0	12	23	83	76	669	1,156	1,550
Average A	23.3a	17.5a	21.9a	74	75	6.7	14.6	15.3	8.2b	21	27	37	34	529	918	1,236
B Unfavorable treatment																
AG Agriculture	19.6	13.6	n.a	n.a.	n.a.	(-2.0)	2.2	7.2	23.7	9	6	9	6	399	715	962
Manufacturing																
Coal	0.2	2.7	5.9	84	87	-2.1	4.1	-8.0	4.9	23	18	1	3	573	829	1,104
Tobacco	4.2	0.2	1.7	53	61	4.2	9.4	18.8	0	0	2	32	24	416	733	933
Food products	7.2	4.9	8.3	47	67	7.0	9.6	5.3	11.1	14	12	17	11	474	794	1,085
Nonferrous metals	9.3	2.6	3.5	91	98	2.4	8.6	10.1	10.0	25	50	53	53	591	970	1,261
Nonmetallic minerals	3.1	2.1	3.2	89	98	3.7	12.7	17.2	17.2	32	55	38	26	476	740	1,033
Building materials	0.2	0	5.4	59	62	0.8	6.2	0	0	1	3	2	1	424	792	1,072
Iron and steel	2.4	9.0	3.7	87	92	1.2	5.6	0.4	16.4	61	72	10	14	619	938	1,253
Metal products and engineering goods	11.9	28.7	18.4	53	56	7.1	10.0	12.0	7.4	46	62	23	14	512	847	1,158
Textiles and clothing	0.9	11.0	14.7	40	47	7.8	9.7	23.8	13.5	28	26	18	19	426	666	857
Footwear and leather	4.5	0.1	3.1	68	69	7.8	11.4	24.9	52.0	3	18	36	37	436	729	942
Average B	41.9a	62.1a	67.9a	67	74	3.7	8.7	10.5	11.6b	23	32	23	19	495	803	1,070

n a. not available. ( ): estimated

a Values shown are total for group, not averages

b The averages calculated exclude the extreme values for wood, tobacco, and footwear

Sources: Havrylyshyn. 1984–6. tables in Parts I and II; Federal Institute of Statistics. *Statistical Yearbook of Yugoslavia*. various issues

least three towns in which plants were located were highly dependent on the iron and steel industry: Zenica in Bosnia, Jesenice in Slovenia, and, to a lesser extent, Smederevo in Serbia.

One other important sector with a moderately high concentration is electrical products, which had a four-firm concentration ratio in 1965 of 84 percent (table 11.2, column 4). This is reflected geographically in the location of the four largest firms in the area of Kranj in Slovenia, Zagreb in Croatia, and Belgrade and Nis in Serbia. While data by city are not available, the three republics respectively accounted for 26.4 percent, 22.2 percent, and 31.4 percent of 1965 employment in the sector. However, in three cases the localities themselves are large and are not dependent on this industry; the exception is Kranj. The problem for Kranj is not as great as it appears, for the industry itself and the large firm in Kranj (Iskra) are internally highly diversified, producing a wide range of electrical products for consumer and industrial uses.

With the exception of iron and steel and wood, the favored (heavy industry) sectors tend to have high capital-to-labor ratios and the disfavored have low ones (see table 7.4). However, the differences are not dramatic, perhaps because aggregation hides many of the characteristics being investigated. Thus, overall, group A has a capital-to-labor ratio of 105 percent of industry average, while group B is just average.

A related characteristic, average "wages" or, more properly, labor income, does show an important difference between the two groups. Average wages in 1965 (table 11.2, column 14) were much lower in the disfavored than in the favored industries – 495 dinars per month compared with 529. This gap persisted through the first phase of liberalization (1965–7) and the reversal (1967–70), even widening in 1970 from a 9 percent to a 16 percent differential. Only the agricultural sector experienced a closing of this gap.

The economic performance of these sectors before liberalization is shown in table 11.2, columns 6–9, which give annual rates of growth of output, employment, exports, and imports. The favored sectors expanded output, employment, and exports much more rapidly than did the disfavored sectors, while imports grew much more slowly, as might be expected given that high protection for priority sectors meant not only protection of domestic markets against imports but also a strong system of export support via subsidies and other measures.

The intention of the 1961 and 1965 reforms was not so much to open the economy for its own sake – indeed many argued that fundamentally a socialist economy could not be open and remain socialist – rather, opening the economy was regarded as an instrument for redressing the sectoral imbalance created by the earlier more autocratic policy. Thus the liberalization was by no means uniform, but entailed sectoral differences to correct previous biases.

The Pattern of Response across Sectors

In this section we continue to use the twofold groupings of table 11.1, but for completeness we add a third group of four "other sectors" (Havrylyshyn, 1988, appendix table 11.1). This third group is quite small (the first two together already account for 89.8 percent of 1964 employment) and excludes several miscellaneous industries for which either the existence of protection is doubtful or data are unavailable. For three of the four sectors – paper products, rubber products, and forestry – relative EER positions shifted only slightly during the course of liberalization. For the fourth sector, petroleum, the EER for imports remained unchanged from 1964 to 1970, though its EER for exports increased sharply. However, this was simply due to an attempt to stimulate fuller use of new refinery capacity by export subsidies. Because the sector is small on all counts (employment, exports, and imports) and its export-to-production ratio remained minuscule despite the rise from 1965 to 1970 (see table 8.2), it is considered too unimportant to be included in either group A or group B.

Was there a "typical" performance of major economic variables over the duration of the liberalization policy? To a limited extent the answer is in the affirmative, but many of the observed responses at the sectoral level point in opposite directions. To help trace such responses, tables 11.3 and 11.4 present detailed information for each of 18 industrial sectors plus agriculture, and table 11.5 summarizes this information for the major groups discussed earlier.

The following economic responses appear to have been typical of most sectors during liberalization in Yugoslavia:

1   output growth slowed down in the first phase of liberalization;
2   imports expanded more than output, that is, import penetration increased in most sectors;
3   in the early phase of liberalization – accompanied by a devaluation – export expansion exceeded both output and imports in many sectors;
4   in the later phase of the reversal, exports grew more slowly than imports, though they continued to outpace output;
5   with very few exceptions across sectors or time periods, employment lagged far behind output and in fact fell in absolute terms in most sectors;
6   related to this, capital stock continued to expand rapidly in all periods and most sectors, apparently independently of output, employment, or trade performance;
7   finally, in all sectors in the first phase inventory build-ups were very high when output slowed and import penetration increased.

Table 11.3 Sectoral evolution of principal economic variables in liberalization, 1965–73 (for sectors receiving unfavorable protection treatment before 1955)

Columns under "Output" through "Imports" fall under the group heading "Cumulative percentage change for subperiods of liberalization"; the two "Study" groups fall under "Annual growth ratio of total factor productivity".

	Relative EERX value change			Relative EERM value change			Output[a]			Employment			Capital stock			Inventories		Exports			Imports			Study 1		Study 2	
	1964	65-7	68-70	1964	65-7	68-70	65-70	68-70	71-3	65-7	68-70	71-3	65-7	60-70	71-3	65-7	60-70	65-7	60-70	71-3	65-7	60-70	71-3	60-5	65-70	65-70	70-5
AG Agriculture	0.76	0	0.03	0.81	0.15	0.04	4.8	0.8	12.1	n a	n a	n a	n a	n a	n a	n a	n a	21.4	-11.4	58.1	1.4	12.9	88.5	n a	n a	n a	n a
B Industry																											
Coal	1.39	-0.03	-0.58	0.80	0.27	0.20	-11.6	2.4	11.6	-14.3	-8.9	3.5	37.4	43.6	55.8	128.5	66.3	-8.5	400.0[b]	-28.5	-32.8	57.6	70.5	2.91	-0.96	-0.44	-2.77
Iron and steel	1.10	-0.01	-0.20	1.09	0.23	-0.08	11.1	38.0	30.4	0.7	9.2	14.2	59.3	-0.4	145.1	80.0	15.3	47.8	51.6	184.9	6.1	76.3	38.6	2.62	2.33	-0.49	-2.04
Nonferrous	1.01	-0.81	-0.81	0.89	0.25	-0.03	13.2	26.3	26.4	12.7	5.3	6.0	66.6	-1.5	95.3	70.5	2.6	30.3	112.9	40.8	103.0	208.0	10.8	1.57	2.15	-0.36	-2.66
Nonmetal products	1.06	0.11	-0.20	0.61	0.35	-0.13	14.9	40.7	18.4	-2.3	5.9	9.6	80.6	40.6	70.2	84.3	6.3	8.9	34.1	26.8	48.5	104.8	28.8	9.19	3.65	1.92	0.51
Metal products	1.15	0.25	0.21	0.81	0.02	0.04	1.9	34.5	20.3	-2.0	16.4	12.2	72.8	7.9	132.3	65.5	4.2	55.9	22.0	117.8	36.8	71.6	50.0	1.13	1.73	0.77	0.02
Building materials	0.92	0.16	0	0.69	0.27	-0.05	8.3	34.6	27.1	-11.4	4.1	4.5	38.4	38.3	145.2	36.1	3.1	89.5	-25.0	9.5	402.8[b]	500.0[b]	-9.5	4.92	4.61	2.50	0.85
Textiles	0.86	0.13	-0.18	0.72	0.18	-0.83	12.1	13.9	25.7	7.2	6.9	19.3	63.2	23.0	90.2	97.8	14.5	53.6	34.4	52.1	23.3	23.3	36.3	4.76	0.04	0.02	-0.34
Footwear and leather	0.85	-0.20	0.71	1.01	0.18	0.23	4.2	6.8	25.3	0.9	8.3	27.2	49.3	48.2	116.4	55.9	2.2	69.2	13.8	103.9	386.9[b]	326.8[b]	47.6	2.90	-1.47	-0.40	-0.14
Food	0.80	0.03	0.07	0.83	0.54	-0.43	19.6	19.7	26.0	-0.3	10.3	21.4	91.8	31.6	207.4	90.4	10.2	11.3	30.3	0.9	26.1	101.3	61.1	5.46	1.08	-0.02	-1.21
Tobacco	0.88	0.03	-0.12	0.06	-0.67	0.83	3.5	6.1	23.4	-21.4	-8.4	4.4	116.9	14.4	95.9	88.0	11.7	-21.1	5.7	7.6	-73.1	400.0[b]	14.0	1.83	-5.11	-5.06	-5.30
Average B	0.99	-0.004	-0.83	0.83	0.16	0.10	7.2	22.3	23.5	-3.0	4.9	12.2	67.6	23.8	115.4	79.7	8.5	33.7	29.8[b]	51.6	24.8[b]	86.1[b]	34.8	3.65	0.80	-0.40	-1.49

n a. not available. EERX, EER for exports; EERM, EER for imports

[a] Constant prices

[b] For calculation of averages, very high rates for sectors with a low base have been arbitrarily set at a value of 100 percent

Sources: Havrylyshyn, 1984:6, tables in parts I and II; Federal Institute of Statistics, *Statistical Yearbook of Yugoslavia*, various issues

Table 11.4 Sectoral evolution of principal economic variables in liberalization, 1965–1973 (for sectors receiving favorable or neutral protection treatment before 1985)

	Change in relative EERX value			Change in relative EERM value			Cumulative percentage change for subperiods of liberalization																
							Output[a]			Employment			Capital stock			Inventories		Exports			Imports		
	1964	65-7	68-70	1964	65-7	68-70	65-7	68-70	71-3	65-7	68-70	71-3	65-7	68-70	71-3	65-7	68-70	65-7	68-70	71-3	65-7	68-70	71-3
A Favored																							
Wood	0.95	0.12	0.24	1.42	-0.45	-0.03	5.6	22.4	22.5	-5.2	-2.4	14.1	118.0	-3.1	27.6	70.7	-13.0	2.7	30.2	115.2	-6.1	324.0	18.1
Electrical products	1.49	-0.89	-0.34	1.22	-0.84	-0.84	13.6	39.1	32.0	3.3	18.8	17.3	126.4	32.8	186.3	113.0	21.4	106.9	48.7	88.6	45.3	71.0	32.3
Chemicals	1.30	-0.31	-0.36	1.49	-0.39	-0.29	40.3	62.1	43.3	12.2	14.0	19.7	76.1	37.1	92.0	44.0	46.6	107.8	35.8	119.1	26.1	61.8	79.7
Shipbuilding	0.95	-13[b]	0.05	3.85	-1.77	-0.26	46.9	50.0	23.5	1.4	14.0	14.9	85.3	22.4	100.9	n.a	18.0	43.8	140.8	25.7	261.7[c]	113.2	65.1
Average A	1.17	-0.06	-0.41	1.00	-0.67	-0.15	35.0	43.4	30.5	2.9	17.2	16.5	95.7	22.3	82.3	76.1	18.0	65.1	63.9	87.2	81.6[c]	142.5	48.8
C Neutral																							
Petroleum	1.62	1.87	0.81	1.13	-0.20	-0.20	54.0	34.5	22.9	13.1	37.3	16.7	43.2	78.3	64.2	70.6	49.4	84.2	-38.4	0.5	106.2	64.4	196.8[c]
Paper products	1.17	-0.24	-0.04	0.82	-0.10	0.11	35.3	22.4	28.2	24.9	10.4	6.9	104.1	5.9	57.7	406.6	-9.2	68.2	29.0	39.5	51.9	181.4[c]	5.2
Rubber	1.08	-0.09	-0.03	0.93	-0.10	0.84	22.0	29.6	32.8	21.6	9.1	15.7	188.2	24.4	186.1	86.1	68.6	76.5	94.1	103.8	42.8	27.8	38.8
Forestry	1.83	-0.84	0.05	n.a	n.a	n.a	2.1	1.0	2.2	-7.1	-11.4	3.2	36.5	13.7	26.6	n.a	n.a	28.2	63.2	87.4	73.8	281.9	39.9
Average C	1.23	0.22	0	0.96	-0.02	-0.02	27.3	21.9	21.5	13.1	11.4	19.6	93.1	12.2	63.7	187.7	36.3	50.2	37.2	57.8	68.7	140.9	68.7
All sectors	1.00[d]	—	—	1.00[d]	—	—	14.3	28.6	25.0	2.3	7.4	16.8	87.3	14.4	111.9	n.a	n.a	41.2	45.1	71.4	32.9	74.1	54.6

— not applicable. n.a. not available. EERX: EER for exports; EER for imports

[a] Constant prices

[b] For 1964 the value for 1967 increased sharply to 1.742, but was quickly revised down in 1968.

[c] For calculation of averages, very high rates for sectors with a low base have been arbitrarily set at a value of 100 percent.

[d] The values of these variables for all sectors are by definition 1.00, that is, individual sector EERs are calculated as a ratio of the overall average

Sources Havrylyshyn, 1984: 6, tables in parts I and II. Federal Institute of Statistics, Statistical Yearbook of Yugoslavia, various issues

Table 11.5 Evolution of principal variables, 1965–1970 (by main sector groups)

Sector group	Change in EER		Change in outputs	Change in employment	Change in exports	Change in imports	Change in capital stocks	Change in inventory
	EERX	EERM						
1965–7								
A	− 0.6	− 0.67	35.0	2.9	65.1	81.6	95.7	76.1
B	− 0.2	0.12	7.2	− 3.0	33.7	24.8	67.6	79.7
AG	0	0.16	4.8	n.a.	21.4	1.4	n.a.	n.a.
C	0.22	− 0.02	27.3	13.1	50.2	2.5	13.1	187.7
All industry (A + B + C)	n.a.	n.a.	14.3	2.3	41.2	32.9	87.3	n.a.
1968–70								
A	− 0.41	− 0.15	43.4	17.2	63.9	142.5	22.3	18.0
B	− 0.04	0.10	22.3	4.9	29.0	86.1	23.8	8.5
AG	0.03	0.04	0.8	n.a.	− 11.4	12.9	n.a.	n.a.
C	0	− 0.02	21.9	11.4	37.0	140.9	12.2	36.3
All industry (A + B + C)	n.a.	n.a.	28.6	7.4	45.1	74.1	14.4	n.a.

n.a. not available: A. sectors receiving unfavorable treatment before liberalization; B. sectors receiving favorable treatment before liberalization; C. sectors receiving neutral treatment before liberalization; AG, agriculture. See tables 11.2 and 11.4 for a list of sectors in each group.

Output Slowdown

The macro story of chapter 10 above has already detailed the extent and causes of the economic slowdown. All sectors experienced the same sharp slowdown except shipbuilding, which, on the strength of ongoing work, maintained about the same pace of expansion as before. Thus, as can be seen in table 11.4, output growth of shipbuilding from 1965 to 1967 was 46.9 percent, much higher than the industry average of 14.3 percent (two other sectors were higher – chemicals, 48.3 percent; petroleum, 54.0 percent – but were not exceptions to the slowdown because their growth in 1960–5 was much higher than for shipbuilding). Later in the study it will be demonstrated that the degree of the slowdown not only differed across sectors, but it was, quite unexpectedly, least for sectors in group A whose favored position was deliberately *reduced* in the liberalization.

Import Penetration

Liberalization certainly succeeded in its immediate objective of increasing the openness of the Yugoslav economy. Although import growth slowed from 9.5 to 7.4 percent, this was far less than the slowdown of output from 6.2 to 3.2 percent. Import penetration increased substantially in most sectors, as was seen in table 8.2 and reflected in the import expansion data in tables 11.3–11.5. Between 1965 and 1970, five sectors did experience a decline in import penetration: coal, textiles, rubber, food processing, and agriculture. However, the reductions were not large and the total import share of these sectors in 1965 was about a third; the overall effect was an increase of the ratio from 26.6 percent in 1965 to 32.7 percent in 1970.

Rapid Response of Exports to Devaluation

In the first phase of liberalization (1965–7) exports in general grew more rapidly than imports which, in turn, grew faster than output. Three facts suggest that this cannot be attributed to the liberalization effect of correcting distortions. First, the policy measures were not fully implemented until some time in 1967; hence, export reorientation could come only later. Second, the immediate impacts on exports should have been negative, if anything, since existing export subsidies were to a large extent removed. Third, the expansion of exports slowed in 1968–70 (below that of imports) when export incentives were introduced and when any indirect effects of corrected distortions might have been expected to take hold. Add to this last the decline in the real exchange rate after 1967 (see table 11.2) as inflation continued, and we have a picture of exports reacting much more to devaluation (or lack of it) than to other measures associated with liberalization.

The early response of exports was not uniform, however. About half the sectors saw a slowing of export growth in 1964–7 (though this was in sectors of lesser importance overall to exports). Some evidence that sectoral variations in export orientation are affected by sectoral export incentives is provided below in this section on correlation of major variables.

Lagging Employment

In many sectors, the first phase of liberalization was one of absolute decline in employment. Indeed, as table 11.4 shows, the group B sectors in which the EER for imports rose in general suffered a decline in employment, while other sectors experienced only a slowdown. In all but three sectors, however, there was an absolute decline in employment in at least one year of this period, and the three sectors which avoided this (nonferrous metals, chemicals, and rubber) accounted for only 11 percent of industrial employment. Thus disemployment during liberalization affected almost all sectors of the economy.

Furthermore, the lag of employment behind output was worse for most sectors in 1965–70 than it had been before 1965, when it was nearly half of output growth (table 11.2); for the period 1965–70 it fell to well below a third in most industries.

Continued Rapid Investment

One objective of the 1965 reforms was to promote modernization via capital-intensive production. The large new investment programs in this period exacerbated unemployment and resulted in excess capacity. Capital stock expanded very rapidly (tables 11.3–11.5), at least in the period 1964–7. This expansion slowed considerably in the next three years as money supply and credit constraint policies were introduced to dampen inflation, but picked up again in the period 1970–3.

The Inventory Cushion

Inventory-to-output ratios almost universally increased in the first phase of liberalization (tables 11.3–11.5). The excess build-up of inventories, of course, would have permitted output and employment expansion in the face of declining demand (whether caused by decline in total demand or import competition). As described earlier, the phenomenon was facilitated by bank credits and an accumulation of interfirm debts (accounts payable).

Resort to this cushion against worsening economic conditions could not be continued indefinitely of course, and, indeed, in the period 1967–70 inventory build-up in most sectors was reversed or at least slowed to a level below output expansion.

Factor Productivity Slowdown

Yugoslavia's long-term decline in productivity growth was noted in chapter 7. The last four columns of table 11.3 provide the data on total factor productivity for three periods. Two separate studies are available with one overlapping period. Differences in method and data preclude comparison between them, but each permits some inferences about the period concerned. With only two exceptions, total factor productivity declined in all sectors after the reform, and continued to decline after 1970.

There are several reasons, however, for suggesting that this phenomenon was not attributable to liberalization. First, as has been discussed earlier, the liberalization was very short lived and incomplete before it began to be eroded in 1967–70, and it continued to deteriorate despite a rescue effort in the early 1970s. Indeed, while the economy remained more open to trade in the 1970s than in the 1950s, internal interventions, distortions, and administrative arbitrariness increased. Visible and understandable central directives were replaced by opaque and unclear decentralized interventionism. The microefficiency implications of this need no elaboration.

Furthermore, certain other explicit objectives of development policy impeded factor productivity improvement. The first easy returns from new technology and experience of industrialization gave favorable results before 1965. Continued growth after 1965 could not come as easily by factor expansion; increased efficiency would have required less capital-intensive expansion and called for more attention to the comparative advantage sectors as opposed to autarkic "key industry" (that is, heavy industry) policies. Yet, even in the 1965 reform, one objective was to increase capital intensity – and this was achieved (see chapter 10)! Note from tables 11.3–11.5 that it continued to be the heavy industries (group A plus certain others) that expanded capital stock most rapidly, experienced greatest output growth, and, thanks to subsidization, experienced highest export growth.

Finally, some rough indication of the correlation between productivity change and trade ratios suggests that increased import openness does contribute to productive efficiency. Estimates of technical efficiency change (TEC) were presented in chapter 7 in a translog production function, which arguably captures microefficiency changes more accurately than general technical progress does (table 11.6).[1] Although none of the correlations with trade ratios is statistically significant, they do suggest that the sectors with the highest increase in import ratios have not been those with the greatest factor productivity change, though they may have

---

[1] See, for example, the results of such an analysis in relation to liberalization for Chile in Condon et al. (1985).

Table 11.6 Correlation of productivity and openness, 1966–1970

	Import ratio change	Export ratio change	Output change	Capital stock change
Total factor	−	+	+	+
productivity (TFP)	n.s.	n.s.	n.s.	n.s.
Technical efficiency	+	+	+	+
change (TEC)	n.s.	n.s.	s.	s.

n.s, not significant; s, significant.
Sources: Author's calculations of factor productivity; Federal Institute of Statistics, Statistical Yearbook of Yugoslavia, various issues

enjoyed the greatest change in technical efficiency. For exports, the correlation is positive in both cases.

What should we expect import penetration to do? If protection has permitted factor-use inefficiencies (which is what a positive EPR implies), this means that production is occurring inside the isoquant. The competition of imports should push production toward the isoquant – that is, a positive TEC value – regardless of what the long-term movement of technical progress may be doing to it. Thus, if capital investment in the long run is not positively related to import penetration increases (see table 11.5), import penetration need not have a positive correlation with total factor productivity but should have a positive correlation with TEC. This is what table 11.6 indeed confirms.

Correlation of Major Variables

In the previous section we traced the differences among sectors in evolution of major economic variables. In this section we isolate some of the major relationships among variables, largely in bivariate correlations. For obvious reasons, such an approach has major shortcomings. The economic causation among variables such as output, employment, investment, exports, imports, and protection is neither bivariate nor unidirectional, and statistical attempts to capture these relations should be cast in the framework of a fuller model.

In a (forgivable?) violation of the spirit of simultaneous causation, it seems most reasonable to posit the following chain of effects. First, liberalization measures directly affect imports and exports, presumably increasing both. Second, for a given level of demand (= absorption) increased imports in the very short run compete with domestic production, causing it, and correspondingly employment, to decline. This can be considered as the direct gross loss in welfare attributable to liberalization. Third, export expansion adds to demand for domestic production, raising output and employment, which can be considered as the direct gross gain in welfare. Fourth are the various indirect effects of improved resource reallocation in response to distortion corrections, increased microefficiency in response to competition of imports and export incentives, and the eventual growth effects of resources released by these efficiency improvements. These can be called the allocation and efficiency gains of liberalization.

There are some difficulties in applying even this simplified description for the observed values of the variables reflect the net effect of all four phenomena plus others. Outside this liberalization paradigm, we have effects of coincidental policies, especially exchange rates, macrostabilization, and development investment programs. Exogenous shocks, such as the gradual closing of EEC markets to Yugoslavia and the increased opportunities for migrant workers, also play a role. Moreover, statistical difficulties complicate attribution of effects. One problem is aggregation. For example, estimates of EERs, output, and employment are available for the very broad sector metal products. However, detailed trade data reveal that the behavior of subcategories varies widely on both the import and export side.[2] Finally, of course, there is an incomplete and only approximate picture of the actual levels of protection and their changes.

Bearing these qualifications in mind let us review the available evidence: first, with a look at the impact of liberalization on imports and exports; second, with an investigation of the relationship between foreign trade and domestic variables. The basic approach will be to correlate sectoral values of changes in one variable with those in another. There are a total of 19 sectors and three subperiods which, with pooling of the time periods, provide up to 57 observations. However, greater aggregation, while statistically less precise, turns out to be more revealing in some cases.

Effects of Liberalization on Trade Volume

Earlier discussion has emphasized the increasingly administrative nature of protection policies starting in 1967, and the consequent difficulty of measuring rigorously the extent of protection or export incentives. Even the direct price comparison procedure used by Pertot (1973) to estimate EERs could not detect all the subtle forms of protection such as delays in paperwork, access to available foreign exchange, various indirect subsidies apparently unrelated to trade, and so on. This difficulty is reflected in the statistical analysis of the relationship between trade policy measures

---

[2] While imports for the entire sector increased in 1964–7 by a total of 36.8 percent, light metal goods nearly doubled and transport equipment increased fourfold.

(EERs) and trade volume responses (exports, imports). Such correlation (not shown) reveals that sectoral variation in import growth or import penetration is not related negatively to the change in relative EERs in imports, nor is the export growth positively related to the change in the relative EERs of exports.

Consider a cruder, but ultimately more revealing, analysis of the policy effects, depicted in figures 11.1 and 11.2, which uses the broad aggregates of table 11.5: favored industry, disfavored industries, agriculture, and others. With two subperiods for which change in relative exchange rates and trade growth can be compared, eight observations are available.

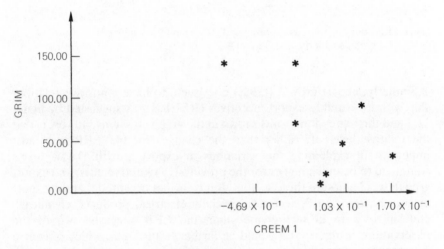

Figure 11.1 Correlation of import growth and change in effective exchange rates (by broad sector groups), 1965–1970

The data of figure 11.2, though limited, indicate clearly that increased protection resulted in less import penetration. (The negative relation is especially strong for the period 1965–7 before administrative restrictions set in.) If we add the further qualification that group A sectors lost less favor in 1964–7 than the values of EER in tables 11.3 and 11.4 suggest, that observation should probably be higher and the negative correlation stronger.[3]

---

[3] These sectors continued to have priorities in various policies, all of them expanded capacity rapidly, receiving favorable credits and/or government funds, and they were large exporters who continued to receive indirect support for investment and operations and easier and probably quicker access to the licenses and foreign exchange which were still needed (Pertot, 1971, pp. 281–303). Thus both the EERM and EERX values are probably understated.

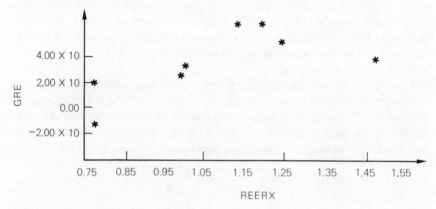

Figure 11.2 Correlation of export growth and change in effective exchange rates (by broad sector groups), 1965–1970

Similarly, export growth (GRE) does seem to have a positive relationship with measurable export incentives (REERX), as suggested by figure 11.2 and the regression results shown in the graph. It seems, however, that the relative level of, rather than the changes in, the EER was most important in explaining the variations in export growth. These levels continued to be much higher for the previously favored sectors, and export growth was highest in these sectors. If it is further accepted that the export incentives to group A sectors (especially electrical products, chemicals, and ships) were in fact greater than the EER suggests, two of the observations in figure 11.2 would be farther to the right, which of course increases the strength of the positive correlation.

To sum up, there is evidence that imports did respond to liberalization as we would expect. In the aggregate, for broad groups of sectors import penetration decreased least where relative protection increased, but this correlation cannot be statistically demonstrated for individual sectors. For exports too, comparing broad groupings, export expansion was greatest where the level (not the change) of EERs was highest, but it is not possible to demonstrate this positive correlation in the sectoral detail.

Impact of Imports and Exports on Domestic Activity

Imports and Employment
The simultaneity problems noted earlier confound any attempt to isolate the negative impact of increased imports, as imports are themselves a function of output and the assumption of perfect substitutability is not completely justifiable. Not surprisingly, correlations between some mea-

sure of import and output do not yield any meaningful results. Simple correlations between imports and output, changes in these, or use of import penetration all suggest either no significant correlation or, if anything, a positive one. However, correlations between imports and employment changes do provide a picture consistent with the short-run gross loss effect. There is a negative relationship between import and employment expansion, and this is particularly evident when change in import penetration is used rather than import growth (Havrylyshyn, 1988, appendix figures 11.1 and 11.2). Thus, in sectors with more rapid import penetration employment is likely to expand more slowly. The same phenomenon is reflected in the time path of these variables within a sector. The simple correlation coefficient r^2 between the import penetration ratio and the employment-to-output ratio is negative and significant in 13 of 18 sectors.

Imports and Capital-to-Labor Ratios
A simple correlation coefficient between the import-to-penetration ratio and the capital-to-labor ratio has been calculated for each sector. In 12 cases out of 18 the coefficient is positive and in ten of these it is significant, while only two of the six negative coefficients are significant. The implication is that import penetration decreased as capital-to-labor ratios increased, or perhaps more accurately that greater increases in capital-to-labor ratios were associated with lower increases in import penetration. If this is so, it suggests protection policy that continued to emphasize import substitution by way of capital-intensive activities, despite the 1965 reform objectives of correcting such biases. This is, of course, consistent with a conclusion that the liberalization was not successful in changing relative protection, although it may well have lowered the overall degree of protection.

Imports and Inventory Build-Up
Many analyses of Yugoslav policy problems emphasize the build-up of inventories as a short-term safety valve against decreased demand or, in the liberalization period, competing imports. (Sirc 1979, ch. 10), stresses this and the financial indiscipline it entails.) The overall picture seen in tables 11.3 and 11.4 seems to support this view. Increases in inventories were extremely high in the period 1964–7. However, the cross-sector correlations (Havrylyshyn, 1988, appendix 11.3) in fact yield a significant negative relationship. Therefore, it is possible that the build-up was a cyclical phenomenon in reaction to the general demand decline and not simply tied to import penetration. Note that for 1967–70 inventory growth fell sharply even though import growth was more rapid.

Imports and Exports
Detailed sector-level correlations between import and export growth do
not reveal any obvious statistical relationship. However, the correlation
between import penetration and export orientation is not only positive but
very significantly so. As with trade incentive measures, a less detailed set
of observations also turns out to be revealing. Thus, figure 11.3 shows the
relationship between export and import growth for the four groups and
three periods of tables 11.3 and 11.4. The 12 observations suggest a
distinctly positive relation; indeed, it is even clearly observable for the four
observations of each of the two subperiods 1964–7 and 1967–70.

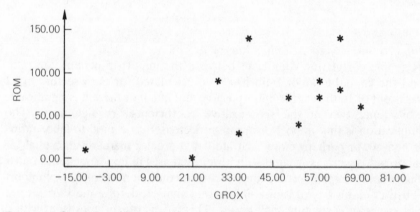

Figure 11.3 Correlation of import and export growth (by broad sector groups),
1965–1973

Taken at face value, this indicates that the groups of sectors that
expanded exports most rapidly also expanded imports most rapidly. This is
not what we might expect in the short run, when liberalization not only
lowers protection but selectively reduces distortions. In such circumstances, sectors that lose high import substitution protection (groups A and
C) should exhibit a rapid increase in imports and a lower expansion of
exports at first. Sectors which had previously been relatively less protected
and less favored by export policies (groups B and A) should experience less
import growth and more rapid exports.

Of course, once the allocation and efficiency gains of liberalization begin
to be felt, the former import substitution sectors may be expected to turn
to efficient lines of export products, and consequently to experience both
high export growth and high import growth. In Yugoslavia, however, as

already emphasized, import-substituting orientation was never fully reversed and soon returned. All indications are that high export performance continued to be in heavy capital-intensive industry, artificially supported by explicit and implicit export subsidies.

The more plausible interpretation of figure 11.3 is that the heavy industries (group A) continued to receive favorable export treatment while facing a decline in protection against imports.[4] In the years 1965–7 exports grew rapidly, as did imports. The other industries, though relatively more shielded against imports than before, did not increase their export orientation markedly because they did not benefit from as much "correction" through relative export incentives (see REERX for AG, table 11.3). By 1967–70, policy corrections began to be reversed and the pre-1965 biases returned. Now, however, there were fewer imports of finished goods competing with domestic output (see chapter 8 on import dependence), and the demand for intermediate and capital goods increased. A more administrative approach to the rationing of imports also began to be introduced, which seems to have favored imports of heavy goods, restricted imports of lighter consumer goods, and involved the reintroduction of subsidies to encourage exports in the heavy industries. This is reflected in a continued positive relation between exports and imports. The capital-intensive industries were favored by export policy, and the same type of industries (or goods) were increasingly the priorities in a macroenvironment of worsening balance of payments.

Exports and Various Domestic Variables

In general, export-to-production ratios declined for most sectors (see table 8.2). In identifying any relationship between export-to-production ratios and other sectoral characteristics, the results are not exactly the same as those for rates of export expansion. There appears to have been a negative relationship between export orientation and capital intensity. Correlation coefficients for 19 sectors between the export-to-production ratio and the capital-to-labor ratio gave strongly negative results in 15 sectors, all but one significant. That is, while heavy capital-intensive sectors were increasing their exports more rapidly, labor-intensive activities were apparently increasing their export orientation more rapidly. ("Apparently," because the correlations noted are not across sectors but over time within a sector.) The two phenomena are entirely consistent, for the output growth of capital-intensive activities was more rapid.

A direct comparison of capital-to-labor ratios in 1965 and the change in the export-to-production ratio from 1965 to 1970 provides further evidence

---

[4] Chittle (1977, pp. 90–3) also shows evidence that trade in the wrong goods was being encouraged. Pertot (1984) emphasizes the conclusion that, despite movement away from import substitution in 1965–70, it was limited and in any event soon reversed.

(see scatter diagram in Havrylyshyn, 1988, appendix figure 11.4). The correlation coefficient for 17 sectors is 0.039, but dropping two outliers (wood products and nonmetallic minerals, with a decline in the ratio of 12.0 and 14.0) gives a correlation coefficient of − 0.353. A direct comparison of the variables shows that the sectors with increases in export orientation were largely labor-intensive (coal, textiles, leather and footwear, rubber products, printing), the only exception being iron and steel.

Characteristics of Outlier Sectors

Since it is difficult to measure accurately any changes in either the degree and timing of protection or export incentives, it is not really possible to identify any given sector as having a rapid or strong trade response. We can only pick out the sectors which had the highest and lowest growth rate, and those that had an early or late expansion relative to the 1965 benchmark period. Even so, a "late" response for exports (for example, building materials) may simply reflect a later introduction of the policy change for that sector or merely a slow response.

Given these qualifications, certain deviants from the typical evolution pattern are identifiable.

Exports and Imports

Typically, exports expanded rapidly in 1965 and 1966, slowed considerably in 1967 and 1968, and then grew much more rapidly in the years 1969–73. For imports, the pattern was decline in 1965, sharp recovery in 1966, and continued rapid expansion until 1970 when there was a slowdown for two years, followed by a rapid expansion once more in 1973. Table 11.7 shows the annual growth rates for the totals and several deviant sectors for the period 1965–8 only.

Taking export expansion first, three sectors show outstanding export growth (above 80 percent cumulative in three years 1965–7): electrical goods, chemicals, and rubber. The first two are quite large (about 5 percent each of 1964 industry exports), while the last is small (about 2 percent). In all cases, export expansion is substantially above the industry average for 1965 and 1966, and continues above average for most cases examined in 1967–8.

By contrast, five sectors, together accounting for 25.6 percent of 1964 exports, were well below average (below 20 percent cumulative in 1965–7) in export performance: coal, nonmetallic products, wood, tobacco, and forestry. Indeed over the four years, six cases out of 20 show a positive growth rate.

Table 11.7 Outliers in export and import performances

Sector	Export growth rates			
	1965	1966	1967	1968
Total	22.2	11.8	2.6	0.9
Industry	26.5	12.1	− 0.5	6.2
High cases (12.1)[a]				
Electrical goods	60.6	23.3	4.6	6.3
Chemicals	64.4	16.5	8.2	3.2
Rubber	30.1	56.9	− 13.1	7.2
Low cases (25.6)				
Coal	− 29.1	− 5.9	34.8	− 31.1
Nonmetallic products	18.2	− 3.4	− 4.4	8.1
Wood	0.8	6.2	− 3.7	11.1
Tobacco	− 7.4	− 5.9	− 9.0	− 15.1
Forestry	− 9.6	− 16.5	− 4.6	18.6
"Slow cases" (20.4)				
Textiles	15.6	15.9	14.9	7.8
Leather	5.9	14.7	39.6	14.3
Building materials	− 3.2	− 1.9	99.0	− 35.1
Iron and steel	− 0.6	12.1	33.1	9.1

Sector	Import growth rates			
	1965	1966	1967	1968
Total	− 2.6	22.3	8.3	5.2
Industry	− 5.0	22.9	14.2	9.3
High cases (4.0)				
Nonferrous metals	39.1	22.5	19.4	21.3
Ships	115.4	112.6	− 20.8	69.8
Leather	93.9	13.1	122.0	76.9
Forestry	43.7	182.7	9.5	6.3
Low cases (15.6)				
Coal	− 2.9	− 11.8	− 21.2	12.8
Iron and steel	− 0.1	19.9	− 11.1	− 15.1
Wood	− 31.6	8.1	26.3	33.4
Tobacco	− 93.0	794.7	− 55.2	− 3.9
"Slow cases" (17.8)				
Paper	5.8	− 14.5	68.2	9.4
(also coal, iron and steel, wood)				

a Numbers in parentheses indicate percentage share of sectors in 1964 exports or imports by industry.
Source: Federal Institute of Statistics, Statistical Yearbook of Yugoslavia, various issues

A sector that is "slow" or "fast" presents problems for the reasons cited earlier. Nevertheless, it is possible to distinguish sectors which are "slow" from those that have low growth. There are four sectors in which exports were neither very high nor very low on average, but in some way lagged behind the typical case: textiles, leather goods (footwear), building materials, and iron and steel. The first and last were quite large contributors to exports, and taken overall the group accounted for 20.4 percent of 1964 exports.

While the typical case showed a rapid response in 1965 and 1966 to devaluation (and other factors, or both) and a subsequent slowdown, textiles stand out as progressing more steadily, albeit at first more slowly. Leather and footwear exports were even more laggard, but then in 1967 and 1968 grew far above average; much the same is true for iron and steel. Finally, building materials exports, though declining at first, boomed in 1967, only to fall again the next year.

Indeed, the last case is perhaps more appropriately assigned to a group designated "erratic," and including also food products, exports of which rose one year and fell the next with great regularity. Interestingly, the trend of imports for the food sector is also somewhat erratic, though not nearly as much for exports. The pattern follows to some extent the trend of agricultural output.

Two final comments on export "deviants" should be added. First, the export share of sectors high above the average is significantly smaller (12.1 percent) than that of sectors well below the average (25.6 percent), reflecting the deteriorating export performance of Yugoslavia in the years since 1965. Secondly, the fact that 12 sectors out of a total of 18 can be identified as exceptional reflects the wide dispersion of export growth rates. Very few sectors were close to "average."

For import expansion, four groups can be identified: high cases with cumulative growth in 1964–7 above 65 percent; low cases with cumulative growth below 20 percent; slow and fast response sectors. (The last two overlap to some extent with the first two.)

Very high growth of imports is observable in nonferrous metals, ships, leather and footwear, and forestry. None of these experiences the 1965 decline observed for all industries, and almost all continue to have import growth well above the average; however, the share of this group in imports was very small.

Coal, iron and steel, wood, and tobacco show very little import growth. With the exception of wood from 1966 on, and iron and steel plus tobacco in 1966, all the values are negative. Three of these sectors (coal, wood, tobacco) have very low output growth in 1965–7 (tables 11.3–11.4) and exceptionally low export growth; the low import growth of these sectors was plainly not "substituted" by high output growth. Nor was it simply a reaction to increased protection, for as tables 11.3 and 11.4 show, while two of these (coal, iron and steel) did enjoy increased protection, the other two suffered decreased protection.

Slow import response has been identified either as a check in the decline responding to devaluation or as a continuation of decline after 1965, contrary to the "typical" upswing. The first type is seen in paper products where imports grew in 1965 and declined only in 1966 but, contrary to the norm, then increased in 1967. A continued decline of course means that the sector has a low growth rate over the period; thus three cases in the low category fall under this heading.

As with exports, it has been impossible to distinguish a fast response from a strong response, unless erratic fluctuations are taken to imply fast. Tobacco, in which imports were moving erratically with very high negatives one year and high positives the next, is such a sector.

While the preceding discussion may shed some light on liberalization timing issues by comparison with experiences in other countries, the patterns appear to have little significance for the Yugoslav experience as such.

Only two points stand out, as mentioned already: the high share of sectors with very low export growth, and the fact that sectors with low import growth did not also experience high output growth.

Employment and Output

While many response linkages could be considered and investigated, only one other in addition to imports and exports will be discussed: that of employment and output, a linkage to the central issues of this project, particularly given the macroenvironment of the liberalization period. The basic approach taken here is to identify sectors which deviate by having an unusually high or low employment-to-output response. If sectors in which employment fell sharply relative to output can be identified, the effect of imports on employment can more easily be isolated by asking whether these sectors also had high import expansion, high import penetration, or both.

Overall, and for most individual sectors, output faltered in 1965 and for some even declined a little in late 1966 or early 1967. Employment began to decline as early as 1965, quarter IV, and continued to fall far more steeply than output, bottoming out only in 1968, quarter I, two quarters after output had hit bottom. However, there is a considerable sectoral variation in this employment-to-output linkage.

The first six (group I) comprise iron and steel, nonmetallic products, metal fabrication, wood products, building materials, and forestry. The second six (group II) comprise nonferrous metals, electrical products, chemicals, textiles, leather and footwear, and rubber. (Their output and employment growth is shown by Havrylyshyn, 1988, appendix table 11.2.)

Of far greater interest than the simple identification of these sectors as special – as with trade responses, the number of "special cases" is very large – is the detection of what causes high or low employment generation in a given sector, and what in particular is the role of trade. Table 11.8 presents some data on the characteristics of these sectors selected with a view to what might turn out to be important, though some characteristics which were investigated and proved uninteresting are not shown (labor income indicators, EERs, inventory change, number of new establishments).

Most striking is the ratio of export expansion to import expansion. Sectors that created more employment relative to output had a far greater ratio of export growth to import growth. A clear exception was leather, though the explanation is simple: leather exports grew at very high rates from a 1964 base of 505 million dinars; imports grew at far higher rates but from a tiny base of 23 million dinars. (The exception of iron and steel in 1965–7 will be dealt with below.) Note that import growth in these sectors was not always low, but even when it was high, export growth was generally higher. Thus, what seemed to matter most was not low import expansion, but generation of enough export growth to compensate. The import penetration and export-to-production ratios are also interesting in this connection. The low employment generation sectors do not have a higher import penetration ratio or a lower export-to-production ratio; indeed, the opposite is true. Similarly, the low employment creation sectors do not have particularly low export-to-production ratios, though they are somewhat lower than for the other sectors.

Greater concentration of undertakings in a sector might be expected to explain higher employment creation, as such concentration means greater lobbying power to obtain job-saving and job-creating privileges. Indeed, some support for this is found in the data, as the ratio is slightly higher in the second group. However, it is far too low in textiles, or even in leather, to have mattered. High concentration does not seem to have helped some sectors such as nonmetallic products and iron and steel, though it may well have contributed to the effect of high export expansion to import expansion in two cases: nonferrous metals and, to a lesser degree, electrical products.

Nonferrous metals is a sector in which Yugoslavia has a strong natural comparative advantage, since it is the only major European producer of several minerals such as copper, lead, and zinc. The export growth was not strong – indeed, the ratio of export growth to import growth is only slightly higher than for group I sectors – yet employment and output expanded (Havrylyshyn, 1988, appendix table 11.2). The key lies in the location: these industries are in less developed parts of Yugoslavia, and as such received considerable federal resources from the special development

Table 11.8 Characteristics of sectors with high and low employment creation

	Employment 1964 (thousands)	Ratio of exports to imports 1965–7	Growth 1968–70	Import penetration 1965	Ratio of exports to output 1965	Four-firm concentration 1965	Ratio of capital to labor 1965	Growth of capital stock 1965–7
I Low employment creation								
Iron and steel	50	7.8	0.67	61.0	10.0	87	200	59.0
Nonmetallic products	43	0.18	0.33	32.3	38.2	89	65	80.6
Metal fabrication	251	1.52	0.31	46.6	23.2	53	90	72.8
Wood products	138	−2.48[a]	0.10	3.1	39.3	49	49	118.0
Building materials	73	0.22	−0.05[a]	0.1	1.6	59	61	38.4
Forestry	89	−0.38[a]	0.22	1.7	12.1	n.a.	40	36.5
Totals or averages of I	644	1.1	0.26	24.1	20.0	67	84	67.0
II High employment creation								
Nonferrous metals	47	0.29	0.54	25.2	53.1	91	146	66.4
Electrical products	77	2.3	0.69	26.8	26.4	84	92	126.4
Chemicals	63	4.1	0.57	43.0	18.0	74	160	126.4
Paper	23	1.3	0.20	17.7	19.1	58	228	104.0
Textiles	201	2.3	1.48	28.3	17.8	40	67	63.2
Leather and footwear	43	0.23	0.05	3.0	36.0	68	67	49.3
Rubber	13	1.79	3.38	53.9	4.5	79	61	188.2
Totals or averages of II	444	1.83	1.11	3.0	26.0	73	98	103.0

n.a. not available.
[a] Export growth negative.
Sources: Havrylyshyn. 1984–6. tables in parts I and II; Federal Institute of Statistics. *Statistical Yearbook of Yugoslavia*, various issues; Four-Firm concentration ratio. Petrin. 1981

funds, and doubtless other privileges also. The concentration of production in four firms no doubt facilitated this.

Electrical products, in contrast, are located in the more developed regions, and could not count on the same treatment. However, once things became difficult in the labor market – and once political rumblings in Croatia and Slovenia began to be heard – this too became an area that could count on privileges. Note that, in the first year, employment lagged far behind output (Havrylyshyn, 1988, appendix table 11.2) but then in 1966 and 1977, when lobbying began in earnest, the gap between output growth and employment growth closed quickly.

Consider finally two measures pertaining to capital. We might expect more labor-intensive industries to experience greater effects on employment generation. The data for capital-to-labor ratios do not support this, as the ratio is higher for the sectors with greater employment generation. In contrast, the growth of capital stock does seem to matter; capital stock grew much more in the sectors with a higher capacity for employment generation.

Another sector in which the geographical and production concentrations may have combined to stimulate employment generation was iron and steel. Overall, employment performance was poor, but note the odd situation of 1967, when output fell by 1.1 percent and employment increased by 4.9 percent. Add to this the above-average growth rate of employment in 1968–70 (9.2 percent versus 7.4 percent, see table 11.3), and the iron and steel sector suddenly became a sector creating high employment.

In summary, it appears that good performance in creating (or saving) jobs during liberalization is determined not by any inherent sectoral characteristic, such as capital-to-labor ratios, size or concentration, but primarily by export performance relative to import exposure. High absolute import growth will not necessarily "cause" unemployment nor will low import growth avoid it. It matters a great deal how exports perform.

Liberalization and the Government Budget

Fiscal Position

Throughout this period, the budget was in general very close to balance, a position not obviously changed by liberalization. Indeed, as emphasized earlier, fiscal policy has been largely unusable as a macromanagement stabilization tool since 1965 because of the decentralization arising from the 1965 reforms. While before 1965 federal budgets were about 60 percent of the total, after 1965 this share fell quickly to 40 percent and even less when extra-budgetary funds are included (Dubey, 1975, p. 424, for years

1967–70; Federal Institute of Statistics, *Statistical Yearbook of Yugoslavia*, 1945–64, p. 266, for pre-1965 data).

It is also noted that the automatic stabilizer of unemployment compensation was too small to matter (chapter 9). In the peak year 1967, outpayments amounted to 83.8 million dinars, about 1 percent of the federal budget and about 0.2 percent of consolidated public expenditures – an increase over 1965, but not a very significant one. In that year, 23,800 of 267,000 registered unemployed received total compensation of 35.4 million dinars, or 0.4 percent of the federal budget and a little less than 0.2 percent of consolidated expenditures.

Revenue Effects

The change from a QR regime to a partially tariff-based regime in fact took place in 1961 rather than 1965: hence the positive impact on revenues from duties is more evident in that period than after 1965. Customs duties more than tripled from 1960 to 1962, rising from a share of 7.7 percent in the federal budget to 23.4 percent. In the combined budget of federal and local governments, this share was much smaller, however, at 4.8 percent and 13.1 percent respectively (Havrylyshyn, 1988 appendix table 11.3).

In 1965 and 1966 customs duties fell, and only regained the 1964 value in 1967. Four separate effects lay behind this net movement. Reductions in tariff levels initially resulted in lower revenues, but their increase in 1967 reversed this. Import liberalization, in the sense of earlier access to licenses and foreign exchange, increased imports and hence revenues. However, the devaluation of 1965 resulted in reduced imports, as did the slowdown of economic activity.

Finally, it is evident that in the grand total of all public funds, customs duties were less than 10 percent, probably throughout the period, but certainly so after 1965.

Expenditure

The link between trade policies and public expenditure is not as easy to make as for revenues, largely because the data are not sufficiently detailed. It has been noted above that not only was unemployment compensation a very tiny fraction of public expenditures, but the increase in this after the 1965 liberalization was a mere 50 million dinars or so, a paltry 0.1 percent.

Grants and subsidies to the economy are lumped together in one line item of the easily accessible public accounts. They do, of course, include export subsidies, capital or nonmaterial purchase subsidies which may affect imports, and general subsidies to cover financial losses which may be partly attributable to the short-run import disemployment effects addressed above. Clearly, however, they include many other elements with no direct or simple connection with liberalization, and must therefore be considered a substantial overestimate of the effect of liberalization (hence, the omission of the word "effect" in this subheading relating to expenditure). Even the *change* in this expenditure after 1965 cannot be taken as a measure of the effects of liberalization because so many other factors were also changing: the pace of economic expansion was slowing: administered prices were being restructured, permitting reduction of subsidies to some enterprises; funding was being handed over to local budgets and extra-budgetary funds, so that these data were no longer comparable after 1965.

While the line item "export credit finance" is directly related to trade phenomena, for two reasons it is of little help in telling the full story. Data are not available systematically before 1966, and in any event these are repayable credits and do not measure the subsidy element. This could not be measured without data on terms of such credit, which, of course, is not available.

Despite these shortcomings, some useful conclusions are possible. First, and most important, is the increasing share of local government and extra-budgetary funds in subsidy payments. Local subsidies were less than 1 percent in 1961–2 but rose quickly to 8 percent in 1964, 30 percent in 1966, and over 40 percent by 1969–70. Subsidies to extra-budgetary funds were less than half as large as direct subsidies in 1961–3, but surpassed these by 1968 and were 30 percent higher by 1970. This tendency was likely to result in greater arbitrariness of such payments, both because decentralization increased the difficulty of control and coordination, and because extra-budgetary funds make it easier to hide such payments.

A second fairly clear trend is the decline in subsidies after 1964. The sum of the two subsidy items (in million dinars) in 1965 was 2,984 (2,075 + 905); this fell to 1,542 in 1965 and was, respectively, 2,053, 2,040, 2,136, 2,430, and 2,881 in the next five years. These figures probably underestimate the amount of subsidization – especially for the later years 1969–70 – as export credits grew in importance and the diffusion of budgets may have hidden many subsidies. Nevertheless, they probably reflect at least the short-run cutback in subsidies immediately following liberalization.

A third related observation is that subsidies began to grow again quite quickly after 1967, especially in the guise of extra-budgetary expenditures. Just as the reduction of subsidies in 1965–7 is consistent with the policies of the first phase of liberalization, so too is the return of subsidies to earlier levels consistent with the reversal.

A fourth tendency is the decline of export credit financing through 1966–8, and the very sharp return in 1969 and 1970. This also accords with the qualitative descriptions (and other quantitative evidence) of the development of policies with respect to export supports: a sharp cutback in 1966–7 and then a gradual reintroduction of supports, perhaps up to or almost up to earlier levels.

12

Employment and Trade Liberalization: Short-run Partial Effects

The term unemployment has a well-established meaning: those willing to work but unable to obtain a job. It may be preferable to coin a different term to refer to the effects of imports upon employment levels: *gross import disemployment*. In this section we attempt to measure only that portion of short-run unemployment attributable to increased import competition, a concept which is quite explicitly narrower than the usual meaning of unemployment. Perhaps the most important reason for making the distinction is that it will be demonstrated that sectors with a high import penetration tend to have a higher import-disemployment effect, but do not automatically have the lowest net employment growth rates. As tables 11.2 and 11.3 and the discussion of them showed, several sectors in fact had high import penetration, but because they also had high export expansion, the growth of output and employment was at least average or better.[1]

An Approach to Measuring Import Disemployment

Disemployment of labor in a given sector arises from general contraction in the economy, reduced sector-specific demand, labor-saving technological progress, increased import penetration, and short-run exogenous disruptions such as supply cutoffs. The actual change in employment in a given year is the net effect of all these plus the possible coincidence of two countering tendencies: government actions to prevent disemployment, and the happenstance of a new entrant whose investment comes to fruition in

---

[1] Yet another reason for using the term disemployment pertains to the calculation of a sectoral unemployment rate. The concept implies labor immobility across sectors, which is a much too rigorous assumption. No such assumption is needed to speak of the number of disemployed in a sector and to label the ratio of disemployment to total (potential) employment as a "disemployment rate."

that year and who may go ahead with production even if the sectoral situation is one of net disemployment.

To isolate the effect of import penetration is obviously not easy; nor is there a self-evident method that suggests itself. A general contraction occurred in the period 1965–7 and a glance at tables 11.4 and 11.5 makes it clear that employment growth fell far short of output growth, implying a trend in labor-saving technical progress. As sectoral disemployment is not a conventional concept, prior studies of the effects of contraction policies on unemployment were not available to give guidance. Indeed, the empirical analysis of the import–employment linkage was the most difficult to resolve in this study and involved many dead-end trails. There is a lesson in this for liberalization policy: the linkage is not a directly observable phenomenon and may be nearly impossible to measure with any reasonable degree of confidence.

The approach finally decided upon was to assume that potential demand growth in each sector was equal to the rate of growth of aggregate final demand $C + G + I + E$ (see equation 12.1) and to use the 1960–4 trend of employment-to-output ratio in order to project labor-saving technological disemployment α_j. As the period considered is very short, the effects of nonunitary demand elasticity at the sector level are minimal. However, the considerable change in relative prices resulting from the 1965 reform might have changed demand structures. As the liberalization process only started during 1965 and was implemented over the next two years, the year 1965 is taken as the benchmark relative to which import disemployment is estimated. Another reason for choosing 1965 is that employment levels for industry peaked in that year, and 1965 is probably closest to a full-employment year.

Perhaps the rationale for the potential demand effect bears a little theoretical elaboration. If we assume that liberalization opens up the economy to imports, then the counterfactual needed is to estimate what output and employment would have been without liberalization but with all other policy and nonpolicy exogenous effects remaining unchanged. Simply put, we assume that import-to-output ratios remain fixed but demand components move, as they in fact did. In addition to any underlying cyclical evolution of the economy, two important policy effects occurred: a contractionary monetary policy sharply curtailed growth of domestic demand components, and the devaluation led to a rise in export growth (table 12.1). The observed change in imports includes these effects of course: some early liberalization may have pushed imports up, and devaluation and contraction may have pushed them down. The demand effect is given by the rate of growth of final demand (0.1 percent in 1965), and at the aggregate level the devaluation effect could be approximated using available GDP elasticity estimates. However, at the sectoral level, the devaluation effect cannot be estimated since elasticity estimates have

Table 12.1 Growth of aggregate output and final demand

Indicator	1964	1965	1966	1967	1968	1969	1970
GDP	9.8	1.4	5.0	0.9	3.5	9.3	5.7
Final demand FD	11.1	0.1	7.7	2.2	4.0	10.0	9.0
(= C + I + G + E)							
Consumption C	9.3	0.6	4.6	5.4	6.1	9.6	5.6
Government expenditure G	6.1	− 2.8	− 2.1	2.6	4.5	4.2	6.0
Fixed inventory + inventory I	15.0	− 9.1	4.1	3.3	5.6	10.7	17.0
Exports	8.4	11.1	12.6	5.2	4.9	11.2	7.4
Imports	17.8	− 6.7	22.7	8.3	6.0	12.9	23.4
		devaluation					
Domestic demand C + G + I	11.5	− 1.7	6.8	1.6	3.7	9.7	9.4
Money supply	9.4	5.0	4.5	− 5.6	25.8	11.6	25.0
			tightening				
Enterprise credit	4.2	3.8	3.2	2.5	4.2	4.8	6.8
			tightening				

—— break in series.
Sources: Dubey, 1975; table 11.3 for money supply and credit

not been possible in the QR regime of Yugoslavia. However, since the benchmark year for the calculations is 1965, this becomes less important as the nominal devaluation effect does not apply and, with inflation low until at least 1968–9, the real exchange rate is little affected.

In sum, at the sectoral level imports fully substitute for domestic production; any increase in imports which raises the import-to-production ratio thus directly reduces domestic output by an equivalent amount. The resultant decline in employment follows, with an appropriate measure of technical progress included. The counterfactual value of output (and employment) can then be estimated by assuming that sectoral output expands at the same rate as final demand as shown in equations (12.1)–(12.3):

$$POTEM_{jt} = POTEM_{jt-1}(1 + \alpha_j RFD_t) \tag{12.1}$$

$$IDE_{jt} = POTEM_{jt} - ACTEM_{jt} \tag{12.2}$$

$$RIDE_{jt} = \frac{IDE_{jt}}{POTEM_{jt}} \times 100\% \tag{12.3}$$

where $POTEM_{jt}$ is the potential employment in sector j, year t, without import liberalization but given aggregate demand and technical progress trends, α_j is the trend ratio of employment to output growth in sector j in the period 1960–4, RFD_t is the rate of growth of final demand in year t, $ACTEM_{jt}$ is the actual employment in sector j, year t, IDE_{jt} is the

Table 12.2 Employment, import disemployment, and import penetration, 1966–1969

Sector	α	1966 (RFD = 7.7)			1967 (RFD = 2.2)			1968 (RFD = 4.0)			1969 (RFD = 10.0)		
		REM	RIDE	RMQR	REM	RIDE	RMQR	REM	RIDE	RMQR	REM	RIDE	RMQR
Coal[a]	—	− 2.2	—	− 13	− 12.0	—	− 25	− 4.4	—	11	− 5.6	—	12
Petroleum	0.30	3.8	− 0	30	− 5.0	− 0	8	17.0	− 0	16	7.6	− 0	− 4
Iron and steel	0.34	− 1.2	0	12	− 4.2	4.3	− 13	0	5.6	− 25	3.6	5.4	15
Nonferrous	0.39	2.3	− 0	17	− 4.2	− 0	14	− 10.0	0	− 13	2.7	0.2	26
Nonmetallic	0.39	0.5	2.8	10	− 3.4	6.8	24	− 2.8	10.0	3	4.6	8.1	12
Metal products	0.61	− 2.8	4.4	22	− 2.0	7.5	29	2.8	7.0	5	6.8	6.4	− 9
Ships	0.20	− 1.6	5.4	60	2.4	3.6	− 30	2.3	1.8	25	3.2	0.9	− 18
Electrical products	0.52	− 4.1	4.9	21	− 1.6	5.2	16	1.1	6.3	2	9.8	2.1	1
Chemicals	0.54	2.4	0	13	− 2.3	2.5	9	− 3.3	− 0	1	8.2	6.4	− 6
Wood	0.41	− 3.0	4.7	5	− 5.0	10.3	30	− 1.3	12.8	25	0.8	15.5	50
Paper	0.56	3.8	− 0	− 22	− 6.8	7.8	50	3.8	0	1	5.9	0.3	25
Textiles	0.61	3.4	1.0	11	− 0.6	2.6	7	1.0	4.8	0	4.5	6.3	15
Leather	0.59	− 0.1	5.0	12	− 1.6	7.7	100	3.3	6.8	70	2.7	9.7	70
Rubber	0.54	2.2	4.7	9	2.6	− 0	− 1	1.0	0	2	5.6	− 0	− 22
Food processing	0.53	2.0	5.5	− 1	4.9	3.9	30	0	20.0	2	4.9	21.0	8

—, not applicable; RFD, rate of growth of final demand; REM, rate of increase in observed employment; RIDE, rate of import disemployment; RMQR, percentage change in import-to-production ratio.

[a] No calculation of RIDE made for coal because of the difficulty of attributing observed employment decline to long-term trends of labor productivity and the substitution of fuels and hydroelectricity for coal.

estimated import disemployment in sector j, year t, and $RIDE_{jt}$ is the rate of import disemployment in sector j, year t.

Since the base for this estimation is 1965, the value of POTEM 1965 is taken to be equal to ACTEM 1965. The assumption that final demand for each sector grows at the same rate is not unreasonable for a short period; it was therefore not thought essential to refine the procedure using annual input–output table data on sectoral demands, since the data are not easily available. The 1960–4 value of the coefficient α_j may be too high for the period 1965–70; the same ratio calculated for later years tends to be much lower, about 0.26 on average compared with 0.40 in 1960–4. This may arise from the policy of technical modernization which pushed capital-to-labor ratios sharply upward, possibly leading to overestimation. However, earlier industrialization policies no doubt created some excess of employment, and the general reform policies toward decentralization should have led to rationalization of employment. This would offset the upward bias.

The random effects of timing of closings, new openings, and so on cannot of course be specified a priori, but are partially reflected in two ways. First, any instance of actual employment exceeding potential is reset to zero uneemployment, shown in table 12.2 as $- 0$. Second, in the discussion of characteristics of high employment or high disemployment sectors in the next section, pertinent references are made to new establishments and capital stock growth.

Table 12.2 summarizes the results of the estimation for the years 1966–9, and also shows the data for the α_j coefficient, the rate of growth of actual employment (REM), and the rate of change of the import-to-production ratio. The data certainly reflect the picture drawn earlier. On the one hand, there was increased import penetration, especially in the years 1966 and 1967 (with some reduction as liberalization reversed in 1968 and 1969), and on the other hand increased disemployment as a consequence. However, the sectoral effects on employment do vary considerably, and there are several cases of negative disemployment – set arbitrarily to zero.

Several attempts were made to find significant statistical correlation between the level or rate of import disemployment estimated in table 12.2 and the change in import penetration by sector. Recall that chapter 11, figures 11.1 and 11.2 showed only weakly that a negative relation exists between actual employment and import growth or change in import penetration. However, long time periods were used in the analysis of chapter 11, compared with the single-year data of this chapter. Thus the negative effect of imports upon employment is even more strongly confirmed by a multiple regression equation in which the two subperiods 1965–7 and 1968–70 are pooled:

$$CEMP = a_{ot}\, a_1(CQ + a_2CM + a_3CX)$$

where CEMP is the percentage change in employment for each sector, CQ is the percentage change in output for each sector, CM is the percentage change in imports for each sector, and CX is the percentage change in exports for each sector. The results are

$$CEMP = 8.181 + 0.472CO - 0.0147CM - 0.160CX$$
$$(-0.72) \quad (4.88) \quad (-1.23) \quad (-0.39)$$

$R^2 = 0.439 \qquad DW = 2.035$
$F = 8.86 \qquad N = 38$

Though it seems clear that employment growth is negatively affected by import penetration, the precise magnitude of the effect is difficult to measure. The estimate in table 12.2, unlike the above equation, explicitly assumes a one-to-one substitution between domestic output and imports. Estimates there suggest that gross disemployment due to imports can be of a considerable magnitude with sectoral rates (percentage of sectoral employment levels) reaching, by 1968 , levels of 5–7 percent in several sectors and over 10 percent in some. The absolute numbers involved, shown in table 12.3, are quite large. By 1966 already, as many as 50,000 jobs or 3.7 percent of employment may have been displaced by imports; by 1968 this may have reached nearly 96,000 or 6.9 percent. These are upper-range estimates: special sectoral situations of long-term decline such as coal and tobacco should probably be excluded from these estimates, lowering the rates to 6 percent in 1969. Further, the estimates may be too high because of greater capital-deepening policies after 1965. With a coefficient of α_j reduced to 0.26 (see earlier discussion), the estimates for total disemployment are reduced to about half that shown in table 12.3 or between 1.5 and 3.5 percent in the period 1966–9.

It should be reiterated that the values of gross import disemployment are estimates of a nonobservable phenomenon. The actual employment changes that occurred in reaction to import displacement, labor-saving capitalization, export growth, and domestic demand are shown in the last two rows of table 12.3. At the peak of unemployment in 1967, a cumulative total of 23,000 jobs had been lost in industry. If we take our range of estimates for gross import disemployment over the three years (43,500–95,700), it is clear that the positive effects of demand expansion (domestic and export) were of the order of 20,000–60,000 jobs. That is, over the period 1965–7, half to two thirds of the jobs displaced by new imports were replaced by demand expansion. As domestic demand growth was very weak in this period (table 12.1), export expansion clearly played a large role. In short, as seen in chapter 11, the critical factor behind employment expansion was not whether there was an increase in import penetration, but how much export expansion there was to offset this.

Table 12.3 Estimates of import disemployment: industry by sector (thousands)

Sector	1966	1967	1968
Coal[a]	5.1	9.5	9.6
Petroleum	0 (− 0.8)	0.7	0 (− 2.0)
Iron and steel	0 (− 0.3)	2.6	0.7
Nonferrous	0	0 (− 1.5)	1.0
Nonmetallic	1.3	3.1	4.6
Metal fabrication	11.7	20.0	19.3
Ships	1.2	0.8	0.4
Electrical products	4.0	4.3	5.3
Chemicals	0 (− 1.0)	0 (− 0.8)	0 (− 0.9)
Building materials	9.2	9.6	9.8
Wood	6.6	14.4	18.2
Paper	0 (− 1.8)	2.2	1.8
Textiles	1.7	5.9	11.0
Footwear	2.3	3.6	3.3
Rubber	0 (− 0.7)	0 (− 0.2)	0.2
Food	5.5	4.7	7.3
Tobacco[a]	2.3	3.3	3.2
Total industry	50.9	84.7	95.7
Total excluding coal and tobacco	43.5	71.9	82.9
Actual employment (1965 = 1,380)	1,372	1,357	1,369
Actual change in employment	− 8	− 15	+ 12
Cumulative change in employment − 1965 base	− 8	− 23	− 11

[a] Coal and tobacco show long-term trend declines of labor; estimates of unemployment are performed as follows: growth of potential employment is given by the rate of growth of final demand value as in table 12.2, less the trend decline of 7 and 8 percent respectively.

An Estimate of Gross Transitory Losses

As discussed at the beginning of this chapter, the negative effects of liberalization need to be carefully (hence inelegantly) described as consisting of the gross short-run displacement of domestic production for a given level of demand and the consequent disemployment of labor as well as capital. Here, the absolute level of disemployment estimated earlier is used to make an estimate of the gross, *ceteris paribus*, transitory loss attributable to import penetration. Note that this excludes the output loss resulting from any decline in aggregate demand occasioned by contraction-ary policies or exogenous factors.

Equations (12.4)–(12.7) summarize the procedure for estimating this loss. It is assumed that the average wage income reflects the marginal product of disemployed labor (equation 12.4) that the disemployment of other factors is proportional to labor, and that their marginal product is unchanged (equation 12.5). The calculations are done only for the socialized industrial sector, excluding a very small private industrial sector and the large nonindustrial sectors agriculture and forestry, services, and handicrafts. Of those excluded, only the private industrial sector and the handicrafts sector were potentially affected by import penetration; to-gether they account for a little over 250,000 employed, compared with nearly 1.4 million for the socialized industrial sector.

Inasmuch as the transitory loss measured here is defined as a very short-run phenomenon and excludes both the export gains and the resource-allocation benefits, it would make most sense to consider only one or at most two years. However, since the liberalization did not reach its fullest implementation until 1967 and since the estimates of disemploy-ment show higher rates for 1968 than for 1966 or 1967, the transitory loss has been calculated for these three years.

The procedure for each year's estimate is given below. We define $ELOSS_j$ as the value in dinars of output lost in sector j due to labor disemployment caused by imports, W_j as the average labor income in dinars in sector j, $KLOSS_j$ as the value of output lost due to under-utilization of nonlabor factors in sector j, $RESHR_j$ as the relative share of nonlabor to labor factors in the distribution of value added for sector j, $TLOSS_j$ as the total loss of output attributable to import displacement in sector j, and $AGLOSS_j$ as the aggregate transitory loss of output in socialized industrial sectors of the economy. Then

$$ELOSS_j = IDE_j \times W_j \qquad (12.4)$$
$$KLOSS_j = ELOSS \times RESHR_j \qquad (12.5)$$
$$TLOSS_j = ELOSS_j + KLOSS_j \qquad (12.6)$$

$$AGLOSS_j = \sum_{j=1}^{17} TLOSS \qquad (12.7)$$

In addition to the obvious general qualifications of such an estimate arising from the assumption made, there are some qualifications peculiar to Yugoslavia. The trend of raising the personal income share of revenues after 1965, thereby perhaps raising "wages" beyond their marginal prod-uct, may make the value of ELOSS too high relative to that of KLOSS. Even without this effect, we cannot be certain how close observed labor income (wages) is to labor's marginal product, given the unique workers' management system. There is a considerable, but not universal, consensus that labor income includes some profits, and that workers maximizing profits per laborer will "hire on" a suboptimal number of colleagues, keeping the average and marginal product of labor higher than in a competitive solution. This also suggests an overestimate of the ELOSS component. However, the data on actual shares of labor in value added do not support these implied biases, as it is quite low, at around 50–60 percent.

With all these qualifications in mind, we consider the face-value implications of such an estimate of transitory losses, summarized in table 12.4. Note that the values of employment loss used for the sectoral estimations are based on the upper-range estimates of employment loss shown in table 12.3. The upward bias possible in this will be considered later.

Table 12.4 gives the value, in millions of dinars, of output losses associated with disemployment of labor caused by import penetration. The largest losses occurred in the sectors with highest disemployment – metal products (which includes engineering goods), building materials, coal, wood, and food, and textiles for the year 1968. These were not the sectors in which import penetration increased most; their large role in the overall

Table 12.4 Upper-range estimate of gross transitory employment loss by sector, 1966–1968 (million dinars)

Sector	1966	1967	1968
Coal	40.8	82.0	94.9
Petroleum	0	10.4	0
Iron and steel	0	26.2	7.9
Nonferrous	0	0	11.6
Nonmetallic	9.9	25.1	40.8
Metal products	99.4	185.0	196.2
Ships	13.2	10.1	5.5
Electrical products	32.5	39.0	56.0
Chemicals	0	0	0
Building materials	64.1	80.9	93.1
Wood	41.5	97.5	143.9
Paper	0	19.5	18.1
Textiles	12.0	42.6	86.6
Footwear	16.7	29.0	28.9
Rubber	0	0	2.0
Food	44.5	42.5	69.5
Tobacco	16.1	25.9	28.1
Total industry	390.7	715.7	888.1
Total excluding coal and tobacco	333.8	607.8	760.1

Source: Wages, Federal Institute of Statistics, *Statistical Yearbook of Yugoslavia*, 1970, p. 265

loss is due to their large workforce. This is especially true for metal products, textiles, and food processing. There was much greater import penetration in the other sectors.

The importance of the metal products sector is also evident in table 12.5, which shows the total transitory loss including the under-use of other factors beside labor. Textile sector losses loom less large and those of tobacco loom larger than in the measure of labor losses alone. This is because the relative share of labor is quite high in textiles (0.56) and very low (suspiciously so!) in tobacco (0.20). Indeed, any of the variations between the relative importance of a sector in table 12.4 and table 12.5 come from the difference in the labor share of value added.

Table 12.5 Estimate of total gross transitory loss by sector (million dinars)

Sector	1966[a]		1967[a]		1968[a]	
Coal	76.7	(9.2)	154.2	(11.1)	178.4	(9.2)
Petroleum	0	(0)	52.0	(3.7)	0	(0)
Iron and steel	0	(0)	57.1	(4.1)	17.2	(0.9)
Nonferrous	0	(0)	0	(0)	27.8	(1.4)
Nonmetallic	18.6	(2.2)	47.2	(3.4)	76.7	(4.0)
Metal products	194.8	(23.5)	362.6	(26.0)	420.7	(21.8)
Ships	24.0	(2.9)	18.4	(1.3)	10.0	(0.5)
Electrical products	67.6	(8.2)	84.1	(5.8)	116.5	(6.0)
Chemicals	0	(0)	0	(0)	0	(0)
Building material	139.0	(16.8)	175.6	(12.6)	202.0	(10.4)
Wood	73.9	(8.9)	173.6	(12.5)	256.1	(13.2)
Paper	0	(0)	42.9	(3.1)	39.8	(2.1)
Textiles	24.5	(3.0)	86.9	(6.2)	176.7	(9.1)
Footwear	34.1	(4.1)	59.2	(4.2)	118.2	(6.1)
Rubber	0	(0)	0	(0)	4.6	(2.4)
Food	98.8	(11.9)	93.7	(6.7)	154.3	(8.0)
Tobacco	77.3	(9.3)	124.8	(8.9)	134.9	(7.0)
Total industry	829.3	100.0	1,393.5	100.0	1,933.9	100.0
Total excluding coal and tobacco	675.3		1,114.5		1,620.6	
As percentage of GDP industry	2.7		4.5		5.9	
(Excluding coal and tobacco)	(2.2)		(3.6)		(5.0)	
As percentage of GDP total	0.8		1.4		1.8	

[a] The numbers in parentheses give the loss as a percentage of the total industrial loss.
Source: Wages, Federal Institute of Statistics, Statistical Yearbook of Yugoslavia, 1970, p. 265

Overall, the transitory loss estimated ranges from 2.7 to 5.9 percent of value added in industry, or from 0.8 to 1.8 percent of value added in the whole economy. While these are not high figures, they are by no means negligible, especially the values for 1967 and 1968. Indeed, if we consider the industrial sector as the major arena of political economy reactions to liberalization, the losses there are not paltry.

However, recall that this is an upper-range estimate of such losses. First, four sectors account for about a third of this value, in which there may be substantial overestimation: coal, tobacco, wood, and building materials. As discussed in the first section, all of these have suffered from secular decline in employment unrelated to liberalization. Table 8.3 shows that import penetration actually fell in one of these (coal) and was quite low in the others.

A second reason for overestimation concerns the assumption that the decline in capacity utilization of nonlabor factors is proportional to labor disemployment. Table 7.3 shows data that suggest otherwise: in 1966 capacity utilization did not decline and in fact increased slightly; it declined only in 1967. This is much less of a downturn than is observed for labor in the liberalization period.

Furthermore, as has already been noted, the estimate of gross import-disemployment losses used the 1960–4 trend for labor-saving effects, whereas 1965–70 was a period of sharp increase in capital deepening and hence even greater labor saving. Use of the actual 1965–70 ratio of employment to output growth (α_j in equations 12.1 and 12.2) gives a lower-range estimate of employment loss, about half as high in aggregate. Thus, such losses might be only 1.5–3 percent of industry GDP, or 0.4–0.8 percent of total GDP.

Nevertheless, disemployment of labor arising from import penetration must have amounted to at least 1 percent and perhaps as much as 3 percent of employment, and the value of production lost to import displacement must have been at least 1–3 percent of value added by the industrial sector. It is useful to contrast this with the commonly known static estimates of the gains from free trade, which are of the order of 0.5–1 percent. Add to this the absolute numbers of disemployed (50,000–95,000, table 12.3) and it becomes clear that the size of the gross negative effect of import penetration was not negligible. Even if it was "relatively" small in the aggregate economy including nonindustrial sectors and even if the net observed effect on employment was much smaller after macro growth effects are added, it was certainly large enough to matter and to worry about. The lesson is simple: whatever the eventual net effects on welfare and employment may be, the transitory short-run negative impacts are not so small that they can be disregarded, especially if slow growth of the economy as a whole happens to coincide with liberalization.

13

Summary and Conclusions

In this chapter we summarize the findings reported in chapters 4–12 on the effects of liberalization and the policy reactions, and then draw some conclusions on the reasons for the eventual failure of the experiment. In the next chapter we will focus on more explicit lessons for the timing and sequencing of liberalization, which may be relevant to other developing countries as well as Yugoslavia.

Effects of Liberalization

The Economic Costs of Liberalization

Even though the 1965 liberalization was never fully implemented before measures were taken to reverse it, some of the likely output and employment costs nevertheless became apparent. Perhaps a first conclusion should be that precise measurement of the disemployment effects of liberalization is very difficult, because many other phenomena (policy and nonpolicy) also affect employment. Nevertheless, after accounting for other phenomena it seems clear that import-related disemployment in industry was at least 1.5–3 percent of employment levels. As the effects in agriculture were probably the opposite, given that liberalization had corrected earlier anti-agricultural biases, and since the nontradeable sector would have been far less affected, this magnitude amounts to well below 1 percent of total employment. However, it was not unimportant because, of course, the political economy spotlight was trained on the industrial sector, as is the case in most developing countries. Other possible costs do not appear to have been important. Income distribution measures show conflicting evidence – some widening and some narrowing, but neither being substantial (chapter 9). Government revenues were little affected by tariff reductions (chapter 11).

The Benefits of Liberalization

Benefits of liberalization were even more difficult to isolate and measure, for, while costs make themselves felt immediately, benefits take longer to surface. There seem to be three benefits: improved export performance as liberalization reduces anti-export bias, better output performance as liberalization removes sectoral distortions and permits more efficient resource allocation among sectors, and finally efficiency improvements at the sector and firm level as liberalization removes the disincentives of government support.

Though liberalization was far too quickly reversed to have had much effect, there is some evidence for each of these developments. Exports initially reacted very strongly in 1965–6, but this must have been due to devaluation since little trade liberalization took place before 1966–7. However, sectoral evidence (chapter 11) shows that at least some previously disfavored sectors improved their export performance considerably over the period 1965–70. Improvements in technical efficiency were also more apparent in sectors which the 1965 liberalization favored. It must be emphasized that the evidence is fragmentary and not very strong statistically. Given the lack of time for these positive effects to develop, this is not surprising.

Increased Openness of the Economy Financed by Debt

One effect that is clear concerns the degree of openness of the economy, as measured by the ratio of trade to domestic output. Both the import-to-GDP and export-to-GDP ratios went up considerably from less than 20 percent before 1965 to 24–5 percent for imports and 20–2 percent for exports in the early 1970s. After the mid-1970s they both declined with exports falling below 20 percent, as before 1965, but imports remaining higher.

The conclusion is that liberalization did succeed at least partially in making the Yugoslav economy more open – a good thing, at first sight, for more openness means more external competition, closer alignment of domestic prices, greater penetration of world technology, and so on. However, while this may be true in most cases, it cannot be claimed with conviction in the case of Yugoslavia, for against the improvement in the import-to-GDP ratio must be set one crucial deterioration: the increase in the export-to-GDP ratio was not sustained and fell sharply after 1974, and hence the gap between the import-to-output and the export-to-output ratios widened (figure 13.1). That is, the increased import-to-GDP ratio was purchased mostly at the cost of increased indebtedness and was not paid for by increased export orientation. It was not that a current account

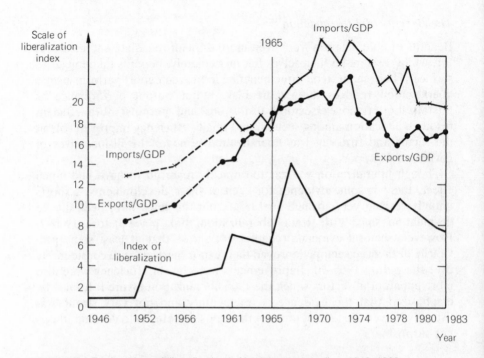

Figure 13.1 Trade ratio and liberalization in Yugoslav trade policy, 1946–1980

Sources: Dubey, 1975; World Bank, 1983; OECD, *Economic Surveys, Yugoslavia*, 1986–7

deficit *per se* was a bad thing, for a healthy developing economy will almost always be characterized by a deficit, reflecting its attractiveness for external capital. It was rather the fact of a widening deficit in the face of a declining export-to-GDP ratio, attributable to underlying sectoral distortions, that was a sign of economic ill health. Thus the higher trade ratios cannot be considered manifestations of beneficial integration with the world economy – a good thing – but rather a growing "import substitution dependence"[1] – a bad thing.

Figure 13.2 depicts this tendency and shows the way in which the goals of output and employment growth continued to be achieved at the cost of growing inflation and widening external deficits. Indeed, the achievement of the goals was increasingly less successful, as the Yugoslav economy, which in 1960–4 seemed tall and lean, became increasingly stunted and stout on a diet of high inflation and foreign debt.

---

[1] The word "dependence" is used here with the modifying phrase "import substitution" to emphasize that the dependence is not caused by external factors but is entirely attributable to internal policies of import substitution.

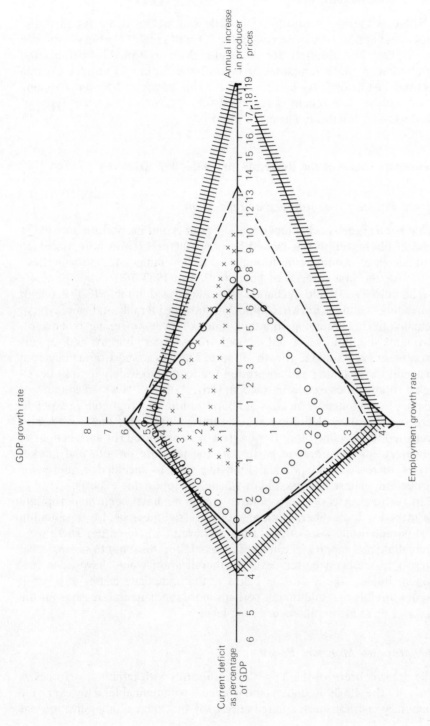

Figure 13.2 Yugoslavia 1960–1982: growing fat and slow on a diet of debt and inflation

Sources: Dubey, 1975; Federal Institute of Statistics, *Statistical Yearbook of Yugoslavia*, various issues

There is therefore unfortunately little satisfaction to be found in the superficial appearance of success in the form of greater openness achieved by the 1965 liberalization, for the eventual reversal of this liberalization resulted in a more fundamental failure: the failure to correct existing sectoral distortions. As a consequence, the Yugoslav economy became more and not less reliant on external sources, both for certain types of products and for the financing of imports.

Immediate Cause of the Reversal: the 1965–1967 Recession

Macro Policies: Inappropriate or Inadequate

It has been argued in chapter 10 that the poor economic performance at the time of liberalization was caused by other factors. It was also concluded that the poor economic performance was the immediate and superficial cause for the first reversal of liberalization in 1967–70.

The macro story told in chapter 10 (summarized in table 13.1) is one of worsening economic growth (output slowed considerably and employment actually fell), continuing inflation, and an ever-worsening balance-of-payments situation, which led the authorities to curb imports and support exports, or cut economic growth, or both. The classic short-term policies of expenditure switching and absorption reduction (so widely used in developing countries, especially in the debt (crises) of the 1980s) ran counter, of course, to the longer-term aims of liberalization. The first policy (expenditure switching) by definition meant reduced liberality; the second indirectly led to the same result, for as growth was reduced (by such actions as monetary restrictiveness in particular) the pressure on jobs and market shares increased and political lobbying for aid included requests for protection against imports and/or financial support for exports.

In restrospect two macro policies appear to have been inappropriate partners for trade liberalization: monetary tightness, and a devaluation that paradoxically was both too early and eventually too little. These were immediate and superficial causes of reversal, but this is not to say that, had these policies been better devised, liberalization would have been sustained. Indeed, the discussion below of the immediate causes of reversal argues forcibly that additional, perhaps more fundamental, reasons for the reversal exist at the microeconomic level.

Inappropriate Monetary Policy

The great concern of the Yugoslav authorities with inflationary forces as early as the 1960s is understandable and commendable. However, the monetary restrictiveness applied during the first stage of liberalization was

Table 13.1 Summary of Yugoslav liberalization, 1965–74

Characteristic	
Broad nature	Reduce QRs, reduce tariffs, export subsidies
Size/duration	Intent of large reductions, over period of 5–10 years
Stages and targets	First stage to 1967 tariffs and export subsidies; second stage 1967–? reduce QRs
Economic circumstances before	
Balance of payments – continuing deficits	Yes, worsening
Prices of major exports	Stable
Rate of inflation	Increasing in 1963–4, but below 10%
Rate of growth	Very high, 6%–7%
Almost closed economy	Yes
Shocks	No
Agricultural output	Good but fluctuating; 1965–6 poor harvest
Political circumstances	
Strong stable government	Yes
Ideological shift	Yes, tendency to liberalize and decentralize
Public perception and debate	Considerable
Administering arm of government	Ministry of Foreign Trade and Central Bank
International influence	Some IMF credits, OECD pressures
Accompanying policies	
Exchange rate	Sharp devaluation 1965; no change in nominal ratio until 1971
Export promotion	Sharp cut in export subsidies, retention quotas remained; subsidies reintroduced gradually after 1967
Monetary policy	Very tight in 1965–7, volatile thereafter
Fiscal policy	None other than some financing of investment; budgets very decentralized and essentially balanced
Capital movement	Considerable growth of debt; private investment allowed on limited basis
Implementation	
Stages departures	Reversal in 1967–70; attempt to restart in 1971, reversed again in 1974
Economic performance	
Employment	Sharp reversal of employment growth; declined 1965–7
Inflation	Sharp up over 10% (20% CPI) until 1967, cut back but restarts
Growth	Reduced in 1965–7, up again briefly 1968–9, then slows
Imports and exports	Import ratio rises from below 20% to about 25%; export ratio from 16–17% to 20–22%
	Exports in 1965 outpace imports, but then always slowed
Wages (personal income)	Substantial increase in real wages 1965–70; slowed later but continues high
Capital-to-labor ratios	Substantial increase in capital intensity

unfortunate and probably excessive in view of the fact that the underlying inflation rates were at most somewhat over 10 percent – not a cause for undue concern. (The actual measured rates in 1965–6 were higher – as high as 30 percent for the CPI – but these were transitory effects of two one-time "shocks:" the 1965 devaluation, and increases in certain controlled prices.) Certainly the restrictiveness was unfortunate in the light of the sharp contraction it occasioned in the economy at the very time liberalization was introduced.

The recession created a very poor environment for achieving the aims of trade liberalization in two respects. On a purely technical economic plane, the sectoral adjustments needed to effect a reallocation of resources were, of course, far more difficult than they might have been with continued high growth. On the political economy side the coincidence of this major policy step in trade liberalization with deterioration in the economy led to a perception that liberalization was at fault and therefore had to be reversed.

Exchange Rate Policy

The large devaluation of mid-1965 was initially a good move as it boosted exports and cut imports enough to provide an external surplus. However, given the importance government attached to inflation it may have been poorly sequenced, as it preceded liberalization of imports. The one-time price shock it caused contributed to observed inflation and the policy reaction just mentioned. The price reduction of import liberalization could have offset this, but it came too late. Had the devaluation been more gradual, or even delayed to coincide with import liberalization, the inflationary pressures perceived by the authorities as calling for monetary restrictiveness would have been much reduced. Certainly, however, the subsequent exchange rate policy also prejudiced liberalization. The 1965 devaluation was quickly eroded by inflation and, with no changes in the nominal rate for five years, the real exchange rate appreciated considerably. Had this been avoided or at least adjusted somewhat, the trade balance would not have deteriorated as much as it did, and there would have been less need for "temporary" restrictions for balance-of-payments reasons.

Underlying Causes of the Failure

Inasmuch as the reversal of liberalization was not sudden or complete, it is fair to say that in the period 1965–74 Yugoslavia was much more liberal than before or after. Thus the long-run "failure" of liberalization was due both to extraneous forces and to failure to attain a degree of liberality adequate to ensure a positive impact. Thus it is rather difficult to distinguish between factors that led directly to reversal measures and factors that prevented the liberalization from making a strong positive contribution to the economy. The list of underlying causes discussed below has some of both elements.

Continued Distortions and Interventionism

The fundamental aim of liberalization is not to lower the barriers to importing *per se*, but rather to allow exposure to world markets to correct internal price distortions and thus lead to an efficient comparative-advantage resource allocation.

The opening-up in Yugoslavia was both too short and retained too many distortions (especially after the reversal) to achieve these. The basic manifestation of continued distortions was the measure of EERs which, despite some lack of data, clearly showed that, while 1965–7 saw distortion considerably reduced, the situation was soon back to what it had been before 1965. However, this may even underestimate the degree of distortion, because the 1970s saw an increase in *ad hoc* administrative interventionism.

It is because distortions continued to exist that the gap opened up between import and export ratios even though both were increasing (see figure 13.1). The gradual return to an import substitution regime based on differential tariffs, import restrictions, foreign exchange allocations, and so on actually encouraged the inefficient allocation of resources to heavy industries and capital-intensive sectors. The interventionist environment with industries pressing for government aid resulted in further inefficiencies associated with noncompetitive and/or rent-seeking situations. Thus domestic industry became less and not more able to compete in world markets, while the renewed disincentive to raw materials industries increased the economy's import dependence.

Excessive and Inappropriate Export Supports

Export performance lagged because the renewed distortions of the 1970s favored domestic production, more often than not in areas of comparative disadvantage. At the same time exports were enjoying strong support in the form of direct and indirect subsidies, export credits, and high foreign exchange retention quotas for exporters. Plainly, these supports were misguided and exports became artificially competitive. What was misguided was the belief that these supports were temporary and would soon assist the industries in question (shipbuilding, machinery, large electrical goods, and other capital goods) to become competitive. There is little reason to suppose that exporters are any less prone to being spoiled by government largesse than are other producers.

However, it was not only that such supports followed a questionable "infant exporters" policy; they were further misguided in respect of the decidedly capital-intensive bias of the industries chosen for support. On the whole they were much the same industries that had received the greatest protection, and much the same ones as had been put in place in the early periods of centrally guided industrialization. In a word, they were the same ones that were at the heart of the so-called structural problem which the 1965 liberalization was supposed to have ameliorated or rationalized.

The failure of this export promotion policy was manifested by the sharp decline of the export-to-GDP ratio from 1974. Indeed, while the import-to-GDP ratio never fell back to pre-1965 levels despite the reversal of liberalization, by the late 1970s the export-to-GDP ratio was as low as it had been in 1962–4 – about 17 percent.

Factor Mobility not Improved

Theoretically, workers' management may have an inherent tendency to reduced labor mobility, though this is arguable. Earlier chapters have given reasons to believe that it is not as inhibiting as the theoretical literature concludes. Data on geographic mobility and turnover indicate considerable movement. Further, the theoretical view that workers will not move because their "share" of the capital is not transferable makes little sense when put against the fact that in the new enterprise they join – presumably a stronger one – they automatically obtain a share – presumably a greater one – without having invested anything. It might equally be said that, as long as expansion is occurring, the workers' management system has greater incentives than capitalism for labor mobility.

Be that as it may, it is indisputable that nothing was done to enhance or facilitate mobility of labor. Compensation mechanisms, retraining activities, and transfer subsidies were all conspicuous by their absence in the 1965 reforms, despite the explicit recognition of the need for resource reallocation and closures of some enterprises. The climate for long-distance inter-regional mobility was also made worse by the more explicit fractionalism and nationalism of the period. As ethnic differences had always played some role in reducing inter-republic migration, the public nature of the regional–national discussions, especially from 1967 to about 1971, no doubt enhanced this. This was not of course a policy error, but rather an unfortunate consequence of decentralization tendencies.

Capital mobility was not helped by the nature of the policies followed. Real rates of interest for investment borrowing were generally negative. Perhaps equally important, there was no adequate financial system for allocating funds, for which there was an excess demand. The 1965 reforms set up a banking system which would do this, but it failed for three reasons.

First, the banks had no incentive to confine lending to the best projects because their performance was based on throughput of activity. They saw themselves as merely passing on a pool of funds that could be expanded by the Central Bank when needed. Second, local banks in the new system were legal entities of which local governments and local enterprises were founder members, so that, in effect, lenders and borrowers were the same people. The third reason lay in the eventual demonstration by the Central Bank (and central government) authorities that in case of difficulty they would indeed step in with "reorganizational support" in the form of new credits.

One last element played a role in limiting factor mobility: the retardation of growth. As many of the world economies have learned in the recent past, adjustment is far more difficult when macroexpansion is slow. Factors of production are loath to move and are most likely to express their resistance politically when the general economic climate is poor, for the obvious reason that it is much harder to find somewhere to move to. Such was the situation in Yugoslavia after 1965.

Enhancement of Decentralized Lobby Powers

Happily for the vested interests that resisted moving as adjustment would require – be it physically or in the sense of rationalizing production in existing locations – the 1965 reforms contained a decentralizing tendency as one important element. The prior period of centrally guided industrialization had established many inefficient industries and, while controlling them, of course sustained them. These same authorities in 1965 now seemed to say: "you are free to make your own decisions." Thus, thrown out of the nest – but with a parting gift in the form of greater freedom to allocate revenues between incomes and reinvestments – these fledglings first gobbled up large chunks of the gift, and then, as they began to realize that freedom to decide meant obligation to survive on your own, quickly turned to their habitual source of succor.

The constitutional changes accorded greater power to enterprises. The political climate encouraged this, and many specific mechanisms (such as the introduction of bottom-up indicative planning, the encouragement of integration, and the formalization by 1974 of obligatory membership in associations) enhanced the power of vested economic interests.

Creation of a Soft-budget Environment

The first reaction by vested interests to problems is almost always to ask for government support or protection. This was the path observed in Yugoslavia. Eventual success or failure of liberalization depended on the will of the authorities to see things through – on their ability to resist the temptation of swooping down from the nest to bring back one or more of the fledglings "temporarily." In actual fact the authorities did not resist, but instead backtracked on the liberalization.

Two motivations can be observed. First, the authorities were not a monolith and the end of the long and heated debate between the "liberalizers" and "centralizers" did not cause the latter to disappear or change their views after 1965. Further, the operating bureaucracy which had held the central-planning powers of implementation continued to have a vested interest in the retention rather than the dispersal of these powers that some interests pressed for positive responses to the cries of distress of weak industries. A second motive was no doubt a sincere belief that such rescue actions were indeed temporary and limited, and were needed economically and politically to achieve liberalization, in the long run.

In any event, the reactions of authorities were clearly to step in again, to reverse some of the liberalization measures, and in general to renew the support for various sectors of the economy. Such a quick positive reaction by the government could only have taught the decentralized units one lesson: "it pays to make an effort at lobbying; the rules of the game are slightly changed and we have to be more explicit and more vocal about our problems and needs and we get, as before, help when we need it."

Thus was born the post-1965 version of what Yugoslav writers have called the "monopoly of the backward," what the trade-development literature calls "rent-seeking activities," and a form of what the public finance literature calls the "moral hazard." Weaker industries are supported because they, unlike stronger ones, need it; the reward structure takes on the perverse form of giving the greatest rewards to those who are least efficient.[2]

The measures taken by the government went far beyond help to industry by means of renewed protection against imports and support for exports. There was also widespread unwillingness to permit bankruptcy, and an

---

[2] Non-Yugoslav examples abound; the current case of Israel (spring 1986) will serve well, as it happens to have presented itself to the author at the time of writing this chapter. Suffice it to quote from an article in *The Wall Street Journal*, April 9, 1986, by an Israeli financial reporter, Pinhas Landau: "Yesterday's failures are being bailed out, and lame ducks of every breed and flavor are receiving aid because their party affiliations, geographic location or plain size make it politically unacceptable to allow them to go under. To nobody's surprise, a growing band of less-well placed but equally bankrupt entities are now clamoring for a piece of the action in the aid program. The logic of the 'me-too' brigade is unimpeachable: 'Why be a sucker, if you can get succor?' . . . Now it appears the best business strategy is to get into as much debt as possible and threaten to dismiss as many workers as possible. If you reach that happy state, ministers of every party will line up for the right to use taxpayer's money to keep you artificially alive." Translate into Serbo-Croat and think of Yugoslavia in 1970–5 (and later), and the statements apply equally well. This criticism of Israel refers to its spring 1986 growth policy budget, which is said by Landau to be a "gimmicky growth." The return to growth stimulation in Yugoslavia in the 1970s was unfortunately equally "gimmicky."

accommodating attitude toward continual financial support from banks for loss-making enterprises. "Restructuring" was the answer, not liquidation. As restructuring had few teeth in most instances, what it all came down to was a "soft-budget" situation. Though the government rarely provided direct financial transfers to cover losses, as in the case of public enterprises, it did resort to other devices. Thus it came to be generally understood that there was no bottom line, that the budget was soft, and that when revenues continued to exceed expenditures, the government authorities could be counted upon to step in.

Growing Lack of Credibility

Some analysts (Sirc, 1979) have suggested that the 1965 reforms had little credibility in Yugoslavia because there had been so many earlier changes. Certainly there was a penchant for experimentation and, starting with the introduction of workers' management in the early 1950s, the rules were frequently changed. The open way in which the 1965 reforms were debated was, however, a new and surprising departure which created some degree of credibility.

However, this was quickly eroded as the various reversal measures revealed the willingness of government to compromise, and by 1971, when it wished to reintroduce liberalization, there could have been little reason to believe that its determination to implement would be any greater than in the preceding five years. Repeated statements in the 1970s about the need to enforce bankruptcies sounded particularly hollow in the light of what had happened after 1965. Lack of credibility certainly played a role in the subsequent failure to renew liberalization.

The Importance of Jobs

The extent of disemployment directly created in the short run by increases in imports is difficult to measure, but it must have been at least 1–2 percent of the industrial labor force. Whether this was large enough to trigger reversal is not clear, but there was an important sense in which disemployment did matter a great deal. Jobs were at the heart of the matter when lobbying by enterprises and local governments began, and it was the critical importance of saving jobs that helped swing the balance in favor of government help for industries in difficulty. While liberalized imports were sometimes considered to be the cause of the problem, and while restrictions on imports were sometimes the solution taken, the two were not automatically coincident. The line connecting import liberalization via job losses to import restrictions was not clear or direct, but the critical political value of jobs was.

In Brief

Broadly speaking, the 1965 measures of decentralization and liberalization were generally sensible, except for the excessive monetary restraint which led to recession. The liberalization experiment failed because the necessary adjustments were never allowed to work themselves out. Instead, measures were taken to ease the shocks, not by compensating the losers or by facilitating their movement from one area of activity to another, but by reversing the liberalization and reducing the pressure to adjust. At this stage, the newly powerful decentralized economic entities (enterprises and local governments) quickly became aware of the "new game:" they were free to make economic decisions, but were not going to be faced by the obligation to live or die by the consequences of those decisions.

Was the liberalization's failure attributable then to the macro error which created a recession or to the micro error of soft-budget indiscipline? While both, as well as other factors, played a role, hindsight suggests that the latter may have been more important. Had macro policy been different and the recession less pronounced, it still would have been necessary to apply micro level discipline to achieve the successful readjustments which were the fundamental aim of liberalization. As it was, a stronger will to enforce the micro level discipline might have been sufficient to ensure a successful continuance of liberalization.

This does not mean that macro policy was unimportant, for there is little doubt that the macroenvironment greatly influenced the general need and will to impose micro discipline. Micro discipline nevertheless remains specially important. Such discipline is always necessary regardless of how favorable other policies or circumstances may be. Such discipline may even be sufficient when other policies are misguided. The "necessary" or "sufficient" syllogism is no great surprise in the context of trade theory. Liberalization *is* a micro policy. Whatever macro policies may do to the position of the production possibility frontier or the unemployment distance from it, if price distortions are corrected and sustained, welfare gains will be achieved. Also, if price correlations are not implemented, macro efforts that push the economy outward will achieve illusory or at best temporary gains in welfare.

14

Some Implications for Liberalization

From the conclusions summarized in the preceding chapter, some inferences can be drawn about policies appropriate for timing and sequencing liberalization, as well as the coordination with accompanying policies. The basis for such inferences naturally makes them most applicable to Yugoslavia; many may, however, be applicable to other developing countries as well. It is left to the reader, and to the comparative analysis which draws on all the different country studies in this project, to assess which of the inferences have general application and to what degree.

Liberalization in One Stage or Multiple Stages

Liberalization in Yugoslavia was originally planned in the early 1960s as a gradual process of at least three stages. The preparatory stage, starting in 1961, was to begin the change from a QR regime with multiple exchange rates to a tariff system with a uniform exchange rate and to introduce some reduction in protection. Later stages were to reduce protection substantially. The period 1961–4 did see some changes, but QRs were by no means completely removed, and while officially a uniform exchange rate was in force, various indirect interventions, such as administered prices and differential export subsidies, effectively brought back multiple exchange rates.

Thus the next and most important stage of liberalization (1965–7) not only included the original objectives of gradually reducing protection but also had to readdress the objectives of reducing QRs and eliminating the unofficial sectoral differences in EERs. The plan was for two stages, and possibly more later. From 1965 to 1967 tariffs were reduced, some reduction of QRs was implemented, and export subsidies were cut. The next step was undefined except as a general intention to reduce protection. A third unplanned stage of liberalization in 1971–4 was merely an attempt to restart the faltering process.

Might a one-stage process have succeeded where the more gradual approach failed? In favor of that proposition is the simple fact that the liberalization did not succeed. The argument is of course not entirely persuasive, for the gradual process might have succeeded had there been no backtracking early on (by 1967–8) and had there been better accompanying policies, such as continued devaluation to stimulate exports beyond 1967, macro policies to encourage growth, and firmer microdiscipline for reallocation of resources.

A more persuasive argument for a one-stage process is founded on a key element in the failure of liberalization: the readiness of the administration(s) (both federal and local) to yield under pressure and permit *ad hoc* particular modifications. The arbitrary exercise of administrative powers was no new phenomenon; indeed these powers were probably stronger before 1961. However, rather than being eliminated as intended, they were simply converted into something that may have been more damaging economically than in the centralist period. Before the liberalization, central power was ubiquitous and its purposes were largely self-generated (that is, not reactions to decentralized pressures), and all economic agents recognized this. Liberalization brought with it a partial decentralization which on the one hand permitted economic agents to influence the purposes and direction of administrative power, and on the other retained enough administrative power at the center (or centers if we include local governments) to make the game of lobbying worthwhile.

Neither the bureaucracy nor the political power centers were willing to give up enough of their powers at the outset to achieve an effective decentralization. The economic disruptiveness of partial liberalization created problems to which these two groups reacted at the urging of affected institutions, and thereby reestablished their power but not their initiative in policy direction. Thus it is argued that the multistage process was worse because it created a breeding ground for a new form of administrative interventionism: a less powerful but also less purposeful (not to say rudderless) administration, reacting more pliantly to the pressures of formerly powerless economic vested interests.

Counterposed to this position is the argument that the problem was not whether liberalization came in one swift move or several gradual stages; the problem was lack of will to persevere in the face of centripetal pressures. However, this lack of will merely reflected the relative importance of trade liberalization in the political power game of the period. Decentralization and other domestic reforms were far more important to most actors in these scenes. Given this, and accepting as immutable the unwillingness of the administration to give up fully its powers, perhaps liberalization could have best succeeded if it had been done in a wide-sweeping single-stage action (which does not mean overnight) from which it would have been more difficult to make gradual retreats and in which it would have been too costly to yield to individual rent-seeking pressures. A fuller trade liberalization could have been imposed by an administration intent on continuing to exercise some power; decentralization of that power in other economic and social spheres could then follow later.

The Length of the Liberalization Process

If there had been a will to persevere with liberalization despite individual lobby pressures – or if there had been compensation mechanisms found to mollify these pressures without reversing liberalization actions – a long period of implementation would not have been a problem. However, with this will apparently lacking, there is reason to argue in favor of a speedier and shorter implementation period. This might have avoided the gradual build-up of precedents demonstrating that the government would respond to special cases and maintained greater credibility for the process. That is not to say that liberalization should have been immediate, but rather that it should have been planned for and implemented fully in a relatively short period of time (two to three years).

Desirability of a Separate Stage for Quantitative Restriction–Tariff Changeover

Yugoslav liberalization did indeed have such a stage, and on the whole it was reasonably smooth and achieved something very useful. While it has been argued in the first section that the gradual staging was not a good idea, especially for the post-1965 episode, there is a case to be made for a prior stage which attempts to transform the basic nature of the trade regime from QRs to tariffs without reducing protection. Problems arose much more in the protection–reduction episode of 1965 and after. Indeed, the apparent success of the preparatory stage in 1961–4 certainly made the concept of liberalization more acceptable. However, it was successful only in the sense that it did not cause much disruption in the economy. This was, of course, because the tariff schedule did not in fact replace the QRs, as both were in force contemporaneously, with the latter generally being binding. Thus the previous protection levels and the distortions were essentially unchanged and were only mirrored in a new formally more open set of institutions.

The resource allocation inefficiencies were not reduced in this stage,[1] nor was the overall level of protection cut. Politically, this was helpful, as it

---

[1] As Pertot (1984) demonstrates, noting that the relative positions of EERs and their range were little changed over the period 1960–4.

gave the impression that liberalization was not harmful and set the institutional stage with a new set of procedures, within which true liberalization could be implemented as of 1965. Note, however, that one paradox existed already: to replace a multiple exchange rate by a uniform one without affecting the absolute or relative level of protection required reintroduction of informal supports (especially export subsidies). Theoretically, this seems like an economically neutral action; in fact, it was the first lesson to economic agents that opportunities were opening up for rewarding rent-seeking lobby activities.

Desirability of a Separate Export Promotion Stage

The experience of Yugoslavia provides some fairly clear lessons about the relationship between export promotion policies and liberalization. The inability of exports to sustain growth close to that of imports had a critical and damaging effect. Insufficient export expansion beyond 1966 exacerbated the disemployment effect of import penetration, and contributed to the demands for special treatment such as increased tariffs or restrictions, as well as export subsidies. The effect on the trade deficit of slow export growth in the face of the rapid import growth allowed by liberalization led to "temporary" reversals which eventually undermined liberalization. Had there been better export performance and less deficit pressure, the need for reversals would have been far less.

Of course, better export performance could have been achieved by applying a realistic real exchange rate policy after 1965. (This point and the nature of export promotion policies are addressed below; here we are considering simply the need for and timing of export promotion measures.) With hindsight we must conclude that to remove export subsidies (even "bad" ones) fully and immediately in 1965, while reducing import restrictions only gradually and partially, was bad timing. The negative effect on exports[2] was immediate, while the positive effects of liberalization (resource allocation and so on), which in any event takes time to surface, were delayed even further. If import liberalization was gradual, export subsidy removal should also have been gradual, if not actually postponed. Even if the kinds of export support provided had been misguided in terms of long-run welfare – and they were – it would still have been preferable politically in terms of public acceptance had export supports been retained in 1965–7 and allowed stronger export performance and less of a deficit. As

---

[2] This was of course a *ceteris paribus* effect given the accompanying devaluation.

it was they were quickly reintroduced, without much deliberation as to their suitability, to help the trade deficit in the years 1968–70.

The Nature of Export Promotion Measures

The obvious conclusion is that much more attention should have been paid to ensuring strong and viable export expansion in conjunction with import liberalization rather than in a separate stage. Export promotion would evidently have been desirable, but it is less obvious how it should have been done. Certainly the Yugoslav trade regime was strongly inward looking, and stories abound about the difficulty of foreign buyers wanting to import but finding great lack of interest on the part of Yugoslav producers.[3] The general bias, with correction in certain sectors and for certain periods (in the form of export subsidies), was to domestic production. Thus import liberalization which reduced the level and disparity of protection would necessarily increase export incentives. In this respect, export promotion cannot be independent of import liberalization.

The two can, of course, be separated by applying export subsidies and other direct export incentives (duty drawbacks, access to foreign exchange, credit facilities) which compensate for the anti-export bias of the trade regime. Not only is this logically feasible, it may be theoretically more "correct" in that it certainly moves the EERs and effective rates of protection toward neutrality. However, in the case of Yugoslavia at least, the consequences of such policies were eventually very negative. The use of such arbitrary and *ad hoc* tools simply reinforced the undesirable climate of administrative interventionism. Further, it did not necessarily help export competitiveness in the long run, for it simply achieved export gains by artificially supporting production, with little incentive for efficiency improvements. Worse, the export support went to candidates with less comparative advantage: ships, electrical generation equipment, machinery, heavy transport equipment. Furthermore, the high capital intensity of favored exports meant low employment generation.

---

[3] *Borba* (October 16, 1966, p. 7) presents an interview with a director of the French department store Sentinel who could not buy as much filigree, glass, ceramics, and pottery as he was willing to, could not find samples of furniture and plum brandies, and so on. In general, it was often stated that it was more profitable to sell at home than to export. Parenthetically, the author was recently told a similar story by a Canadian retailer of shoes who was constantly promised but never received samples of Yugoslav footwear – in the early 1980s! Clearly, the problem of inward orientation continues to the present day.

Uniform versus Discriminatory Sectoral Treatment

No clear conclusion presents itself on whether uniform liberalization across sectors is more desirable than discriminatory treatment. The advantage of the discriminatory treatment that was applied in the 1965–7 liberalization was that it quickly addressed the distortion problem and, at least initially, narrowed the distortions. However, given the reactions to and reversal of liberalization in the form of *ad hoc* discriminatory reintroduction of protection, there is a case to be made for uniform treatment despite the huge distortions. First, equal reduction of protection would have reduced the relative disparities in effective protection to some extent. Certainly, if the liberalization had consisted of a gradual move of all tariffs to an equivalent amount, this would have achieved the same result as discriminatory correction of distortions. The second argument in favor of uniform treatment concerns credibility and the ability to resist exceptions. If all sectors are to face a uniform cut (or a move toward a uniform tariff by a certain date), it is far easier to deny any requests for exceptions. If, instead, exceptions are already built in to the original liberalization, it is far more difficult to deny such pressures.

Alternative Forms of a Uniform Process

The Yugoslav experience did not involve a uniform process of liberalization and therefore yields no direct lessons on alternative methods of applying uniform liberalization. However, the preceding discussion does suggest some possibilities. A uniform process, when applied to an existing regime of differential protection, might take several forms.

First, transformation of QRs to equivalent tariffs can precede reduction of protection, or the two can be combined. The difficulties of determining what a uniform reduction of QRs is, given initial differences in treatment, argues against a combined approach. Further, the discussion of QRs above gives reasons why a prior stage of transformation from QRs to tariffs is desirable, despite the technical imprecision of finding tariff equivalents of QRs.

Secondly, the reductions in tariffs can be effected by an equal percentage cut across the board, or a proportioned harmonica formula with higher percentage cuts for products with higher initial levels of protection. While the latter more quickly reduces the distortions of the system, the former may minimize the negative impacts on employment in highly protected sectors and reduce the potential political economy forces leading to reversal. Although Yugoslav experience sheds no light directly upon these alternatives, the evidence on the link between the degree of import penetration and the degree of employment expansion (or reduction) is more supportive of a proportional formula. A proportional tariff cut may lead to a larger gross effect on employment of high tariff sectors than does a uniform percentage cut. However, it reduces distortions more and is thus more likely to generate export growth which will absorb the disemployment.

The Nature of Desirable Discrimination

Given discrimination in the liberalization process, what was most desirable is clear: reduction of protection for the capital-intensive sectors, heavy industry and capital goods industries, and the raising of relative incentives for raw materials, labor-intensive industries, and consumer goods. While this in fact was done in the first stage (1965–7), the extent of such corrections was limited and in any case shortly undermined. However, there is nothing in the Yugoslav experience that would suggest that such discrimination was ill designed and led to the eventual failure of the liberalization. If anything, the facts suggest that inadequate implementation of sectoral objectives rather than their incorrect design led to the failure. For example, some (but very little) export strength was revealed by the labor-intensive light goods sectors; they received some early incentives (by correction of distortions), but these neither were strong enough nor lasted for long enough.

Appropriate Economic Circumstances for Liberalization

External circumstances in the mid-1960s would appear to have been very propitious for introducing liberalization. The world economy was growing strongly, international trade opportunities were expanding, and the Yugoslav turn to the West was welcomed by the West and supported by credit from bilateral and multilateral sources. The only drawback was the formation of the EEC and the relative rise in protection there, especially against agricultural goods. However, the economic boom in the EEC provided a compensating benefit – the potential for labor emigration and the consequent reduced unemployment pressures and increased foreign exchange from remittances. This was a net benefit only to the extent that any "Dutch disease" effects were avoided; since there is some reason to believe that they were not avoided in the long run, this plus may have been turned into a minus.

Domestic circumstances were less clearly ideal. On the one hand, there was a general spirit of decentralization, greater reliance on market mechanisms, and a build-up of industrial capabilities in the form of infrastructure, capital, and increasingly skilled labor. On the other hand, the existing industrial structure was highly distorted by the heavy industrialization and import substitution policies, factor mobility was limited, especially for capital but perhaps also for labor, and the system was overlaid with a heavy long-standing bureaucracy accustomed to controlling prices and new investments. The constraints on factor mobility, and the vested bureaucratic interests, played no small part in limiting the success of liberalization. Most important, however, the decentralization of powers was eventually abused in the sense that firms were allowed the freedom to make production decisions, but were not in the final analysis obliged to live by the consequences. Lobbying requests for help by weak firms were met by favorable responses, bankruptcy was never enforced, and financial discipline was eroded. Not surprisingly, governments soon reclaimed some of the decision-making powers.

The Role of Other Policy Measures

Two "other" policies – export promotion and financial discipline – have been dealt with earlier. Here we consider exchange rate, investment, and macrostabilization policies.

Initially, devaluation came at the right time – just as liberalization began in all three stages: 1961, 1965, and 1971. However, in all cases the devaluation was either not enough (1961) or was quickly eroded by inflation (1966–70 and 1973–4). The possible export stimulus and import restriction that may have come with a closer alignment of the real exchange rate cannot be overstated. Liberalization was curtailed and reversed for two reasons: the growing trade gap, and the restrictive monetary policy aimed at curbing inflation. Less important was the trade gap; had this been avoided by continued devaluation, especially in 1966–70, liberalization might have been more sustained. Alternatively, a more gradual phasing of the devaluation of 1965 would have contributed less to observed inflation and might have resulted in a less restrictive monetary policy.

Investment policies had two conflicting effects on liberalization. On the one hand, continued direct control or influence over a large proportion of investments by the government (15–16 percent directly, but wielding considerable influence over the 40–50 percent financed by banks) generated new jobs, often in areas with the greatest employment problems. This helped to offset the short-run disemployment effects of import liberalization. On the other hand, the long-run effect was to reinforce the structural misallocation of capital stock and undermine the disciplinary effect of liberalization on productive efficiency. This, like the export subsidies to the least export competitive, was another instance of moral hazard effects, or the monopoly of the backward.

Finally, stabilization policies were doubtless ill designed to support the objectives of liberalization. It is one thing to argue that the situation in many countries in the late 1970s and early 1980s predicates contraction at the same time as liberalization of imports because government policies have been excessively expansionary and public deficits are far too large. Such a bullet did not have to be bitten in Yugoslavia in the mid-1960s. For one thing, external finance credibility was high and such financial discipline was not being requested of Yugoslavia. Further, the budgetary situation was strong and balanced. The only indications of a need for restrictiveness were some worsening of inflation and of the current account deficit in 1961–4. The latter was initially corrected by the mid-1965 devaluation, so that only inflation remained a problem.

In the circumstances, the very tight restrictionist policies (mostly monetary) of 1965–7 seem excessive in retrospect. To have domestic demand components actually decline, or grow at a very modest rate, just at the time that imports were being liberalized was, to say the least, unfortunate timing. While the combined effect of domestic demand and export expansion in reaction to devaluation was to give some positive growth of output (and presumably employment), this was not enough to absorb all the disemployment caused by liberalization.

Had macro policy been somewhat less restrictive, the net disemployment and the pressures for reversing liberalization might have been avoided. While this may have created even greater inflationary pressures, continued devaluation could at least have minimized the effect on the trade deficit until such time as the more subtle longer-run gains from liberalization began to take hold in the form of increased efficiency, and hence increased competitiveness, at once increasing exports and reducing imports as domestic industries approached world cost levels.

Timing of Liberalization and of Other Policies

This point has essentially been addressed. Suffice it to say here that it was a mistake to have such a strongly contractionary policy in the initial phase of liberalization, for this simply exacerbated the employment problem liberalization is bound to create instead of minimizing its impact. A slightly looser policy and somewhat of a delay in handling the inflation problem, which was not so serious, was certainly called for. Devaluation policies, while initially sensible, were either not enough or were not sustained in the face of inflation. It must be concluded that a gradual and more sustained devaluation would have been better than the substantial one-time devaluation of mid-1965. Finally, government investment policies were not at all well timed. Continuing the same basic policies of the past – albeit with a reduced share of total investment – was not helpful to the aims of liberalization. At the very least, such investments should have been planned to fit the likely new orientation of incentives and comparative advantage a little better, even if the government did not wish to wait and see what signals were thrown up by the market. There is no indication of such a coordination between allocation of investments (sectorally or geographically) and the intended direction of incentives in the liberalization process.

References

Books and Articles

Amacher, Ryan C. (1972) *Yugoslavia's Foreign Trade*, New York: Praeger.

Bajt, Alexander (1969) "Privredna kretanjna ekonomska politika u 1969 i 1970 godine." *Aktuelni Problemi Ekonomske Politike Jugoslavije, 1969–70*, Zagreb: Informator.

Balassa, Bela and Laura Tyson (1983) "Adjustment to external shocks in socialist and private market economies." Washington, DC: Development Research Department, World Bank, Discussion Paper, Report no. DRD61.

Balassa, Bela and Laura Tyson (1984) "Policy responses to external shocks in Hungary and Yugoslavia: 1974–76 and 1979–81." Washington, DC: Development Research Department, World Bank, Discussion Paper, Report no. 111.

Barton, Allen H., Bodgan Denitch, and Charles Kadushin (1973) *Opinion-Making Elites in Yugoslavia*. New York: Praeger.

Bicanic, Rudolph (1973) *Economic Policy in Socialist Yugoslavia*. Cambridge: Cambridge University Press.

Breznik, Dusan (1969) "Demographic and other aspects of labor force formation in Yugoslavia for the next 20 years." *Ekonomist*, 1.

Burg, S. L. (1983) *Conflict and Cohesion in Socialist Yugoslavia*. Princeton, NJ: Princeton University Press.

Burkett, John P. (1983a) "The effects of economic reform in Yugoslavia: investment and trade policy, 1959–76." Berkeley, CA: Institute of International Studies, University of California, Berkeley, Research Series no. 55.

Burkett, John P. (1983b) "The impact of ecomonic reform on macroeconomic policy in Yugoslavia: some econometric evidence." *Economic Analysis and Workers Management*, 17(3), 213–43.

Canapa, Marie-Paule (1971) *Reforme Economique et Socialisme en Yougoslavie*. Paris: Armand Colin.

Chenery, Hollis and Moises Syrquin (1975) *Patterns of Development 1950–70*. Oxford: Oxford University Press.

Chittle, Charles R. (1977) *Industrialization and Manufactured Export Expansion in a Worker-Managed Economy: The Yugoslav Experience*. Tübingen: J.C.B. Mohr (Paul Siebeck).

Cohen, Lenard and Paul Warwick (1983) *Political Cohesion in a Fragile Mosaic: The Yugoslav Experience*, Boulder, CO: Westview Press.

Comisso, Ellen Turkish (1979) *Worker's Control under Plan and Market: Implications of Yugoslav Self-Management*. New Haven, CT: Yale University Press.

Condon, Timothy, Vittorio Corbo, and Jaime de Melo (1985) "Productivity growth, external shocks and capital inflows in Chile during 1977–81: a general equilibrium analysis." *Journal of Policy Modeling*, 7(3), Fall, 379–405.

Dimitrijevic, Dimitrije (1973) "Mekanizam finansiranje Yugoslovenske privrede." *Ekonomska Misao*, 22–45.

Dubey, Vinod (1975) *Yugoslavia: Development with Decentralization*. Baltimore, MD: The Johns Hopkins University Press for the World Bank.

Ekonomski Institut (1965) *Metode Bilansiranja Strukturnih Proporcija u Planu Privrednog Razvoja*. Belgrade: Ekonomski Institut.

Ekonomski Institut, Pravne Fakultete (1972) "Efektivna carinska zascita u Jugoslaviji." Ljubljana: Ekonomski Institut.

Estrin, Saul (1983) *Self-Management: Economic Theory and Yugoslav Practice*. Cambridge: Cambridge University Press.

Estrin, Saul, Jan Svejnar, and Carolyn Mow (1982) "Market imperfections, labor-management and earnings differentials in a developing country: theory and evidence from Yugoslavia." Ithaca, NY: Department of Economics, Cornell University, Working Paper no. 276.

Fabinc, Ivo (1969) "Ekonomski odnosi s inostranstrom u reformi I ekspanzikja privrede." *Urbzanje Rasta Jugoslavenske Privrede u Uslovima Stabilnosti*. Zagreb: Informator.

Fabinc, Ivo and Olga Lazic-Djerdj (1973) "Proracum efektivne zastite u Jugoslaviji." Belgrade: Institut za spoljnu Trgovinu.

Fabinc, Ivo, et al. (eds) (1976) *Sistem Ekonomskih Odnosa sa Inostranstvom*, II (Sintesa rada – II faza Makro-projekta, Privredni Sistem SFRJ). Zagreb. Informator.

Federal Institute of Statistics (1963) Privredni bilansi Jugoslavije, 1952–1962. Belgrade: Federal Institute of Statistics, Studije, Analize i Prikazi, no. 19.

Federal Institute of Statistics (1966a) "Medjusobni odnosi privrednih delatnosti Jugoslavije u 1962, Godini." Belgrade: Federal Institute of Statistics, Studije, Analize i Prikazi, no. 26.

Federal Institute of Statistics (1966b) "Privredni bilansi Jugoslavije 1962–1965." Belgrade: Federal Institute of Statistics, Studije, Analize i Prikazi, no. 29.

Federal Institute of Statistics (1967a) "Kretanje privrede u prve dve godine reforme: statisticki podaci." Belgrade: Federal Institute of Statistics, Studije, Analize i Prikazi, no. 34.

Federal Institute of Statistics (1967b) "Privredni bilansi Jugoslavije, 1962–1965." Belgrade Federal Institute of Statistics, Studije, Analize i Prikazi, no. 40.

Federal Institute of Statistics (1968) "Privreda u godinanama reforme." Belgrade: Federal Institute of Statistics, Studije, Analize i Prikazi, no. 40.

Federal Institute of Statistics (1968, 1970) "The economy in the years of the reform." Belgrade: Federal Institute of Statistics, Studije, Analize i Prikazi, no. 19.

Federal Institute of Statistics (1969) "Kretanje drustvenog proizvoda i narodnog dohotka Jugoslavije 1952–1966, Republikama u cenama 1966." Belgrade: Federal Institute of Statistics, Studije, Analize i Prikazi, no. 45.

Federal Institute of Statistics (1970a) *Kretanje Narodnog Dohotka, Zaposlenosti i Produktivnosti Rada u Privredni Jugoslavije, 1947–1967* (National Income, Employment and Labor Productivity in the Economy of Yugoslavia, 1947–1967). Belgrade: Federal Institute of Statistics.

Federal Institute of Statistics (1970b) "Mediusobni odnosi privrednih delatnosti Jugoslavije, 1962 i 1966." Belgrade: Federal Institute of Statistics, Studije, Analize i Prikazi, no. 50.

Federal Institute of Statistics (1970c) *Privredni Bilansi Jugoslavije, 1964–1968*. Belgrade: Federal Institute of Statistics.

Federal Institute of Statistics of Yugoslavia. *Foreign Trade Statistics*, various years. Belgrade: Federal Institute of Statistics.

Federal Institute of Statistics of Yugoslavia. *Indeks*, various issues. Belgrade: Federal Irstitute of Statistics.

Federal Institute of Statistics of Yugoslavia. *Statistical Yearbook of Yugoslavia*, various issues. Belgrade: Federal Institute of Statistics.

Federal Institute of Statistics of Yugoslavia. *Statisticki Bilten*, various issues. Belgrade: Federal Institute of Statistics.

Federal Institute of Statistics of Yugoslavia. *Studies, Analyses and Reviews*, various years. Belgrade: Federal Institute of Statistics.

Fisher, Jack C. (1966) *Yugoslavia – a Multinational State. Regional Difference and Administrative Response*, San Francisco, CA: Chandler.

Frkovic, Marko (1957) "Disparitet spoljnotrgovinskih kurseva u nasoj privredi." *Ekonomist*, 70–7.

Gluscevic, B., H. Hadziomerovic, B. Horvat, N. Kljusev, B. Soskic, and D. Vojnic (1971) *Ekonomske Funkcije Federacije*, Dokument 2. Belgrade: Institut Ekonomskih Nauka.

Havrylyshyn, Oli (1977) "Ethnic affinity and migration flow in postwar Yugoslavia." *Economic Development and Cultural Change*, 26 (1), October, 93–116.

Havrylyshyn, Oli (1984–6) "Timing and sequencing of trade liberalization policies: the case of Yugoslavia" Part I, 1984, Part II, 1985, Part III, 1986. From the World Bank, Washington, DC.

Havrylyshyn, Oli (1985) "Issues of price policy in Tunisia." Washington, DC: World Bank, Report no 5328-TU, vol. II, October.

Havrylyshyn, Oli (1988) "Timing and sequencing of trade liberalization policies: the case of Yugoslavia, statistical appendix." Available from the Brazil Department, World Bank, Washington, DC.

Horvat, Branko (1969) *Tehnicki Progres u Jugoslaviji*. Belgrade: Institut Ekonomskih Nauka.

Horvat, Branko (1971a) *Business Cycles in Yugoslavia*. White Plains, NY: International Arts and Sciences Press.

Horvat, Branko (1971b) "Yugoslav economic policy in the post-war period: problems, ideas, institutional developments." *American Economic Review*, 61(3), 71–161.

Horvat, Branko (1976) *The Yugoslav Economic System*. White Plains, NY: International Arts and Sciences Press.

Institute of Industrial Economics, *A Survey on Production Capacity Utilization in Industry – Yugoslavia*, various years. Belgrade: Institute of Industrial Economics.

Ivanovic, Mjomir (1968) "Carinski sistem SFRJ [Socijalistika Federativna Republika Jugoslavija]." Mimeo. Seminar o Carinskom Sistemu, Bled, Slovenija.

Jugoslovenski Institut za Ekonomska Istrazivanja (1969) *Ocjena Economske Situacije i Predvidjanja Daljnjeg Razvoja*, Radovi 12, Belgrade.

Kerim, Srdjan A. (1983) *Strategy of Self-Reliance: Developing Countries and the New International Economic Order*. Belgrade: Poslovna Politika.

Knight, Peter T. (1983) "Economic reform in socialist countries: the experiences of China, Hungary, Romania and Yugoslavia." Washington, DC: World Bank, Working Paper no. 579.

Kovac, Oskar (1974) "Ekonomski odnosi s inostranstvom na Pragu 1974 godine." *Aktuelni Problemi Privredrih Kretanja Ekonomska Politika Jugoslavije, 1973–74* (*Ekonomist*, special issue), Zagreb.

Kovacevic, Mladen (1979) "Elasticnost izvozai uvoza Jugoslavije." *Vanjskotrgovinsko Poslovanje*, 155–71.

Kovacevic, Mladen (1980) *Faktori Konkurentnosti Jugoslavenskoj Izvoza*. Belgrade: Institut Economskih Nauka.

Madzar, Ljubomir (1979) "Problemi perspektive razvoja Yugoslovenske privrede," *Ekonomska Misao*, 1, 9–39.

Mencinger, Jose (1979) *Zatvaranja Jugoslovenske Privrede i Sistem Zastite*. Ljubljana: Ekonomski Institut Pravne Fakultete.

Mrkusic, Zarko (1972) *Teorijska Osnova Deviznog Sistema*. Belgrade: Institut Ekonomskih Nauka.

Mrkusic, Zarko, Oskar Kovac, and Franka Filipi (1968) "Uslovi i kriteriji za optimalmo ukljucivanje u medinarodnu podelu rada i proizvodna orijentacija Jugoslavije." *Ekonomska Analiza*, nos 3–4, 243–63.

The New Yorker (1984) "Tito's legacy." March 5, pp. 110–25.

Nishimizu, Mieko and John M. Page Jr (1982) "Total factor productivity growth, technological progress and technical efficiency change: dimensions of productivity change in Yugoslavia, 1965–78." *Economic Journal*, 92, December, 920–36.

Nishimizu, Mieko and Sherman Robinson (1984) "Trade policies and productivity change in semi-industrialized countries." *Journal of Development Economics*, 16, 177–286.

Organization for Economic Cooperation and Development, *Economic Surveys, Yugoslavia*, various years. Paris: OECD.

Organization for Economic Cooperation and Development (1970) *Foreign Investment in Yugoslavia*. Paris: OECD.

Pertot, Vladimir (1969) "Neki strukturni problemi: nase medjunarodne robne razjmene." *Vanjskotrgovinsko Poslovanje Radnih Organizacija*. Zagreb: Fakultet Ekonomskih Nauka.

Pertot, Vladimir (1971) *Economika Medunarodne Rozmjene Jugoslavie*. Zagreb: Informator.

Pertot, Vladimir (1972) *International Economics of Control*. Edinburgh: Oliver and Boyd.

Pertot, Vladimir (1973) *Anketa O Tendencijama Promjena Odnosa Vrijednosti u Nasem Vanjskoj Rozmjene 1955–1970*. Zagreb: Ekonomski Institut.

Pertot, Vladimir (1980) *Teorija Dispariteta Troskova, Cijena i Valuta*. Zagreb: Skolska Knjiga.

Pertot, Vladimir (1984) "The Political Economy of Trade Liberalization in Yugoslavia." Mimeo. Zagreb.

Petrin, Tea (1981) "Analiza vgrokov koncentracije organizacijskih enot 1954–1976." Doctoral dissertation, Universita Edvard Kardelj, Ljubljana.

Pleskovic, Boris and Marjan Dolenc (1982) "Regional development in a socialist, developing, and multinational country: the case of Yugoslavia." *Report, International Regional Science Review*, 7, May, 1–24.

Plummer, James (1969) "Production function analysis of resource allocation in Yugoslav industry." *Dissertation Abstracts International*, 30/09-A; Ithaca, NY: Cornell University, dissertation.

Puljic, Ante (1980) "The impact of technological progress on the growth of the industrial social product." *Economic Analysis and Workers Management*, 14 (2) 181–217.

Puljic, Ante (1982) "Kriticki osvrt na clanak Sapira." *Economic Analysis and Workers Management*, 16 (4), 369–76.

Rajkovic, Velimir (1970) "Ocjena ostvarivanja privredne reforme i aktuelni problemi." *Aktuelni Problemi Privednih Kretanja Ekonomske Politike Jugoslavije, 1969–70*, (*Ekonomist*, special issue), Zagreb.

Robinson, Sherman, Laura D. Tyson, and Mathias Dewatripont (1984) "Yugoslav economic performance in the 1980s: alternative scenarios." Washington, DC: Development Research Department, Economics and Research Staff, World Bank.

Rusinow, Dennison (1977) *The Yugoslav Experiment: 1948–1974*. Berkeley, CA: University of California Press.

Sacks, Stephen R. (1972) "Changes in industrial structure in Yugoslavia, 1959–1968." *Journal of Political Economy*, 80(3), Part 1, May–June, 561–74.

Sapir, Andre (1980) "Economic growth and factor substitution: what happened to the Yugoslav miracle?" *Economic Journal*, 90, June, 294–313.

Sapir, Andre (1981) "Economic reform and migration in Yugoslavia: an econometric model." *Journal of Development Economics*, 9, 149–81.

Savezni Zavod Za Privredno Planiranje (1965) *Metode Bilansiranja Strukturnih Proporcija u Planu Privrednog Razvoja*. Zagreb: Ekonomski Institut.

Savicevic, Milorad (1970) "Protective tariffs and other measures of protection of the national economy." *Yugoslav Survey*, 11 (1) May, 56.

Schrenk, Martin (1981) "Managerial structures and practices in manufacturing enterprises: a Yugoslav class study." World Bank, Staff Working Paper no. 455.

Schrenk, Martin, Cyrus Ardalan, and Narval A. El Tatawy (1979) *Yugoslavia Self-Management Socialism: Challenges of Development*. Baltimore, MD: The Johns Hopkins University Press for the World Bank.

Sekulic, Mijo (1978) *Kretanje Uvoznih Za Cijena, Intervalutanih Odnosa i Konkurentnosti Jugoslavenski Privrede*. Zagreb: Ekonomski Institut.

Sirc, Ljubo (1979) *The Yugoslav Economy under Self-Management*. New York: St Martin's Press.

Socan, Lojze, et al. (1983) *Strategic Issues of the Yugoslav Development Policy*. Ljubljana: Institute for Economic Research.

Srdar, Srdam (1974) "Vanjskotrgovinska politika i povecanje izvoza." *Aktuelni Problemi Privrednih kretanje Ekonomske Politike Jugoslavije, 1973–74 (Ekonomist*, special issue), Zagreb.

Tyson, Laura D. (1977a) "The Yugoslav economy in the 1970's: a survey of recent developments and future prospects." Washington, DC: US Congress, Joint Economic Committee, pp. 941–996.

Tyson, Laura D. (1977b) "The Yugoslav inflation" *Journal of Comparative Economics*, 1 (2), 113–46.

Tyson, Laura D. and Egon Neuberger (1979) "The impact of external economic disturbances on Yugoslavia: theoretical and empirical explorations." *Journal of Comparative Economics*, 3 (3), 346–74.

ULG Economic Consultants Ltd (1977) "Yugoslavia: agricultural prices and subsidies case study." Prepared for World Bank Economic and Policy Division of Agriculture and Rural Development, Division Working Paper no. 8, vol. I.

United Nations, Economic Commission for Europe (1985) "Economic survey of Europe in 1984–85." United Nations, Document Id. 0985f.

Vanek, Jaroslav (1970) *The General Theory of Labor-Managed Economies*. Ithaca, NY: Cornell University Press.

Vukina, Tomislav (1982) "Activizacijski period investicija u industriji Jugoslavije." *Economic Analysis and Workers Management*, 16 (3), 273–86.

Wachtel, Howard M. (1973) *Workers Management and Worker's Wages in Yugoslavia*. Ithaca, NY: Cornell University Press.

World Bank (1966) *Current Economic Position and Prospects of Yugoslavia*, vol. II. Washington, DC: World Bank, Europe, Middle East, and North Africa Department.

World Bank (1970) *Current Economic Position and Prospects of Yugoslavia*. Washington, DC: World Bank, Europe, Middle East, and North Africa Department.

World Bank (1972) *Current Economic Position and Prospects of Yugoslavia*, vols 1 and 2, Washington, DC: World Bank, Europe, Middle East, and North Africa Department.

World Bank (1980) "Yugoslavia: Export Performance and Policies." Washington, DC: World Bank, Report no. 2972-YU.

World Bank (1981) "Raising productivity in Yugoslav Industry: some issues." Washington, DC: World Bank, Country Programs Department, Report no. 3383a-yn.

World Bank (1983) "Yugoslavia adjustment policies and development perspectives." Washington, DC: World Bank, Country Study.

World Bank (1984) *World Development Report*. New York: Oxford University Press.

Yagci, Fahrettin (1985) "Macroeconomic policies and adjustment in Yugoslavia: some counterfactual simulations." Mimeo. Washington, DC: World Bank, Department of Economic Analysis and Projections.

Yugoslavia, Socialist Federal Republic (1983) *Economic Stabilization Programme*. Belgrade: Yugoslovenski Pregled.

Zarkovic, Jelena (1969) "Jedan pokosaj utvrdjivanja dejstva carinskih stopa na uvoz." *Finansije*, 576.

Newspapers and Journals

Borba, Belgrade, daily.
Delo, Ljubljana, daily.
Economist, London, weekly.
Ekonomska Politika, Belgrade, weekly.
Jugoslovenski Pregled, Belgrade, monthly.
Politika, Belgrade, daily.
Vjesnik, Zagreb, daily.
Vjesnik u Srijeda, Zagreb, weekly.

Index